Contemporary China – An Introduction

"This is a very clear, well written and highly readable book that will be used widely in undergraduate courses. It is also up-to-date including much content on developments in the past couple of years. Michael Dillon has done an admirable job. This will be a comprehensive text for survey courses."

–Rachel Murphy, *University of Oxford*

This book presents a concise introduction to contemporary China. It is intended as a first book for those coming new to the subject, providing the essential information that most people need to know, without going into excessive detail. Its coverage includes the economy, society, politics and international relations; China's history, especially the twentieth century; and Taiwan and Hong Kong as well as the People's Republic of China.

The book provides an up-to-date and clear guide to the often bewildering changes which have taken place in China in the late twentieth and early twenty-first centuries. It draws on the enormous body of empirical and theoretical research that is being carried out by economists, political scientists and sociologists on contemporary China, but is itself written in non-technical and accessible language. It does not assume any previous knowledge of China and explanations of Chinese terms are provided throughout the book. It includes a map, a chronology, a glossary of Chinese terms, biographical notes on key figures, and a guide to further reading.

Michael Dillon is a frequent commentator on Chinese affairs for the BBC and other broadcasters. He was formerly Director of the Centre for Contemporary Chinese Studies at the University of Durham, UK, where he taught Chinese and Chinese history. His previous publications include *China: A Historical and Cultural Dictionary*, *China's Muslim Hui Community: Migration, Settlement and Sects* and *Xinjiang: China's Muslim Far Northwest* (all published by Routledge and RoutledgeCurzon).

Contemporary China – An Introduction

Michael Dillon

Routledge
Taylor & Francis Group

LONDON AND NEW YORK

First published 2009
by Routledge
2 Park Square, Milton Park, Abingdon, Oxon, OX14 4RN

Simultaneously published in the USA and Canada
by Routledge
711 Third Avenue, New York, NY 10017

Routledge is an imprint of the Taylor & Francis Group, an informa business

© 2009 Michael Dillon

Typeset in Times New Roman by Pindar NZ Ltd, Auckland

British Library Cataloguing in Publication Data
A catalogue record for this book is available from the British Library

Library of Congress Cataloging in Publication Data
Dillon, Michael, 1949-
Contemporary China: an introduction/ Michael Dillon. — 1st ed.
   p. cm.
  First published 2007 by Routledge, Abingdon, Oxon
  Simultaneously published in the USA and Canada by Routledge.
  1. China. I. Title.
  DS706.D55 2008
  951.06--dc22   2008021680

ISBN 10: 0-415-34320-8 (hbk)
ISBN 10: 0-415-34319-4 (pbk)
ISBN 10: 0-203-48294-8 (ebk)

ISBN 13: 978-0-415-34320-6 (hbk)
ISBN 13: 978-0-415-34319-0 (pbk)
ISBN 13: 978-0-203-48294-0 (ebk)

Contents

Preface

Is the People's Republic of China (PRC), as some would argue, a nightmare realm of human rights abuses? It can be criticised on many grounds. It has one of the highest rates of death sentences and executions in the world; many peasants and other rural workers suffer desperate exploitation; dissenting opinions and unorthodox political, religious or social attitudes are severely repressed; there is no independent judicial system and the track record of the state in dealing with ill-treatment or torture in prison and police custody is at best mediocre; some of the poorest children in the country are neglected in ill-equipped orphanages; no genuine independence for Tibet or Xinjiang can be countenanced; corruption exists on a vast scale at all levels of society and there is nothing that approaches political democracy as it is understood in the West.

Alternatively, is China a country with a dynamic economy that is finally allowing its population to break out of a decades-old torpor, making it possible for millions, both peasants and urban dwellers, to improve their opportunities for work, education, travel and family life? The banal answer, but the only appropriate one, is that it is both of these and much more. Chinese society and the state that (up to a point) controls it are a mass of contradictions and complexities that render useless any attempt at a simplistic analysis. That does not prevent commentators and analysts from attempting to characterise it as either heroic or villainous, according to their own political or cultural perspectives and prejudices.[1]

It is a commonplace today that China is a major international economic force and an influential, if not entirely predictable, actor on the international scene. An informed understanding of the often bewildering changes in the Chinese world is not the exotic indulgence that it was once erroneously thought to be, but a practical necessity.

This introduction to contemporary China focuses primarily on the PRC but also covers developments in Hong Kong and Taiwan in the late twentieth and early twenty-first centuries. It draws on the vast body of empirical and theoretical research that has been carried out by economists, political scientists, anthropologists and sociologists on contemporary China but deliberately avoids the technical, and at times inaccessible, language of the specialists. It does not assume any previous knowledge of China or the Chinese language: any Chinese terms used in the text are explained as they occur and romanised versions of some terms are included for the convenience of readers who have some knowledge of Chinese.

One of the most important assumptions underlying the approach of this book is that contemporary China cannot be understood adequately without an appreciation of both its immediate historical past and how this past is perceived by Chinese people today. Today's China of reform – the land of concrete, glass and steel and the realm of bizarre youth cultures and extraordinary contemporary art – is still the same China as that of Mao Zedong and the Red Guards. Many of the students and secondary school pupils of the Red Guard generation have grown up to be the managers, teachers, Chinese Communist Party (CCP) officials or senior civil servants of today. This may create conflict between them and the younger generation, many of whom are apathetic and deeply cynical about ideology and politics, but the influence of their past, and China's recent history, is still immense.

Although the study of contemporary China has been well served by many humane and balanced enquiries, it has also been bedevilled by simplistic and ill-informed, but nonetheless strongly held, political opinions and allegiances. In the tradition of the Cold War, China-watchers have often been divided – frequently with very little justification – into pro-China and anti-China. That automatically suggested that they must be respectively either anti-Taiwan or pro-Taiwan. In the current politico-academic jargon, particularly popular in North America and not entirely intended as tongue-in-cheek, they are either 'panda-huggers' or 'dragon-slayers' – more recently, people considered to be particularly critical of, or unsympathetic to, China have also been labelled 'panda-muggers'. All good knock-about entertainment perhaps, but it does mask real professional anxieties. Scholars and analysts of the Chinese world spend far too much time looking over their shoulders for fear that they may be accused of being too hard or too soft on China.

It is probably unrealistic to hope that the dragon might lie down with the panda: what is essential is a level of understanding and analysis that looks at the whole of the Chinese world critically, without the straitjacket of political preconceptions or the fear of being labelled a 'friend of China' or a 'cold warrior'. Such grossly oversimplified classifications do not encumber studies of, say, Indonesia or India (and developing China has many similarities with both of these countries) in the same way, so why should they be considered so important in China studies?

It is essential for the Western analyst or observer to be able to step into the shoes of the people of China, including those who are in positions of power, and to endeavour to understand how they perceive their country, their society and their institutions. This does not necessarily imply sympathy with, or support for, those in power: the converse is frequently the case. However, it is both arrogant and dangerous not even to attempt to see the world from a Chinese point of view. There is, of course, no single Chinese point of view: the ways that peasant farmers in Henan, Westernised intellectuals in Beijing and Tibetan nuns in Lhasa think and feel about China and the world are far from identical, and it is important to appreciate this range of viewpoints, even although they may be inconsistent and mutually incompatible.

This book has grown out of a critical engagement with China, its language, culture, history and politics that stretches back over forty years of study, teaching and research. During that period, the PRC has experienced the rise and fall of the Cultural Revolution; the death of its founding leader, Mao Zedong; a war with its former Communist ally, Vietnam; the introduction of the 'reform and opening policy' under Deng Xiaoping and the brutal suppression of the Democracy Movement in Beijing on 4 June 1989. As a backdrop to these events the people of China have been witnesses to and participants in: a dramatic process of urbanisation and modernisation; the large-scale migration of men and women from the countryside to the cities in search of work; conflicts in the villages over taxation, land ownership and the one-child policy; the escalation of underlying ethnic and cultural frictions between the Han majority and minority groups; the constant tension between the mainland and Taiwan; and a growing awareness of the dreadful potential of military conflict with the United States as China seems set to emerge as the second superpower of the twenty-first century. All of this has happened in the presence of the international media, which had virtually no access to China between 1949 and 1980.

More Chinese people than ever before have travelled abroad for work, study or leisure and they take back to China (and to Taiwan) informed opinions, both positive and negative, about the West and detailed information about the outside world – a level of knowledge and understanding of which the preceding generation could not have dreamt. The dramatic transformation of the mainland has brought into sharp focus enduring questions about the nature of the Chinese state and Chinese society. China today certainly does not look or behave like a traditional Soviet-style Communist state and yet the CCP remains firmly in control. Neither is it anything approaching a liberal democratic system with a completely free-market economy. The economy remains mixed, and state-owned enterprises continue to dominate in the key sectors. Nevertheless, migration and changes in working and living patterns are fundamentally and rapidly altering the social structure of both towns and villages.

In the same period, Taiwan has evolved from a one-party state dominated by the former mainland government party, the Kuomintang (Guomindang), and its military adjuncts into a multiparty democracy, albeit one wracked with discord, corruption and ethnic and social divisions. There has been an upsurge of popular support for a formal declaration of the legal independence of Taiwan from China: this angers Beijing and, without careful management and sophisticated diplomacy, the independence issue has the potential to develop into a serious political, and even military, conflict.

Hong Kong, the last British colony in Asia, was returned to China in 1997 and became a Special Administrative Region of the PRC. Superficially, it retains its individual character and much of its old colonial charm: in reality, it is grappling with the challenge of retaining its own identity and traditions while operating within the PRC and dealing more closely with the government in Beijing than at any time since 1949.

The observations offered in this book have been informed by regular travel to China and other parts of the Chinese world – not only travel to the major urban centres such as Beijing, Shanghai and Guangzhou, but also research visits to carry out intensive programmes of fieldwork in the rural areas and small towns of Jiangxi and Anhui in southern China; in the remote (their word, not mine) Hui Muslim regions of Gansu and Ningxia in the northwest and the border regions of Xinjiang and Inner Mongolia; as well as to China's inner Asian neighbours, Mongolia and Kazakhstan, and to Hong Kong and Taiwan.

The range of topics covered is such that no individual can possibly claim to be an authority on them all and the views offered have been influenced by the work of many others, including academics and the more serious journalists, not all of whom will agree with the conclusions drawn from their efforts. Condensing complex and controversial topics into a few pages will inevitably have resulted in some degree of oversimplification, although strenuous efforts have been made to avoid oversimplifying in a way that might run the risk of misleading the reader. Every attempt has been made to ensure that this book is as up-to-date as possible but economic, social and cultural changes in twenty-first-century China are rapid and often unpredictable. Caveats aside, this book is offered by an unrepentant parachutist with grateful acknowledgement to all the truffle hunters.

Acknowledgements

I began the serious study of what was then a very different contemporary China in the Departments of Chinese Studies and Sociology at the University of Leeds in the United Kingdom during the late 1960s and early 1970s. It was the era of the Cultural Revolution and there was virtually no opportunity for direct contact with the PRC. Staff in the departments, who came from very different backgrounds in China and in Western Sinology, had between them an extraordinary range of expertise and interests which they communicated in their teaching. An acknowledgement of the inspiration of all the staff in Leeds who introduced me to Chinese studies is long overdue.

At Durham University, I am grateful to the undergraduates who followed my Chinese language and history courses in the Department of East Asian Studies for keeping me on my toes with lively, challenging and often irreverent questions. Postgraduate students brought to seminars and to discussions about their research practical experience of life and work in China, intelligent questions, and the necessary scepticism and humour. I am grateful to those staff members of the university who were supportive when the Department was forced to close down in 2007.

In China, I have been fortunate over a period of twenty-five years in having had the opportunity of working with historians and other scholars at the Institutes of Modern History, Economics, World Religions and Minorities of the Academy of Social Sciences in Beijing, and its regional academies in Shanghai and Guangzhou and in the provinces or autonomous regions of Anhui, Jiangxi, Gansu, Ningxia and Xinjiang. I have also found great profit and pleasure in cooperation with colleagues in many universities, including Renmin University of China in Beijing, Fudan University in Shanghai, the Universities of Xinjiang in Urumqi and Ningxia in Yinchuan and the Hong Kong University of Science and Technology. In Taiwan, I have carried out research at the Academia Sinica in Taipei and have benefited from cooperation with colleagues at National Chengchi University.

These academic partnerships have been absolutely vital in enabling me to shape my understanding of China and none of my visits to these institutions would have been possible without financial and organisational support from the British Academy and the Universities' China Committee in London. This book, and the other publications which have resulted from these exchanges, would have been much poorer without these academic exchanges and it is a great pleasure to be able to acknowledge the generous support of these organisations over many years.

Last, but certainly not least, I am very grateful to Peter Sowden of Routledge who has skilfully steered the book though the production process with exactly the right combination of encouragement, firmness and tact. I am also grateful to the anonymous reviewers who have been both critical and constructive. The sole responsibility for any inaccuracies and omissions in the text rests, as it properly should, with the author.

Durham
August 2008

Abbreviations

APCs	agricultural producers' cooperatives
CAAC	Civil Aviation Administration of China
CC	Central Committee
CCP	Chinese Communist Party
CCTV	Chinese Central Television
CMC	Central Military Commission
CPPCC	Chinese People's Political Consultative Conference
CYL	Communist Youth League
FECs	foreign exchange certificates
GATT	General Agreement on Tariffs and Trade
GMD	Guomindang, Nationalist Party (also Kuomintang)
HPC	higher-level producers' cooperatives
NDRC	National Development and Reform Commission
NGOs	non-governmental organisations
NPC	National People's Congress
PAP	People's Armed Police
PLA	People's Liberation Army
PRC	People's Republic of China
RMB	*renminbi* (people's currency)
RMRB	*Renmin Ribao* (*People's Daily*)
SAFE	State Administration of Foreign Exchange
SAR	Special Administrative Region
SASAC	State-owned Assets Supervision and Administration Commission
SEPA	State Environmental Protection Administration
SOEs	state-owned enterprises
TVEs	township and village enterprises
WTO	World Trade Organisation
XPCC	Xinjiang Production and Construction Corps

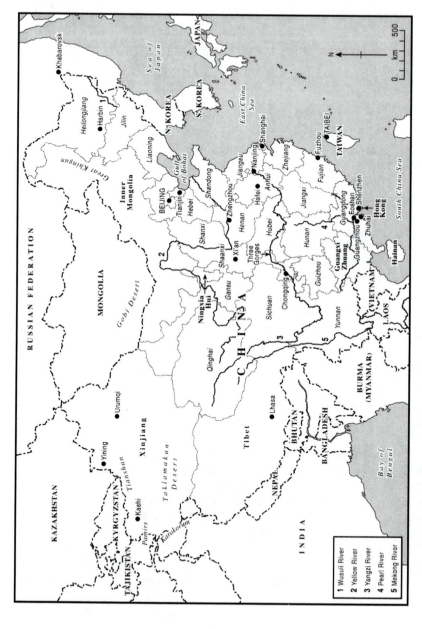

Map of the People's Republic of China and its neighbours: Shows provinces and autonomous regions (in bold), major cities, rivers and mountain ranges.

Chronology

Key imperial dynasties

Qin	*221–207 BC*
Han	*206 BC–AD 220*
Tang	*618–907*
Song	*960–1127*
Yuan	*1271–1368 (Mongol)*
Ming	*1368–1644*
Qing	*1644–1911 (Manchu)*

Modern period

Qing dynasty	*1644–1911*
Republic of China	*1912–1949 (continues on Taiwan)*
People's Republic of China	*1949–*

1839–42	Opium War
1842	Treaty of Nanjing – Hong Kong ceded to Britain
1898	New Territories ceded to Britain
1899–1901	Boxer Rebellion
1908	Death of Empress Dowager
1911	Revolution overthrows Qing dynasty
1912	Republic of China proclaimed
1912	Sun Yat-sen relinquishes Presidency to Yuan Shikai
1915	Japanese Twenty-One Demands for control over China
1919	May Fourth Movement – modern Chinese nationalism born
1921	Chinese Communist Party (CCP) founded
1923	Guomindang (GMD) (Kuomintang) reorganised
1923	CCP and GMD cooperate in First United Front
1925	Death of Sun Yat-sen
1926	Northern Expedition to unify China
1927	CCP and GMD split after Shanghai massacre
1928	GMD National Government in Nanjing
1929–34	CCP establishes rural bases in Jiangxi province

1931	Japanese invasion of Manchuria
1934–36	CCP Long March to Xi'an base
1937 (July)	Japanese invasion of China proper
1937 (September)	CCP and GMD Second United Front
1945	Japanese surrender
1946	Civil War breaks out between CCP and GMD
1949	People's Republic of China founded
1950–53	Korean War
1955	Bandung Conference of non-aligned nations
1956	Hundred Flowers movement
1957	Anti-Rightist campaign
1958	Great Leap Forward and creation of People's Communes
1959	Lushan conferences and dismissal of Peng Dehuai
1966	Cultural Revolution begins
1969	Ninth Communist Party Congress
1971	Death of Lin Biao
1972	US President Nixon visits China
1975	Death of Chiang Kai-shek
1976 (September)	Death of Mao Zedong
1976 (October)	Arrest of Gang of Four
1978	Third Plenum of Eleventh CCP Central Committee
1978	Reform period begins under Deng Xiaoping
1980–1	Trial of the Gang of Four
1987	Hu Yaobang dismissed as CCP head
1987	Zhao Ziyang replaces Hu as CCP head
1989 (4 June)	Tian'anmen Square demonstrations suppressed
1989 (24 June)	Jiang Zemin replaces Zhao Ziyang as CCP head
1989	Deng Xiaoping retires
1997 (February)	Death of Deng Xiaoping
1997 (July)	Hong Kong returns to China
1999 (May)	Chinese embassy in Belgrade hit by NATO bombs
1999 (July)	Falungong demonstrations
2001 (April)	US fighter plane incident off Hainan island
2001 (December)	China enters the World Trade Organisation
2002 (November)	Severe acute respiratory syndrome (SARS) epidemic
2002 (November)	CCP Sixteenth Congress – Hu Jintao President
2003	Avian influenza epidemic
2006 (January)	Agricultural taxation abolished
2007 (October)	CCP Seventeenth Congress – Xi Jinping tipped as future leader
2008 (August)	Olympic Games in Beijing

Part I

Introduction

1 Land, people and culture

China as a subcontinent

China is in many ways a country like any other – say, Denmark or Ecuador or Nigeria – but in view of its size and diversity, it is often more practical and fruitful to think of it as a subcontinent. It is commonplace to speak of the countries of South Asia as the 'Indian subcontinent' – a term which accurately reflects the size of the land mass; the geographical diversity; the variety of peoples, languages, religions and cultures; and the political differences of the states of which that region is composed. China has all of these, including the political antagonism that divides the mainland and Taiwan, but it is usually treated, both by Chinese and by foreign observers, as a single homogeneous entity. Thinking of it as a subcontinent, as well as a nation, makes it possible to understand more clearly the geographical and cultural complexity that has influenced its history and the evolution of its political structures.

There is resistance, often intense resistance, by some Chinese people, to the idea of considering China as anything other than a nation. This is invariably motivated by a sense of national pride or patriotism. In their view, to regard China in any other way appears to leave the door open to federalism or worse still to separatism – the possibility, however unlikely, that Tibet, Xinjiang, Inner Mongolia or even one of the more prosperous southern provinces might achieve independence from the mainland. Many citizens of China are acutely aware of the historical legacy of division and weakness that made it possible for a disaggregated China to be colonised partially by the West and then to be invaded by Japan which occupied much of its territory between 1931 and 1945. A strong, unified China, it is argued, is the only way of preventing a repetition of that period of national humiliation. Attitudes such as these severely inhibit any discussion of possible alternatives to the existing configuration of China's polity, such as federalism, but they are a very significant part of China's political culture.

Size

China is vast by any standards: it extends from a point 54° North, on the Wusuli (Ussuri) River in the northern part of Heilongjiang province, which has a border with the Russian Far East, to 18° North, the southern point of the semi-tropical island of Hainan. It stretches for three thousand miles across the eastern part of the Eurasian land mass from the most westerly part of Xinjiang at 74° East to a point 135° East, which is to just to the west of the city of Khabarovsk, a reminder for Westerners, especially Europeans, who tend to assume that all of Russia lies to the west of China. China occupies an area of 3,657,765 square miles and has a land border of some 13,800 miles, mostly with Central Asia: it has a coastline that is over 9,000 miles long and functions as an important maritime frontier. Some of these figures may be disputed because of long-standing and unresolved boundary disputes but nevertheless they give a clear sense of the orders of magnitude involved in considering the geography of China. Because of the size and diversity of the country, it is essential that great care be taken when making generalisations about any aspect of Chinese society.

The population of China, which was 582 million when the 1953 census was carried out (the first in the entire history of China that had any degree of credibility), has grown at a rate which is either impressive or alarming according to the observer's point of view: it currently stands at approximately 1.3 billion. This makes China the most populous nation on earth, a distinction it has held for decades, although India with a total population of 1.1 billion is gradually catching up. It is instructive to compare figures for China's population with other countries and regions. In 2005, the United Kingdom had an estimated population of 60.5 million, compared with the population of the Chinese province of Hubei which alone is over 60 million; the whole of Europe (East and West) is home to 728 million people who live in 6,500,000 square miles of land shared between twenty-seven separate nation-states; the United States has a total population of 300 million. The land area of North America as a whole is 9,450,000 square miles and it has a combined population of over 514 million. Taiwan has a population of 22.8 million and a declining birth rate,[1] while in the former British colony of Hong Kong there are only 6.86 million inhabitants. Population size is far from being the only determinant of a nation's character and prospects for development and stability but it is a critical factor.

Great rivers

In common with all civilisations of great antiquity, China owes the earliest development of its agriculture and settlement to great rivers which run through its territory. The two best known, and by far the most important in the story of China's development as a nation, are the Yellow River, and the Yangzi.

The source of the Yellow River, the Huanghe, is 14,000 feet high in the mountains of Qinghai province close to the Kokonor: in the Mongolian language, *Kokonor* means 'Blue Lake', which is also what *Qinghai* means in Chinese. The Yellow River runs for over three thousand miles through northern China and into the Gulf of Bohai to the north of the promontory of Shandong province. On its long journey to the ocean, the Yellow River describes a magnificent arc through the deserts and plains on China's border with Mongolia and then bends sharply into the low-lying farmland of the eastern seaboard – farmland that the might of the river has been instrumental in creating. It is called the Yellow River because it carries yellow (more accurately, brown) silt from the mountains down to the plains. The silt is deposited to contribute to a fine-grained, easily worked loess soil that has enabled China's farmers to till the land for centuries.[2]

The waters of the Yellow River then irrigate this loess terrain. However, the silt that has been such a boon to rural China has also destroyed it periodically: the accumulation of silt deposits builds up over time and causes the river to burst its banks, flooding the farms and villages of the North China Plain and causing great loss of life as well as physical devastation and economic and social disruption. In one fateful year, 1851, the spectacular intensity of the flooding forced the river to change its course. Before the inundation, it flowed into the ocean south of the Shandong Peninsula; afterwards it emerged to the north, at its present exit point. Not for nothing has the Yellow River been called 'China's sorrow'.

The river that the world knows as the Yangzi (Yangtse) is known in China as the Changjiang, which simply means 'Long River', which it is – its total length is 3,964 miles. It flows from its source high on the Tibetan Plateau through spectacular gorges, passes through the very centre of China and spills out into the Yellow Sea just to the north of Shanghai. Its great breadth is as significant as its great length. For centuries it was impossible to bridge the torrent for a distance of hundreds of miles and, in many places, it is still necessary to use a ferry to cross from one bank to the other. The construction of the great bridge at Nanjing, which was completed in 1969 during the Cultural Revolution, was proclaimed a major triumph for Chinese engineers and for the collective spirit of the People's Republic.

Because of the difficulty that there has always been in crossing the Changjiang, the river was a major physical barrier and it is the natural boundary between northern and southern China – a separation which accounts in part for the pronounced cultural differences between the north and the south. The productive rice-growing areas of the south were traditionally known as Jiangnan ('south of the river', that is to the south of the Changjiang) and these areas have retained distinctive spoken languages and cultures which, especially in the rural areas, are quite unlike those of the northern, Mandarin-speaking part of China.

The Three Gorges hydroelectric project which dams the upper reaches of the river is a colossal and controversial feat of engineering which began in 1993, has submerged some 1,200 towns and villages and has displaced thousands of local residents. It has been criticised by environmental campaigners and many have blamed it for the increased pollution of the river. A more detailed consideration of the Three Gorges project can be found in Chapter 14.

Another important watercourse which is vital to the regional economy of south China is the Pearl River or Zhujiang. The Pearl River is China's third longest and it is produced by the confluence of three smaller rivers: the Xi Jiang (West River), the Bei Jiang (North River), and the Dong Jiang (East River). The river and its tributaries flow through the provinces of Hunan, Jiangxi, Guizhou, Yunnan, Guangxi and Guangdong before emptying into the South China Sea in the great Pearl River Delta.

The Pearl River Delta is home to some of the most dynamic and enterprising urban economies of contemporary China, including the pioneering Special

Economic Zone of Shenzhen, where Deng Xiaoping's reform policies were first displayed to the outside world, Zhuhai with its modern high-tech industries and the old iron and porcelain town of Foshan. It has become one of the economic boom centres of post-Mao China and specialises in manufacturing, notably electronics and other consumer goods for the export market.

Mountains

Mountain ranges have always been the historical and the natural boundaries for many of the provinces in southern China. Mountainous terrain which is difficult to farm and challenging to cross has hampered communications and economic development over the centuries although the lack of land routes has, to some extent, been compensated for by the abundance of natural waterways – lakes and rivers – which have played an important role in communications and commerce in the south.

The Tianshan (Mountains of Heaven) and the Pamirs mark the geographical frontiers of western China. They form the boundary with Kazakhstan, Kyrgyzstan and Tajikistan although the Tianshan range (Tengri Tagh in Uyghur and in the other Central Asian languages) also extends into northern Xinjiang to the north of the Taklamakan Desert. The Karakorum mountain range, part of the Himalaya chain and home to K2, the second highest peak in the world, separates China from Kashmir and Pakistan; the eastern ranges of the Himalayas are the boundary between China and India. In the northeast of China, the Great Khingan (Xing'an in Chinese) range of volcanic mountains forms the geographical boundary between the plains of Manchuria and the high plateau of Mongolia.

Geography and development

Economic and social development in China has never been uniform. There are major differences between the north and south of the country. This is partly due to geographical factors: the northern climate is drier, it is difficult to guarantee regular sources of water for agriculture and there is a constant underlying threat of desertification. The south experiences rainfall in much greater abundance. This makes it possible to grow sufficient rice to feed large populations, in some areas by multiple cropping, but the drawbacks are the risk of flooding and the threat of tropical storms and typhoons which regularly assault the coastal regions of the southeast, often with devastating effect on settlements, lives and crops.

Geopolitical factors have also played a significant role: throughout recorded history almost all the capitals of unified Chinese states have been in the north and the paramount strategic necessity of defending agricultural China from the nomads of the steppes of Inner Asia shaped communications and settlement for centuries.

There is a striking contrast between the relatively high level of development in the eastern and southeastern coastal regions and the economic and cultural backwardness of the interior (the western regions). Although this disparity has a historical pedigree that can be traced back for hundreds of years, it was exacerbated

Table 1.1 GDP per capita in RMB* 2002

Shanghai	40,646
Jiangsu	14,391
Zhejiang	6,838
Fujian	13,497
Shaanxi	5,523
Gansu	4,493
Ningxia	5,804
Guizhou	3,153

* Renminbi (people's currency)

by the creation of the treaty ports and their hinterlands under the influence of Western colonisation in the nineteenth century. The discrepancy in levels of development between eastern and western China has increased dramatically during the economic expansion that has taken place since 1978. One economic marker that illustrates the different level of development is gross domestic product (GDP), which broadly speaking represents the total value of all goods and services produced. Per capita figures for the GDP of individual provinces and cities illustrate the difference between the coastal (the first group) and the inland western regions of China (the second group).

Provinces, autonomous regions and municipalities

The major administrative subdivisions of China are its twenty-two provinces and five autonomous regions (ARs) – Tibet (Xizang), Xinjiang, Inner Mongolia (Nei Monggol), Ningxia Hui and Guangxi Zhuang – which are provincial-level administrations that exercise a degree of autonomy (arguably only token autonomy) in deference to the large populations of non-Han Chinese people who have lived in them for centuries. Provinces and autonomous regions are further subdivided into prefectures and, below those, counties: prefectures and counties are always based on an urban administrative centre. In areas where there is a concentration of ethnic minority communities, there are also autonomous prefectures and counties.

Towns and cities may serve as provincial, prefectural or county centres, but the largest cities – Beijing, Chongqing, Shanghai and Tianjin – are municipal administrations in their own right and also have responsibility for large tracts of rural areas that surround the cities as well as for the central urban areas.

Languages and cultures

Chinese is the principal language of China, but it is not the only language and, more importantly, it is not even one single language. The official language of the country is known today as *Putonghua*, which translates as the 'common language' or *lingua franca* and which purists tend to call Standard Chinese. In Taiwan, it is still known as Kuo-yu (in pinyin, *Guoyu*) which translates as the national language, a term that was common on the mainland in the 1930s and 1940s. Standard Chinese is almost universally known in the English-speaking world as Mandarin, an even more old-fashioned term than Kuo-yu and one which was used of the court language of the Qing period (1644–1911). At the time this was known in Chinese as *Guanhua*, 'official language'.

Mandarin, or Standard Chinese, is in fact a standardised form of the spoken language of the region of northern China that includes the capital, Beijing. It is not, however, spoken universally, even in the capital itself where there is a dialect (*Beijing tuhua*) used by the local people and which can take some time for even seasoned speakers of Standard Chinese to get used to. Mandarin is the official spoken language of television and radio and it is taught in all schools: in theory, everyone in China should understand *Putonghua* even if they are more comfortable speaking a dialect of Mandarin or one of the southern variants of Chinese.

There are various dialects of Mandarin throughout the north and northwest of China, with the most noticeable difference being between the northern and southern dialect areas, but anyone who has ventured far from the major urban centres will have become aware of the great variations in pronunciation within the rural population of the Mandarin-speaking area. Because of the awareness of the existence of dialects within Mandarin, it has become more usual to see the other varieties of Chinese, which were once referred to as 'dialects', now promoted to the status of 'languages'. This recognises the linguistic reality since they are as different from each other as the languages of, say, the Romance family in Europe – Portuguese and Romanian, for example. Regional forms of speech that are spoken a great distance apart, especially in the rural areas, are mutually incomprehensible, have quite distinct vocabularies and to some extent different grammars.

The most important non-Mandarin Chinese languages are: Cantonese, which is spoken in Guangdong province and in Hong Kong and is also used very widely as a *lingua franca* among the communities of the Chinese diaspora in Europe and North America; the Shanghai or Wu language of eastern China; and Fujianese or Hokkien from the southeastern province of Fujian, which is also spoken by a majority of the population of Taiwan, whose ancestors migrated from Fujian in the eighteenth and nineteenth centuries. In Taiwan, this form of Chinese is often referred to as Taiwanese to distinguish it from the Mandarin or Kuo-yu spoken by the ruling mainlander elite. Technically it is Minnan or Southern Min: both Northern Min and Southern Min are spoken in Fujian on the mainland. Fujianese is also important in the Chinese communities of Indonesia, Malaysia and other parts of southeast Asia.

What is unusual about the condition of language in China is that, while each of these regions has its own distinct spoken vernacular, they all use one single form of written Chinese – based on the grammar and vocabulary of Mandarin Chinese – for most practical purposes. This is possible because Chinese characters are essentially non-phonetic.[3] There are in existence variant written forms which are used in certain circumstances to represent the local idiom in, for example, popular regional drama, but newspapers, magazines, books (including textbooks for schools) and the internet all use the standard written language.

This standard written language appears in one of two forms of script: the older form which is retained in Taiwan and Hong Kong, as well as in many expatriate communities, and the simplified script which was adopted in the People's Republic of China as part of a programme of language reform in the 1950s. This reform was part of the Chinese Communist Party's (CCP's) efforts to grapple with the serious problem of illiteracy. Simplified Chinese characters, which are based on the original characters but with a reduced number of brush or pen strokes, are disliked and even rejected by many Chinese who live outside the mainland. In particular, they are avoided in Taiwan because of their association with the CCP, although these objections are often couched in terms of aesthetics and readability rather than politics. Written styles also vary: Taiwan and Hong Kong favour prose styles that have echoes of the classical Chinese tradition and tend to be terser and arguably more elegant, whereas writing on the mainland has deliberately remained closer to the spoken vernaculars as part of a policy of popularisation and in the hope that this would help to improve the spread of literacy.

As China has opened culturally to the rest of the Chinese world, there has been greater contact between these styles. Writers on the mainland have felt able to use more complex styles of writing that would once have looked out of place. In Hong Kong, the simplified script is used alongside the traditional version.

Chinese is not unique in this separation of standard written and local spoken forms: the near universal use of a standard form of written Arabic throughout the Middle East disguises the fact that there exists a variety of very different and often mutually unintelligible spoken vernaculars, but the separation between spoken and written Chinese is much greater than that between spoken and written Arabic.

2 China's past in the present

Without some appreciation of the historical background to the colossal changes of the twentieth and twenty-first centuries, it is very difficult to make sense of what is happening in China today. The historical legacy, which continues to influence attitudes in contemporary China, includes: the Opium War and the impact of the West in the nineteenth century; peasant rebellions; cultural nationalism which was in part a response to challenges posed by the West; the abortive Republican experiment of 1912–13 and the collapse into balkanised regional regimes under the rule of warlords; the military occupation by Japan during the Second World War; Civil War between Communists and Nationalists; the rise of Mao Zedong and the radical experiments of the Great Leap Forward and the Cultural Revolution. Some of these events are still fresh in the minds of the older generation and are also familiar to the younger age group from studies at school and in popular culture, although some may wish to reject the political heritage of their parents' and grandparents' generations.

Two thousand years of imperial tradition

From 1644 to 1911, China was ruled by the Qing dynasty, the last in a long line of ruling houses that, by Chinese convention, stretches back in an unbroken line to the unification of the feudal warring states by the First Emperor, Qin Shi Huangdi, in 221 BC. A list of all of the dynasties of imperial China in chronological order provides a comforting illusion of continuity and stability but the transition from one dynasty to another was rarely peaceful. Typically the ruling elite of the declining dynasty lost the confidence of all or part of the population and its authority waned, during a period of perhaps scandal at court or a peasant rebellion, and a new elite came to power. The victors would claim that they now possessed the Mandate of Heaven (*tianming*), which the vanquished court were deemed to have lost by virtue of their defeat.

Not all of the dynasties that ruled China were Chinese, in the sense that they were not all of ethnic Han Chinese origin. The Chinese state and Chinese society have evolved through the perennial conflict between the steppe and the sown; between the nomad stock breeders of the northern and western high pastures and the settled rice and millet farmers of the fertile basins created by the Yangzi and the Yellow River. Some of the most important dynasties in Chinese history were of non-Chinese (or, as far as many Chinese were concerned, 'barbarian') origin. The ruling elite of the Yuan dynasty was Mongolian and the aristocracy of the Qing dynasty was Manchu; both of these came from people who had their origins in nomad tribal confederations of the vast regions to the north of China. Their languages, cultures and traditions were quite unlike those of the Han Chinese although proximity, trade and conflict had led to linguistic and cultural borrowing in both directions over the centuries.

Manchus and Chinese

The relationship between the Manchu elite and the Han majority is vital for understanding the forces that led to the break-up of the Chinese empire: it was the wellspring of the nationalist movement of the late nineteenth and early twentieth centuries. Although the Manchus brought able Mongols, Muslims and Han Chinese into their administration – they had little option, as it was impossible for them to rule on their own – their garrisons, which were stationed strategically throughout China, were a visible reminder that the country was under the control of alien rulers. There were conflicts between the Manchu and Chinese members of the elite (there were far fewer Mongols), particularly over the most important issues such as relations with the West and the development of the economy. When there were serious difficulties or dangers, blaming the alien Manchus was the obvious solution for some of the most sophisticated Chinese thinkers as well as for less well-educated peasant leaders. The most obvious target for the denigration of the Manchus was the Empress Dowager, Cixi, frequently demonised but, on the basis of the available evidence, unquestionably culpable of many of the crimes of which she was accused. As a woman who ruled in what, according to Confucian orthodoxy, could only ever be a man's role, she could be blamed for bringing down the wrath of heaven on China and endangering the Qing dynasty's entitlement to the Mandate of Heaven. It was not forgotten that she was Yehonala, of the ruling Aisin Gioro clan of the Manchus, a foreign tribe holding sway over the sacred territory (*shenzhou*) of the Middle Kingdom.

The position of the Qing dynasty was already under attack from rural religious rebels, influenced by Buddhist and Daoist popular tradition, as early as the late eighteenth century in spite of the successes of the Kangxi and (particularly) the Qianlong emperors in military conquest and territorial aggrandisement. However, it was not this internal conflict but the increasing demands of the West for trade that were to precipitate both a crisis of state and a crisis of confidence.

Unable to obtain by negotiation the trading privileges that they desired, and after the failure of several costly diplomatic missions including the Macartney Embassy of 1793, the West, or, to be more specific and accurate, Great Britain, engineered a military confrontation, the Opium War of 1839–42. The Opium War is called by this name because it was the determination of the Qing court to bring to an end the British sale of opium to China that led to hostilities: on both sides, however, it was widely accepted that the issues in contention were far greater than just the trade in a narcotic, however much this was resented by China. China's territorial integrity and the question of who should exercise control over its foreign trade were at stake.

Defeat in the Opium War forced the court in Beijing to sign the Treaty of Nanjing in 1842, the first in a series of what were to become known in China as the 'unequal treaties'. Under this and subsequent agreements, most of which were imposed on China by force or the threat of force, a number of coastal and river cities – the treaty ports – were opened to trade with the West, Christian missionaries were permitted to proselytise among the predominantly Buddhist and Daoist population of the hinterland and, perhaps most important of all, the island of Hong Kong was handed over to Britain. For Britain, Hong Kong was to become a productive colonial possession; to China, it was an ever-present reminder of its defeat and humiliation. China was never completely colonised in the way that Britain had earlier taken control of India, but European (and later American and Japanese) merchants, administrators and military personnel established themselves in the foreign-controlled concession areas in ports such as Shanghai, Tianjin and Guangzhou, governing great swathes of territory with embassy-style privileges and keeping the locals at arms length, unless of course they were required for trade or menial work. This 'semi-colonialism', as some called it, rankled with many thinking Chinese, although it also provided a source of economic and social advancement for a small class of merchants and entrepreneurs who were prepared to transact business with the foreigners and who also remained on good terms with the local Chinese administration.

Rise of the Chinese Communist Party

The Chinese Communist Party (CCP) has been in power on the mainland of China since 1949. There has been no effective organised opposition to it since that date and, until the suppression of the Democracy Movement in and around Tian'anmen Square in June 1989, CCP rule appeared to be completely unassailable. The CCP recovered even from that trauma: it has reformed and restructured itself and evidently has every intention of retaining power in the long term. Whether it will succeed in this and what will happen if it does not are the key questions for understanding the future of China.

The rise of the CCP and the revolutionary movement that it spearheaded can be traced back to the colonisation of parts of Qing dynasty China by the European powers and later by the United States and Japan in the late nineteenth and early twentieth centuries. This encroachment culminated in the scramble for territorial concessions in 1898, the suppression of the Boxer uprising by foreign troops in 1899–1901 and, in 1911, the collapse of not only the Manchu Qing dynasty, which had demonstrably failed to deal with pressure from the foreigners, but also the two-thousand-year-old Chinese empire.

After the revolution of 1911, which began as a small-scale mutiny among units of the army based in the garrison of the town of Wuchang (part of present-day Wuhan) but spread like wildfire throughout the whole country, the centralised bureaucratic administration of Qing China disintegrated. A Republic was proclaimed in 1912 to replace the Qing dynasty but it was never able to take a firm hold of the country and, when the first President, Yuan Shikai, who had seized power from Sun Yat-sen, attempted to have himself declared Emperor in 1916, the fragile basis of the new system was obvious. It collapsed into a network of regionally based warlord kingdoms which formed fluid alliances with each other but were also in constant conflict. From 1917 to 1927, these warlords were the *de facto* rulers of China: central government was either weak or non-existent. China, a predominantly peasant society, was subject to endemic poverty and disease as well as to periodic and widespread famines, some of which had catastrophic effects on the land and the people. Educated Chinese were conscious of the plight of their country and many were deeply ashamed and angry at the degradation and humiliation of what they continued to believe was a great nation.

A nationalist movement developed in response to this sentiment, with supporters advocating the overthrow of the warlords and the restoration of a unified national political structure. Most of them rejected the old imperial structure, even in a revised form such as a constitutional monarchy, and looked to some kind of republic as the most appropriate form of government for China. Two strands of nationalism, one associated with the Guomindang (GMD) (Kuomintang or Nationalist Party) and the other with the CCP, emerged at about the same time.

The catalyst for the growth of this nationalism was the treatment of China by the major international powers in the peace settlement that followed the Treaty of Versailles, which was signed in June 1919 after the end of the First World War (1914–18). Most educated Chinese who followed international developments had assumed that territorial concessions which had been secured by Germany at the end of the nineteenth century would be returned to China after the Allied victory, since China had been at least nominally an ally of Britain. However, these concessions were in fact handed over to Japan, in recognition of Tokyo's pact with Britain, the Anglo-Japanese Alliance, which had been agreed in 1902, and also its nominal alliance with France during the war. The Japanese army and navy had played little part in the conflict, but the parties drawing up the treaty were conscious of Japan's emerging status as the next great power in the Pacific. In China, the renowned demonstrations of 4 May 1919 which followed the announcement of the treaty provisions were accompanied by a widespread and profound questioning of the nature of Chinese society and China's place in the world – a phenomenon which was to become known as the May Fourth Movement or the New Culture Movement.

Trade unions were developing rapidly in Hong Kong, Shanghai, Guangzhou (Canton) and many other major Chinese cities, and they flexed their muscles in a series of strikes, which Marxist activists helped to organise. It was in this setting that the CCP was formally established in 1921 with advice and support from the Comintern in Moscow, and it held its first conference in the grounds of a girls' school in Shanghai. The twelve delegates who attended represented a total membership of fifty-seven and the conference was obliged to repair to a boat on a lake for fear of informers. This was a small and inauspicious beginning for the party that was to take control of China within less than thirty years.

At the same time, Sun Yat-sen, the leading nationalist revolutionary in China, also accepted offers of support from the new Soviet Union and its international arm, the Comintern. This was not because of any ideological attachment to Marxism but because he admired the success of the Communist Party of the Soviet Union, a success that he attributed to its discipline and organisation. The GMD under Sun Yat-sen was reorganised on the basis of the centralist and Leninist model of the Soviet Communist Party in 1923. However, Sun died on 12 March 1925 and his place as political and military leader was taken by Chiang Kai-shek (Jiang Jieshi), who had been commandant of the Whampoa Military Academy in Guangzhou, a college that was charged with the responsibility of creating a modern officer corps for the GMD's new army.

It is ironic, in the light of their subsequent history of conflict and enmity, that both the CCP and the GMD in their early days were supported by the Moscow-based Comintern. This was partly because Stalin's theories of national revolution required an alliance between a bourgeois and a proletarian party and partly because of the practical consideration that the CCP was perceived as far too weak to be an independent political force. The policy of the Comintern was that the two Chinese parties should cooperate and, during what was known as the First United Front (from 1923 to 1927) CCP members joined the GMD while still retaining membership of their own party. They supported the National Revolutionary Army, which was controlled by the GMD and which Chiang Kai-shek led on what he announced was to be the movement's Northern Expedition from his base in Guangzhou in southern China to recover China from the warlords and establish a national government. This alliance came to an abrupt and grisly end in Shanghai in April 1927 while the Northern Expedition was still under way. Nationalist troops, assisted by members of Shanghai's criminal underworld, imprisoned and killed Communists and suspected Communists and broke up the trade union organisations which had been their main source of support.

The immediate response of the CCP to what they would from that time onwards regard as a historic betrayal was to launch a series of urban insurrections. When these failed disastrously, the CCP was forced to abandon its offices in the cities and it gradually regrouped in China's vast rural interior. Cut off from the urban labour movement, from the nationalists, and from Western and modern ideas, the CCP underwent a profound transformation, first in its base camp at Jinggangshan on the border of Jiangxi province in south-central China, and then during a period of experimental independent government in the Jiangxi Soviet. This was the name given to a region in the south of Jiangxi province which the CCP controlled and governed from 1930 to 1934. GMD siege tactics, known as 'encirclement campaigns', finally forced the CCP to abandon its base in Jiangxi and it embarked on its legendary Long March, the epic strategic withdrawal that took it to the remote mountainous region of Yan'an in northwest China's Shaanxi province.

The Communists, or to be more precise one contingent of the CCP, arrived in the small town of Yan'an between September 1935 and October 1936 and it was in the traditional peasant cave houses of this mountain redoubt that Mao Zedong consolidated his leadership over what was to become the most successful section of the Party. The CCP also acquired a new ideology in Yan'an – Marxism-Leninism-Mao Zedong Thought. This was a highly idiosyncratic synthesis of crude mechanical Marxism drawn from such editions of the works of Stalin (and other theoretical studies from the USSR) as were available in the isolated community of Yan'an, underpinned by the romance of the Chinese rebel and revolutionary tradition which particularly attracted Mao Zedong. This mixture of philosophy and political dogma is often known in the West as 'Maoism' for the sake of brevity, although this usage has never been popular in China.

The CCP that emerged from these harsh experiences was very different from the one that had grown up in the metropolises of Shanghai, Hong Kong, Tianjin (Tientsin), Guangzhou (Canton) and Beijing in the 1920s. By this time, its orientation was almost entirely rural. There was a constant drive to recruit peasants through a series of campaigns for land redistribution and rent reduction and, after the Japanese invasion of China in September 1937, the emphasis changed to a movement of patriotism and resistance. The transformation in the CCP was so profound that for many orthodox Communists it was difficult to see how it could be treated as a Communist Party in the accepted sense of the term at the time. In addition to the Party itself, the Communists had created the Workers' and Peasants' Red Army in 1927: the Red Army had a close and symbiotic relationship with the Party and the membership of the two overlapped.

The Japanese invasion of China in 1937 dramatically altered the balance of power in China. The GMD government under Chiang Kai-shek was forced to flee from its capital, Nanjing (Nanking in the spelling current at the time), and it established a temporary base in Chongqing (Chungking) in the southwestern province of Sichuan. The Japanese armies of occupation controlled the most populous parts of China, the east and the southeast, or at least they held the main towns and cities and the railway links between them. The Communists consolidated their power base in the northwest and developed a strategy of guerrilla resistance behind enemy lines. A formal agreement between the GMD and CCP to combine their forces in a Second United Front for the War of Resistance against Japan led to only limited military cooperation. From 1937 onwards, the military units of the Workers' and Peasants' Red Army were nominally under unified national control, adopting neutral names such as the Eighth Route Army and the New Fourth Army, but in practice they retained considerable operational and political independence.

With the defeat of Japan in August 1945, the war of resistance metamorphosed almost imperceptibly into a bitter civil war between the GMD and the CCP: this lasted from 1946 to 1949 in spite of ill-fated attempts by United States diplomats to broker a coalition government of the two parties. The Civil War ended with the defeat of the GMD and their flight to the island of Taiwan. They continued their government in Taiwan, with a regime that was led by Chiang Kai-shek until his death in 1975, and maintained their claim to be the only legitimate authority for the whole of China.

Communist Party in power

The CCP emerged victorious from the Civil War in 1949, largely because of the patriotic reputation that it had acquired through its guerrilla resistance to the Japanese invasion (even though this was somewhat exaggerated), its land reform policies which earned it widespread support from peasants, and the sheer incompetence and corruption of the GMD political and military leadership. A close reading of sources published in the late 1940s suggests that there was no realistic alternative to the CCP, whatever anyone might have felt about their background or their policies.

The CCP had to make a difficult transition from acting as a military revolutionary force to establishing a civilian administration – a transformation that had many antecedents in the history of the rise and fall of Chinese dynasties. A series of political campaigns in the cities eradicated GMD supporters from influential positions and the old urban elite was gradually replaced with a new cadre of CCP sympathisers. In the rural areas, land reform teams led by the military and by educated young CCP activists secured Communist control over outlying areas by means of the land reform strategy of confiscating land from the wealthy and redistributing it to the poor. This was implemented throughout almost the entire country and guaranteed for the CCP the support of a great many of the poorest people in the rural areas.

The supremacy of the CCP was further strengthened by China's participation in the Korean War on the side of North Korea. The domestic prestige of the People's Liberation Army (PLA), already great after its victory in the Civil War, rose even higher. The perception of an external threat, and a genuine and justified fear that UN troops led by the USA might take the opportunity to put Chiang Kai-shek back in power on the mainland, created a combination of patriotism and paranoia that enabled the state to equate opposition to the CCP with treason. When the Korean War came to an end with the armistice that was signed in 1953, China, though isolated from the West, was unified under what appeared to be a strong government with extensive popular support for its creation of a 'New China'.[1] Popular policies, which included land reform and a marriage law that aimed at equality between men and women, were followed by a Five-Year Plan to develop the economy on the basis of the Soviet model.

However, this apparent sense of solidarity and unity of purpose masked significant differences in the attitudes and approach of individuals and groups within the CCP elite. During the 1960s, divisions began to appear in the leadership over the appropriate strategy for developing China. The 1958 Great Leap Forward was an attempt by Mao Zedong, as he would have seen it, to drag China kicking and screaming into the age of industrialisation. Mao's strategy in his Great Leap was to strengthen the collectivisation of agriculture while at the same time attempting to increase the national output of iron, steel, coal and electric power as a means to industrialise China. More cautious members of the CCP hierarchy were opposed to this audacious but impractical approach to development and, although many went along with the Great Leap in public, there was forthright criticism and robust opposition in private. Far from succeeding in overtaking the level of industrialisation of Great Britain, which had been one of Mao's stated aims, the manner in which the Great Leap was carried out was probably the main cause of at least twenty million deaths, over and above what would normally have been expected, in 1959–60, three years when rural China was devastated by terrible famines. The famines were not caused solely by the Great Leap – there had been dreadful famines in China long before Mao and the CCP – but far from mitigating the effects of the famines as some claimed at the time, the transfer of farmers from agriculture to the production of iron and steel in the over-enthusiastic drive to industrialise made it more difficult to produce food crops and to share what was available.

After this catastrophe, the 'Maoist' approach of mass mobilisation and the politicisation of every aspect of daily life was temporarily replaced by the more cautious and pragmatic approach of Liu Shaoqi, Deng Xiaoping and others who were more inclined to think and behave like Soviet-style central planners. Mao was personally held responsible for the catastrophe, although he was not criticised publicly at the time, and for several years his power and influence were diminished. In the early 1960s China appeared to be reverting to a more conventional planned economy under a conservative bureaucratic structure.

The Great Proletarian Cultural Revolution was launched in the summer of 1966. At the time it was presented as a mass movement to rid the country of old-fashioned bourgeois culture (although an authentic bourgeois culture of the type that flourished in Europe had never developed in China) and to replace it with genuine proletarian culture. This was exemplified by vituperative criticism of traditional Beijing opera with its mandarins, mannered scholars and fragile heroines and the creation of alternative revolutionary operas to replace them. The resilient protagonists of the new operas were workers, peasants and soldiers and some were even women: their milieu was no longer the court or the wealthy landowning family but the docks or the mountains during the war of resistance against Japan.

The Cultural Revolution had never been primarily about culture, although attacking those in the cultural elite who were also his political enemies suited Mao Zedong's purpose well. The movement was his attempt to stage a political comeback. He attempted to use the troops of the PLA, which he had been cultivating under the leadership of his *protégé* and ardent supporter ('close comrade-in-arms' was the phrase at the time) Lin Biao, together with the poorer peasants and young and idealistic urban students, to overcome his factional opponents. What began as an ideological dispute spilt over into street fighting and violence in factories and universities: chaos ensued. Within a year it was necessary to deploy the PLA to police the cities and also to take over the leading role in local government in many parts of the country, to such an extent that much of China in 1968–69 was effectively under martial law. Lin Biao, in a spectacular and still largely unexplained escapade, apparently attempted to seize power in 1971 and was killed when his aircraft crashed in Mongolian territory while flying towards the Soviet Union.

An alternative and more sophisticated, political programme began to emerge after Lin's death. This programme was associated initially with Zhou Enlai, an enigmatic and ruthless, but enormously popular, character. Zhou had managed to survive the Cultural Revolution relatively unscathed without having been publicly criticised and was not linked too closely with either faction, although documents that have been subsequently released make it clear that he played a leading role in the organisations that were responsible for some of the callous purges during the period. Zhou's first successes were in the field of international relations and diplomacy. His willingness, in conjunction with Mao, to talk to the United States after China and the Soviet Union had fought a series of border skirmishes was undoubtedly the main cause of the fatal rift with Lin Biao. China replaced Taiwan in the United Nations in October 1971, giving China a way out of its international isolation. Deng Xiaoping, whose mentor Liu Shaoqi had died in 1969 as a result of persecution during the Cultural Revolution, gradually became more influential as Zhou Enlai became seriously ill, but his return to power could not immediately be made public for fear of offending Mao and his supporters.

Although many of the more radical policies had already been abandoned, the Cultural Revolution period only came to a complete end in 1976 after the deaths of some of the key political figures of twentieth-century China. The GMD leader, Chiang Kai-shek, died in Taiwan in 1975 and Zhou Enlai, Zhu De (the veteran Long March military leader) and finally Mao Zedong passed away in the following year.

Mao died on 9 September, following what was regarded by the more traditional and superstitious element of the Chinese population as a celestial portent – the devastating earthquake which had struck the northeast city of Tangshan the previous July. Within a month, Mao's closest Cultural Revolution supporters (including his wife Jiang Qing) had been arrested and accused of operating as a counter-revolutionary Gang of Four against the CCP.

First decade of reform 1979–89

The members of the Gang of Four were not put on trial until November 1980, by which time the political battle against supporters of the Cultural Revolution within the CCP had to all intents and purposes been won. The Gang of Four and many of their junior aides and acolytes were sentenced to long terms of imprisonment: this included a life sentence for Jiang Qing who later died in prison, almost certainly by her own hand. Deng Xiaoping's position was now more secure and he had already begun to implement the policies of Four Modernisations (the modernisation of agriculture, industry, science and technology, and defence) that had been bequeathed to him by Zhou Enlai. These policies, which evolved into the broader approach of reform and opening (*gaige kaifang*) that was Deng's own political trademark, launched the reform decade that was to change Communist China out of all recognition.

In essence, and although this could never be admitted openly at the time, Deng's policies undid virtually all the work that Mao Zedong had done in the period from 1949 until his death in 1976. Officially the reforms were subject to the Four Basic Principles: the dictatorship of people's democracy; leadership by the CCP; socialism; and Marxism-Leninism Mao Zedong Thought. In practice, the third and fourth of these principles were mere rhetoric: the only principles that mattered were the first two and these should be read as making it clear that whatever reforms were to be carried out, the CCP would remain in power.

The earliest, and one of the most fundamental, of the reforms was the implementation of the Responsibility System or Household Responsibility System in agriculture in 1979. This anodyne term concealed a programme to return land to individual families, essentially privatising Chinese agriculture and thereby ending twenty years of the People's Communes, the distinctive Chinese form that collectivised agriculture had taken in 1958 during the Great Leap Forward. Private trade, privatised industry and the emergence of a new class of small entrepreneurs (*getihu*), gradually reduced the state's absolute monopoly over industry and commerce. Special Economic Zones with preferential taxation and financial packages for foreign investors became a back-door way of introducing European, American and Japanese capitalism into China.

Reforms did not proceed without opposition and, during the 1980s, tensions continued between senior political figures who were pressing for deeper and faster reforms and others, many of them elderly former military officers, who could not accept that everything they had fought for against the Japanese and the GMD might be destroyed by the reforms. Modernisation looked too much like Westernisation to many of the older members of the elite.

One of the leading reformers, Hu Yaobang, who had been CCP Secretary-General and a *protégé* of Deng Xiaoping, was dismissed by Deng in 1987 after it was alleged that he had been too accommodating to the organisers of student demonstrations which took place in December 1986 against corruption and the restriction of freedom of speech. He was also thought to be too close to the liberal elements of the Chinese intelligentsia and, more bizarrely, was accused of leading a pro-Japan faction in the CCP. He was replaced by Zhao Ziyang,

Hu's death, from natural causes, on 15 April 1989, was the catalyst for a wave of demonstrations from which the Democracy Movement eventually emerged. The demonstrations, and the temporary camp that students and local citizens had established in Tian'anmen Square, were crushed by troops and tanks of the PLA on the night of 3 and 4 June 1989 and the whole endeavour was denounced afterwards by the Chinese authorities as a counter-revolutionary movement. The brutal suppression of a youthful domestic political movement was a clear indication that the gerontocracy could still tip the balance of power in a crisis. The decision to use the military to clear the demonstrators from Tian'anmen Square was by no means unanimous and it left the CCP and PLA desperately divided for years. Chinese thinkers were once again asking, as they had during the nationalist demonstrations of May 1919, how such a betrayal could possibly happen in China. The old soldiers, products of the Long March, and the war of resistance to Japan, were by this time all in their eighties and nineties and their influence was destined to die with them, as few people in the succeeding generations shared their perspectives or their fears. Deng Xiaoping himself, the man whose name will be linked indelibly with both the reform programme and the brutal suppression of the demonstrators in Tian'anmen Square, died on 19 February 1997. The chapters that follow are the story of his successors.

Part II

The economy

3   Economic growth and the changing economy

Dramatic growth

The most dramatic aspect of China's reform programme since its inception in 1979 has been the rate of growth of the economy. International economic analysts have frequently used words such as 'breakneck' to describe the pace of reform and concern has been expressed at regular intervals that the economy might overheat. Chinese economists and social planners have been acutely aware that this success in economic growth has been achieved at a price: the ever-increasing gap in income and standard of living between the rich and the poor; and between the wealthy eastern and coastal regions of China and the vast and often impoverished western territories.

After the plenary meeting of the Chinese Communist Party's (CCP's) Central Committee that came to an end on Tuesday 11 October 2005, it was clear from the concluding communiqué that China would continue its economic expansion and that the CCP was determined that the country's gross domestic product (the generally accepted measure of an economy's growth) should be doubled by the year 2010. However, the Central Committee also formally recognised the existing and potential social and environmental costs of the dash for growth and the communiqué included a statement on the need to improve China's system of welfare and social security and an indication that the leadership favoured the adoption of policies that were more responsive to environmental needs, almost certainly a sign of the influence of Premier Wen Jiabao.[1]

During 2006 there was no reduction in the speed of economic growth: the expanding export sector was the major contributor to an overall 10.4 per cent increase in the size of the economy in the third quarter of the year, although domestic consumption also played a significant role. This was a reduction on the 11.3 per cent growth of the second quarter but all the indications were that, for the fourth year running, China's economy would still be growing by over 10 per cent. At the same time the government had been restricting speculative investment. Some regional development projects did not receive the necessary government approval as part of a plan to slow what the leadership considers to be excessive growth in certain areas. This was achieved partly by the use of anti-corruption measures which allowed the central government to examine what it claimed was the misuse of public funds, including allegations of the abuse of pension funds in Shanghai which developed into a major scandal.[2]

Data from the National Bureau of Statistics that became available on 19 July 2007 revealed that, in spite of the government's measures, growth for the second quarter had not reduced but had in fact increased to 11.9 per cent. This growth was accompanied by a higher level of consumer inflation, attributed mainly to the increase in food prices. Chinese analysts, including economists at the Chinese Academy of Social Sciences and members of a specialist committee reporting to the National People's Congress (NPC), warned that the economy was on the brink of overheating. The response of the Chinese government, through the People's Bank of China, was a dose of fiscal engineering. The bank announced an increase in interest rates of 0.27 per cent and a cut in the taxation of interest earned in savings accounts: these measures were designed to reduce consumption and promote savings, the reverse of the policy that had been adopted in 1999.[3]

Economic legacy

China's economy, when the CCP came to power in 1949, could be characterised as essentially pre-modern. The Middle Kingdom was predominantly an agricultural society and in many parts of the country peasants were still using traditional technology, some of which had been in place with little change for hundreds of years.[4] This was not 'unchanging China' and there had been technical and organisational improvement in some regions and in the production of particular crops over the centuries, but the level of agricultural development was still far too low. The scarcity of arable land made it extremely difficult for China's farmers to produce sufficient food to meet the demands of population growth: this was a significant cause of the famines that the country had experienced in the 1920s and 1930s. War and civil war had also played their part in this. In 1949, the amount of grain produced was a mere 113 million tons, a quantity that was completely inadequate to feed the population. Urban China amounted to only some 20 per cent of the total population of the country but the towns and cities had to be fed from the surpluses generated from the countryside, surpluses that were seldom large enough even to feed the peasants.

Industrial development before 1949 had been patchy. There had been advances in modern heavy industry in the provinces of the northeast (Manchuria), largely as a result of the Japanese Occupation in the 1930s and 1940s. Manchuria was considered by the government in Tokyo to be vital to the development of the Japanese economy since it possessed immense resources of coal and iron, resources that Japan lacked. Coal mines and iron workings had been developed by Japanese enterprises since the 1920s, as had the railway infrastructure which was required to transport their products back to Japan. There had also been significant developments in the treaty ports, which were spread along the southeast coast and inland along the banks of the Yangzi River. The manufacture of textiles, food processing and other light industries was widespread but the development of these industries was hampered by the low level of technical skills among the workforce and by major problems in transport and distribution. The 'foreign matters' movement that followed the Tongzhi Restoration in the early 1860s had also left a legacy of industrial development to underpin the naval and armament industries that had been created by the modernising proto-warlords of the late Qing period and which were the highest priority of the Qing government. This type of development was localised in certain of the treaty ports and other coastal cities, including Fuzhou and Shanghai.

The problems of underdevelopment and rural poverty had been further exacerbated, not only by decades of war and civil war, but also by the hyperinflation of the 1940s. The first significant fiscal action taken by the new People's Government in 1949 was the centralisation of finance and taxation together with severe restrictions on the circulation of foreign currency. These measures, outlined in a Government Administration Council (GAC) document entitled *Decisions on the Unification of the Nation's Financial and Economic Work* were published on 3 March 1950 and had the effect of breaking the inflationary spiral.[5] China had no inflation between that date and the beginning of the reform programme in 1978.

Planned economy to mixed economy

When it was established in 1949, the government of the People's Republic of China (PRC) based its plans for economic development on the model that had been tried and tested (even if it had also often been found wanting) in the Soviet Union. The PRC had no other significant allies and was effectively obliged to follows this model. Essentially this involved creating a national planning system with targets and production quotas that were set centrally: subsidiary quotas were allocated to regions, provinces and, at the base of the planning hierarchy, to individual enterprises. These quotas were allotted on an annual basis but this was expressed within five-year plans, a system that had been borrowed almost without change from the Soviet Union. China's first Five-Year Plan began in 1953 and from that time onwards, China has had a Five-Year Plan for the economy. No plans were as high profile as the first one: subsequent plans were overshadowed by political developments including the Great Leap Forward and the Cultural Revolution and when the reform era began they assumed less immediate significance in the day-to-day economic life of the country. They continue to exist although they have not been referred to as frequently since the beginning of the economic reform programme in the 1980s. In 2007–8, China was working through the Eleventh Five-Year Plan.

The First Five-Year Plan (1953–57) was regarded by many contemporary analysts, Communist and non-Communist alike, as having been broadly successful. It was the only Chinese plan during the Mao era that followed its natural economic course completely without interruptions by political upheavals and it is therefore a good measure of the efficacy of this type of economic management in the Chinese context. Planning on a national scale could only begin in 1953 when the outlying provinces had been conquered and mass campaigns in rural and urban areas had assured the CCP that it was able to exercise political control. Initial attempts at long-term planning had been limited by lack of expertise in both planning and statistics; by the demands that the Korean War made on the Chinese economy; and by difficulties that China had encountered in negotiating an aid package with its ally, the Soviet Union. At first, plans had been made on an annual basis only, but by 1953, when the Korean War had ended and aid negotiations with the USSR had finally been concluded, realistic long-term planning was possible. The general principles of the First Five-Year Plan were published in 1953, but it was not until April 1955 that a full version was made publicly available.[6] In 1952 two government bodies were established to assist in the implementation of the plan, the State Statistical Bureau and the State Planning Commission, both of which were to become highly influential in the management of the Chinese economy. The fundamental role of the State Statistical Bureau was to generate the data needed for planning; the State Planning Commission, which reported directly to the State Council under the 1954 Constitution, was responsible for both long-term and annual plans until 1956 when short-term planning was devolved to the State Economic Commission.[7]

The central body that oversaw the early plans, the State Planning Commission, was renamed the State Development Planning Commission in 1998 in recognition of its changing role in an economy that was becoming more mixed in character. In 2003 it merged with the Office for Restructuring the Economic System, a department established by the State Council with special responsibility for moving China towards a market economy, and with a section of the State Economic and Trade Commission. It was renamed again, became the National Development and Reform Commission (NDRC), and its role was defined as being to oversee 'the transition from the planned economy to a socialist market economy'. Unlike the earlier bodies which had generated targets for local organisations, the NDRC is responsible for macroeconomic management, including the Five-Year Plans, which it is required under the terms of China's constitution to present to the NPC on behalf of the State Council. It is also responsible for the structural management of the national economy, for regional development strategies, including for example the Western Region Development Programme, and for major construction projects which have implications for the national economy. It is a key government body, has almost 1,000 employees working in twenty-six departments and is ideologically committed to economic reform under CCP control.[8]

An example of its specific, rather than its general, planning authority can be seen in the case of the steel industry in the province of Hebei, which is adjacent to the area directly under the control of the capital, Beijing. The NDRC accused the Hebei provincial government of having allowed the steel industry in the province to develop in an uncontrolled fashion and to expand in a way that was contrary to the national interest: in particular, it was argued that it duplicated industrial development in other regions. The NDRC instructed its office in Hebei province to prepare a report on overcapacity in Hebei which was due to be submitted to the NDRC and other central government bodies by the end of November 2006 and, in an unusual move, drew this to the attention of the central and the local media. The Hebei steel industry was seen as a test case and it is a good example of the type of problems that have arisen in economic relations between the centre and provinces and how they might be resolved. The measures proposed to bring Hebei into line included forcing the Hebei provincial government to decide on the closure of a number of steel plants in its own province.[9]

4   Rural economy

China is a Third World country: its economy is developing dramatically from a low base and its society is evolving rapidly. Its status as a developing country is often forgotten or ignored because it also a large Communist country. For thousands of years in the pre-historical period and under the successive dynasties of the empire, China was an almost exclusively rural and agricultural society: well into the twentieth century, as much as 80 per cent of the population lived in the countryside and worked on the land.

That proportion declined significantly in the second half of the century. Since 1949, China has undergone a remarkable process of industrialisation and urbanisation, both in the age of the planned economy of 1949–78 and in the reform era that followed. At the start of the twenty-first century, Chinese society is changing rapidly and, as a result of industrialisation and migration, the rural economy today probably employs less than 60 per cent of the total population. If the present government's plans for economic development are carried through, this proportion will continue to decrease.

Rural tradition and the village economy

The population of traditional China consisted almost entirely of peasants who owned their own land, tenant farmers, agricultural labourers and landowners. There was only a small urban sector. County towns were established as the seat of magistrates (*zhixian*) who were civil servants entrusted with the dual role of administering their county on behalf of the emperor and enforcing the law. The term 'magistrate', by which they are always known in the West, is somewhat misleading as their main function was local administration: there was, however, no tradition of separating the legal system from government. There were some important towns which grew up around specialised industries, such as the porcelain centre of Jingdezhen and Suzhou which was renowned for its silk manufacture, but these were few and far between, islands of industry in an ocean of agriculture.

The village economy was the foundation and the backbone of rural Chinese society for centuries. It had a complex social structure that incorporated the individual household; the extended family which is also known as the clan; neighbourhood groups which conventionally extended to five residences each side of a household; religious groups which worshipped the local gods and the village government under a headman who had probably risen to that position because of his seniority and experience. This structure, which was identified and described lucidly by the distinguished anthropologist Fei Xiaotong in the 1930s, persisted throughout the twentieth century and, although many believed that it had been eliminated during the Chinese Communist Party's (CCP's) land reform, collectivisation and commune programmes in the 1950s, it proved to be remarkably tenacious and has re-emerged since the destruction of the People's Communes in 1978.

Agriculture was naturally the mainstay of the rural economy. It was the regular occupation of most of the population and, in the traditional Chinese world view that for convenience is usually labelled 'Confucian', it was the only morally and socially acceptable calling for those born into peasant families. The vast majority of rural families devoted their lives to growing crops, although some also raised livestock: in certain areas of southern China, fishing was an important economic activity. Rice was, and remains, the main staple crop. It is especially abundant in the south and is also a powerful symbol of the Chinese rural economy, and indeed of Asian economies in general. In the north, however, wheat and millet are more easily grown, although there are also some productive rice-growing areas. Whereas people in the south will fill up on bowls of rice, in northern villages and towns, the main source of carbohydrate is the steamed or baked roll or, in the far northwest, varieties of flat bread similar to the *nan* of Pakistan and Afghanistan.

In imperial times, the agricultural year was regulated according to the traditional Chinese calendar which is in essence a lunar calendar – although it also takes into account the position of the earth in its solar orbit and should properly be termed a lunar–solar calendar. This calendar provided a framework for the seasonal cycles and was used to determine the correct time for the vital activities of the farming year such as sowing, transplanting and harvesting, but it also had a central social function as it served as a reminder of the dates of local community and religious activities.[1] Even though the Western calendar is now used in China for most purposes, the dates of the traditional calendar are still included on the mastheads of many newspapers. Almanacs that contain the lunar–solar calendar are widely consulted on the mainland, in Hong Kong and Taiwan and in Chinese communities in the West. Chinese almanacs (in common with Western publications such as *Old Moore's Almanach*) typically contain predictions which, in the case of China, are likely to be of particular interest to farming communities – such as trends in the weather and natural disasters; practical advice on crops and livestock; health, relationships and business, as well as much astrological material.

Handicraft industries were an important subsidiary economic activity in the rural areas, especially at quiet times for farming and when the weather made it impossible to work in the fields. Most handicrafts were produced by families in their houses or in small workshops rather than in larger units such as factories. The manufacture of farm tools and simple pots and pans was almost universal but some regions specialised in high-quality craft products that could be sold to outsiders for cash. These and other items were traded by pedlars or sold in the periodic or permanent markets with which traditional China abounded.

As the Civil War between the Communists and the Nationalists drew to an end in the 1940s, rural China was suffering from severe poverty, backwardness and underdevelopment: the need for reform was obvious to foreign and Chinese observers alike, whether or not they were sympathetic to the policies that the CCP eventually adopted to deal with the problem.

Land reform

Of all the policies adopted by the CCP in the rural areas that came under its control during the periods of civil war and the Japanese Occupation, land reform (*tudi gaige*) was by far the most important. Without land reform and the support that the CCP derived from it, none of their other policies could have been implemented. It had initially been tried out in the Jiangxi Soviet during the early 1930s and it later became part and parcel of the CCP's strategy for recruiting a mass army of sympathetic peasants during the dark days of the Japanese occupation. The term 'land reform' is sometimes used in a broad sense to indicate reforms that benefited the rural poor, including the reduction in rents and the interest rates on loans that the CCP compelled landlords and money-lenders to accept during the 1946–49 Civil War. Strictly speaking, however, it should be used in a more restricted way and refers primarily to the confiscation of land from landlords and rich peasants and the redistribution of the land that had been seized in this manner to the poorest of the peasants. The economic rationale for this compulsory redistribution was that the release of under-used assets could then enable the poor to feed themselves. The political rationale, not always made explicit, was that this would guarantee the support of the lowest socio-economic group in the countryside for the CCP. Land reform began in earnest, albeit in an uncontrolled and frequently forceful and brutal manner, in the areas that the CCP took from the Guomindang (GMD) armies in the closing years of the Civil War. When the People's Republic of China (PRC) was established in October 1949, one of the first pieces of legislation enacted by the new government was the *Agrarian Reform Law*, which came into force on 28 June 1950. From this time onwards, land reform was carried out throughout the whole of China and the law set out precise regulations for methods of confiscation and redistribution, although these were not necessarily adhered to with great care.

Mutual-aid teams, cooperatives and People's Communes

Even before the land reform programme had been completed, the second phase of agricultural reform – cooperation – was introduced. On the face of it there was a complete contradiction between the confiscation of land and its redistribution to peasant households and the subsequent policy of creating cooperatives, but the CCP argued that cooperation had always been its long-term goal. In the early 1950s, China's isolation from the West after the Korean War meant that its only allies were in the Soviet bloc: that alliance committed China to following, at least in broad terms, the style and approach of the Soviet Union in its development and management of the economy, albeit with some modifications to take into account social and cultural differences. China did, however, attempt to avoid what the CCP believed to have been the errors and excesses of forced collectivisation in the USSR and above all the attempt to exterminate the *kulaks*, the wealthiest peasant farmers, during the 1930s. Between 1949 and 1956, China to a large extent followed the Soviet model but as relations between the two governments began to sour in the late 1950s, Beijing evolved its own independent strategies – a Chinese style – for agricultural development as in other areas of policy.

The first stage in the process of bringing together what were essentially small family-run farms into larger units that were deemed to be more productive and more efficient was the creation of mutual-aid teams. These were family and village groups which were initially encouraged by CCP activists to cooperate in seasonal tasks by pooling their labour and farm tools, the latter of which in many cases they had very few. Ploughing, spring sowing and harvesting were among the key tasks undertaken by the teams. They were not an entirely new phenomenon: in many parts of the country they were based on traditional forms of community and clan cooperation on which the CCP activists could build. Once the teams were established, they were encouraged to continue on a more permanent basis and to work all the year round rather than solely when seasonal work demanded it.

Agricultural producers' cooperatives or APCs (*nongmin shengchan hezuoshe*), the second stage in the programme of collectivisation, were created by amalgamating the permanent mutual-aid teams. The first APCs appeared in 1954 but most of them were created during the movement that was dramatically launched as the High Tide of Socialism in the Countryside (*nongcun shehuizhuyi gaochao*), a political campaign orchestrated by the most enthusiastic supporters of Mao Zedong in the central bodies of the CCP. Documents published by activists during this campaign claimed that there was a demand from the poorer peasant farmers that they should be included in the drive towards cooperation and there is some evidence that Mao was persuaded by this and that he, in turn, demanded that there should be greater urgency in the creation of APCs. By the end of 1956 it was claimed that as many as 90 per cent of rural households were members of an APC, but it is not clear how much genuine change in the management of agriculture this brought about. Members of this new interim body had an income that derived in part from wages that were paid for the work they did for the cooperative and in part from rent payable for the land that they had contributed, whether willingly or otherwise.

Higher-level producers' cooperatives (HPCs) were created during 1956 and 1957 by the further amalgamation of APCs to produce even larger collective units. In the HPCs, the land was considered to be owned communally and no rental income was payable to the former owners of the land that had been collectivised.

In 1958, the HPCs were in turn amalgamated into yet larger units that became known as People's Communes (*renmin gongshe*), a form of organisation favoured by Mao partly because he conceived of it as a distinctively Chinese-style administration for the countryside. For the next twenty years, the communes dominated the life of China's peasants. Not only were they the organisations responsible for managing the farming cycle and the production and distribution of agricultural goods, but they also became the basic administrative unit in the countryside. Education, child care, retirement homes, medical clinics and hospitals, banking and the building and maintenance of roads, bridges and many other public works and services were all the responsibility of the People's Communes.

In an attempt to abolish market forces within the communes, it was intended that the system of paying wages in cash would be replaced by a system of work points. The reality was much more complicated. The work point system, under which jobs and responsibilities were graded in terms of points rather than cash, had been developed in the cooperatives and was formalised in the 1956 *Regulations for Collectives*. Peasant members of collectives at first received a portion of their income in rent, a portion in cash and a portion in kind: that is, they were entitled to an allowance from the grain harvest and other crops in proportion to the number of work points that they had earned. The rent element disappeared when higher-level cooperatives were created and, when the communes were established, it was also assumed that the wage element would disappear. There were attempts to abolish the system of cash wages but by the early 1970s this was still in existence or, if it had been abolished, it had subsequently returned. Members of a family working in a production brigade in one commune in Henan were said to be receiving 'a share in the distribution of its income in the form of food grain, vegetables and other necessities and nearly 1,000 yuan a year in cash'.[2] The level of cash income suggests rather a prosperous family for the time but the publication of this information indicates official recognition that this was then the norm.

Critics of the commune system point to the lack of financial incentives in a structure where it was possible to obtain the necessities of life by a system of work points. The work point system created a complex internal bureaucracy with specially trained commune accountants who became powerful because they were able to manipulate the system and thus the supply of food and other products.

The People's Communes did have positive aspects, notably economies of scale when compared with small family farms and the ability to engage in the long-term planning of agricultural production. Under a government policy that emphasised 'grain as the key link' in its struggle to feed the urban population as well as the rural one, this was considered by some in the Chinese leadership to have been a considerable advantage.

Responsibility system

The collectivisation programme that led to the establishment of the communes was ineradicably associated with Mao Zedong and his radical supporters and it did not long survive his death in 1976. Dismantling the commune system, which by then was widely regarded as inefficient and inimical to economic development, was the first priority of Deng Xiaoping and his reformers when they took hold of the reins of power in the late 1970s.

There had been a degree of decentralisation within the communes in response to the disastrous famines of the early 1960s but it was felt necessary to dismantle them completely. The mechanism that was introduced to accomplish this was the Responsibility System for Agricultural Production (*nongye shengchan zeren zhi*), sometimes known as the Household Responsibility System or simply the Responsibility System, under which individual households were given contracts that permitted them to cultivate land, although they did not formally become the titular owners of the land that they farmed. In effect this was a complete repudiation of the commune system but, although Mao was dead and his most powerful supporters in the higher echelons of the CCP, the Gang of Four, had been arrested and were awaiting trial, there was considerable opposition within the Party to anything which explicitly contradicted Mao's policies. A workable formula had to be found to embrace the formal retention of collective ownership while at the same time handing over to families the management of farms. This was not entirely a return to the system of family farms that had existed before the land reform programme of the 1950s. The contract system involved the local administrative bodies of the state, which were able to impose production and tax quotas on farmers, although peasant families were still able to sell their surplus production.

A pilot scheme for the Responsibility System was carried out in Fengyang county in Anhui province in 1979 and it was then extended across the country. Contracts were originally issued on an annual basis but from 1984 a contract could remain in force for fifteen years. Individual families were allowed to retain the surpluses produced on their own land, rather than hand them over to the commune authorities. The direct outcome of the new system was a dramatic (and immediately obvious) economic boom in the rural areas, especially in the southeast. The economy began to take off, building sites sprang up everywhere and, in the 1980s, it was common to see roads in the countryside partially blocked by piles of bricks and timber that had been deposited close to bridges for transfer to boats on the rivers and destined for new house-building programmes in distant villages.

When a new post-Mao constitution of the PRC was being drafted in 1982, it was openly acknowledged that communes, irrespective of whether they had been beneficial for agriculture, had not been a success as organisations of local government: there had been an over-concentration of power and inappropriate management. The former system of township administrations, with their own People's Governments and local People's Congresses, was reinstated as the basic level of state power, although the name 'commune' did persist for some time as a form of agricultural management organisation, and possibly for sentimental reasons.[3]

Rural–urban migration

The commune system had provided work and a livelihood for the vast majority of China's peasants. The management bodies of the communes, the Revolutionary Committees, had also been able to discourage migration from the countryside to the cities, which was in any case difficult because of poor rural transport facilities and the household registration (*hukou*) system. Under the *hukou* system, which is dealt with in more detail in Chapter 8, individuals in families were registered according to their place of residence and their occupational category, with the most important distinction being between agricultural and non-agricultural categories. The *hukou* functioned as an internal passport system and registration was essential for access to rationed foodstuffs such as oil and rice. The *hukou* documents, which are still issued to every family in China with copies held in the local police stations, indicate where an individual is registered and therefore where he or she is allowed to live: in the past, it was extremely difficult for people from the countryside who had an agricultural *hukou* to find work, accommodation and even food in the cities without 'going black' (*zou hei*) and living on the fringes of the criminal underworld.

One of the most dramatic outcomes of the dismantling of the communes, and the economic reforms in general, was the creation of a vast population of migrant workers. This was unprecedented in the period since 1949, since the priority of the government had been to keep peasants on their farms to increase food production. The smaller decentralised farms that were created under the Responsibility System could not sustain the number of workers that the communes had been able to absorb and the economic development that was taking off in the cities of the east and southeast created opportunities for the enterprising, the desperate and the adventurous. In the mid-1980s, gangs of peasants from Shaanxi could be seen building new hotels and office buildings in Beijing and the housemaid, nanny or *au pair* (*baomu*), who was employed to look after the children and the households of the newly rich in the cities, became an iconic figure. Most of the *baomu* in Beijing came from the south, particularly the province of Anhui, and they were even the subject of a popular film. However, the greatest migration was not northwards towards the capital but in the direction of the coastal provinces of the southeast where the economic boom was most dramatic. Although it is difficult to give precise figures for such a phenomenon, there is broad agreement that as many as 120 million rural residents may have been working in, or travelling to seek work in, the urban areas at any given time. This is the equivalent of the entire population of Japan being on the move in the interior of China.

However, by early 2007 it was beginning to appear that the wave of migration might be slowing down. In some villages everyone who was physically able to migrate had already migrated and new industries that had been created in the countryside had absorbed as much surplus rural labour as they could. A survey by the Development Research Centre of the State Council suggested that, in as many as 74 per cent of the villages that they had examined, there were no longer any able-bodied workers available for employment in the cities. The Chinese Academy of Social Sciences warned that the Chinese economy was facing a labour shortage and that by 2009 this would generate wage increases in all sectors.[4] This potential rise in labour costs began to be a matter of some concern to foreign bankers and employers in China in late 2007, for whom cheap labour was the major attraction in relocating factories to China, but whether this was a temporary phenomenon or the beginning of a long-term trend remains to be seen.

Land ownership in the reform era

The question of the ownership of land, and indeed of property in general, remains an area of great confusion in China. In a formal and legal sense, land in the urban areas is the property of the state while rural land is still considered to be collectively owned even though it is almost thirty years since the dismantling of the People's Communes. In practice this means that land in the countryside is also controlled by the state, although it is the local government, in the shape of the township administration, rather than central state bodies, that has the authority to decide on its usage and disposal. The township is the lowest level of the hierarchical government structure. It normally has political and economic control over several villages and in practice it is not always strictly controlled by the higher tiers of government.

Peasant families were given the right to cultivate their farms under the Responsibility System of 1978 and were awarded long-term contracts. However, since they do not own the land that they farm they do not have the inalienable legal right to sell it or to retain it. While this was not thought to be a major problem in 1978, it became one as the pace of development escalated.

Because there is no private ownership of land, it has been relatively easy for agricultural land to be bought or requisitioned for industrial development, for the expansion of urban housing or for extending the transport network. Although this type of expansion is deemed by the state to be imperative for the overall process of urbanisation and the much-needed development of the economy of rural China, it has also generated numerous opportunities for corruption. Local officials have been bribed by developers or have siphoned off compensation that was intended for peasants who had been forced off their land: this state of affairs has created a climate of dissatisfaction that has frequently boiled over into violence. The reduction of the burden of agricultural taxation, and the final abolition of the land tax in 2006, assisted peasant families greatly but at the same time it significantly reduced the income of the local authorities and made the sale of land to developers an even higher priority for township officials. A survey of 1,962 peasant households in 1,773 villages that are located in seventeen of the provinces of China found that 27 per cent of farming families had been affected in some way by land seizures and it is clear that there was a significant increase in the requisitioning of land from the late 1990s.[5] At the beginning of the twenty-first century, disputes over the sale of land began to replace protests against high taxation as the main source of unrest in the Chinese countryside, especially in the more prosperous villages that are close to urban centres.

Premier Wen Jiabao on rural stability

Wen Jiabao, the Premier, who, towards the end of 2005, was openly associating himself with populist causes, including the environment, opposition to corruption and the plight of the peasants, made a speech on the problems of stability in the countryside. The speech was unusually candid and the text was not published until 19 January 2006, which was almost three weeks after he made the speech. Speeches by the leadership are normally made public immediately.[6]

Wen Jiabao observed that the development of the rural areas was a key factor in China's national revival and its stability in the long term. The rural revival was envisaged by Wen as 'the construction of a new socialist countryside', a policy that had been approved by the Fifth Plenum of the Sixteenth Central Committee of the CCP. In practical terms, this involved the improvement of living standards and working conditions in rural areas and also the implementation of 'institutional reform at township level and financial reform at county and township levels' and ensuring the success of the compulsory education policy. Wen pointed out that the popular abolition of agricultural taxes, which began in 2006, did not resolve the problem of financial burdens on farmers and went on to say that 'We must guard against the re-emergence of random charging of farmers under various pretexts'.

Wen Jiabao indicated that preferential policies would have to be put in place to encourage peasants to grow grain, a contemporary version of the 'grain as key link' argument of the Maoist era. He also argued that the acquisition of agricultural land for construction projects should be strictly regulated and that the rights of farmers to their own property should be respected. These issues have been the root causes of much of the rural unrest in China in the early years of the twenty-first century.

Acknowledging that migrant workers from the rural areas now played a key role in the country's industrial labour force, 'the Premier called for the improvement of their treatment, including pay, social security, vocational training opportunities and their children's education'. He also contended that a range of public services in the rural areas, including education, medical care and cultural services, would have to be improved.[7]

Fiscal decentralisation and local decision-making powers

Prior to the reforms of the 1980s, China's fiscal or budgetary system had been strictly controlled by central government. Taxes and other revenues were collected by the local authorities and passed on to the central government. A proportion of the tax that had been collected was then repaid to the local government according to formulae that were drawn up and controlled by central bodies.

During the 1980s the fiscal system was gradually decentralised and local authorities were allowed to retain more of the taxation that they had collected. The decentralisation policy was designed to devolve responsibility for economic planning and decision-making to local authorities. Some central control was retained to allow for the redistribution of funds from poorer to wealthier provinces but overall the policy of decentralisation encouraged local authorities to search for ways in which they could maximise their tax income. This was achieved by a variety of methods, some legal and some less so. The tax burden on farmers during the reform period has been a heavy one and, after the implementation of the policy of fiscal decentralisation, the potential for conflict between farmers and the state at the local level increased, and contributed to widespread unrest.

Agricultural taxation and the roots of peasant unrest

The highly unpopular agricultural tax was gradually reduced in many areas of China, particularly in the poorest counties. Far from being an invention of the CCP, this tax was in many ways the continuation of a centuries-old tradition of taxing the peasants and thus in many ways a legacy of the Chinese empire.

The Standing Committee of the National People's Congress (NPC), at its meeting in Beijing in December 2005, decided unanimously (160 votes to 0, with one abstention) that the modern version of this tax, which had been introduced by the NPC on 3 June 1958, would finally be abolished from 1 January 2006. The main headline of *People's Daily* on the day that it was announced read: 'Chinese peasants bid farewell to the agricultural tax in the New Year'.[8] This move was intended to lessen the financial burden on farmers, to reduce the income gap between the rural and urban areas and to calm down the increasingly violent rural protests that had arisen in response to heavy taxation and to some of the corrupt practices associated with tax collection. However, without the income from this tax, local government was driven to find other ways of raising revenue.

Peasant protest, twenty-first-century style

During the 1990s a series of rural protests erupted and these disputes, often intense, have continued into the early twenty-first century. Publicising the discontent of the peasants was tolerated by the authorities to a far greater extent than previously and reports of demonstrations, sometimes violent, became frequent during 2005. Disputes over taxation had affected the poorer and remote interior counties, but conflict over land requisition and corruption was more prevalent in the wealthier and developed coastal areas, including Guangdong province, the economic dynamo to the north of Hong Kong where land for development is scarce and prices are at a premium. Many of these protests were suppressed with considerable force by police, or in some cases by armed private security units who gained a reputation for brutality; many peasant protesters were injured and some lost their lives.

Some major rural protests 2004–06

- **September 2004–February 2005** Yuncheng District, Yunfu City, Guangdong province. Farmers' land was requisitioned with little compensation.Fields and burial plots were bulldozed and impoverished farmers were forced to withdraw children from school. Villagers sent petitions to the government in Beijing.
- **June 2005** Maxinzhuang village, Shunyi, Beijing. Peasant farmers protested against the requisition of land to build a water sports complex for the Olympic Games.
- **11 June 2005** Shengyou, Dingzhou municipality in Hebei province. Villagers resisted armed private security guards who seized land on behalf of developers wanting to build a waste-processing plant.
- **December 2005** Dongzhou, Guangdong province. At least three deaths were reported but the total may have been as high as twenty. Twelve villagers were sentenced to up to seven years imprisonment in May 2006 for illegal assembly, disturbing public order and the illegal manufacture of explosives.
- **14–16 January 2006** Sanjiao township, Zhongshan, Guangdong province.

20,000 protesters blocked major roads after complaints that farmers had not been paid enough compensation for land that had been requisitioned to build a road.

- **29 April 2006** Zhaowenmin village, Ninghe county, Tianjin municipality. At least 200 villagers clashed with police outside the offices of the Ninghe county government to protest against what they alleged had been rigged elections the previous day. They claimed that there had been intimidation and bribery and that counterfeit ballot papers had been issued.
- **8 November 2006** Sanzhou village, Shunde, Guangdong province. Villagers blockaded a warehouse built on land that they claimed had been requisitioned illegally. Officials had arrived for the opening and as many as 5,000 protesters were dispersed by riot police using teargas.
- **10–11 November 2006** Further protests took place in Dongzhou when villagers were arrested after putting up posters against corruption.

This outbreak of unrest has exposed serious problems caused by the failure of the government to resolve the complex question of rights to the ownership of rural land and the residential property that stands on such land. In particular, farmers and the local government have wrangled over the question of compensation and whether compensation for property should be at the market price if the land on which it stands is sold by the state.[9] Legislation on property rights has been under discussion in the Chinese government for some years and on Wednesday 18 January 2006, Sheng Huaren, the vice-chairman of the Standing Committee of the NPC, announced that a revised draft of this legislation was being prepared. The aim of the legislation was to protect assets owned by the state and to clarify the status of collective and individual property and the rights of peasant farmers.[10]

The Ministry of Public Security issued statistics to show that the number of protests during 2006 had declined in comparison with the unusually high number recorded in 2005. According to the official announcement, in the first nine months of 2005, there had been 17,900 'mass incidents', but the number of 'public order disturbances', a term which is normally used to refer to small-scale and less serious incidents, had increased by 6 per cent to 87,000. It is not clear whether the reduction in serious disorder was a genuine figure or a result of underreporting or redefinition by local officials, but the number of serious incidents that were acknowledged and the fact that they were being reported publicly, in a society where the tendency had been to keep silent about embarrassing issues, indicates the level of concern felt by the authorities.[11]

Township and village enterprises

The disparity between poor and backward rural areas and rapidly developing cities is not as simple or as stark as it might appear. In response to the problems of rural unemployment and underemployment, and as part of a strategy for managing internal migration, China has developed a nationwide network of township and village enterprises (TVEs) which, unlike the state-owned enterprises (SOEs), are primarily orientated towards the market. TVEs tend to be small community enterprises which can draw on the pool of surplus labour in the countryside and are often engaged in businesses that are connected closely with farming, such as the manufacture of farm tools and machinery, the production of fertiliser and the processing of grain and other food products. Although they have been publicised as a brand new type of rural industrial development, they are clearly the descendants of the cooperative and commune industries that were promoted in the 1950s and even of the small rural industries such as the backyard furnaces that were a much-criticised feature of the Great Leap Forward. The crucial difference between the TVEs of the reform period and their predecessors is that they are market oriented. The household responsibility system that was adopted for the management of agriculture was adapted so that it could be applied to TVEs which usually operate as cooperatives, although that term which was associated with the Mao period is not in favour. In these cases, ownership rights are often distributed among employees who own shares in the business, but some TVEs appear to be privately owned.

TVEs are regarded as a major success story by the Chinese government and they are popular because they can be presented as a distinctively Chinese response to the rural–urban divide. A recent study has referred to them as a 'leading force that has propelled China's market economy forward, a vital pillar of the rural economy and an important component of the national economy'. Statistics gathered in 2005 indicate that there were at least twenty-two million businesses that could be classified as TVEs and that between them they employed more than 138 million people.[12]

There is no doubt that township and village enterprises have made an important contribution to the economy, although there are concerns about their impact on the environment and on the health and safety of their employees because of the low level of technology, education and expertise available to them, the lack of regulation and, in many cases, their serious undercapitalisation.[13]

5   Urban and industrial economy

Although the urban economy and the industrial sector have constituted only a small proportion of the total until recently, they are important symbols of China's success in its drive for modernisation. China today possesses almost all of the types of industrial and manufacturing capacity that are found in developed economies elsewhere but the geographical spread of industries is patchy and the level of development varies considerably. One of the greatest economic challenges faced by China in the twenty-first century is the successful transition from an industrial sector that was almost entirely state-owned to one that is dominated by private or mixed ownership.

State-owned enterprises

In common with the Soviet Union and other members of COMECON, the economic union of the Soviet bloc, China developed a large state-owned industrial base in the 1950s and 1960s. There is a widespread conviction, often based on little evidence or understanding, that the impact of these state-owned enterprises (SOEs) was wholly negative and that they hampered rather than assisted China's economic development. This belief is based on another assumption which is not always articulated clearly: that there is only one viable model for economic development, a Western individualistic and free-market model. The SOEs can certainly be criticised for inefficiencies, for conservative working practices and for their inability to compete with international firms. They also limited the opportunity for individuals to develop their own careers since most staff were directed into a firm on leaving school or college and did not leave unless they were transferred for some reason connected with the interests of the industry or the state. This system of lifetime employment, which became known as the 'iron rice bowl' (*tie fanwan*), provided job security but it inhibited movement between different types of employment and different parts of the country and restricted the sharing of skills and information.

What the SOEs did provide was a considerable level of stability, security and social cohesion and these were of great value in a country that had endured years of occupation by the Japanese military and a bitter civil war. SOEs provided continuity and security of employment, cheap and decent accommodation, health care that was usually free of charge and education for the children of employees.[1] The SOEs could not provide both social stability and competitiveness at the same time. The decision to reform them was a decision to put the need for international competitiveness over the need for security.

In the 1980s, the reform of the SOEs was perceived, particularly by overseas business and finance interests, as the key indicator of China's ability and willingness to make a successful transition from a planned (some prefer the description 'command') economy to a mixed or wholly commercial industrial and financial system. Since these enterprises constituted the core of the industrial economy – mines, iron, steel and chemical plants, machine manufacture, automobile industries and thermal, hydro and nuclear power, for example – it was vital that they were able to continue to function and to produce the materials needed to power China's economy even while they were being transformed. What is usually described as the 'reform' of the SOEs is far more radical than that term suggests: the process involves the wholesale dismantling of a significant part of the state-owned industrial sector and the radical reform of the remainder.

The Chinese government decided that it was essential that such a complex process should be carried out gradually. Between 1980 and 1986, more and more economic enterprises were given the authority to manage their own affairs autonomously – that is, without direct control from the ministries in Beijing. A 'dual price' system was established as part of the strategy of creating a market system that had not existed since the 1950s. Under this twin-track pricing system, some goods and services were made available at prices fixed by the state while others were allowed to enter the market, which determined their prices. The proportion of goods available at market prices was gradually increased.

From 1987 to 1992, a system labelled 'contract responsibility' was put into operation and under this new system SOEs were required to be profitable. A third stage in the reform process ran from about 1993 to 1997, and at this stage the most significant change was the separation of ownership and control from management: managers of individual enterprises were given additional powers and profit incentives. A capital market was also introduced to stimulate the reform of property rights. During the fourth stage, 1998–2001, although the state retained overall control of the largest SOEs, it was prepared to relinquish its authority over the more competitive small and medium-sized enterprises and in 2001 the sale of these SMEs was seriously considered for the first time. This was not a simple process of privatisation since state organs retained a considerable degree of control during what was intended to be a transitional period.

The standard method for reforming SOEs has been the creation of a new board of directors and board of supervisors and the issuing of shares in what was then deemed to be a new company. State organisations, however, retain a majority of the shares in the largest of the SOEs, so this process is not directly comparable with European privatisation programmes. Unreformed SOEs continue to play a considerable part in China's economic development but their financial status has changed. Direct funding from the state has been reduced and they have been obliged to seek financial support from the banks, increasingly at commercial rates of interest.

The state has retained complete control over SOEs in certain sectors, particularly those that were considered to have a strategic role. Industries in the fields of defence, telecommunications and finance were ring-fenced for state-run organisations although finance was opened to private firms to a degree from 2003 onwards as a condition of China's entry into the World Trade Organisation. There has been considerable reluctance to allow SOEs to be taken over by foreign companies.

One of the main outcomes of the dismantling of the state-owned conglomerates was the winding down of the 'iron rice bowl' system which had guaranteed employment for life in the major state enterprises. This system had provided a large measure of social stability since the 1950s and employees benefited from a range of community provisions made by the SOEs, including housing, education and medical and social care and there was also a system of welfare provisions for the children of employees and for elderly retired employees. On the debit side, as has already been noted, the SOEs did not provide any freedom of choice for employees, who were typically transferred to an enterprise at the conclusion of their secondary or tertiary education and remained there for the rest of their lives unless they were transferred to another plant. The concept of advertising opportunities for employment or applying for jobs was virtually unknown.

The dismantling of the SOEs has led to many instances of labour unrest in the cities, sometimes on a large scale, and there have been concerns about the impact of this dramatic change on the pensions of former employees. The social problems that this process could create are illustrated by an incident in October 2005 when a protest by workers who had been laid off from the Chongqing Steel Mill became violent. Workers who had been made redundant by management at the plant, which had formerly been one of China's top companies but had declared itself bankrupt in July 2005, began a series of demonstrations on 12 August. They demanded severance payments of 2,000 *renminbi* (RMB) – the Chinese currency – each and alleged that the collapse of the company had been a consequence of corruption and maladministration by the management: in particular, there were criticisms of the sale of the land on which the factory stood for less than the market price at the time.

Hundreds of former employees of the steel mill blocked main roads in the city of Chongqing and brought traffic to a standstill. Negotiations between factory management and representatives of the workforce were also taking place at this time but were not making any progress. The situation came to a head because workers' organisations were planning to continue their protests during a summit meeting of town and city mayors from the Asia–Pacific region which was due to take place in Chongqing during 11–14 October. However, police arrived in the early morning of 7 October to bring the protests to an end. Two police vehicles were overturned – the demonstrators claimed that this was a provocation carried out by plainclothes police officers – and riot police were called. In the disturbance that followed, two women, aged fifty and seventy, were reported to have died.[2]

China's determination to press ahead with the reform of the SOEs, but to do so in a gradual and controlled fashion, is demonstrated by the role of the State-owned Assets Supervision and Administration Commission (SASAC), a body operated by the State Council. In accordance with the *Company Law of the People's Republic of China*, SASAC has been given the responsibility of pushing forward the reform and restructuring of SOEs. Its formal duties include the preservation and augmentation of the value of state-owned assets in enterprises under its supervision and the development of modern business systems and methods in SOEs in general. It has the authority to despatch supervisory panels to enterprises on behalf of the state and can takes control of the daily management of enterprises through these panels if it deems it to be necessary. It has the authority to appoint and dismiss executives and to evaluate their performances and can also draft legislation and administrative measures on the management of state-owned assets. On 24 January 2006, Huang Ju, one of China's Vice-Premiers, issued written instructions to SASAC, emphasising the importance of restructuring and calling for an increase in the pace of SOE reform.[3]

In parallel with the dismantling of the state sector, there was a significant growth in private industry, at first on a very small scale. The private sector had been almost eliminated in the early 1950s during the movement for the 'socialisation of industry', although some smaller-scale handicraft workshops remained outside state control. The importance of the private sector for the development of China during the reform era has been formally recognised by the state: entrepreneurs have been cultivated by local Party committees and, under Jiang Zemin, were even encouraged to join the CCP. However, restrictions on the areas of the economy in which private industry can operate remain in place, notably in matters that involve defence and national security.

A new class of small entrepreneurs (*getihu*) emerged during the 1980s. Former employees of the SOEs were encouraged to cast themselves into the sea (*xiahai*) of private enterprise. This opportunity was seized by many entrepreneurially minded individuals who established new businesses, but there were also many social casualties.

The government was obliged to create a social security structure to support families living in towns and cities who did not have income from work or whose income was very low. There is an urban minimum living standard guarantee (*dibao*) and this has had some effect on mitigating the problems of urban poverty. This benefit is payable to twenty-two million Chinese citizens living in the urban areas: these are the unemployed, those unable to work and the elderly who have no other means of support. The minimum income level varies from city to city – in Beijing in 2007 it was RMB 330 (£21.5 or US$43) per month – and eligible families receive a payment to bring their income up to RMB 330 if their regular income is below that level. Inflation has hit the urban poor hard, above all the steep rises in the cost of food, and the government authorised an increase of RMB 15 per month in these benefits to take effect from the end of August 2007.[4]

6 Banking, finance and foreign trade

The banking system in China in the period between the foundation of the People's Republic of China (PRC) in 1949 and the decision to implement the major reforms of the 1980s was relatively simple. In the rural areas, markets did not operate to any extent and many transactions were made by administrative transfer within communes or between communes and state organisations. Money existed of course but was in fairly short supply and there was no question of individuals investing or saving, other than secretly. Foreign trade was limited and carried out by means of transfers from the People's Bank of China.

Foreigners visiting China, including diplomats, business people and other long-term residents, were not even officially permitted to use the normal Chinese currency, the *renminbi* (RMB): they were restricted to foreign exchange certificates (FECs) which, as the name implies, were issued in exchange for the foreign currency that China desperately needed. This was a measure designed to protect the RMB in a hostile financial market. FECs were the only currency accepted in the Friendship Stores, special shops that sold high-value and imported goods which only wealthy foreigners could afford and from which most Chinese were barred.[1] In theory, FECs were not supposed to be used in normal shops or by Chinese citizens but they attracted a premium from Westerners who were working in Chinese organisations and from Chinese citizens who sought them to buy foreign imports.

As the overall standard of living improved in Chinese cities, people increasingly wished to acquire FECs so that they could buy the goods that had been the privilege of the foreigners and a flourishing black market developed. It was impossible for a foreigner to walk for more than a few minutes in Beijing without being approached to 'change money', the one English phrase that everyone understood. As confidence in the RMB increased, the FEC system gradually became more trouble than it was worth and FECs were abolished in 1995 by the simple stratagem of the government setting the exchange value between FEC and RMB to 1:1. FECs had only really been usable in the major cities. Shopkeepers in the farther flung parts of China did not recognise them and some even assumed that they must be some sort of foreign currency.[2]

People's Bank of China

The People's Bank of China (*Zhongguo renmin yinhang*) was established by the Chinese Communist Party (CCP) on 1 December 1948 during the closing months of the Civil War. Inflation had reached such a level that the old currency that had been circulating, the *fabi* ('legal currency') issued by the Guomindang government (GMD), was completely worthless. The first act of the new bank was to issue a new currency, the *renminbi*, which means literally 'people's currency', universally abbreviated as RMB and still in use today. The unit of this currency is the *yuan* but it is usually referred to in speech as a *kuai*, literally a 'piece' of money.

The People's Bank was, and remains, the only bank allowed to issue notes and coinage and it functioned as a central bank, albeit one under the strict control of the government and the CCP. It was also the accounting arm of all government, military and cooperative organisations, which were obliged to maintain accounts at the bank and to deposit reserves with it. It effectively had a monopoly over credit for the non-agricultural sector and rapidly established a network of branches throughout the whole of the country in the 1950s.

The People's Bank came directly under the control of the State Council rather than the Ministry of Finance. In turn it controlled two subordinate banks, the Bank of China, which had its origins in capital confiscated from a semi-official organisation run by the GMD in the 1940s and the Joint State–Private Bank, which was the result of the merger of dozens of private banks during the nationalisation of the private sector in the 1950s.

The special and critical needs of the agricultural sector were met by various specialist banks, the most important being the Agricultural Bank which was established in November 1963 after the decentralisation of management in the communes. Like the People's Bank, this was also directly answerable to the State Council. The People's Construction Bank of China functioned as a subsidiary of the Ministry of Finance and its main role was managing the payment of state investment to construction units and other enterprises. The model for these banks was plainly the system of banking that had been created in the Soviet Union and had also been exported to Eastern Europe: it was used, as well, in other Asian Communist countries including China's near neighbours, North Korea and North Vietnam.[3]

Reforming the state banks

The reform of the financial sector has been much slower than corresponding reforms in the agricultural and industrial sectors. As suppliers of credit to the state-owned enterprises (SOEs), the banks are contractually and organisationally bound to these organisations which are being dismantled and this has restricted their ability to function in the same way as banks in the developed world. They have a portfolio of non-performing loans and are considered by some economists to be technically insolvent according to international criteria: it has been estimated that bad debts make up between 40 per cent and 50 per cent of their total loans.

The process of reforming the state-owned banks has been twofold. On the one hand, they have been reduced in size: the number of staff employed by the state-owned banks was reduced from a total of 1.6 million in 1997 to 1.4 million in 2001. On the other hand, the proportion of their dealings that involves loans to the SOEs has been reduced. Loans to private companies and to individuals, including mortgages and car loans, which were virtually unheard of until very recently, increased dramatically during the 1990s.[4] Concerns about abuses in the banking sector have been raised frequently, but the most direct criticisms were made in December 1999 by the deputy auditor-general of the Audit Office, Liu Jiayi, after an investigation had been carried out into the operations of 4,600 branches of the Industrial and Commercial Bank of China and 1,700 branches of the China Construction Bank. The main problems that were highlighted were claims that assets had been overstated but there were also allegations that some bank managers were running unofficial lending operations in parallel with the bank's legitimate loan transactions and that they were diverting the interest from these illegal deals for their own use.[5]

Creating a modern financial sector

In December 1999 Zhou Xiaochuan, the president of the China Construction Bank (one of the old PRC banks, founded as the People's Construction Bank in 1954), outlined the options for banking reform that were being imposed on China by its application to gain admission to the World Trade Organisation. He suggested that banks could become shareholding companies and that the major institutions – Bank of China, Agricultural Bank of China and Industrial and Commercial Bank of China, which together control 80 per cent of banking assets – could be decoupled. Joint ventures with foreign banks and listing on the stock market were also under consideration at that time.[6]

When the government became concerned in 2003 that the Chinese economy was overheating, it was to the central banks that it turned to operate one of the few effective levers available to deal with the problem. Restrictions on lending were imposed but with no certainty that these would be adhered to by bank managers who had been enjoying their new-found freedom to lend in the property and personal car loan markets.[7]

Stock market and stock exchanges

No stock market existed on the Chinese mainland between 1949 when the PRC was founded and 1990: during that time the Chinese economy was a planned economy and the private sector was either non-existent or strictly regulated by the state.

China now has three official stock exchanges: one in Hong Kong, and the others in Shanghai and in Shenzhen, the latter of which lies to the north of Hong Kong and was the first of the Special Economic Zones created at the birth of the reform era. There is also an informal and unregulated market for trading shares. The novelty of share-buying has attracted a great deal of attention, not to say an atmosphere of mass hysteria, and the first bankruptcy of a listed company was treated by some sections of the Chinese media as if it were a rite of passage for China's entry into the market economy.

The Hong Kong Stock Exchange is the largest within China and one of the largest in the world: it has operated almost continuously since the end of the nineteenth century. It was established during the colonial period and its traditions and history are comparable with those of the London or New York Stock Exchanges or the Bourse in Paris, whereas the other two institutions, established recently on the mainland, have been obliged to create their own credibility and confidence.

The Shanghai Stock Exchange has a history which also dates back to the nineteenth century and it perhaps reached its peak during the 1930s when Shanghai, controlled to a large extent by European business interests, was the financial hub of China. It continued to operate in the early years of the Japanese occupation of China but ceased trading in 1941 when the international settlement in which it was based was overrun by the Imperial Japanese Army. It reopened briefly in 1946 after the surrender of Japan, only to close again in 1949 when the CCP took control of China, including Shanghai. It has the history and the tradition, but it does not have the continuity, that the Hong Kong exchange enjoys and it is essentially a new organisation. In its most recent incarnation, as one of the flagships of Deng Xiaoping's economic reforms, it opened for trading in 1990 and a long-standing rivalry was reignited between Hong Kong and Shanghai for supremacy in financial markets. The Shanghai Stock Exchange deals in two types of shares, which are designated 'A' and 'B' shares. The most significant difference between them is that prices for 'A' shares are quoted in RMB, whereas 'B' shares are priced in US dollars. When the system was established, only Chinese investors were permitted to trade in 'A' shares; 'B' shares could be bought and sold by overseas investors and from 2001 onwards by locals. There has been some relaxation of these restrictions and the long-term plan is for the two types of shares to be consolidated.

Concern that China's stock exchanges were overvalued was reinforced by the revelation in November 2007 that PetroChina had suddenly emerged as the world's largest firm in terms of its market value. PetroChina began trading on the Shanghai Stock Exchange on 5 November 2007 and, within hours, the price of its shares had tripled. Stock market analysts had been expressing concern for some time that overenthusiastic investors were pumping money into Chinese shares with unrealistic expectations of potential earnings and some were warning of a possible crash in the markets.

Foreign exchange and *renminbi* convertibility

The reform of the foreign exchange system has played a critical role in China's economic modernisation. The high-profile disagreement between China and the United States over the convertibility and valuation of the RMB is only the most public of the problems that has arisen with this complex reform.

Under the centrally planned economy, the state retained a complete monopoly of China's imports and exports. Import and export quotas were determined according to the needs of the Five-Year Plans and there was hardly any scope for the operation of a price mechanism. The supply of foreign exchange before 1956 had been controlled by the People's Bank of China and by approved foreign exchange banks under the overall political direction of the government's Central Financial and Economic Committee. The system of control was further strengthened in 1956. The state had control over decisions on setting the rate of exchange of the RMB and the regulations that governed foreign exchange, and these were governed by the annual foreign exchange plan produced by the State Planning Commission. In the past, major changes to the rate of exchange could only be made with the specific approval of the State Council but in 1993 it was agreed that the RMB would be 'pegged to a basket of international currencies'.

There is a degree of consensus among international economists that the RMB has been undervalued, although economists working for Chinese state and banking organisations would not necessarily concede this in public. China has certainly had a long-term problem with a shortage of foreign exchange. Technical measures were implemented to resolve these problems: the RMB is now partially convertible and decisions about the exchange rate and the allocation of foreign exchange are made to some extent on the basis of a price mechanism. China's reserves of foreign currency reached a total of US$1,000 billion in October 2006.[8]

Since the RMB is not completely convertible, Beijing continues to face demands from the international banking community for currency liberalisation. China revalued the RMB on 21 July 2005, discontinued the strict peg to the US dollar that it had been following and moved to a system that is known as the 'floating peg'. Since that date, the RMB has appreciated against the US dollar, reaching its highest relative value on 4 December 2006 at 7.82 to the dollar, a gain of 3 per cent since revaluation. Under the regulations set by China's central bankers for the 'floating peg', the US dollar/RMB rate is not permitted to vary more than 0.03 per cent in any single day's trading and the RMB can only move by 3 per cent against other currencies in any single day.

The United States and other countries remain dissatisfied with the valuation of the Chinese currency. They claim that the RMB is still undervalued and that this allows China to sell its exports more cheaply, giving it a competitive edge and enabling it to develop a large trade surplus.[9]

Foreign trade

After the CCP took control of China in 1949, foreign businesses, many of which had been established in the country for decades, some of them for over a hundred years, were targeted. Under the policy of the 'socialist transformation of industry', which was effectively the nationalisation of private companies and which reached its height in the mid-1950s, the assets of foreign companies were sequestered and their businesses transformed into state-owned enterprises. Many foreign-owned companies, realising the possible implications of a takeover by the CCP, had already removed their assets and relocated to Hong Kong or elsewhere. Between the 1950s and the 1980s there were no foreign-owned economic enterprises in China and this meant that when the reform programme was launched in the 1980s there were no models and no recent or acceptable precedents for the involvement of Western companies in the Chinese economy.

China's external economic relations before 1980 had been almost entirely with the Soviet Union and other members of COMECON, the Council for Mutual

Economic Assistance, which had been established to promote cooperation between the economies of the Communist world. China had been accorded observer status in COMECON in the late 1950s but never became a full member and withdrew in 1961 as relations between Beijing and Moscow soured.

Trade with the West did continue although there were severe restrictions that affected both sides. The Canton (Guangzhou) Trade Fair, formally known as the Chinese Export Commodities Fair, which was first held in 1957, became the most important conduit for business between China and the West. It has taken place twice a year, every year, since then, in the spring and autumn. The irony of the setting, the city of Guangzhou to which Western traders had been restricted until the Opium War of 1839–42, was not lost on either side.

Part of the rationale behind the great political changes that were launched under the slogans of Four Modernisations and Reform and Opening in the 1980s was the need to attract foreign investment, although without jeopardizing state and CCP control over the economy as a whole.

This was initially achieved by the creation of joint-venture companies which combined Chinese management and foreign capital, often from overseas Chinese investors in Hong Kong (which was still outside the PRC), Singapore, Taiwan and Southeast Asia, but also from Japan and the West. This method was initially successful in the development of large-scale enterprises which China had previously lacked, such as steel plants, factories for the volume production of automobiles of a Western standard and high-quality hotels (such as the White Swan in Guangzhou) for both the business and tourist trade. However, joint-venture companies frequently encountered problems because of government regulation, tensions over management styles and cultural differences. Wholly owned foreign enterprises were more attractive to overseas investors and, as China's foreign trade grew and the government became accustomed to the idea of sharing its economic power with private foreign companies, the joint-venture approach became less and less popular.[10]

China's accession to the World Trade Organisation

China's application to join the World Trade Organisation (WTO) was deemed, both within the PRC and by the international community, to be the most important indication of the modernisation of China's economy, or at least of the acceptance by worldwide opinion that it was a system that other advanced industrial economies could deal with.

The origins of the WTO were in the peace settlement that followed the Second World War. A conference was held in Bretton Woods, New Hampshire in the United States in July 1944 to set out the parameters for the post-war economic and financial order. It was attended by representatives of the victorious Allied powers. The conference failed to agree on the creation of an international trade organisation, which had been one of its key objectives, but instead set up the General Agreement on Tariffs and Trade (GATT) and also the International Monetary Fund and the International Bank for Reconstruction and Development. GATT's role was to regulate international trade and to encourage the growth of free trade by reducing tariff and other barriers. Technically, it always remained an agreement rather than a fully fledged international organisation, although it exercised much greater authority than this status might suggest: it was replaced on 1 January 1995 by the WTO.

Membership of the WTO confers many benefits but there are also rigorous conditions and China's accession to the organisation was delayed because of concern by both sides over the implications of these conditions, particularly the requirement that the PRC be opened to the international financial market. There were reservations as to whether China, as a 'socialist market economy', was in a position to fulfil the conditions. The thorny question of the status of Taiwan *vis-à-vis* the WTO was also a stumbling block. Nevertheless, China's accession was essential for the Chinese government, not only as a prerequisite for economic modernisation but as a matter of national pride. The PRC had been excluded from the United Nations for twenty-two years until 1971 and becoming a member of the WTO, this powerful new international economic club, was a matter of self-respect as much as economic necessity. It was also extremely important for the international community as it was the only mechanism available to oblige China to open its commercial and financial sectors to overseas businesses and banks and to hold Chinese companies to international agreements.

The PRC finally joined the WTO on 11 December 2001, after protracted negotiations which were fraught with technical and diplomatic difficulties. The complete application process took a total of fifteen years, which was the longest on record in the history of either GATT or the WTO. Taiwan also became a member but not until 1 January 2002. It did not join as the PRC, which would have been completely unacceptable to Beijing, but as the Customs Territory of Taiwan, Penghu, Kinmen and Matsu (Penghu, Jinmen and Mazu in the *pinyin* romanisation, although Jinmen is also known as Quemoy), the latter three being the names of islands under Taipei's control.

Foreign banks

As part of the negotiations to join the WTO, China was required to agree that it would open its financial markets to foreign banks within five years. Regulations for the operation of foreign banks in China were not published until 2006 and this publication followed a prolonged internal debate on the wisdom of allowing foreign banks into China at all. During the negotiations on China's accession to the WTO there had been strong arguments against allowing international banks to establish themselves in China, even though this was a fundamental and necessary condition of accession. These arguments were to a certain extent inspired by patriotic or nationalist sentiment, but there were also practical and realistic economic concerns, including the fear that, because foreign banks had greater status and higher standards of service, they would attract investment away from the state-owned banks, and the home-grown Chinese banking sector would be seriously undermined.

More optimistic supporters of economic reform hoped that competition with efficient foreign banks would oblige the state-owned Chinese banks to reform and adopt international norms. A more balanced scenario suggests that the banking sector might well divide into two, with smaller savers preferring to remain with the traditional Chinese banks while the larger corporations would incline towards the major international financial organisations which have greater capital and lending power at their disposal. Foreign trading partners, especially the United States, have consistently argued that China has failed to liberalise its financial markers and that it has effectively restricted the import of goods, partly by its determination to keep the RMB at a low level compared with the US dollar to increase its ability to export. Arguments over the degree of progress in the liberalisation of the banking sector are the next stage in negotiations between China and its foreign economic partners.[11]

With the advent of the reform period and the growth of foreign investment in China, overseas banks which had been prohibited from operating in the PRC began to establish a presence in the country. However, it was not until China's accession to the WTO in 2001 that foreign banks could begin to operate effectively.

The operation of non-Chinese banks is overseen by the State Administration of Foreign Exchange (SAFE). It is part of SAFE's remit to control the flow of overseas capital into the country because this is an important weapon in the government's armoury of measures to control the growth of the Chinese economy. In June 2007, it was reported that a number of international banks operating in China, including well-known names such as HSBC and Standard Chartered, had been penalised by SAFE, which accused them of ignoring regulations on the import of large amounts of capital and of speculative activity under the guise of investment. Many domestic Chinese banks also suffered penalties at the same time. Most of the capital involved was being invested in either the stock markets or in China's booming property market.[12]

The extent of financial links between Chinese and foreign banks was revealed in the wake of the crisis in the US banking industry caused by problems with high-risk (sub-prime) mortgages for low-income would-be homeowners in the United States. In August 2007, the Bank of China revealed that it held securities that were underpinned by sub-prime mortgages to a value of nearly US$10 million. Although the total capitalisation of Chinese banks was high enough for this not to be a cause for concern, the degree of exposure to some of the more risky mechanisms in the international credit market surprised many financial analysts in the West, particularly since it had come relatively early in the process of reforming the Chinese banking system.[13]

7 Tourism and transport

Tourism

One major and very visible development after China's opening was the expansion of tourism. Tourism had been possible since the late 1970s but only by a small number of organised tour groups and with considerable restrictions on the areas that could be visited. This changed year by year during the 1980s and tour groups from Japan, overseas Chinese communities and the West could be observed regularly in many parts of China. Individual tourism also developed and it suddenly became possible to visit China as an independent traveller and to book hotels and hire cars (with drivers) as in most other countries. The growth of tourism was assisted by the building of luxury joint-venture hotels in the main tourist centres and by improvements in transport but mostly by changes in the official attitude towards foreigners who wished to travel independently and off the beaten track. At first this was done within the concept of the group tour booking with the individual bizarrely treated as a group of one.

Modernising transport

Transport has been an inhibiting factor in China's economic development for centuries. In a country which is the size of a subcontinent, it has always been easier to develop local systems of transport that assist local economies than to construct long-distance systems nationwide. Imperial China had road networks and a national postal system but in the south most trade and travel had to be carried out by water-borne transport on the intricate and widespread network of rivers, lakes and canals, including the Grand Canal that was used to transport grain from the rice bowls of the south to the imperial court and its capital city in the north.

In the 1920s and 1930s, the government of the Nationalist Guomindang (GMD) embarked on a programme of improving China's transport infrastructure, partly in order to enable the swift transfer of troops in their attempt to control the whole of the country, partly to enable the development of the economy. As with all the reforms of this period these developments were cut short by the Japanese invasion, although some Japanese transport projects such as the South Manchurian Railway were eventually of use to the Chinese.

Railways had been a controversial development in the late nineteenth and early twentieth centuries as they were regarded by some as an alien development which would enrich the government and impoverish local businessmen: they were the focus of nationalist or proto-nationalist protest and disruption and this was fuelled by superstitious fears that the construction of railways could damage the natural balance of the landscape.

When the People's Republic of China (PRC) was established in 1949, transport was an important part of its development plan both under the planned economy and since the beginning of the reform period. In the 1950s and 1960s there was significant growth in the rail network and also in domestic air travel: the roads were relatively neglected and there was no long-distance road network worth speaking of. Air travel was little used except by senior officials and later by foreign tourists. For most people in China, long-distance travel meant long hours on slow trains, travelling in hard-seat, soft-seat or hard-sleeper class; for the important, the relatively wealthy or the foreign tourist, there was the luxurious soft-sleeper class.

Rail

China's railways are undergoing modernisation and this means that the magnificent black steam engines, some manufactured in the United Kingdom, that in the 1980s used to draw long-distance trains southwards from Beijing into the Yangzi delta region and westwards out to Lanzhou and Urumqi, are a thing of the past. Diesel and electric engines have replaced them and new types of railway are being developed.

The Beijing–Shanghai Express Railway will eventually cut the journey time for the 800-mile journey between China's political capital and its commercial and financial centre from nine to five hours in a system that is designed to rival the Japanese Shinkansen Bullet Train. Construction of the line was due to begin in 2006 but it has been dogged with difficulties including disputes over the budget. *China Daily* reported in March 2007 that work on the line would begin later in the year. On 12 October 2007 the National Development and Reform Commission announced that a feasibility study had been approved by the State Council and *Xinhua* news agency interpreted this to imply that the high-speed railway had finally been given the seal of approval. Construction will take at least five years and there has been much speculation over the possible involvement of specialist foreign companies in what will be a prestigious national project.[1]

Roads

Roads began to emerge as a priority for development in the late twentieth century and government plans to connect the major regions together in a national motorway or expressway system have made a good start. This development has both been driven by and resulted in an increase in the ownership of private transport, both cars and commercial transport. Whereas in 1988 a reasonably well-informed academic in Xi'an could say with some confidence that China would never become a society in which people owned their own cars because there was 'nowhere to park', in 2005 that same academic's university had a sizeable carpark which had been created by demolishing local buildings because private car travel to the city had become such a high priority for the university's more senior staff.

Toll roads remain an inhibitor on the growth in the use of private cars but the number of vehicles on the roads is still growing rapidly. The expansion of traffic in Beijing and other cities has been so rapid that the road network is at times scarcely able to cope. Frequent gridlock in Beijing during the 1990s was eased to some extent by the construction of four concentric ring roads, but this in turn has encouraged the use of cars. Similar developments have taken place in other major cities and the construction of inter-city highways proceeds apace. The eventual outcome will be a comprehensive national network of highways, most of them radiating from Beijing and many of them of motorway or expressway standard.

Private cars are still the preserve of the wealthy minority and are seen mainly in the towns and cities; in the rural areas, while there are some cars belonging to wealthy individuals, there are still also many *danwei* (work unit) cars that are used by Party and government officials. For the poorest section of society, transport is overwhelmingly public: cramped and overcrowded buses are used for short- or long-distance travel and within their local areas people move around by bicycle or, in the countryside, on noisy tractors with trailers that double up as people carriers for small families.

Underground and light rail

China is also developing underground (subway) or light rail systems to help ease the crowded roads of its major cities. Beijing has had an underground system for many years. This was originally constructed with a view to securing communication between government offices during a possible conflict with the Soviet Union. It opened in 1969 for the use of government officials only and it was not fully available to the travelling public and foreign visitors until the 1980s. It is cramped and uncomfortable to travel in but not much more so than the buses and trolley buses that were the only alternative for crossing the capital at the time of its construction. It is a relatively small system which links only a few stations in central Beijing but it was due to be expanded as part of the colossal construction programme for the 2008 Olympics.

Shanghai is developing an ultra-modern high-speed Maglev (magnetic levitation) railway built by a German company, which opened in 2004 and carries travellers on a short journey from the Longyang Road underground station to the main international airport in Pudong. It has been criticised as an expensive and inefficient prestige project but extensions to other parts of the city are being planned.

Hong Kong's Mass Transit Railway (MTR), which came into service in 1979, is clean, efficient and popular. It links the commercial districts of Central with the residential and rural areas of the New Territories and also the new airport at Chek Lap Kok, which is in the north of the island of Lantau.

Aviation

Civil aviation developed in the 1980s and after a number of serious accidents was improved considerably in the 1990s.

The first, and for a long time the only, Chinese airline, CAAC (Civil Aviation Administration of China, *Zhongguo minyong hangkong zongju* and known universally by the abbreviation *minhang*), was established in 1949 as China's answer to Aeroflot and was responsible for all domestic civilian flights. It was initially under the control of the military but responsibility for civil aviation was transferred to the government in 1980. As the national economic reform programme progressed, it was transformed into a regular airline operating both domestically and internationally.

In 1987 CAAC was broken up. CAAC itself retained overall control over the management and regulation of the industry but the operational elements were divided into separate airlines. Air China would operate international flights and five regional airlines were created to operate domestic internal schedules: China Eastern Airlines, China Southern Airlines, China Northwest Airlines, China Northern Airlines and China Southwest Airlines. As international travel to and from China has developed, the main international air transport hub, Beijing Capital Airport, has been refurbished to international standards and many regional airports have been rebuilt and updated.

Part III

Society

8   Rural and urban social change

China has always been, and remains, a predominantly rural society: consequently, social change in the countryside has had a critical impact on China's overall development. During the implementation of the radical policies of land reform and collectivisation in the 1950s, the old pre-revolutionary rural social structure was attacked and it appeared that it had been destroyed. In its place were installed social organisations that could be controlled more effectively by the Chinese Communist Party's (CCP's) bureaucratic and military machine. The history of these developments was outlined in Chapter 4.

Land Reform, the confiscation of land that was in the possession of landlords and the wealthier peasant landowners and its redistribution to the poorest farmers, was part of the CCP's successful strategy in the countryside during the 1940s. By the time that the Party came to power as the government of the People's Republic of China (PRC) in October 1949, the Land Reform process was already well advanced and the Party and its cadres had amassed considerable experience in implementing it. The priority of the new government in its promotion of agrarian reform was to consolidate and codify the practice and, in many cases, to restrain overzealous activists who were redistributing land and killing people who they alleged were landowners with little regard to their actual status or individual track records. The legislation designed to carry out this policy was the *Agrarian Reform Law*, promulgated in 1950. The general principles were expressed in Article 1 of the law:

> The land ownership system of feudal exploitation by the landlord class shall be abolished and the system of peasant landownership shall be introduced in order to set free the rural productive forces, develop agricultural production and thus pave the way for New China's industrialisation.[1]

The campaign to implement land reform led by work teams was designed to break down the traditional social patterns of dominance, deference and interdependence that had characterised rural China for centuries. Work teams identified landlords and sought to isolate them from the poorer members of their extended families. Landlord families would often find ways to reduce their apparent standard of living dramatically so that they seemed to be no wealthier than middle-ranking peasants: some killed and consumed their livestock, rather than have cattle and sheep calculated as part of their wealth; others deliberately discontinued their customary participation in traditional social or charitable activities that would have clearly indicated their status as landlords.

> 'The old village institutions of clan, temple and secret society had been re-placed by the new, which assumed their education, mediatory and economic functions.' A new elite of village cadres from the poorest peasant backgrounds had emerged and the members of this new elite owed their positions entirely to the CCP.[2]

The policy of Land Reform led to collectivisation, as has been outlined in Chapter 4, but what were the social consequences of this economic policy and what precisely did collectivisation mean for the families involved? In most cases there may have been very little physical displacement, if any: they continued to live where they had always lived and they farmed the same fields. The changes that did take place were essentially in the management of agriculture and in the impact that this had on the local government in the rural areas. They were organisational changes to ensure that control of agriculture was firmly in the hands of local supporters of the CCP. With the move to larger collective units, decision-making was further divorced from the farming families so that planning could be carried out over a wider area. The names attached to the sub-divisions – brigades and divisions – are interesting as an indication of the changes in the style of management. They are essentially military terms and would have been familiar to many peasants who had served in the People's Liberation Army (PLA) or even in the old Guomindang (GMD) army. They certainly reflected the organisational style with which the PLA work teams that had spearheaded land reform would have been comfortable. The rhetoric that accompanied the push towards collectivisation was frequently also militaristic although it could also be construed as patriotic or nationalistic. To a certain extent this can be perceived as the militarisation of the Chinese countryside, but it would probably be more appropriate to consider it as a movement towards the centralisation of decision-making and control by the CCP and its local government.

After problems were encountered in the management of cooperatives, there was a move to decentralise the decision-making process and to return a degree of control to the lower levels of management, but this tension between centralisation and decentralisation remained a constant feature of cooperatives and of the even larger People's Communes that were to follow in 1958.

Demise of the People's Communes

The People's Communes were part of a broader politico-economic strategy devised by Mao, the Great Leap Forward (*da yuejin*), which was an attempt to galvanise China into speeding up its economic development and catching up with the West. Inspection tours in outlying regions of China, after the fashion of some of the Qing emperors, were an important part of Mao's style of leadership. They enabled him to claim that he was acting on the basis of first-hand knowledge of local conditions and also gave him the opportunity to broaden his personal support by winning round local Party leaders to his own radical policies. At the beginning of August 1958, Mao was undertaking one of these tours in Hebei, Henan and Shandong, three provinces in north-central China. While in rural Shandong he discussed the creation of agricultural cooperatives with local party leaders and said, 'People's Communes are good. Their advantage is that they can combine industry, agriculture, commerce, education and military affairs, making it easier to exercise leadership.' This was the cue for an upsurge in the merger of cooperatives with local township administrations to create People's Communes. The term People's Commune (*renmin gongshe*) was probably not Mao's own creation. It had first appeared in the monthly theoretical journal of the CCP, *Red Flag*, on 1 July 1958 in an article written by his political secretary and adviser, Chen Boda, about the merging of cooperatives that was already being implemented by some county authorities in Henan province. When Mao spoke approvingly of the Commune idea, he was telling the Shandong leadership that they should adopt the model that was being tried just over the provincial border in Henan.[3]

Most communes were rural and were often identical to the previous *xiang* or township administrations but there were also larger communes which were closer in size to a whole county. Urban communes were also created, mostly based on either a large factory or a residential district, but they never achieved the support or the status which rural communes enjoyed and they died out very quickly.[4]

The rural People's Communes have been mythologised and reviled in turn. They were the normal way of life for the majority of China's farming families for twenty years. The manner in which communes were created and the way that they operated across China varied greatly: all had their own local characteristics and idiosyncrasies that reflected geographical conditions, local agricultural traditions and social and ethnic differences. The commune system came to an end in 1978 with the introduction of the Responsibility System and rural China reverted to a version of the system of landowners and peasants that had existed before collectivisation and before the advent of the PRC. The role played by Party and government cadres in the lives of the peasants changed drastically. No longer in absolute command, although they still had considerable power through their ability to tax, members of local Party committees sought a new accommodation with the peasants, some of whom had become extremely wealthy, and some CCP officials joined in business ventures with the most influential landowners in their area. In the course of time some of these business ventures, wishing to expand, bought or requisitioned land that was being farmed by poorer or less influential peasant families. This has been a major factor in the outbreak of rural unrest that China experienced in the first years of the twenty-first century.

Migration and urbanisation

Urbanisation has been one of the most important features of China's development since the inception of the reform programme in the late 1970s. During the previous two decades, the CCP had sought to control the development of the metropolitan centres, partly for practical reasons and partly because of an abiding prejudice against the cities among an aging leadership that had established its powerbase in the rural areas and felt that it owed a debt of loyalty to the peasant masses. When migration to the cities began in the 1980s, there were serious attempts to create buffer zones, including, for example, the designation of a ring of small towns around Shanghai as satellite towns to absorb the demand from the large numbers of rural people seeking a better and brighter life. The household registration system (*hukou*), which is considered below, also prevented rural people from moving to the cities in search of jobs. This was because their agricultural role as producers of grain to feed the cities was seen as vital, 'the key link', by the government.

At the beginning of the reform period something like 18 per cent of China's population lived in towns and cities. By 2006 it was of the order of 40 per cent, at least. These figures are difficult to interpret precisely as there is a vast floating population of migrant workers, estimated at something of the order of 120 million, who have a notional rural base but who work in the cities and whose remittance earnings form a vital part of the income of their rural families. It is far from clear what proportion of this migrant population will eventually return to the countryside and by 2007 it was becoming clear that the rate of migration from the villages was beginning to slow down. Nevertheless, many rural migrants will remain in the cities and will become part of the new urban social structure that is emerging. China is now home to some of the largest cities in the world, including Shanghai with a population of 9.8 million, Beijing with 7.4 million and Hong Kong with 6.1 million. Another problem in estimating the change in the urban population is that the designation of some substantial cities has also been modified and many cities include large areas of farming land in the territory under their jurisdiction.

The cities began to change in character with the rise of a new urban middle class and also new urban workers who may have originated in the countryside but in many cases were settling in the cities and acquiring the new skills required for the modern economy. These included technical expertise and foreign languages, primarily English, which was viewed more and more as an essential requirement in the tourist trade and for attracting foreign trade and investment.

New people needed new housing and the Beijing skyline changed completely, and not necessarily for the better, with the appearance of high-rise blocks of flats. Houses and flats began to change hands (sometimes at exorbitant prices) and the Western concept of buying and renting replaced allocation by the *danwei*, at least at the top end of the market. The habits of urban residents also began to change. The *nouveaux riches* rapidly acquired cars, and the iconic Chinese bicycle, although still ubiquitous, has become a symbol of the poor or the elderly. New restaurants and cultural amenities provide for the leisure activities of the rising new elite and internal tourism has taken off as people travel to see the parts of their country that they had not been allowed, and probably could not afford, to visit for decades, often beginning with the ancestral homes (*guxiang*) of their extended families.

The *Hukou* system

At the centre of the restrictions on movement in pre-reform China was the fifty-year-old *hukou* or household registration system. Proposals to reform or even abandon the system have stimulated an intense debate in political circles in Beijing as China strives to increase its urban population to 45 per cent of the total by 2010. The system of requiring the entire population to register as either rural or urban residents has been criticised as discriminating against China's rural majority. It is also seen as a barrier to the mobility of labour necessary to urbanise and modernise the country. Opponents of reform point to fears that the unfettered migration of rural workers to the cities will impose impossible strains on social services. They also predict that it will cause a further rise in crime and disorder, which has in any event already increased as the economy has developed.

Origins of the hukou *system*

When the Communist Party emerged from its rural bases to take control of China in 1949, one of its major concerns was the threat of massive uncontrolled migration from the poor countryside to the cities. Provisional regulations for registering urban residents were introduced in 1951 and quotas for the urban and rural population ratio were fixed in 1955. However, the need for labour mobility to supply the needs of heavy industry ensured relatively free population movement until 1958. During the Great Leap Forward, which was launched in that year, the *Regulation of Household Registration* laws were passed to ensure strict control over internal migration.

The *hukou* household registration document, which every family is obliged to have and to keep safely, is a combination of residence permit and an officially accredited family history. It contains personal information on the family, including details of the births, marriages, deaths and divorces of all family members. It has been particularly important in migration control and in the enforcement of the one-child family planning policy. It is not simply a creation of the CCP as it builds on elements of historical Chinese systems of social control that operated in different ways in most periods of imperial China and combines them with similar policies that were copied from the former Soviet Union. Taiwan, Japan and the two Koreas also have similar systems and this has led some observers to suggest that an East Asian or a Confucian attitude towards social control is in operation.

In order to live and work in the towns and cities, migrants were required to have an urban *hukou*, rather than the documents that were issued to members of farming families which restricted them to residence in the rural areas. Urban *hukou* became increasingly difficult to acquire. Without this permit, no access was possible to basic services such as accommodation, education, health and welfare payments. This even extended to rationed food supplies during times of scarcity. The *hukou* system exacerbated the great disparity that already existed between living standards in the cities and in the countryside. It also reinforced a traditional Chinese urban prejudice against the rural population by forcing them to stay in their native villages where social, economic and cultural services were at a low level, if they existed at all.

Breakdown of the hukou *system in reform period*

The system began to break down in the early 1980s at the beginning of the reform period. Migrant workers left the rural communes, which were being dismantled and needed far less unskilled labour than under the previous system, and they sought work in the cities. These workers were subject to quota systems and were often the victims of discrimination, intimidation and violence by the authorities. They were also restricted to the most unpleasant and dangerous jobs – jobs that many of those who already possessed an urban *hukou* were not prepared to do. Employers were able to stipulate that the possession of an urban *hukou* was a prerequisite for the more desirable jobs. This was an effective way of excluding outsiders. Migrants to the cities who were unable to obtain the permit frequently had to pay higher prices for accommodation, education and other services. Their lack of legal status often led to problems in getting paid and poor employment conditions.

By 1998 it had become clear that urbanisation and labour mobility were being stifled by the household registration system. The State Council introduced reforms, initially allowing outsiders to acquire urban *hukou* by marriage and permitting children to inherit this status from their parents. Centrally imposed urban and rural quotas were phased out in 2000, and in 2001 the responsibility for granting urban *hukou* was devolved to local governments. This led to inconsistency and confusion. Of the twenty-three provincial-level administrations, eleven, mostly in the booming southeast, produced plans to abolish *hukou*. However, the large cities, particularly Beijing and Shanghai which are the greatest magnets for the urban poor, are resisting the reforms because of the potential pressure of migration and concerns about the impact on crime and security. At a conference on the problems of the floating population in November 2005, the Ministry of Public Security proposed the abolition of the demarcation between rural and non-rural residents in favour of a unified registration system.

Opponents of the reform have pointed to problems that have been revealed during pilot projects. In 2001 the city of Zhengzhou, the major rail hub of north-central China, offered to issue residence permits to people whose relatives already lived in the city. This was reversed in 2004 because of claims that demands on the transport, health and education systems had become unmanageable and that crime had increased. Prejudice against rural migrants undoubtedly played a part.

Beijing's Public Security Bureau has argued that reform of the system would lead to demands for places in the capital's schools that would be impossible to meet. They also predict a rise in crime and disorder and argue that the city could not meet the costs of medical care and social security. At worst, the local administrations of the biggest cities fear the development of shanty towns of the type that have grown up in other parts of the developing world. The relaxation of the *hukou* policies also risks increasing the impoverishment of the rural areas.

Current hukou *practice*

In practical terms, the *hukou* is not the absolute barrier to migration that it once was. It is estimated that the migrant population has mushroomed to at least 120 million, which indicates that peasants desperately in search of work are finding ways around the regulations. Even in the absence of the implementation of any reforms, the authorities began to relax the enforcement of the regulations. Some legal restrictions on workers without urban *hukou* were lifted and in Beijing the practice of fining or deporting migrants without a permit was discontinued. Some rural migrants were also permitted to transfer from a rural to an urban *hukou*. This reduced the level of discrimination and intimidation experienced by migrant workers, at least temporarily, but the uncertainly persists. It remains to be seen whether these restrictions will be re-imposed as the Beijing authorities concentrate on presenting their city in the best light for the Olympic Games of 2008.

Rural migrant labourers have effectively become an underclass in the major cities. They have no security and are excluded from many of the benefits enjoyed by permanent residents. As such, they are at risk from exploitation, casual violence and summary expulsion from the cities by the police. They are also vulnerable to being drawn into urban criminal gangs and prostitution. The problem of rural migrants is now a major concern for the authorities in the cities and fully integrating them is a high priority. Not all migrants are able to settle in the cities and many return to poverty in the countryside. The reform, or even the complete abolition, of the *hukou* system will remove an outdated and unworkable formal barrier to migration. It will not, however, without further reforms, remove structural discrimination against rural dwellers and rural migrants in the cities and the potential for conflict and social disorder that this creates.[5]

9 Education and health

The provision of education and health services is generally considered to be a good indicator of the level of development of any society. Societies governed by Communist parties, as China has been since 1949, have always made a point of providing universal education, either free of charge or at a cost that could be afforded by the majority of the population. Educational provision in the early years of the People's Republic was limited and the content of the curriculum was often skewed and used to serve a partial and partisan view of society. However, basic literacy was accorded a high priority and the government was able to point to this as a significant advance on the system that had been offered under its predecessors.

Healthcare on a national scale was also a declared priority of the Chinese Communist Party (CCP) and some of the more idiosyncratic provisions, particularly the intriguingly named 'barefoot doctors', and the reliance on traditional indigenous medicine attracted considerable interest internationally. After the reform of the 1980s, both sectors were obliged to confront the impact of greater commercialisation.

Education

Traditional education

Before the middle of the twentieth century, the provision of education in China was underdeveloped and uneven. For most of the imperial era, instruction had been provided only for the landed elite and its primary function was to ensure that potential administrators acquired a thorough grounding, not only in the literary Chinese language, the language of administration, which was a considerable challenge in its own right, but also in the philosophical and historical classical texts of the Confucian tradition, familiarity with which was believed to be essential for the correct governance of the empire. This *literati* education proceeded through a series of examinations at local, provincial and finally national level, a process which took many years to complete. Only candidates who were able to devote themselves full-time to the study of the classics had any prospect of being awarded the degrees and as a result the candidates were drawn almost exclusively from the landowning class, the gentry, and most were from families that were connected with existing official post holders. The process was one of indoctrination in the prevailing Confucian orthodoxy rather than anything approaching liberal, critical or scientific education: questioning conventional wisdom or advocating alternative approaches were on the whole discouraged as iconoclastic and dangerous.

There was no central or state-administered education: all teaching was provided at the local level and financed by individual families, clans (extended families) or other social organisations, including religious foundations. Teaching might be carried out in the home of the student or at the house of a private tutor and could be at the student's own pace. It initially consisted of the directed reading of basic educational texts such as the *Thousand Character Classic (Qianziwen)* before the student was considered capable of proceeding to the *Four Books* and *Five Classics*, which collected together the major books of the Confucian canon of philosophy and literature. Girls were almost never allowed to attend school: exceptionally the daughter of a wealthy family might be educated at home.

For the overwhelming majority of the population, whether farmers, craftsmen or merchants, there was virtually no opportunity to gain a formal education, although some small traders did acquire the rudimentary skills in reading and writing that were necessary to run their businesses. There was no public education but religious bodies did offer education to young novitiates. The Buddhist monasteries were notable for this, both in the Chinese tradition and the Tibetan, since facility with spiritual texts was central to the performance of religious duties. For Muslims in some parts of China, the *madrasas*, religious schools that were run by mosques or Sufi orders, also provided an education. In all of these institutions, the education that the students received was essentially religious in nature. At the end of the nineteenth century as the Chinese empire began to collapse, China was sadly lacking in secular, liberal and, above all, scientific and technical education. More seriously, a large part of the conservative elite did not even recognise that this problem existed.

Missionary contribution to educational reform

Christian missionaries arrived in China in considerable numbers in this period: the China Inland Mission alone had 641 missionaries on its books in 1895. The majority of missionaries in China were Protestant, although Catholic missions had established a small but influential presence much earlier, and education (together with medical care) was one of their most important activities after the initial task of establishing churches and preaching the gospel to attract converts. Although Christian missionary education, like that of the monasteries and mosques, had a substantial religious component, it did introduce other aspects of Western education to China. Missionaries who began to understand Chinese culture and sympathise with the predicament of the Chinese people embarked on a programme of secular education: to a certain extent this was for altruistic and humanitarian reasons but it was also viewed as part of a strategy to create a body of sympathetic followers. Missionaries supported schools, hospitals, libraries and the press: some colleges and universities that were set up under the auspices of European and

American churches were to become very influential, including the forerunner of Beijing University.

The traditional Chinese educational system fell into decline towards the end of the nineteenth century and in 1905 the imperial examinations, which had been the cornerstone of the *literati* educational system, were abolished, signalling the final demise of the old educational order. Reforms that were introduced at this time reduced the role of the Confucian classics in schools and emphasised the ability to read and write the modern Chinese language. The new reformed schools had a strongly patriotic or even nationalist ethos and were to a large extent modelled on the successful educational reforms that had recently been implemented in Japan. Chinese students began to travel to Japan to complete their higher education but many also studied in Europe and the United States.

Education and the New Life movement

Education in the Republican period under the Nationalist Guomindang (GMD), which ruled most of China from its capital in Nanjing between 1928 and the Japanese invasion of 1937, was constructed to a certain extent on the model established by missionaries. Under the New Life Movement inaugurated by the GMD in 1934, there was also an attempt to reintroduce the application of Confucian principles in a manner that was deemed appropriate to the society of that era, in the belief that this would promote harmony and social order. This approach demonstrated a preference for indoctrination rather than education, following the Confucian tradition, and, although it was the creation of the nationalists, it also laid the foundations for the educational system that was to develop later under the CCP.

The original ill-fated attempt at a Confucian revival gave way to a Western Christian and particularly an American style and an American citizen, George Shepherd, became director of the New Life movement in 1935. The day-to-day implementation of the aims of the organisation – such as courtesy, cleanliness and social order – was to a large extent left to the police, the military and even the scout movement. Gradually the New Life movement became more militaristic until it began to look uncomfortably like the right-wing youth movements that were springing up in Europe in the 1930s and showed signs of blatant borrowing from the style and trappings of European fascism.

Education and the Chinese Communist Party

When the CCP came to power, with an agenda that was radical but also at times xenophobic, the missionary schools fell under suspicion and a new type of education was created, an approach that was considered to be more suitable for a 'New China'. Schools and colleges that had been established by foreigners were the object of a campaign launched by the new Chinese government in 1951 and by the following year all of these institutions had been brought under government control. The authorities encouraged students to criticise foreign, particularly American, cultural influences: this campaign was of course closely connected to the conflict in Korea between China and United Nations forces which were dominated by the United States.

An important aim of the Communist Party's new strategy for education was to redress the social balance, to right a historical wrong and to create a system of schools for the peasant farmers who had been completely neglected by governments for centuries, in education as in so much else. Peasants had been the greatest supporters of the CCP in its rise to power and the Party considered that it owed them a political as well as a moral debt.

Before 1949, the greatest educational problem was illiteracy: this may have been as high as 80 per cent according to government data although sources sympathetic to the GMD tend to claim that this figure was exaggerated. Nevertheless the combination of basic education with a programme to reform the use of the Chinese script dramatically reduced the level of illiteracy in China.

Basic education was in any case the top priority and establishing a universal system of education was one of the CCP's key aims. In the early 1950s, it was the Soviet Union that provided the model for China's system of primary, secondary and higher secondary schools and colleges and universities in the tertiary sector. Soviet influence in the structure of education and the curriculum was strengthened by the presence in China of teachers from the Soviet Union and Eastern Europe (part of the larger group labelled 'Soviet experts' who provided technical and other expertise) who taught in schools and universities and who also trained many of China's teachers. Moreover, many Chinese students had studied in the Soviet Union and Russian was by far the most important foreign language studied by young Chinese during the 1950s and 1960s.

Cultural Revolution period education

Within a few years of the establishment of the PRC, the differences between Mao and Moscow that were to lead to the Sino–Soviet dispute were already prompting some powerful CCP members to question the nature of the education being provided in China's schools. There was pressure for more political education and there were demands that the schools should emphasise the importance of participation by students in physical labour. The chaos of the Cultural Revolution led to the breakdown of the centrally organised educational system although schools did continue to function in spite of the difficult conditions.[1]

Education during the Cultural Revolution period was intensely political. Teaching and learning in all schools, from kindergartens to senior high schools and also colleges and universities, was focused on the study of Mao Zedong thought: it was an exercise in rote learning and the parroting of short texts that had been memorised rather than a critical approach, an uncanny echo of the imperial educational system. The school and college day was frequently disrupted by political demonstrations and periods of physical labour which were intended to express the closeness of students to the peasants and workers, but especially to the peasants. While some Western true believers who visited China during that period were impressed by the degree of political activity in schools, the vast majority of well-informed Chinese now view this as having been at best a complete waste of time and at worst an absolute disaster, both for their own educational opportunities and careers and for the creation of a modern, educated Chinese society. It created a 'lost generation' whose education, either at secondary school or at university, was so disrupted by the Cultural Revolution that some individuals have never recovered.[2]

Educational reform in the 1980s and 1990s

When Deng Xiaoping's reform programme began in the 1980s there was increased investment in public education with the aim of rebuilding a national system, although at this juncture what the leadership envisaged was a system that would also be flexible enough to respond to varied conditions in different regions of the country. The political and ideological content that had dominated education in the 1960s and 1970s was drastically reduced: it was never completely eliminated although the subject matter and the style have changed radically and there is now far less dogmatic Marxism and more material of a patriotic or nationalist nature. However, the Young Pioneer (*shaoxiandui*) organisation, which recruits children between the ages of seven and fourteen and had a membership of 130 million in 2005, exists in parallel with the school system to promote patriotic and socially responsible attitudes among children. Its function and approach are reminiscent of the Boy Scouts or Girl Guides and church Sunday school but the ethos is primarily political and patriotic.

Hu Jintao, speaking at a gathering of Young Pioneers in 2000 shortly before he was formally identified as the next leader of China, told them that they were 'expected to be strict with themselves, to be good students at school, good children at home and good children in society. They must strive to become talented young adults.' He went on to say that the Young Pioneer organisation was 'a cradle for nurturing China's children and provides a school where children can learn socialism and communism'.[3]

In April 1986, legislation setting out plans for a nine-year compulsory education system, a system similar to the one that exists in many other countries, was passed by the National People's Congress (NPC). The intention was that this would be in force in the cities and the more economically developed rural areas by 1990 and that it would spread to the rest of the country by 2000. This nine-year system is the core of primary and secondary education: in addition to this, three years of pre-school teaching may be available before the compulsory core and three years of higher secondary afterwards: higher education is also available, but only for a talented minority. The reforms also permitted the re-introduction of private education and, by the end of 1993, there were 4,030 privately run primary schools, 851 secondary schools and 800 higher secondary schools in operation.

Primary education normally lasts for six years although in some poorer rural communities children begin school at the age of seven rather than six and follow a five-year curriculum. Primary schools teach for forty weeks each year and the children usually attend classes for between twenty-four and twenty-seven hours each week. The study of the Chinese language necessarily occupies a high proportion of classroom time (up to 50 per cent) and considerable emphasis is placed on moral and ethical education, but children also study mathematics, science, history, geography, physical education, music and art.

Secondary education is compulsory for three years in junior high schools and the subjects studied are broadly the same as those taught in primary schools, with the addition of foreign languages and more specialised science subjects: the students spend approximately thirty hours in the classroom each week. In order to proceed from this junior level to senior high school, students must pass a competitive examination.

There is an attempt to run all schools throughout the country on exactly the same lines although in practice there is considerable variation, a situation that is oddly reminiscent of the system in France. Every morning schoolchildren sing the national anthem as the national flag is raised on the flagpole that is found in every playground. Primary-age children throughout the country tend to wear the same practical standard green tracksuits as a school uniform and they are rewarded for achievement with red stars rather than the gold or silver ones traditionally awarded in the West. For secondary schools the uniform is a different colour, with light blue tracksuits often being favoured. Some schools have provision for boarding pupils. Sporting activities are an important part of the curriculum and basketball courts and table tennis tables are usually in evidence.

To European eyes the system might appear regimented, but it would not be strange to Taiwanese or Japanese students and teachers: similar school regimes can also be found in other Asian countries. At the end of the school day, when the children tumble noisily out of the gates of a school, it could be anywhere in the world.[4]

The reform programme conceded a degree of devolution to local authorities but the idea of a centralised and standardised system has not been abandoned and this was the responsibility of the State Education Commission which once again became the Ministry of Education in 1998 when the ministries of the State Council were restructured. Among its most important objectives were an expansion in the number of schools, especially at the middle school or junior high school level and the training and certification of a body of appropriately qualified teachers. There was also a desire to maintain uniform national criteria for the curriculum, for textbooks and other teaching resources, and for examinations.

The key piece of legislation was the *Compulsory Education Law of the People's Republic of China*, which was approved by the NPC on 12 April 1986 and came into force on 1 July of the same year. The eighteen clauses in this brief act included an outline of the nine-year compulsory education programme from the age of six years, or seven where six is not possible: this alternative was offered in recognition of the problems involved in bringing education in the rural areas, particularly in poor or minority areas, up to the level of the urban areas. There were also instructions to local authorities to provide education in their own areas in accordance with local conditions. The law recognised that, of the two stages of compulsory education, the primary stage would become universal long before the middle or junior high school stage. It stipulated that *Putonghua* (Standard Chinese, but usually called Mandarin by Westerners) should be promoted in schools but allows the use of non-Chinese languages in schools in ethnic minority areas. The law also specifies that there should be no tuition fees and that grants should be made available to support students from less wealthy families. It also provides for an expansion in the number of colleges to train teachers.[5]

While this in many ways has the appearance of an admirable and progressive approach to national education, the implementation of the policies has exposed many problems in the educational system, especially in the more remote rural areas. There are not enough schools; attendance is often very patchy; and, although there is a clear prohibition on the levying of tuition fees, many schools have managed to circumvent this regulation by inventing other fees or charging for the provision of textbooks and other services. In some instances this makes the cost of school attendance prohibitive for children from the poorest families, replicating conditions that existed in the rural areas and poorer towns before the government of the People's Republic first attempted to introduce compulsory education in the 1950s. For wealthier families, this is less of a problem and it is widely acknowledged that many better-off families spend more on the education of their children than on any other single item of expenditure. The introduction of fees, both legal and illegal, is a direct result of the budgetary decentralisation that is a key feature of the economic reform programme. As central government funding has been reduced or withdrawn, schools have been faced with the need to find alternative sources of financial support.[6]

Key schools

Key schools emerged in the 1950s as a way of concentrating the most able students in schools that already had an outstanding track record of achievement and these institutions were provided with additional funding. This system was designed with the intention of steering the most able students into the higher education sector. Key schools were abolished during the Cultural Revolution because they ran counter to the prevailing mood of egalitarianism. They were reintroduced in the 1980s as part of the drive to reform the educational system but rapidly fell out of favour as the creation of a universal national system of education was preferred and they were abolished in the summer of 2006.

Private education in the reform era

With the advent of the reform era, private schools, colleges and universities began to make an appearance, partly in response to the real or perceived inadequacies of the state sector and partly as newly liberated entrepreneurs spotted a business opportunity. It was not, however, until 1997 that the existence of the private sector was formally recognised by the Ministry of Education. There were conferences on independent or non-governmental education in a number of Chinese provinces in 2000 and 2001 and the NPC discussed its first draft legislation on private education in November 2001. Concerns were expressed over the standards of education provided by some of these institutions and the government recognised the need to regulate the private sector. This was the topic of a heated debate at a meeting of the NPC Standing Committee held in June 2002 when members of the NPC clashed over whether the provision of education for profit, rather than as a public service, should even be permitted. Legislation on promoting what were termed 'non-state educational institutions' was passed by the NPC Standing Committee on 28 December 2002 and came into effect on 1 September 2004.[7] At a news conference held in Beijing in November 2005, the Minister of Education, Zhou Ji, emphasised the necessity for China to develop private education to reduce the pressure on the public system, which was having great difficulty responding to the demands placed on it by the dynamic economic reform programme. Statistics produced by the Ministry of Education indicated that in 2005 there may have been as many as 70,000 independent schools in existence, catering for as many as fourteen million students in all age groups from primary to college level.[8]

The growth of private schooling in China is a pragmatic response to the new demands created by the economic reforms rather than an attempt at constructing a political or ethical alternative to the existing state educational system. The creation of the independent sector has been almost entirely a result of practical needs and commercial opportunity and does not appear to be explicitly ideologically driven.[9]

Further and higher education

China has a system of vocational and technical schools which recruit students of secondary age but provide the kind of education that is often the responsibility of the further education sector in the West. There are also colleges for agricultural and technical education and a thriving and increasingly competitive university sector.

The higher education system ground to a halt in the Cultural Revolution of the 1960s. The time and energy of students was diverted into the conflicts between Red Guard factions that helped to facilitate the intra-Party struggle instigated by Mao Zedong and it was impossible for most institutions to operate anything approaching a normal curriculum. When the universities and colleges were permitted to reopen, the spirit of the Cultural Revolution still prevailed and admissions were dependent not on educational ability or potential, but on the political track record and family background of the applicants. Students who were blessed with good 'worker, peasant or soldier' pedigrees took precedence over those who had enjoyed a bourgeois upbringing: this effectively precluded anyone from a family with any history of higher education. The result was a demoralised and largely ineffective higher education sector.

Scientific and technological advance was one of the cornerstones of the Four Modernisations programme put forward by Zhou Enlai and later by Deng Xiaoping. This prioritisation led to renewed investment in education and an emphasis on quality and professionalism rather than political attitude or family background. Universities were granted considerable autonomy in developing their own curricula and appointing their own staff and a national examination system was established. These examinations are taken by all candidates for higher education establishments and are extremely competitive. In many households all normal family activities are suspended during the examination season and the combined efforts of all family members are directed at getting talented sons or daughters into the right university. Elite institutions are able to select the most able applicants, which is a complete reversal of the position in the Mao era. During the 1980s the system under which all graduates were allocated jobs by the state began to break down and employment choices expanded.

China has a total of over 2,000 universities, colleges or other institutions of higher education: some are familiar names with international reputations while others are completely unknown, even within China. Among the universities that are consistently rated most highly are Beijing University, Qinghua University (which is also in Beijing and has begun to revert to the older spelling of Tsinghua), Renmin University of China (People's University, which was at one time a CCP training school), Fudan University in Shanghai, and the Chinese University of Science and Technology, which is based in Hefei, the capital of Anhui province, and which according to some educationalists in China aspires in time to be a serious rival to the Massachusetts Institute of Technology. In addition to these there are many provincial universities and teacher training colleges (normal schools), many of which are sound institutions, but there are also new names, many of them privately run, whose status and academic respectability is in considerable doubt.[10]

In the summer of 2006, the problems of private universities were brought to the attention of a wider public when there were serious disturbances among students at a college campus just outside the Henan provincial capital of Zhengzhou. There were angry demonstrations at the college, property was damaged and police cars were attacked. Although there were reports that the trouble had been caused by student dissatisfaction at a Spartan regime which included early morning physical exercises, a prohibition on drinking and smoking and restrictions on when students could leave the campus, it was first and foremost the status of the degrees offered by the university that was behind the protests.

The college, the Shengda Economics Trade and Management College of Zhengzhou University, is run by a partnership between Zhengzhou University and a Taiwanese educational foundation. Because it was sponsored by Zhengzhou University, which is a respected and prestigious establishment of national standing, it was considered to be part of the public education sector. Students who were not able to gain admission to Zhengzhou University itself were able to pay for admission to Shengda. Their tuition fees were five times the normal level but they claimed that they had been led to believe that their degree certificates would be those of Zhengzhou University. Government regulations imposed in 2003 made it mandatory for the name of any subsidiary college (Shengda, in this case) to be included on the certificates and when the cohort that graduated in 2006 discovered this they took the view that they had been short-changed. The college principal resigned but the institution continues to operate as a college of Zhengzhou University. The Shengda case was the most prominent but it was not an isolated incident. Demonstrations also took place in a textile college in Jiangxi province and in the PLA Artillery Academy in Hefei in Anhui province when changes to diplomas were announced.[11]

Hong Kong has several universities including Hong Kong University (HKU), the Chinese University of Hong Kong and the Hong Kong University of Science and Technology, as well as several which have been promoted from polytechnic or college status. Although they are formally within the PRC, they function and are administered independently, for the most part as they did when Hong Kong was a British colony and HKU played a key role in the Association of Commonwealth Universities.

Health and family planning

Barefoot healthcare

In the pre-reform era, medical treatment and healthcare was generally provided free of charge or at least at a very low cost. For the majority of peasant farmers it was provided by the commune clinic or by the legendary 'barefoot doctors', partly qualified medical auxiliaries who did sterling work in rural areas, often the more remote regions, that had no Western-style professional medical provision. The term 'barefoot doctor' attracted a certain amount of derision in the West, but the work that they were doing was vital. Their role was similar to that of a district nurse or health visitor in the United Kingdom, combined with the first-aid skills of the Red Cross or the St John's Ambulance Brigade. In communities where the alternative was no healthcare at all, they were a boon. In the towns and cities, medical care was generally much more advanced and was the responsibility of the work unit (*danwei*), and diagnosis and treatment were generally provided free of charge for its employees.

Traditional Chinese medicine

The quality of care, and certainly the level of resources available, was usually very poor in comparison with the developed West but it was no worse than in other developing countries in the same period and was better than in many. There was an emphasis on traditional Chinese medicine including herbal treatments, acupuncture and moxibustion, which is the burning of the herb mugwort on the skin. This was partly a pragmatic response to the impossibility of providing Western scientific medicine in a vast, poor country and partly a patriotic response, taking pride in the traditional treatments that were distinctive or sometimes unique to China. Western specialists who were trained in conventional medicine initially tended to dismiss Chinese claims for these treatments but some were inclined to be impressed when it was demonstrated, for example, that acupuncture worked on livestock. It is ironic that clinics offering traditional Chinese medical treatments are now commonplace in many Western cities where they are offered as complementary to Western scientific medicine.

In the 1950s the provision of healthcare was a high priority of the government and it was claimed that major endemic diseases such as cholera, typhoid, scarlet fever and schistosomiasis (bilharzia), a debilitating disease caused by parasites that pass to humans through freshwater snails in drinking water, had been completely eradicated. Details of epidemic diseases and other health problems that beset rural China during the 1950s and 1960s are difficult to verify but it is likely that epidemics played a large part in the high number of excess deaths recorded in the famines that followed the Great Leap Forward of 1958.

Reform era medicine

One of the consequences of the economic reform programme that began in the 1980s is that medical care is no longer free of charge, except for employees of state-run organisations and government and Party officials. Everyone else has to pay and a recent but increasingly common way of doing so is by taking out medical insurance, either through a state-run system or, for a small number of people, private insurance.

Paying for healthcare is not a serious problem for the newly rich elite but the cost of consultations and medication is a heavy burden even for relatively well-paid white-collar workers in the cities. In the rural areas, the premiums are far beyond the means of the vast majority of the peasants, who simply pay cash if they cannot avoid seeking medical treatment. Many people do not consult doctors at all and this has caused great concern, particularly in the light of epidemic health scares such as SARS and AIDS. For the unemployed and the migrant workers, who are thought to number at least 120 million, there is virtually no possibility of paying for healthcare. An additional source of disquiet is that under-attendance at clinics may lead to the under-reporting of serious conditions and this, in turn, suggests that official statistics are even less reliable than they should be.[12]

In 1998, the government announced a plan for making medical insurance universally available for urban residents, the *Decision on Establishing a Basic Medical Insurance System for Urban Employees* which, following the usual pattern, was implemented nationally after regional pilot studies. According to *People's Daily*, 'By the end of 2003, some 109.02 million people around China had participated in the basic medical insurance program, including 79.75 million employees and 29.27 million retirees'.[13]

Sichuan healthcare disturbances

The serious predicament that China faces in healthcare provision, especially in the rural areas, was graphically illustrated by a case in the southwestern province of Sichuan. Sichuan is a relatively prosperous province in what is otherwise the generally underdeveloped western region. It profited from the relocation of resources during the 1960s under the Third Front policy that was designed to protect China's strategic industries in the event of an attack from the United States or the Soviet Union. It was also the provincial political base of the reforming premier Zhao Ziyang who strengthened the economy of his region.

In November 2006, a four-year-old boy was admitted to the No. 2 People's Hospital in Guang'an after having accidentally drunk pesticide. Guang'an is in the east of Sichuan province and coincidentally is also the birthplace of Deng Xiaoping. The boy's family and the hospital disagree about what happened next but the family claimed that he was refused treatment, in this case having his stomach pumped, because they did not have sufficient funds. They alleged that the hospital demanded RMB 800 but the family could only afford RMB 100. The boy died two hours after having been brought to the hospital. The hospital maintain that appropriate treatment was given and that the family only paid RMB 123 after the child's death rather than the full fee of RMB 639 which the hospital could have insisted on.

The family set up a shrine outside the hospital, demanded compensation and tried to petition the local government but were rebuffed roughly by security staff. Believing that the boy had died because the hospital had refused to treat him, schoolchildren from a nearby secondary school and then other local residents began to demonstrate in front of the hospital. Up to 2,000 protestors came to the hospital, windows and equipment were broken and the hospital was obliged to close. Police who were called to deal with the riot used tear gas and arrested at least twenty demonstrators. There were reports that three people had been killed during the disturbances, including one police officer. These deaths were never confirmed but it was accepted by the authorities that a large crowd had gathered and that there had been a serious disturbance.[14]

The Guang'an city government investigated the incident in consultation with the Huaxi Hospital which is attached to Sichuan University. Their joint report concluded that the boy had drunk enough pesticide to kill '500 children' and that he may have done so because it had been placed in a soft drink bottle when it was bought by his grandfather. Staff at the Guang'an No. 2 Hospital were exonerated: it was accepted that they had pumped the boy's stomach and put him on a drip which was all that was possible in the circumstances.[15] The willingness of the local populace to assume that an injustice had been done is a clear indication of the crisis of confidence in the healthcare system.

Medical insurance for the countryside

In 2003, in an attempt to provide at least a partial solution to the costs of healthcare in poorer rural communities, the government launched a medical insurance scheme targeted at peasant farmers. As is the normal practice in China, this scheme underwent trials in a few counties before being extended nationwide after it became clear that it was extremely popular. It requires large-scale government investment in a scheme to which individual farmers also subscribe, at a premium that can be as low as RMB 10 per annum: the government then provides matching funds and up to 50 per cent of the medical fees incurred by patients are covered. Even though farming families will still have to pay part of the cost of their medical care under the new scheme, it is expected that the financial support from the government will ease the burden on them sufficiently to overcome the reluctance of many peasant families to seek medical advice. This rural medical insurance scheme is one of Premier Wen Jiabao's pet projects and in his speech to the NPC in March 2006 he announced his intention of making it available to 80 per cent of the rural population by the end of that year.[16] The Minister of Health, Chen Zhu, claimed in October 2007 that 83 per cent of the rural population, some 720 million farmers, had enrolled in the plan, now entitled the Rural Cooperative Medical Care programme, and that by 2008 it would have been extended to cover all of China's countryside.[17] Not all medical costs are covered by the scheme and its success depends to a large extent on the willingness of hospitals to limit their fees and on the ability of the authorities to keep a tight rein on corruption.

HIV/AIDS and SARS

International concerns about health in China have focused on the major epidemic diseases particularly HIV/AIDS and SARS (severe acute respiratory syndrome) which was identified in 2002, largely because these were judged to present a significant risk to people living outside China. HIV/AIDS has been a growing problem that is associated with the greater mobility of the labour force, the re-emergence of prostitution on a large scale and the appearance in certain areas of intravenous injection of heroin and other narcotics. The SARS epidemic began in Guangdong province in November 2002 and lasted until July 2003. Out of a total of perhaps 8,000 people identified as having been infected with the SARS virus, 800 died. Both of these outbreaks generated criticism at the way the Chinese government has handled medical issues, and there has been concern at the slowness with which resources were deployed to the affected areas and the lack of transparency about the prevalence of the diseases. There was inadequate reporting of the problem within China although the level of discussion in the media was consistent with the treatment of other controversial and difficult issues.

Tobacco smoking was almost universal, at least among men, in China until the 1980s and for many years it is said that it was effectively a taboo subject because Mao Zedong had been a chain smoker. At academic and other meetings it was routine for cigarettes to be handed out with the ritual cups of tea. After Mao's death in 1976, posters proclaiming the health risks of tobacco began to appear and the popularity of smoking has declined.

In spite of the problems that China faces in developing an effective healthcare system it should be noted that average life expectancy has risen from thirty-two in 1950 to seventy-three in 2006.

Contaminated blood

In 1995 a scandal emerged which highlighted both the shortcomings of the Chinese healthcare system in the countryside and the desperate poverty of many peasant families. Officials and businessmen in Henan province established a network of unofficial and illegal blood banks to supply hospitals and pharmaceutical companies with blood and plasma products. The creation of these blood banks coincided with the appointment of a new director of the provincial Bureau of Health, Liu Quanxi, who among other projects created a central blood collection facility and a pharmaceutical company. He encouraged all health professionals in Henan to concentrate on providing services at a profit, an approach that was in tune with the early days of the reform programme. As many as 300 blood collection stations were set up in the south and east of Henan, which are the poorest regions of the province. Poor peasants were encouraged to sell their blood and many did so.

Liu is alleged to have argued that there would be an international market for Chinese blood since there was no HIV/AIDS in China, but whether this was from ignorance or simply a ruse to make money is not clear. Conditions at the blood banks were insanitary, needles were reused and there were no facilities for screening donors for diseases. Much of the blood that was collected became contaminated with the HIV virus and also with hepatitis B. This contamination was then compounded by poor practices in processing the blood and by donors who presented themselves at multiple collecting points to maximise the amount of money they were paid, often using false names to conceal the number of times they had given blood. In addition to the authorised blood banks, there were illegal collection points, some of which were eventually closed down by the local Bureaux of Health.

To add insult to injury, many peasants were persuaded that it would be beneficial for their health if they had their own blood reinjected after the plasma had been removed. By the time this was done the blood had already been mixed in centrifuges with other blood. They were charged RMB 5 for this procedure.

Not surpisingly there was a major epidemic of HIV/AIDS and hepatitis B in Henan: this outbreak was on a much greater scale than the spread of these diseases in the rest of China, which was already at such a level that it was a serious cause for concern. The numbers involved cannot be determined with any certainty because of the culture of secrecy in China and attempts by the local authorities to cover up the disaster: some government officials have conceded that as many as 30,000–50,000 people were infected when they paid for contaminated blood but academic researchers have argued that the total number of people who contracted HIV/AIDS or other diseases as a result of the contamination could be of the order of 300,000.

When the magnitude of the problem became apparent in 1995, the local government moved rapidly to close down the operation but it also attempted to cover up the whole scandal, harrassing and arresting journalists who had tried to investigate the outbreak of unexplained sickness and deaths among rural families.[18] Although the sale of blood was not an entirely new phenomenon in China and there is evidence of poor people having previously sold blood and possibly even organs, it had never before been organised on such an industrial scale.

Although the most severe problems were in Henan province there is concern that the blood supply in the rest of China was still not being monitored adequately over ten years after the Henan scandal. There is a shortage of blood for transfusions and this increases the risk of illegal and unchecked blood being used in hospitals. In November 2007, reports began to emerge of demonstrations by victims of the Henan blood scandal demanding compensation from the hospital that had been responsible for infecting them. Campaigners for compensation and doctors who have attempted to publicise the problem and the cover-up have been harassed and threatened with prosecution, including the retired gynaecologist Dr Gao Yaojie, now in her eighties, who has become a national and international heroine for her activism. Dr Gao has been nominated for international awards for her work but has been put under increased surveillance and has been unable to obtain permission to travel abroad.[19]

One-child families: population policy and family planning

Outside China, by far the best known, but not the best understood, policy of the PRC is the planned birth (*jihua shengyu*) policy which was introduced in 1979 and is universally known in the West as the 'one-child' policy. Mao Zedong had believed, at least in the early years of the PRC, that the more Chinese there were, the better: he refused to consider any artificial limitation on China's already spiralling population growth. The economic planners who came back into power in the Deng Xiaoping era saw population control as a vital part of their development strategy. The one-child family was promoted nationally as the ideal or 'model' family and in the urban areas the idea of planning to have only one child was enforced strictly, often with relatively little resistance as new urban professionals looked to career and wealth enhancement as an alternative to traditional large families.

In the rural areas, the situation was very different and there was considerable resistance to the control of family size. What had started as an advisory policy was deemed mandatory in some areas and families with more than one child faced punitive sanctions including fines and were made to pay for education and healthcare for second and subsequent children. The overenthusiastic enforcement of the policy by local officials led to serious abuses including forced abortion and sterilisation. Families that wished to have more than one child devised a variety of subterfuges including travelling to remote villages to stay with relatives when a child was due to be born in order to avoid the family planning inspectors.

The impact of the one-child policy varied from region to region but it is generally accepted that it has exacerbated distortions in the sex ratio of the population. Boys greatly outnumber girls in a ratio of 117:100. A traditional preference for male children has meant that if families were obliged to have only one child, they would try to ensure that it was a boy, either by gender-selective abortion or by female infanticide, although it is extremely difficult to establish how widespread this latter practice was. The policy also led to public alarm at the creation of a generation of 'little emperors', one spoiled child in a family.

Following demographic changes in China that are associated with the economic reforms and increasing longevity that is leading to a greater proportion of older people, there has been a considerable relaxation of the policy. The revised policy was consolidated in legislation, the *Law on Population and Family Planning*, which was approved by the Standing Committee of the NPC on 29 December 2001 and came into force in September 2002. This legislation continued the existing policy of encouraging families to have only one child but conceded that they were permitted to have a second child if their economic circumstances were suitable.[20]

However, the State Family Planning Commission cautioned against the overhasty relaxation of the one-child policy, emphasising the need for China to keep its population below 1.4 billion.[21]

Given what appeared to be a more relaxed attitude to the one-child policy following the abolition of many targets and quotas since 1998, news of demonstrations and riots related to the policy that erupted in May 2007 in the Guangxi Zhuang Autonomous Region in southern China came as something of a surprise. The disturbances took place in Bobai county in the southeast of the region. For many years the family planning regulations had not been enforced in the county with any great enthusiasm but in spring 2007 the authorities organised family planning work teams to crack down on families that had ignored the regulations: fines were increased and families that could not or would not pay faced the confiscation or destruction of their property. In one case it was alleged that a farmer had his house bulldozed. To make matters worse, the work teams were intent on collecting fines retrospectively, in some cases relating to births that had taken place in the 1980s. The new level of enforcement was carried out with a considerable degree of force and the villagers responded by attacking staff in the family planning office, overturning cars and setting local government offices on fire.[22] In a further attempt to reinforce its commitment to the policy, the provincial government of Hubei has expelled many people from the CCP for disobeying the one-child rule.[23]

It is not clear whether these were intended to be local responses to a re-intensification of government policy at a national level or local initiatives to enhance the status and the finances of the family planning officials, whose regular income of fines had been drastically reduced by a more liberal interpretation of the policy. The overall finances of local governments had in any case suffered as a result of the policy of fiscal decentralisation.

The one-child policy was never intended to be permanent and some of its supporters predicted that it would only last for one generation. The government's aim, to control China's population, remains unchanged and the policy appears to have delivered the goods. Nevertheless there is a growing consensus that it is now time for draconian penalties to be replaced by the pressure of social and economic realities.

10　Law and human rights

Absence of the rule of law; lack of respect for human rights; restrictions on the freedom to dissent and the absence of any tradition of independent print or broadcast journalism – these have been among the main criticisms of Chinese society, not only by Western commentators but by Chinese thinkers, many of whom do not feel able to express their views publicly. These issues are closely connected. Without the creation of a legal system that is both formally, and in practice, separate from the Communist Party and the state – a system with an independent judiciary – it is difficult to see how even the most basic human rights can be guaranteed in China.

Law

Traditional legal system

China has had a sophisticated legal system and a comprehensive written legal code for centuries: some of the earliest extant legal documents date from the Qin (221 BC–207 BC) and Han (206 BC–AD 220) dynasties. The monumental legal code of the Manchu Qing dynasty (1644–1911) was the culmination of this long tradition. In addition to the *Da Qing huidian* (Administrative Statues) which set out the functions and authority of all the institutions of Qing government, the *Da Qing lüli* (Penal Code) was a comprehensive treatise on prohibitions, restrictions, crimes and the appropriate punishments for these crimes. It also covered matters that in other societies would be treated as part of the civil law.[1]

Punishments were, by and large, administered by the local magistrate, whose functions, in spite of the usual English translation of the Chinese term, were primarily administrative: his role was essentially to be the Emperor's representative in local government. Punishments that could be imposed by the magistrate included imprisonment, flogging, the wearing of the cangue (a wooden halter) around the neck, and the death penalty. Trials were often perfunctory and the results arbitrary: pressure during interrogation, sometimes amounting to torture, could be used to extract a confession. There was no right to legal representation in the court, although licensed notaries could submit a written defence to the magistrate.

When Westerners, particularly missionaries, came into contact with China in the nineteenth century they stimulated a drive to reform the legal system and some reforms were enacted in the early years of the twentieth century. After the Revolution of 1911, the new Republican government continued to introduce reforms and began a system of registering lawyers, a system that was consolidated in the *Lawyers Act* brought in by the Guomindang (GMD) administration in 1941. The years of war and civil war from the 1920s to the 1940s impeded the establishment of an effective legal system, in the same way that they held back many other social reforms.

PRC legal system 1949–78

On coming to power in 1949, the Chinese Communist Party (CCP), under the terms of its proto-constitution, the *Common Programme*, abrogated all laws that had been enacted by the defeated GMD and effectively dismantled what remained of the existing legal system. Lawyers as a category were viewed with deep suspicion because it was assumed that they were, or might have been, supporters of the old regime and many were dismissed or not reappointed when the new system was created.

In 1950 the Central Ministry of Justice was established and there was an attempt to create a 'socialist legal profession' following the model already in existence in the Soviet Union. The *Organic Law of People's Courts* was enacted in 1954 at the same time as the first Constitution of the People's Republic of China (PRC), but the judicial system that it legitimised was not entirely new. It was based partly on courts, known as People's Tribunals, that had been in existence for many years in the revolutionary base areas that were controlled by the CCP and its armies during the Civil War. The lawyers who staffed the courts were appointed as public servants and there was no attempt to separate government and judicial functions. In addition to the courts, a system of extra-judicial instruments evolved: these included provisions for administrative detention that did not require a decision by a court. The new legal profession that was beginning to find its feet was criticised during the Anti-Rightist Campaign of 1957 and after the onset of the Cultural Revolution, when all professions were regarded as suspect, there was effectively a legal vacuum which was not filled until the 1980s.[2]

Part of the 'reform and opening' programme, the policy shift that is always associated with Deng Xiaoping, was the restoration of a legal system and the development of a modern legal profession, although initially all lawyers continued to be state-appointed officials rather than independent practitioners. During the 1980s and 1990s the number of qualified lawyers increased significantly and the quality of legal practice and the level of professionalism also improved. China's rapid economic development created a new market for legal services, including a demand for practitioners in areas of the law that related to the operation and investments of foreign businesses in China. Private legal practice became possible, Chinese law firms were created and major international legal practices began to establish branches in China. However, the operation of the legal system remains dependent on the state and ultimately on the consent of the CCP.

PRC legal system since 1978

China's modern system of law is still immature and underdeveloped. The construction of a legal system and of a cadre of legal professionals began in the 'reform and opening' period of the 1980s. This followed the chaos of the Cultural Revolution (1966–76) during which the previous legal system, based on the Soviet model that had operated since 1949, collapsed. Neither the courts nor the Supreme People's Procuracy, which had overall responsibility for criminal prosecutions, were able to function during this period.

Since 1978 a new legal system has been established and the National People's Congress (NPC) and its Standing Committee have enacted a substantial body of legislation. The courts and the procuracy (the prosecuting authority) now operate across the whole of the country: both were originally staffed by former army and police officers with relatively little legal training but they have subsequently recruited large numbers of graduates from law schools.[3]

Although significant progress has been made, the system is still evolving and the operation of the rule of law as it would be understood in the West is still patchy. It is more highly developed in urban than in rural areas with the most advanced developments having taken place in the major cities of Beijing, Shanghai and Guangzhou (Canton). In the rural areas, particularly in the economically backward interior, there has been little progress. The lack of separation between the legal, government and Party structures remains a serious concern to both independent lawyers in China and the international legal community. The operation of the legal system is subordinate to, and to a significant extent controlled by, central and local government, both of which are themselves dominated by members of the CCP.

According to Jerome Cohen, one of the most respected Western specialists in Chinese law:

> Legislation is frequently inadequate, and many conflicts between national and local norms, and the proliferation of regulations, interpretations and other edicts often produce incoherence and inconsistency. There are too few able lawyers and those who are not afraid to undertake sensitive cases sometimes lose their licence to practice law or are detained and punished for 'damaging public order' and similar offences. Judges are often vulnerable to corruption, political control and the pressures of *guanxi* (social connections based on family, friendship, school or local ties). Since their appointment, promotion, assignment, compensation and removal are all at the pleasure of government and Party leaders rather than the Supreme People's Court or provincial High Court, they and the litigants who appear before them are subject to the abuses of 'local protectionism'.[4]

Chinese criminal law

> The weakest link in the PRC legal system is criminal justice. The codes of criminal procedure and criminal law...lend themselves to abuse by law enforcement authorities.[5]

Chinese citizens who are suspected, or accused, of criminal activities have none of the protection afforded to citizens in the developed West in relation to detention, bail, searches or the right to silence. They do not have the right of access to lawyers that would be the case in the West. In some cases neither the accused nor his or her family can afford to engage a lawyer. Even when a lawyer is appointed, access to the client and to information about the case being brought is frequently obstructed. Witnesses are rarely summoned to court for cross-examination. Although China claims that torture is not used in the interrogation of criminal suspects, there is a substantial body of evidence that this stricture is far from being universally observed.

On Wednesday 31 August 2005, the Chinese government signed an agreement with the United Nations High Commissioner for Human Rights, Louise Arbour, under which the UN agreed to assist China in improving the implementation of human rights policies that had already been agreed and facilitating China's 'ratification of the International Covenant on Civil and Political Rights'. The Special Rapporteur of the United Nations Commission on Human Rights with responsibility for investigating torture and other cruel, inhuman or degrading treatment, Manfred Nowak, visited China for two weeks in November 2005 to meet officials of the Chinese government and representatives of non-governmental organisations (NGOs) and to inspect detention facilities. This visit had been requested by one of his predecessors in 1995 but it was not until 2005 that the terms of reference were finally approved by the two sides. He found that torture was 'on the decline – particularly in urban areas – [but] remains widespread in China' and complained of attempts by Chinese officials to obstruct his investigation. He concluded that it would be impossible to outlaw torture completely without reforming the legal system and creating an independent judiciary but put forward a series of recommendations which included the abolition of programmes of forced re-education.[6]

Such reform as there is within the system is slow and cautious. Revisions made to legislation on the status and practice of lawyers that was approved at the end of October 2007 by the Standing Committee of the NPC stopped short of allowing legal organisations to operate independently and had the effect of keeping them under the political control of the court bureaucracy. However, the new legislation did formally concede the right of defence lawyers to have access to their clients without having to seek formal approval from a judicial department, a major concession. It was also made clear that:

> conversations between a lawyer and his client will not be monitored and neither will whatever a lawyer says in defence of his or her client in court be

used as evidence leading to his or her prosecution. The amendment specifically stipulates that a lawyer has the right to consult all files and materials related to the case he or she is dealing with and also has the right to collect evidence himself or herself.[7]

These amendments reflect a significant shift in attitudes towards a more independent legal system but there is no robust procedure to ensure that any of these rights will be enforced.[8]

People's Courts

The court system in China has four levels. The Supreme People's Court which sits in Beijing is the highest judicial organ in China and is formally responsible to the NPC and its Standing Committee. It tries the most significant cases, hears appeals against the decisions of lower-level courts and supervises the operation of local courts and special courts. The second tier consists of approximately thirty Higher People's Courts which sit in the capital cities of provinces and autonomous regions and in the major cities which have been accorded independent municipal status.

The third tier courts are the 400 or so Intermediate People's Courts which are based in the administrative centres of prefectures, certain other towns and the districts of larger cities. Intermediate People's Courts try criminal cases and have jurisdiction in cases carrying the death sentence, subject to any appeals to the Higher Court. Basic, or primary-level, People's Courts, of which there are over 3,000, are the lowest level courts and sit in all counties and in many cities. In addition they have the authority to establish People's Tribunals to handle local cases and it is estimated that there are as many as 20,000 such tribunals.[9]

Lawyers from China participate in a number of cooperative training programmes with their counterparts from the United Kingdom, United States and Canada – programmes designed to examine ways of implementing a fairer and more transparent judicial system in China. The fact that such programmes exist and are considered necessary by both international and Chinese lawyers is an indication of the problems faced by China in creating a system that is considered fair and open by international standards. Until the recommendations that have emerged from these programmes have been fully implemented there is no guarantee that any criminal trials in China will be fair and there is substantial evidence that many are not carried out fairly.

Prison and pre-trial detention

Prison conditions in China are generally acknowledged to be extremely grim. The few modern prisons in the more advanced cities may approach Western standards of hygiene and security, but this is far from the norm. Amnesty International and other organisations have consistently expressed concern about conditions in prisons and in the *laogai* (reform through labour) and *laojiao* (education through labour) camps and the harsh regimes in these camps has also been revealed in research by academics and human rights campaigners.[10] Information on conditions in prisons and labour camps is deemed to fall into the category of state secrets and it is therefore a treasonable offence to publish such information. As a result of this state of affairs, judgments about conditions have to be made on the basis of far less documentation than is desirable. Information collected from former inmates supports the view that conditions are harsh and there is no public scrutiny of the behaviour of prison staff towards inmates. There are regular reports of detention regimes that amount to inhuman or degrading conditions, but without access to prisons and other detention facilities by independent inspectors it is extremely difficult to verify this. There are also frequent reports of unexplained deaths in custody but this information is not published officially.

Political control and the reporting of court cases

Although there have been many changes in the Chinese media since the 1980s, the state still exercises firm control in many areas, particularly over matters which are judged to have an impact on national security. This is not restricted to the reporting of controversial political issues or questions related to defence: social disorder and organised crime and its consequences may also fall into this category. This does not mean that there is no reporting, as was the case in the past, but it does mean that whether a matter is reported and how it is reported may have to be approved by a senior political body.

Court cases are not routinely reported in the press in the way that they are in the West. They are only reported in the national and provincial daily press when they are of political significance and if the government intends that a lesson should be drawn from them. There are often more detailed reports in the local daily and evening newspapers and on local television stations, so that local residents will have access to this information about their own locality but not about the neighbouring province. Many trials, if not most, are effectively held *in camera*.

Local newspapers, particularly those published in the more remote regions, have always been classified as *neibu* (internal) rather than *gongkai* (open or public). *Neibu* approximates to 'classified' or 'restricted' in Western government concepts of document availability and, although these restrictions are frequently ignored in practice and local newspapers have regularly made their way abroad, high-profile cases have demonstrated that the government continues to regard the information published in them as 'state secrets'. The transmission of 'state secrets' to foreigners is considered to be a serious crime punishable by long terms of imprisonment.[11] Newspapers from Xinjiang and Tibet are subject to more stringent controls than, for example, those from Shanghai. However, other areas are also problematic, such as the southeastern coastal province of Fujian, from which many emigrants to the West originate. It is an especially sensitive area in military and political terms, not only because of the recent history of illegal emigration but also because it faces the island of Taiwan, which has been in political (and occasionally military) conflict with China since 1949.

There is considerable local variation in the application of legislation, up to and including the death penalty, and the fact that there are agreements on good practice at national government level does not guarantee that the provisions of such agreements will be carried out at the local level.[12]

Petitioning the government

China may be working its way slowly towards the creation of a modern legal system that is influenced by the most advanced international practices, but an older and more traditional approach to redressing grievances, the petition to the government, is still in existence: it is often the preferred, and sometimes the only available, route for desperate individuals and communities from the most remote corners of the country. It is a system with a long historical pedigree and it can also be found in societies in the Middle East and Africa which retain traditional systems of social control: however, it sits oddly with the formal structures of a society like that of China under the control of a Communist Party. The Chinese term for petition is usually *shangfang*, which implies a visit to one's superiors, but there is also the *xinfang*, a letter of complaint to superiors. Party and government institutions usually have a petition department (*xinfang bumen*) which deals with both letters and visits.

Petitioners are typically peasant farmers from the more remote regions who make the long and uncomfortable journey to Beijing after having failed in attempts at persuading local officials that their grievances should be redressed. These grievances are often connected with the ownership and sale of land. Many petitioners have gravitated to the Fengtai district, which is situated in the southwest of Beijing. Until the 1980s Fengtai was mostly rural, with many small farms, and urbanisation is a recent phenomenon. A petitioners' settlement has grown up in Fengtai and houses perhaps as many as 4,000 individuals, a small proportion of the thousands who attempt to petition the government each year. Many petitioners find that they have to remain in the capital for extended periods to have their grievances heard. Conditions are poor and parts of the area resemble a shanty town. In September 2007, notices appeared requiring all petitioners to vacate their rundown accommodation by 19 September and demolition began shortly after that date. This was presumed to be part of an operation to make the area look immaculate in advance of the beautification of Beijing for the Olympic Games of 2008, because attempts to clear out the transitory population in other parts of the capital had already been made. Petitioners are routinely harassed by police and detained, but desperation and possibly a naive belief that the central authorities would be willing and able to deal with local maladministration continue to attract them to the capital.

Human rights

The question of human rights, or more precisely the lack of human rights, in China did not become an issue of serious international concern until the 1980s when China became more open and accessible to foreign visitors including academics, journalists, and the employees of international NGOs. The military suppression of the Democracy Movement in and around Tian'anmen Square on 4 June 1989 concentrated Western attention on the more brutal aspects of the government of the PRC. In the aftermath of the occupation of Tian'anmen Square by the army, who had been told that they were protecting the Party Centre, the precise number of civilian deaths and injuries was never clearly established but it certainly ran into the hundreds.

Subsequently, concern has been raised about the suppression of political dissent; the repression of ethnic and religious minorities; the widespread use of capital punishment; the physical abuse of inmates in prisons and labour camps; and the treatment of orphans in nurseries. Attention has also focused on shortcomings in the legal system more generally and the impossibility of fair trials, as has been outlined above, particularly for impoverished litigants.

This does not mean that the problem of human rights abuses only began in the 1980s. From the inception of the PRC in 1949, reports of mass trials during political campaigns and the incarceration and execution of people for what were essentially political offences had seeped through to the West, usually as a result of information gleaned from a steady flow of refugees from the mainland who escaped to Hong Kong and other places. Although there was some scepticism and a suspicion that problems on the mainland were being exaggerated by Taiwanese propaganda organs for their own political ends, in time, the publication of PRC documents and the testimony of many eyewitnesses confirmed beyond any reasonable doubt the broad outlines of the repression.

There were also reports of the existence of a large-scale prison and labour camp system in China during the 1950s and 1960s and of the brutal regime that operated in China's *gulag*, but solid and reliable information did not begin to appear until after the end of the Cultural Revolution when there was a significant change in the attitude towards the publication of official data. It should be remembered that widespread knowledge about the network of Soviet prison camps only dates back to the 1970s following the publication of Alexander Solzhenitsyn's *The Gulag Archipelago*.

Confucian tradition

The problem of human rights abuse in China did not begin with the victory of the CCP in 1949. There had been no tradition of respecting individual rights in the imperial political and legal system. In the Confucian world-view the emphasis, for the *laobaixing* (the mass of the population), was almost entirely on collective responsibility rather than individual rights and indeed on collective culpability in the case of instances of individual wrongdoing.

The 'Confucian world-view' is a rough and ready shorthand way of referring to the complex traditional culture that developed over 2,000 years and that informed the policy decisions of the imperial court, its ministers and its provincial governors and local magistrates. This culture was based on detailed knowledge of immense collections of documents which contain deliberations on political and social issues by scholars and the ruling elite and which were consulted selectively, when decisions were needed.

The modern Chinese word for 'human rights', *renquan*, did not appear until the end of the nineteenth century. Like so much of the modern vocabulary of science and social science, it migrated to China from Japan, where the concept of the Japanese equivalent, *jinken*, was being developed in debates about Japan's modernisation during the Meiji period. The meaning of *renquan* in the late nineteenth and early twentieth centuries is somewhat ambiguous. At times it was used to signify individual rights, but on other occasions it meant something like 'popular power'. The republican revolutionary, Sun Yat-sen, did not employ the term in his writings on democracy, preferring the term *minquan,* 'people's power'.

Chinese values, Asian values and world opinion

China's response to the criticisms of its human rights record has been vigorous. Beijing has argued that its successive constitutions have made adequate provision for the freedom of speech, assembly and publication: technically this is correct, although in practice these rights have always been honoured more in the breach than in the observance. The government of the PRC also argued that, as a revolutionary regime replacing the Guomindang, it was championing the rights of the peasants and other groups that had been disadvantaged under the former regime.

These arguments were deployed at a time when there was a backlash in Asia more generally against international demands for the universal application of Western-style human rights legislation. Many Japanese commentators contended that Japan was a unique form of society and that it did not fit into the normal Western social categories and could not be judged according to a Western value system. In Singapore, the ruling elite vigorously defended its paternalist and authoritarian attitudes, pointing to the economic success and social stability of the island city-state and arguing that the suppression of dissent was a small price to pay for this. Malaysia, under its abrasive Prime Minister Mahathir Mohammed, and supported by many members of the political elite of Southeast Asia, professed a belief in the existence of a separate category of 'Asian values'. Supporters of the idea of 'Asian values' maintained that these were values that were specific to Asia, although to what extent they were representative of the whole of Asia was left rather vague in the debate. The implication, however, was that they were of more lasting significance in East and Southeast Asia than were Western concepts of human rights or individual rights.

China's position was essentially a special case of this 'Asian values' argument and official publications contended that 'socialism with Chinese characteristics' (*juyou Zhongguo tese de shehuizhuyi*) was an alternative framework which would provide appropriate local solutions for China's social problems. The Asian values argument, which is probably best understood as part of a movement of cultural nationalism in response to the post-war economic and cultural dominance of the West, died down and international standards of human rights are now more generally accepted in the region. In China, they are accepted privately by many individuals and they are also increasingly recognised in some government and academic circles. There is an awareness within the political elite that many institutions in China do not live up to these international standards and there have been effective measures to block the access of international observers to prisons and labour camps to inquire into allegations of torture or other physical mistreatment. The obstruction has been greater in the most politically sensitive regions of China, notably Tibet and Xinjiang, where visits by foreign politicians, academics and journalists and the operation of NGOs are more restricted than in other areas.

China has issued a series of White Papers on human rights since 1991. These have been unfailingly positive and have emphasised China's economic development under the PRC and the benefits that this has given to the poorest sections of the population. The rights of ethnic and religious minorities are presented almost entirely in terms of their economic progress; progress in the development of other social and political rights is presented solely in terms of legislation, with little evidence of how this has effected social development in practice. These White Papers have been dismissed by most international human rights organisations, although the very existence of documents of this nature, which are reported in the Chinese domestic press, means that there is at least a rudimentary debate on human rights within China.

In November 2006, the government of the PRC unveiled an exhibition in Beijing to demonstrate its commitment to the protection of human rights. The exhibition – which consisted of hundreds of photographs, legal documents and published books – was organised jointly by the Information Office of the State Council, the Chinese Society for Human Rights and the Chinese Foundation for the Development of Human Rights.[13]

Political prisoners

There is no internationally agreed figure for the number of individuals imprisoned in China for political offences. This is partly because detailed information of this nature is regarded as an official secret in China and the penalties for communicating it to foreigners are draconian. It is also partly because there is no agreement on the concept of political offences in China and because many prisoners whose offences are political in nature may have been convicted on other, criminal, charges. It has been estimated that the number of individuals detained or imprisoned for political or other reasons that are contrary to the international understanding of fundamental human rights runs into the tens of thousands. Even people who have been tried under the evolving Chinese legal system may not have received a trial that would be accepted as fair under international norms. There is also considerable evidence of the existence of torture and ill-treatment of prisoners in the network of labour camps which often appear to be run under brutal regimes.[14]

Death penalty

The death penalty is applied very widely in China and in some cases the decision on whether a death sentence should be called for appears to be completely arbitrary. China executes offenders who are convicted of murder and other violent crimes, as do Japan (where at least ten convicted murders have been hanged with very little publicity since December 2006) and the United States among other countries, but there are also death sentences for offences that involve no violence at all, including embezzlement, tax evasion and drug trafficking. Political offences, including those associated with separatist movements in Tibet and Xinjiang, attract the death penalty as well. Death sentences can be commuted by suspension for two years and in effect this is equivalent to the sentence of life imprisonment in many Western legal systems.

The number of death sentences in the PRC, often for those crimes – including financial crimes – that have never carried the death penalty in most Western societies, has been a matter of concern to Western lawyers and human rights activists for decades. The total number of executions carried out in China is a closely guarded secret although individual death sentences and the trials that precede them are regularly reported by the local press, radio and television. The best informed estimate for 2004 suggests that 6,000 people were sentenced to death and that 3,400 were executed in that year. However, it is widely assumed that this is an underestimate and in 2005 a senior member of the NPC, China's legislative body, claimed in public that there were normally over 10,000 executions a year. There is a long-standing tradition in China of using seemingly precise numbers, especially large numbers, to indicate a vague figure so it cannot be assumed that this was based on precise statistics, but it was an unusual official acknowledgment of the scale of executions.[15] The state is able to use the broad and vague provisions of the criminal code to impose the severest sentences on anyone accused of 'endangering state security', a catch-all phrase which can be applied to any political and religious activities of which the government or the CCP does not approve, in addition to criminal activities.

During an official visit in August and September 2005, the United Nations High Commissioner for Human Rights, Louise Arbour, met the president of China's Supreme Court and government ministers and called on China to release data on the extent of the use of capital punishment. She also expressed concern about China's use of the death penalty for offences 'that do not meet the international standard of "most serious crimes"'.[16] Constant international pressure of this nature was one of the reasons for China's decision in 2006 that all death sentences would in future be reviewed by the Supreme People's Court and would not be left solely to the discretion of the lower courts, which had been able to pass death sentences for decades. The ruling was a breakthrough: since that decision was taken, there has been compelling evidence of a significant reduction in the number of sentences of death. In September 2007, according to the English language newspaper *China Daily*, which is aimed at expatriate foreigners living in China and overseas readers, officials of the Supreme People's Court declared that the number of executions was at a level lower than at any time in the previous decade. The Vice-President of the Supreme People's Court, Jiang Xingchang, explained that this was because the criteria for applications by lower courts for capital punishment had been made stricter and court proceedings had become fairer and more efficient. The Supreme Court made it clear to judges in lower courts that the death penalty should be restricted to 'an extremely small number of serious offenders': instructions were issued to judges that they should avoid the death penalty in the case of economic crimes and some difficult personal and family cases.[17] There is no suggestion that China intends to abandon the death penalty in the foreseeable future: Jiang Xingchang, indicated in January 2008 that China was intending to move to a system of execution by lethal injection rather than shooting convicted criminals in the back of the head, which has been the normal procedure for decades.[18]

Contrary to popular myth, there are no public executions in China. Sentences may be announced at public rallies, particularly during political campaigns, such as recent drives against corruption, when the authorities feel the need to use the execution and the threat of further executions to warn the populace against specific crimes such as embezzlement or separatism. There have also been persistent reports that members of the family of an executed criminal are obliged to pay for the bullet that ended their relative's life. Although this story is so prevalent that it may well have happened, there is no real evidence that it is routine or that it is authorised.

Torture and other ill-treatment in custody

The anecdotal evidence of brutality and ill-treatment throughout China's police and prison system is far too widespread to be dismissed or ignored, as the Chinese authorities often appear to wish. China formally proscribed torture in 1996 but evidence suggests that this has had little effect on practices at the township and village level. Even if senior Party and government officials in Beijing wish to eliminate torture, the centre does not necessarily have the authority to compel the local organs of state to do so. The evidence for this could only be verified or countered by giving international organisations open access to police cells and prisons and the Chinese authorities are unwilling to grant this type of access. In November 2006, in what was a most unusual admission by a senior legal official, Wang Zhenchuan, the Deputy Procurator General, agreed that at least thirty verdicts in the Chinese legal system that year might have led to wrongful convictions following illegal interrogation techniques, sometimes amounting to torture, because of local police and court procedures. Interrogations by police are already recorded in some instances although the practice is not yet widespread.[19]

China's prisons

China has a prison system which is based both on the system that it inherited from the Nationalist Guomindang government and on its own prisons that were run in the Jiangxi Soviet in the 1930s and the border base areas that were under the control of the CCP in the 1940s. In addition to this largely urban prison system, it has a network of prison camps which are either 'education through labour' (*laojiao*) camps or 'reform through labour' (*laogai*) camps.

The *laojiao* camps were a Chinese innovation and were developed to deal with the tens of thousands of citizens who were designated as 'rightists' during the Anti-Rightist campaign of 1957. Rather than handle their cases through the extremely rudimentary court and prison system that existed at the time, this new form of administrative detention enabled the police to send people who were accused of social or political offences directly to labour camps. The continued existence of the "education through labour" camps is criticised by international legal bodies and many Chinese lawyers and legislators are aware of the international opprobrium that it attracts and are pressing for the abolition of this system, which is one of the main stumbling blocks to the establishment of the rule of law in China. Legislation to make this possible has been discussed by committees of the NPC for several years but has never been enacted. It is widely believed that this is simply because of the opposition of the powerful Ministry of Public Security, which is reluctant to relinquish such a powerful instrument of control.

"Education through labour" institutions take prisoners mainly for short-term sentences, up to four years, and these are individuals who have been sentenced to undergo a period of administrative detention which has not normally been ordered by a court. The offences are usually minor and include prostitution, drug use and small-scale theft, but detention in the *laojiao* camps has also been used for dissidents and the victims of political campaigns, although some of these have also been sent to the *laogai* camps. The regime in the *laojiao* camps is tough but not as tough as in the *laogai* system and time served in *laojiao* does not have the same stigma that is attached to a prison or a *laogai* sentence. International concern has led to pressure on the Chinese authorities and in March 2007 it was announced that the future of this system was being reconsidered.

The *laogai*, also known as China's *gulag* (GULAG was the Russian acronym for the Main Administration for Collective Labour camps, the Soviet system of forced labour camps), were modelled on the prison system of the former Soviet Union. Just as the Soviet camps were typically located in Siberia and other regions far from metropolitan Russia, China's forced labour camps are mainly in the farthest flung regions with a significant concentration in the western part of China, especially in Xinjiang and Qinghai. The operation of these camps is a state secret and the extent of the system was hardly known in the West until the 1990s, partly because the names of labour camps are very similar to those of state farms or other non-penal institutions. There was much confusion, some of it deliberate: in many cases, labour camps operate under two names, one being the formal name within the penal system and the other the name used for commercial transactions. There is consistent evidence of brutal regimes and severe ill-treatment in these institutions but what is unusual about the Chinese labour camps, in comparison with other similar penal systems, is the way that they have been incorporated into the national economy. Labour camps produce a wide range of commodities, including tea, wine, coal and industrial equipment, and are required to run at a profit or at least to be self-financing. Until the 1990s there was very little awareness that these goods, many of which were exported to the West, were produced by forced labour.[20]

11 Mass media

Successive Constitutions of the People's Republic of China (PRC) have formally claimed that freedom of expression and the freedom of the press are guaranteed in China, but as with many other constitutional provisions, this has been honoured more in the breach than in the observance. It has been difficult for Chinese citizens to express independent or controversial views publicly during even the most tolerant of political climates and even more difficult, if not impossible, for them to reach a wide audience if their views are at all individual or eccentric.

The Chinese Communist Party (CCP) has endeavoured to maintain its control of the whole of the mass media (*chuanbo meijie*), from the press and domestic broadcasting to satellite television and the new media of the internet, fully recognising the force of the maxim that information is power. Since the onset of the reform era in the late 1970s, Communist Party control over certain aspects of the media has been relaxed appreciably and there is far more diversity and variety than there was during the Mao period. However, many topics, particularly domestic political issues, Tibet, Xinjiang, Falungong and the suppression of the June Fourth Democracy movement in 1989, are still completely off-limits: the mass media in contemporary China is far from being independent. Although the nature of the media has changed dramatically since the early years of the PRC when there were only two state-controlled national newspapers, a handful of state-controlled magazines and a state-controlled radio network, it still does not stand comparison with the best of the Western media in terms of breadth, independence and openness. It is far more diverse and livelier than it was in the pre-reform era but it is still dominated by organs of the state and, more importantly, the state retains the ultimate sanction of closing down publications or other outlets of which it does not approve.

China has not been able to throw off the legacy of central control, even in the age of the internet and other new media, and although there has been a proliferation of information sources in print and other formats, there is still great tension between the purveyors of information and the state. While some areas, particularly entertainment, advertising and fashion, are relatively free from political restrictions, other fields are still strictly controlled, notably the reporting, printing and broadcasting of news. The reporting of issues that are considered by the CCP to be sensitive is constantly monitored and can be rapidly and effectively suppressed in the interests of state security. As has been noted previously, this concept encompasses a much wider field than would be found in the West. It is not only issues such as defence, which would be deemed to be genuinely sensitive in most countries, that are outlawed. Additionally, it is not possible to report in any detail on the inner workings of the government or of the CCP, particularly in the case of internal conflicts or dissent, and it has been difficult to report openly on business relationships that involve any relatives of senior government figures, although information on these commercial involvements has surfaced from time to time as a result of corruption trials. Comment on developments in Taiwan, Tibet and Xinjiang is also subject to rigorous scrutiny and restrictions.

The greatest change in the media has been the removal of the substantial financial support that the state previously provided to many of the key outlets, with the result that they have been compelled to find funding elsewhere, mainly from advertising. Journalists have expressed concern that they were exchanging one patron for another and that news coverage has had to be tailored so that it did not upset the advertisers. This does not apply to the major publications sponsored by the state and the CCP, including *People's Daily*.

Xinhua

Government news management is achieved primarily through the New China News Agency, which is increasingly referred to abroad by its Chinese name of Xinhua. Xinhua is a colossal bureaucratic machine, said to have over 7,000 employees, and is directly under the control of the CCP's Propaganda Department: it has offices in every province of China as well as branches abroad. Its wide coverage and its status and authority within China has obliged all Chinese newspapers to rely on it for national and international stories. As an agency of the CCP Propaganda Department its international remit is to propagate news about China as well as to gather news and information about the countries in which it is based.

Xinhua's close connection with the political establishment is illustrated by the peculiar case of Hong Kong, where for decades the Xinhua office functioned as the *de facto* Chinese embassy because the PRC was unable to recognise formally the status of the colony. After 1997 the Xinhua office, which had played an invaluable role in negotiations with Beijing, was renamed the Liaison Office of the Central People's Government in Hong Kong and continues to function as a point of contact between a wide range of organisations and the government of the PRC.

Newspapers

The main sources of news in the early days of the PRC were *People's Daily* (*Renmin Ribao*), the official gazette of the Central Committee of the CCP, and *Guangming Daily*, which was the only other newspaper published. The relationship between them was modelled on the relationship between *Pravda* and *Izvestia* in the Soviet Union. One of the earliest signs that reform was taking hold in the late 1970s was the change that could be detected in the style and format of *People's Daily*.

This newspaper was revitalised in the late 1970s under its reforming managing editor, Hu Jiwei. These changes were possible because of the improvement in the political climate and the positive influence of the reform-minded CCP Secretary General, Hu Yaobang. However, according to Liu Binyan, one of China's best known journalists who worked as an investigative reporter on the paper, none of this would have been possible without 'the moral courage of editor-in-chief Hu Jiwei and his deputy, the philosopher Wang Ruoshui, and their loyal staff', who came under constant pressure from conservatives in the CCP hierarchy who were opposed to the reforms.[1] The outcome was that *People's Daily* became more readable (or at least less unreadable) and, although it continued to cover major political and economic developments from the point of view of the CCP, the coverage became broader. Hu Jiwei also introduced a letters page, which at the time was regarded as nothing short of revolutionary.

Guangming Daily (*Guangming* means 'light' or 'bright', as in 'bright future', but the paper is invariably referred to by its Chinese name, even by foreigners) was originally published by the China Democratic League, one of the token minority parties still permitted to exist in the PRC, but it was taken over by the CCP Central Committee's Propaganda and United Front Work Department in 1959 when the minority parties lost all influence, and is now run by the CCP. It retains a distinctive tone which marks it out from *People's Daily*: its more sophisticated and literate style, and the wider range of topics that it covers, make it more appealing to educated professionals.

China's provinces all have their own daily newspapers as do major towns and cities, and many also have evening newspapers with a small local circulation, such as the *Beijing Evening News* (*Beijing wanbao*), a chatty but readable small paper that circulates in the capital. In the past these newspapers formed part of a centralised and hierarchical news organisation controlled by the CCP from Beijing: the provincial dailies would typically publish the same key policy articles that appeared in *People's Daily* with the addition of local editorial and news material. This tradition has not entirely died out but there is less central control and a greater degree of independence in the local press: some regional newspapers have acquired a reputation for fearlessness in the exposure of malpractice and corruption. The *Southern Metropolitan Daily* (*Nanfang dushi ribao*) in Guangzhou is noted for its trenchant and critical approach, and its supplement *Southern Weekly* (*Nanfang zhoumo*) has a track record of investigative journalism. Newspapers and magazines frequently carry stories of successful police actions against criminals, separatists and organisations such as Falungong, and publications published by the police or legal bodies that specialise in this area are openly available. *Legal Daily* (*Fazhi ribao*) is the leading example of this type of publication. Criminal activity was rarely reported before the 1980s and certainly not in the detail with which it is now covered.

These state-controlled newspapers are still published although they do not have the monopoly that they used to enjoy and it has been estimated that over 2,000 titles are published in China today, many of them local, tabloid in style if not in format, and with a low cultural content. Some sensational and shoddy publications are even published under the auspices of government or Party newspapers and are used simply to generate revenue. The publication of magazines and books has increased exponentially, with the only control being the registration system under which all publications are required to register with the state, occasional campaigns against pornographic and other unacceptable material and a highly effective culture of self-censorship. Chinese citizens are eager consumers of the print media: newsstands are ubiquitous and carry a range of both serious and popular titles.

It is possible to read English language versions of the government's newspapers. *China Daily* has been published in English since 1983. It has no Chinese-language equivalent and is not the English version of *People's Daily*, although it does carry translations of articles from Xinhua news agency and from other Chinese newspapers. It has always had a relatively open and liberal approach and its somewhat idiosyncratic English style has over the years been polished by a succession of staff from all over the English-speaking world.

People's Daily itself is also available online in Chinese, both in the domestic edition which is circulated within China and the overseas edition which is significantly different. The online English-language edition contains a summary of the main news stories and editorials but it is not by any means a full translation of the paper that is still read by millions of members of the CCP and government officials every day. Both the content and flavour of the English version are very different from the main Chinese edition.

China Youth Daily (*Zhongguo qingnian bao*) is an interesting publication. Formally it is the official organ of the Chinese Communist Youth League (CYL), which created it in 1951, and it built up a huge readership among young Chinese because all colleges, universities and secondary schools were obliged to subscribe to it. In spite of its official connections, it has succeeded in establishing an important niche as a publication with an independent voice and has published many articles critical of corruption and maladministration. It came into direct conflict with the government early in 2006 when its weekly supplement *Freezing Point* (*Bingdian*) published an article by a historian from Zhongshan University in Guangzhou, Yuan Weishi, who criticised the content of history textbooks used in Chinese secondary schools. Specifically he complained about the treatment of the Boxer Rebellion of 1899–1901, which is always presented positively as a patriotic movement but which, he argued, should also be criticised for its violence and xenophobia. Publication of the supplement was suspended and the editor, Lu Yuegang, and the editor-in-chief, Li Datong, were transferred to other duties. When *Freezing Point* reappeared in March 2006 it appeared without Li and Lu in charge. The paper enjoys the patronage of the former head of the CYL, President Hu Jintao, but this did not prevent the suspension of the journalists and the episode is a clear indication that there are still strict limits as to what can be published.[2]

Internal newspapers

China has for decades operated a system of internal publications, that were originally intended solely for Party and government officials, and contain news, analysis and data considered unsuitable for wider publication. These internal newspapers were graduated in terms of security and access and the best known were *Reference News* (*Cankao xiaoxi*) and *Reference Material* (*Cankao ziliao*), both of which are published by Xinhua. They have evolved and are no longer all distributed as restricted internal documents available only to certain cadres: *Cankao xiaoxi* is on sale to the public on news stands. Other classified internal newsletters have included *Internal Reference* (*Neibu cankao*), which is only available to senior political leaders, and *Big Reference* (*Da Cankao*), which was circulated only to the very highest authorities.

Television and radio

Chinese Central Television (CCTV) is responsible for China's national television network of sixteen channels. It is managed jointly by a Party and a government organisation: the CCP Propaganda Department oversees programme style and content and the State Administration of Radio, Film and Television, an office of the State Council, has responsibility for day-to-day management. There are other broadcasters in China, mainly provincial stations which are extremely popular as they give considerable coverage to local events and personalities, but only CCTV is allowed to import programmes from abroad.

While it no longer has the absolute monopoly on news broadcasting that it did before the reform era, CCTV is able to dominate the news agenda. Channel 1, the main news channel, produces national news programmes three times daily and all regional networks are required to carry its main daily news broadcast which comes on air at 7.00 every evening. The other channels cover a wide range of topics including business, the arts, international affairs, sport, films, drama education, society, the law and Beijing opera. Channel 9 is an international channel broadcasting English-language programmes. Regional television stations also originate their own programmes, often in the local variants of Chinese such as, for example, Cantonese and the Wu language of Shanghai. There are also programmes in ethnic minority languages: for example, in Yining in the far northwest of Xinjiang it is possible to receive television broadcasts in Standard Chinese as well as the local Uyghur and Kazakh languages. Regional stations broadcast local news programmes in addition to the central news and also feature cultural and educational programmes and, increasingly, light entertainment. Long-running soap operas and series based on traditional and historical themes are particularly popular.

When the reform era began in the late 1970s there were probably fewer than ten million television sets in China and many of these were only viewed by groups of people in work units, clubs and other communal social facilities. Television is now almost universally accessible, even in the remotest rural areas and, as in the developed world, is mainly viewed by families and in individual households.

The reception of international cable and satellite TV varies greatly. There is easy access in the top-of-the-range hotels that are run mainly for the benefit of foreigners but otherwise coverage is very patchy. Attempts are still made to restrict the sale of satellite dishes that are capable of receiving broadcasts from Hong Kong and Taiwan, but these measures have been largely ineffective and many Chinese viewers have access to programmes in Chinese from broadcasters such as CNN and Star TV. Cantonese speakers in southern China were ahead of their northern compatriots and had regular access to Hong Kong television programmes long before the handover in 1997.

Radio was by far the most common broadcast medium in the early years of the PRC and, although television is now almost universal, radio has experienced a new lease of life. There is still heavy coverage of political news but it is now possible to listen to popular music for much of the day. Among the most popular programmes have been innovative phone-in shows which address personal and social matters that were almost completely neglected by the traditional media. Some of these programmes are hosted by agony aunts whose forthright style has turned them into national stars – because callers can be anonymous, there is free and frank discussion about many controversial issues.

New media

The internet is popular and some estimates suggest that access is now available to as many as 100 million people, although even this figure would mean that less than one-tenth of the total population of the country is able to access the web. Internet sites are monitored regularly by the authorities and many are blocked either permanently or temporarily if they are considered to be morally or politically suspect or otherwise unsuitable. There are also government restrictions on the growth of internet service providers. There are many websites in Chinese, both in simplified and traditional characters, which carry news and comment on the Chinese world, some of them extremely well informed; among the most popular search engines are Baidu, Sina and Sohu. There is also material for entertainment and much that is of a sensational or trivial nature. Access to the internet is possible through internet cafes, although these often seem to be monopolised by teenagers playing online video games. Internet cafes are also subject to periodical crackdowns by the authorities whenever there are government concerns about unsuitable material being placed online.

The government is not solely concerned with the possibility of Chinese citizens having access to Western ideas on the internet. There is also a worry, voiced by the Deputy Director of the Chinese National Administration for the Protection of State Secrets, Cong Bing, that the internet could be used to leak state secrets, which are, as has been argued, defined far more broadly in China than they are in the West. Cong Bing specifically referred to the use of bulletin boards, chat rooms and newsgroups on the internet as channels through which classified information could find a way out of China.[3]

Despite the continuing restrictions there has been a significant reduction in government control over the media during the reform period and, at the same time, an increase in cynicism about the official media. However, the products of the newly emerging media are often of low quality and offer content that is trivial and ephemeral.

Journalists

Chinese journalists in the past were state employees and, with a few honourable exceptions, did not enjoy a reputation for independence and fearless investigation. This is changing, partly because Chinese journalists have been exposed to Western media and in some cases have been trained in the West, but also because the expectations of their audience have altered with increased commercialisation and competition. It is increasingly common for journalists from China to take qualifications in media studies in Western universities at both undergraduate and postgraduate level.

The existence of an independent-minded tradition in the media was demonstrated in 1989 when groups of journalists were prominent among the demonstrators in Tian'anmen Square who were calling for greater democracy and openness. Inevitably they also suffered disproportionately in the political repression that followed the military suppression of the protests, but the tradition of independence persists in spite of the fact that journalists can be, and regularly are, fined or imprisoned for reports that criticise the government.

Globalisation and the Chinese media

Media academics in China are conscious of the tension between the CCP's attempts to control the mass media in the way that it has done for decades and the pressures of globalisation, which has exposed at least the educated portion of the Chinese population to foreign newspapers, magazines, radio and above all satellite television and the internet. In 2002 Tsinghua (Qinghua) University published a collection of articles in Chinese under the English subtitle *Globalisation and Mass Media: Clash, Convergence and Interaction*. Contributors included media researchers from Hong Kong and the West in addition to academics working within the PRC. The discussion covered the impact of the global media on China and the global market for television products; protection and openness in the Chinese media; nationalism and internationalism in the media; the diffusion of the internet in China and the reporting of China by foreign broadcasters. The breadth of issues discussed showed a keen understanding of the issues that face Chinese media professionals: the greatest challenge, however, may well be for media academics to communicate these concerns to their political masters.[4]

12 Religion and ethnic minorities

Religion, which many people believed had become irrelevant in a Communist society, has emerged as a significant social issue and a challenge for the Chinese Communist Party (CCP) and the government since the beginning of the reform period. China has been criticised regularly by international human rights activists for its attitude to religious freedom in theory and in practice. While some religions are practised irrespective of ethnic affiliations, others, notably Islam and Tibetan Buddhism, are closely tied to specific ethnic groups and are an integral part of their national and cultural identities.

Religious movements in China

Religious institutions and religious movements have become more influential in China as the ideological and moral authority of the CCP (although not its political power) has weakened. Religion survived decades of rule by an atheist government against the expectations of many observers and experienced a dramatic revival during the immediate post-Cultural Revolution period of 'reform and opening'. Religious leaders who were willing to work with the government and the CCP were appointed to advisory positions in local and central government, although their institutions were also subjected to a considerable degree of surveillance and state control. Underground religious groups attract wide support in spite of (or possibly because of) the fact that their activities are officially proscribed.

Religious freedom is formally guaranteed under the Constitution of the People's Republic of China but it is no secret that such freedom as is allowed applies only to bodies approved by, registered with and monitored by the state. Individuals and congregations that are not registered with the government's Religious Affairs Bureau (the central body controlling the local bureaux was renamed the State Administration for Religious Affairs in 1998) face significant restrictions. These can range from political pressure and obstruction to the compulsory closure of churches, temples, mosques and religious schools; the seizure of devotional literature (books, audiotapes and videotapes); and the imprisonment of priests, monks, nuns and imams.

Since the 1980s there has been a remarkable increase in overt religious activity. Religious buildings that had been closed down or commandeered for secular use during the Cultural Revolution were reopened and religious communities that had maintained their traditions and organisations informally and in secret have emerged from the shadows. While many of these groups would be recognised as authentic religious bodies anywhere in the world, there are others which have the characteristics of religious cults with questionable spiritual and ethical values, particularly some of those that have sprung up in the more remote rural areas. Between these two extremes are the 'new religions', which have emerged from a selective synthesis of Buddhism, Daoism (also spelt Taoism) and traditional folk religions: Falungong is the most prominent of these. Although some of these groups are considered to be legitimate by both Chinese and Western commentators, others are more questionable and it has been alleged that some sects practise psychological manipulation, the breaking-up of families and economic and sexual exploitation.[1]

Daoism and Buddhism

Attendance at traditional Daoist and Buddhist temples and the presentation of votive offerings have increased over the last twenty years. In some remote rural areas, secret societies which draw on the popular tradition of Daoism and Buddhism have also revived. In some cases, these are treated as criminal bodies by the police and local officials, but they persist and their thinking and organisation blend religious symbolism and rituals that are reminiscent of the secret societies of the nineteenth century. As the income and wealth gap between the cities and the villages widens, these societies have been shown to appeal to the poor and marginalised and there are suggestions that in some areas they may have become involved in protests by villagers against unpopular land deals and corrupt officials.

Daoism is (together with popular and folk religions, from which it is sometimes difficult to distinguish) the indigenous religion of China. Shinto occupies a similar position in Japan and there are parallels between the two religions, particularly in their sympathetic attitude towards the natural world. Daoism, especially in its popular form, overlaps at a popular level with Buddhism, a second-century import from India that, in spite of its foreign origins, is also regarded as a native Chinese religion.

Daoism has two aspects which often appear to sit uneasily together: on the one hand, there is the literary and philosophical tradition of the educated elite; on the other, there are the popular practices which are part of China's folk religion. Literary and philosophical Daoism, exemplified by the oblique and often mystifying classical texts, the *Zhuangzi* and *Daodejing* (*Tao-te Ching*), advocated the belief that human beings should accommodate themselves to the flow of the natural world, the *Dao* or the 'way'. Popular Daoism, on the other hand, was a religion with its own texts and rituals, focused on 'immortals' and the quest for everlasting life. It was fragmented and frequently at odds with authority and this popular tradition of Daoism persists today. It is quite open in Hong Kong and Taiwan, but on the mainland it remained underground until the 1980s and was frequently linked with new religious sects and clandestine organisation that were branded as criminal by the CCP.

Wing-tsit Chan, a distinguished expatriate Chinese scholar of philosophy who revisited China in 1948 and 1949 during the period when the Guomindang (GMD) regime was collapsing and making way for the CCP, concluded that Daoism, together with folk religion in general, was defunct: 'Since [D]aoism underlies the religion of the masses, its decline is tantamount to the collapse of the people's religion as a whole'. Temples, shrines, idols and priests were still in evidence, although their numbers were in decline and Chan felt that 'the real spirit of the religion [was] dead, and its vitality [was] fast disappearing.' When the CCP established the Chinese People's Political Consultative Conference in 1949 to provide a forum for – and simultaneously a means of controlling – political, ethnic and religious minorities, there were delegates representing Protestant Christianity, Buddhism and Islam but none from the world of Daoism. The Daoists had no effective leadership and no programme to address their needs in the mid-twentieth century: Daoist influence was limited largely to art, rituals and festivals.[2]

According to the sceptical Chan,

> The chief reason for the Daoist collapse is, of course, its total devotion to the search for earthly blessings – wealth, health, longevity, happiness, children. With the advancement of science and education in China, the Chinese masses learn that the fulfilment of human desires does not come from chasing away evil spirits and praying to benevolent deities. Modern medical science is fast replacing the God of Medicine, and rural schoolchildren go to the temple of the God of Literature, not to pray but to play.[3]

With hindsight it is clear that Chan overstated the decline of Daoism and his negative view of the religion and its extinction in the twentieth century, in line with modernising Chinese scholars of his day, is challenged by other scholars. It can be argued that the collapse he witnessed was superficial and that the importance of Daoism lies in the fact that it is inseparable from the rituals of daily life in China, rather than its usefulness as a shortcut to wealth and longevity.

Daoism survived by metamorphosing into a variety of religious bodies, usually secret societies which also drew on Buddhist tradition and had their own political agendas. These societies included the White Lotus and the Guiyidao (the Way of Returning to, or Following, the One). Many of these religio-political associations had been in decline since the 1930s, but one, the Yiguandao (Way of Pervading Unity), had, as Chan put it, 'gained strength and extended its activities during the Second World War'. It probably grew out of the Boxer Uprising (1899–1901) but developed rapidly under its teacher Zhang Tieran, who died in 1947. Many religious groups including the Yiguandao flourished during the Japanese Occupation of China and provided a degree of support and self-defence for the rural population.[4]

After the victory of the CCP in 1949, Daoism was forced to abandon its apolitical and detached position and was obliged to adapt to the new political conditions of the 1950s. Daoist temples lost much of their land during the land reform movement, as did other religious institutions, and this considerably weakened their economic position and their social authority. Monks had no option but to take manual jobs to support themselves: this was seen as a positive change by the CCP but it undermined the mystique and the prestige of the clergy among their followers. Even official Communist Party publications accept that during the Great Leap Forward of 1958, now described as an ultra-leftist deviation, many ancient and precious Daoist artefacts such as bells and cauldrons were melted down in the 'backyard furnaces' campaign to produce steel at any cost.[5] In spite of this repression, the Daoist tradition continued, particularly in the countryside, sometimes underground and sometimes openly. In the 1980s the police were openly reporting the arrest of members of the Yiguandao which was believed to have been wiped out during the 1950s.

Daoist temples and monasteries re-opened in the 1980s, initially in some cases as tourist attractions, but they gradually regained their religious functions. Monks were recalled from retirement, from the farms or from other work units to which they had been assigned. Funds were raised to pay wages and to buy materials to rebuild or repair temples; local seminaries were set up to train priests but some novices were also sent to Beijing. The Chinese Daoist Association, which was originally founded in 1957 but had ceased to operate during the Cultural Revolution, was re-established in 1983 and is based in Beijing at the Baiyunguan, the White Cloud Temple, which is the largest Daoist temple in northern China. The Baiyunguan was closed in 1966 when the Cultural Revolution started and only reopened in March 1984, by which time it had over thirty resident monks who were training Daoists from over a hundred monasteries that had registered with the Chinese Daoist Association.[6]

In the southeastern province of Fujian, one of the areas that has benefited most from the economic reforms of Deng Xiaoping, Daoist temples were reconsecrated by former monks who were brought back from the secular jobs to which they had transferred. Rituals and local cults that had been assumed to be extinct were revived and once again began to play a significant role in local politics.[7]

In October 2000 there were reports that officials at a rural People's Court had engaged a Daoist priest to carry out a five-hour-long ceremony of exorcism after a guard had fallen to his death from a window. Higher authorities launched an enquiry into these activities which contravened government policy on the avoidance of superstition.

Although Buddhism, which originated in India, is technically a foreign religion, it has been established in China for so long that it is to all intents and purposes regarded as Chinese. Its scriptures were translated into Chinese, its practices assumed a Chinese form and it became an integral part of the lives of the majority of Chinese people.

Buddhism was well established in Central Asia by the first century BC and began to spread to China in the early Christian era. During the Han dynasty (206 BC–AD 220), the first great dynasty of the empire and one of the formative periods of Chinese culture, the main centres of Buddhism in China were at Pengcheng in the south of what is now the province of Hebei and Luoyang. Another centre, Tonkin, is now in Vietnam. Buddhism acquired great political influence during the Tang dynasty (618–907) when it attracted support from the imperial court. In the words of Kenneth Ch'en, a leading scholar of Chinese Buddhism, in the Tang dynasty 'Buddhism finally came of age in China; it was supported by all elements of society – by the imperial household, the nobility, the great and wealthy families, and the common people'. Temples became social and entertainment centres as well as places for worship. Buddhist monasteries accumulated great wealth on the basis of donations from believers and acquired land: this gave them social influence and economic power in their immediate area. By the later years of the Ming dynasty (1368–1644), prosperity and stability had created a large landowning gentry class, far larger than was needed for official positions, in either central or local government. For many people from this background, Buddhist monasteries were to become the focus of their social lives, either as patrons and supporters or as monks. Consequently monasteries enjoyed immense wealth, prestige and authority. In addition to the Buddhist establishment, there were many popular sects linked with secret societies, such as the millenarian and messianic White Lotus which drew on the tradition of the Maitreya, the Buddha of the future, and which took part in rebellions against the Manchu Qing dynasty in the eighteenth century. White Lotus ideas were influential in the Boxer Rebellion of 1899–1901 and remain influential in parts of rural China to this day.[8]

In the early years of the People's Republic of China (PRC), hundreds of thousands of monks were compelled to leave their orders and to work in farms, workshops or factories. At the same time the CCP recognised Buddhism as an official religion and allowed two Buddhist delegates to attend the meetings of the Chinese People's Political Consultative Conference (CPPCC). Holmes Welch, the author of major studies of Buddhism in China, neatly summarised the official status of the religion in the first seventeen years of the PRC: 'until the Cultural Revolution began in 1966, it was the policy of the Chinese Communist Party to protect Buddhism, while at the same time keeping it under control and utilizing it in foreign policy'.[9] This did not prevent damage to temples and their contents and physical attacks on Buddhist clergy during the campaigns for land reform (in spite of clauses in the *Land Reform* law specifically prohibiting this) and during the movement for the suppression of counter-revolutionaries. Although the general tenor of Marxist writing in China was anti-clerical, there was some ambiguity, even in the writings of Mao Zedong, where it is possible to detect some respect for peasant religious beliefs and an acknowledgement that if those beliefs were to be overturned it should be the peasants themselves who decide to do so.

The career of Juzan (Chü-tsan) is instructive for an understanding of the position of Buddhism in the early years of the PRC. He was considered to be 'modern and progressive in outlook' and was one of the two Buddhist delegates to the CPPCC. Juzan became a monk in 1931 having studied under Taixu, 'the leading Buddhist reformer of the Republican era'. He moved to Hong Kong in 1948 and came into contact with a group of people who were to be extremely powerful in the PRC, including the writer Guo Moruo. As the CCP came to power, he lobbied for the preservation of a reformed school of Buddhism under the Communist state by placing the religion at the service of New China. In June 1950 he became the editor of the journal *Modern Buddhism*; this journal, unlike either its predecessors or other contemporary publications, was highly influential and became the nucleus of a powerful Buddhist organisation and the origin of the Chinese Buddhist Association which was founded in 1953. The journal and the association were part of the CCP's system for controlling religious activity, and to a lesser extent soliciting feedback from believers.[10]

Land reform was the single most important policy implemented by the CCP in its early years in power. Designed to alleviate dreadful rural poverty and to distribute land, albeit temporarily, to peasant families who had been the Party's power base, it also undermined the traditional social structure of rural China and effectively abolished the landowning class. Buddhist monasteries had acquired large holdings of land over a period of many centuries and were treated as landlords. During the land reform process, many of them lost all or part of their land and thus their means of an independent livelihood, although the *Agrarian Reform Law* was implemented unevenly and not all monasteries suffered to the same extent.

As collectivisation succeeded land reform, some monks formed themselves into cooperatives and farmed or worked in craft industries to avoid being criticised as parasites. In 1958, the year of the radical Maoist Great Leap Forward, donation boxes at Buddhist temples and shrines were outlawed and monks were forbidden to carry out divination for money.

Many monks and nuns left their monasteries and became lay people, working in agriculture or industry. Monasteries and temples were taken over by the government and some were converted into schools, museums, administrative offices or even army barracks. This was not unprecedented as there were instances of the previous Nationalist Guomindang government having requisitioned monasteries. Some smaller temples were also destroyed during the 1950s. The net effect of these policies was a dramatic decline in the *sangha* (the community of Buddhist clergy) which, along with the Buddha and the *dharma* (or doctrine), are the Three Jewels, the essential components, of Buddhism. However, monasteries and temples remained open and were visited by foreign Buddhists who travelled to China.

With the Cultural Revolution of 1966, the destruction of Buddhism appeared almost complete. Mao Zedong's youthful political shock troops, the Red Guards, were encouraged to attack the Four Olds: old ideas, old culture, old customs and old habits. Although Buddhism was not specifically named as a target, by the end of September 1966 almost all Buddhist monasteries and temples had closed down (at least in the cities), as had mosques and churches. Many of these were converted into flats or to other uses. Buddhist icons were damaged or destroyed, if they had not been carefully concealed, and monks were arrested and ill-treated. Many were criticised in public meetings and the work of the Chinese Buddhist Association came to a halt although it was able to resume some of its responsibilities in 1972 after the intervention of Premier Zhou Enlai.

When China began to return to some kind of stability in the late 1970s and early 1980s, Buddhist temples were once again opened and, although initially there were very few monks in evidence, it was common to see votive offerings of money or fruit that had been left in the outstretched hands of the statues of Bodhisattvas.

Official estimates suggest that there are now over 13,000 Buddhist temples in China and more than 200,000 monks and nuns. This total includes 120,000 lamas and nuns in the Tibetan Buddhist tradition, which has over 3,000 temples and 1,700 Living Buddhas.[11]

Tibetan and Mongolian Buddhism

Buddhism remains an especially potent force in Tibet and Inner Mongolia. Distinct from Chinese Buddhism, although drawing ultimately on the same inspiration and scriptural sources, it is also a means of expressing ethnic and cultural differences and has a political and national dimension. In the past, the traditional religious elite in both regions exercised considerable temporal power in addition to its spiritual authority: there is still much support for the Dalai Lama, who is venerated in Mongolia and Inner Mongolia as well as in Tibet and this is anathema to Beijing. Temples in Inner Mongolia remain closed and some are primarily museums although it is not uncommon to come across worshippers even in these.

The Yonghegong Lama Temple in Beijing, which dates back to the eighteenth century, reopened in the post-Cultural Revolution period and has a thriving community of monks, many brought in from Qinghai province. It is clearly a showcase designed to persuade visitors to Beijing that the CCP practices religious tolerance but there is no doubting the genuine convictions of Tibetan, Mongol and Chinese Buddhists visitors who prostrate themselves before the statues of the Buddha.[12]

Protests in Tibet by Buddhist clergy against the lack of religious freedom have been treated as nationalist disturbances by the government. Many monks and nuns have been imprisoned and there are consistent and credible reports of brutal treatment.[13] The Tibetan issue is explored more fully in Chapter 17.

Islam

Islam has had a presence in China since the earliest days of the religion but, unlike Buddhism which is considered to be essentially Chinese in spite of its origins in India, it is treated as a foreign religion. Han Chinese often express negative stereotypes about the Hui, suggesting that they are ill-educated, interested only in trade and not highly cultured. Some consider the older, traditional mosques to be dark, alien and forbidding. Chinese-speaking Hui Muslims are assumed by the state to be basically loyal to China whereas the Uyghur Muslims of Xinjiang are suspected of sympathy for the independence movement. Not surprisingly, the reality is more complex.

Hui Muslims are free to worship at registered mosques and to study at registered *madrasas* (Qur'anic schools) in the Hui areas of Ningxia and Gansu and elsewhere. They are also able to make the *hajj* pilgrimage to Mecca although there is considerable monitoring and supervision by state bodies. Islamic organisations other than mosques, including the influential Sufi orders, which are usually based at the shrines of their founding fathers, are treated with great suspicion.

Nevertheless they prosper and pilgrimages to the shrines are generally permitted. Sufi organisations have a history of involvement in violent conflict, both with other Muslim groups and with the authorities, and have often been the focal point of activity against the state. They are carefully monitored by the state but their leaders are also included in the deliberations of local government, often through membership of local branches of the CPPCC.

Xinjiang is different. The Uyghurs speak a Turkic language and only have Chinese as a second language, if at all. There are severe restrictions on attendance at mosques, especially for anyone under the age of eighteen, and on formal religious education. There are periodic campaigns to compel imams and other religious professionals to undergo training to ensure that they remain 'patriotic' and students and staff in schools and colleges are under pressure to eschew religion if they wish to have a career in public service. An interest in Islam is believed by government organisations to be associated with the movement for independence. Although active support for an independent Xinjiang is not universal, there is some justification for this belief. Uyghurs have family, business and religious ties with communities in the former Soviet Central Asian States, and the independence of these states after the collapse of the Soviet Union in 1991 stimulated hopes for the revival of an independent Eastern Turkestan, which had existed briefly in the 1940s. Many Uyghurs do favour an independent state and some would like an Islamic state: most realise that this is unlikely if not a complete impossibility in the foreseeable future. Xinjiang is discussed more fully in Chapter 18.

Protestant Christianity

China treats Protestant Christianity (*Jidu jiao*) and Roman Catholic Christianity (*Tianzhu jiao*) as if they are two completely separate religions but in both cases the government attempts to restrict the participation of Chinese Christians in the wider religious community beyond China. Orthodox Christianity which has a long history in certain ethnic Russian communities in the northwest and northeast is also often treated as a separate religion.

The Three Self Patriotic Movement (self-governing, self-supporting and self-propagating) which was established in the 1950s is the vehicle for Protestant Christians who are willing to worship in churches that are approved and monitored by the state. Many Chinese Christians reject this system and belong to underground or 'house' churches. Some of these churches are treated by the authorities as if they are cults: they are subject to periodic suppression and their ministers who are not recognised by the authorities have been arrested and confined in labour camps. The geographical location of both types of church, registered and underground, is related to the activities of pre-1949 missions: the Church is significantly stronger in the Yangzi valley which was within relatively easy reach of the nineteenth-century treaty ports.

Christianity was suppressed during the Cultural Revolution as were other religions but it was not entirely extinguished and it began to reappear in the early 1980s. The first wave of this revival was most dramatic in the provinces of Zhejiang and Henan and particularly in the poorer and more remote rural areas of Henan where a 'Christianity fever' was reported. Because the leadership of the Three Self Patriotic Movement, the official church, had lost its authority and credibility during the Cultural Revolution, in most cases the revival took the form of the re-creation, or creation, of autonomous house churches.[14]

The Lord's Recovery Church is an example of one of the underground Protestant churches and its history illustrates the difficult relationship that unofficial congregations have had with the Chinese state. This church is one of the unregistered and therefore illegal underground Protestant groups of which there are many in China and its closest parallel in the West is something like the Plymouth Brethren. It belongs to the revivalist and ecstatic tradition of dissenting Christianity, hence its nickname, the Shouters, which is a name given to it by its critics and not one used in general, or particularly liked, by the church itself.

Watchman Nee, a legendary figure in the Chinese dissenting Christian tradition, is credited as the founder of the church and it regards itself as indebted to his religious legacy, although, like many in the dissenting tradition, it has a complex history. Watchman Nee, Ni Duosheng (1903–72) was born in Guangzhou but brought up and educated in Fujian province where he came under the influence firstly of Methodist missionaries and then of certain members of the Church Missionary Society who were associated with the Exclusive Brethren, although he himself was later to be closer to the Open Brethren. He was baptised at the age of nineteen and established a church in Shanghai where he wrote what were to become important texts in the indigenising theology of Christianity in China. Watchman Nee's church was originally known as the Little Flock.

An autonomous and arguably more elitist Local Church broke away from the Little Flock: this was led by Witness Lee, Li Changshou (1905–97), who had been a disciple of Watchman Nee. This sect became very popular and spread through Christian communities in China and among overseas Chinese. Witness Lee moved to Taiwan in the 1940s in the wake of the military victories of the CCP and subsequently relocated to the United States. Chinese followers of the Local Church movement in the twenty-first century refer to their church as the Lord's Recovery (*Zhu de huifu*) Church, a term which to its members signifies the recovery or rediscovery of the true meaning and practice of the early church fathers. As it is to a large extent based in the United States, its involvement in China is seen by the government of the PRC as an example of outside interference in the religious policy of the Chinese state.

Watchman Nee came into conflict with the CCP very soon after the foundation of the PRC. Because of his conservative and fundamentalist theological stance he was unable to comply with the CCP's policy on the registration and control of religious organisations. He was arrested in 1952, for his opposition to the CCP but also on charges of financial irregularities, was transferred to a labour camp in Anhui province during the Cultural Revolution and died there in 1972.[15]

Contact between the official church in China and the wider Anglican communion has increased since China began to open to the outside world in the 1980s, although these contacts have been characterised by caution on both sides. Dr Rowan

Williams, the Archbishop of Canterbury and the head of the worldwide Anglican community, visited China in October 2006. His impressions of the development of Christianity in China were positive and his interviews in China inclined him to the view that estimates of fifty to eighty million Protestant Christians in China were a reasonable guess. He acknowledged the existence of a cultural Christianity – that is, a sympathy for and interest in Christianity particularly among students and staff in institutions of higher education. He rejected the easy assumption that China was 'a field ripe for missionary harvest', arguing that the Chinese church should be permitted to manage its own development.[16]

Catholic Christianity

Catholic Christianity in China is similarly divided. The Chinese Catholic Patriotic Association is the official body and there is an underground Catholic church, which is usually characterised as being loyal to the Vatican. Under Pope John Paul II, the decision by Rome to canonise Chinese Catholic martyrs appeared to exacerbate the dispute between the two churches: given the Polish Pope's hostility to Communism, this was not surprising. In contrast, during the early days of the papacy of Benedict XVI there has been a mood of reconciliation and a move towards the re-establishment of diplomatic relations between the Holy See and Beijing which were severed in 1951.

A papal letter addressed to Roman Catholics in China on 27 May 2007 initiated a fresh dialogue with both the Chinese Catholic church and the secular authorities. It acknowledged the difficulties that had been faced by Catholics in China who had been put in the position of having to decide whether they should accept the authority of government bodies. It affirmed that underground activities were not considered to be usual or desirable in the Catholic church but accepted that some Catholic bishops had 'felt themselves constrained to opt for clandestine consecration'. The Pope's letter was couched in dense theological and legal language and endeavoured to demonstrate that there was in fact a considerable element of continuity between his policy on China and that of the papacy of John Paul II, although the tone of the new Pope's approach was markedly different. Pope Benedict acknowledged that some bishops had 'consented to receive Episcopal ordination without the pontifical mandate', but had subsequently asked to be received into communion with the Vatican and that these had been retrospectively legitimised as bishops: in some cases this had not been made public, so congregations and even priests did not know and this had cause great confusion. Even bishops who had not asked for or obtained this legitimate ordination could be recognised as 'illegitimate but validly ordained'. This acknowledgment confirmed rumours that had been circulating for some time and clarified some oblique remarks that had been made by Pope John Paul II about covert consecrations during the final years of his papacy, which can now be understood to mean that the process of reconciliation had been underway even before the Papacy of Benedict XVI.

The relationship between the official and the underground Catholic Church is complex: some Catholic bishops who were not formally approved by the

Vatican, but are nevertheless considered to be acceptable to Rome because of their background and training, may have been selected and authorised by the Patriotic Association in what was probably both a gesture of accommodation and a face-saving exercise. Likewise, it appears that the Vatican has accepted the authority of many of the bishops who were consecrated by the Patriotic church.[17]

An underground Catholic bishop, Han Dingxiang, of Hebei province, who had spent almost thirty-five years in prison, died in September 2007 while still in custody. He had been suffering from lung cancer for some time and it appears that his funeral was arranged hastily and was carried out without the presence of any Catholic priests. However, almost simultaneously in the southern city of Guiyang a new bishop was ordained jointly by clergy from the underground church and the state-sponsored Catholic Patriotic Association.[18] That was a low-profile ordination, but the ordination of Father Joseph Li Shan as Bishop in the Cathedral of the Immaculate Conception in Beijing (the Nantang or Southern Cathedral, as it is known in the city) on 21 September 2007 was a much more public occasion and, although he was the candidate of the Patriotic Association, his consecration was carried out with the express approval of Pope Benedict. This consecration marked a new phase in the relationship between the underground and the official church and a recognition that the two churches were now operating closely together and had many shared activities. The Vatican hopes that this will herald a full unification of the Chinese church and permit the establishment of full diplomatic relations with Beijing.[19]

There was further evidence for the trend towards closer relations between the official and the underground Catholic churches late in 2007 when two bishops were installed with the approval of both traditions. Joseph Gan Junqiu was consecrated as Bishop of Guangzhou, the most important city in south China, while Lu Shouwang became Bishop of Yichang, a city in the west of Hubei province. In both cases the ceremonies were low key and not open to the press or television. A spokesman for the Catholic Patriotic Association insisted that the appointments had been made by Beijing, but he also expressed his satisfaction that the Vatican had approved of the individuals who had been chosen.[20]

Overseas churches

Churches outside China that attempt to support churches on the mainland are viewed with great suspicion: these include evangelical Christians from South Korea who have been involved in smuggling North Korean refugees into China and the Cardinal Kung Foundation based in the United States which is vociferously critical of the Catholic Patriotic Association. Some evangelical Christian organisations in the United States have an explicit policy of 'planting churches in China', a policy that is resented and resisted by the CCP, more from a sense of national pride and affronted dignity than for strictly ideological considerations. Outside interference of this nature is perceived as an attempt by foreign powers to undermine the state's policies on religion.

There is potential for considerable conflict between those religious groups that are registered with the state and unofficial religions. The state tolerates religion if it is locally controlled but abhors any suggestion of foreign interference. There are families who have been believers for generations but religion has also found new adherents among those sections of society that are disillusioned with the CCP. Christianity appeals to some educated Chinese today, just as it did in the 1920s and 1930s: it is perceived as Western and modern as well as anti-Communist. There is also the growing phenomenon of cultural Christians – individuals who identify themselves with Christianity to demonstrate that they are modern and fashionable but who do not necessarily believe or practice.

Unofficial branches of all religions continue to grow in popularity as confidence in the ideology of the state declines. While some of these groups have the familiar spiritual and social functions that are found in religious organisations in the West and elsewhere, others resemble messianic cults which may come into conflict with the Chinese state in the future, as they have in the past.

Falungong and the 'new religions'

Falungong has been the *bête-noire* of the government of the PRC since April 1999, when it organised large-scale demonstrations outside Zhongnanhai, the residential and administrative compound that is home to senior leaders of the CCP in Beijing.

Falungong, which draws on Buddhist and Daoist beliefs and on other spiritual traditions (or superstitions, depending on one's point of view) that have been popular among the less-educated rural population, stands out as by far the most widespread of the many new Chinese religions. It has also attracted educated urban dwellers, including retired members of the CCP, police and armed forces (which greatly alarmed the authorities) and spread rapidly across China. Many of its followers are middle-aged and elderly and there appear to be many more women than men. It represents itself as a group that is primarily interested in achieving spiritual enlightenment through exercise and breathing techniques and it encourages particular combinations of *qigong* breathing and physical training, which links it to the martial arts tradition; it also propagates bizarre superstitions about health. Because it was ostensibly a Chinese organisation rather than a foreign import, it was not initially considered by Beijing to be a serious threat.

Falungong was formed by Li Hongzhi in May 1992 and at the time appeared to be just one of many *qigong* groups that were organised or revived throughout China. There is a great deal of uncertainty and obscurity about Li Hongzhi's background, much of it manufactured to give him an air of mystery or even sanctity but, according to some accounts, he served in the People's Liberation Army (PLA). *Qigong* is a traditional Chinese practice of exercise and deep breathing which, it is claimed, enhances physical, mental and spiritual fitness, but it is also associated with ancient and esoteric Buddhist and Daoist religious practices. Groups of this nature had been suppressed immediately after the founding of the PRC and, after a period during which they revived, they suffered further repression during the

Cultural Revolution, but many were allowed to operate with some restrictions in the more tolerant atmosphere that prevailed after the death of Mao Zedong in 1976. In 1985 the China Qigong Scientific Research Association was created as the national regulatory body for all *qigong* groups.[21] Falungong was initially recognised by this national body and Li Hongzhi gave seminars in Beijing and in his place of origin, northeastern China, with official approval.

Relations, however, broke down during the 1990s for reasons that are not entirely clear and Falungong withdrew, or was expelled, from membership of the China Qigong Scientific Research Association. The Association continues to function but Falungong is no longer authorised by it and, to the extent that it is active at all, it operates outside of any government regulation.

Falungong attempted to establish its legality by registering with other government bodies but was unsuccessful and in 1996 its publications were banned by the State Press and Publications Administration, partly because of concern at the rapidly growing number of Falungong adherents, but also because of the contents of its publications which attacked modern science and promoted what the Chinese government considered to be superstitious ideas. Particular concern was expressed at the Falungong attitude to sickness and health, its rejection of modern medicine and the substitution of *qigong* exercises for medical treatment, even in the case of severe and life-threatening illnesses. The philosophical vision which underlies Falungong's teachings sees humanity moving towards an apocalypse, after which only a small number of true believers will achieve salvation.

Having failed to secure legitimacy, Falungong decentralised into local associations and made its presence felt by dramatic demonstrations. It also acquired a large body of supporters outside China, both in the Chinese-speaking world and in the West. It is clear from Falungong's own documents that it is not simply an organisation promoting *qigong* exercises but is developing as a sect with apocalyptic ideas, similar to those that have been found in Buddhist and Daoist secret societies in China for many centuries, as well as in new religions and cults in the more developed world.

Li Hongzhi, the founder of Falungong, continued to spread his teachings in China after the publication ban but he relocated to the United States in 1996. This allowed the Chinese government to assert that Falungong was no longer a native Chinese religious movement but had evolved into an organisation with a foreign base and foreign funding which threatened the existence of the Chinese state.[22]

In China, Falungong attracted a significant number of professionals into its membership, many of them at or near retirement age but who are still part of China's educated and influential elite. Of particular concern to the authorities were reports of the level of interest in Falungong among senior officers of the PLA and the police. Since the demonstrations of 1999, many members of Falungong have been arrested and detained. Information on the scale and the nature of this detention is extremely difficult to obtain and almost all of it comes from sources close to either the Chinese government or Falungong supporters. There is very little independent or objective data. Nevertheless, a coherent pattern has emerged. Very few members of Falungong have been brought to trial under the normal judicial processes: those who have been taken to court are the most senior activists and those associated with publishing and fund-raising. Far more Falungong supporters, numbering possibly tens of thousands, may have been subjected to administrative detention – that is, they have been sentenced to short periods of 'reform through labour', effectively terms of imprisonment. These sentences do not require the intervention of the courts and there are no public records of the numbers of supporters of Falungong who have been detained in this way.

Supporters of Falungong have claimed that members of the group have been tortured in detention and there have been a small number of high-profile instances where detained Falungong members are reported to have committed suicide in prison, but it is extremely difficult to verify these. Foreign observers do not have access to prisons and 'reform through labour' camps except on occasional, carefully controlled, visits by international bodies. Although there is no evidence of a systematic policy of torture in any of these detention facilities, there is substantial and consistent anecdotal evidence of ill-treatment and brutality towards minority groups, especially those that are designated as a threat to the state, which is certainly the case with Falungong.[23]

In Falungong, there is a core leadership, partly outside China, and a wide body of supporters or adherents, within China but also in Chinese communities elsewhere, who are attached to local groups. The Chinese authorities are more concerned about the organisation of Falungong, both centrally and at the local level and its finances, than the practice of individual adherents. By the summer of 2007, the number of reports of prosecutions simply for practising Falungong had decreased but, if there were to be a renewed campaign against the organisation, arrests on a large scale could take place once again.

The *Epoch Times*, which has been published from an office in New York in hard copy editions in Chinese since May 2000, and in English since September 2003, represents itself as an independent newspaper for the communities of the Chinese diaspora. It also appears in Chinese and English internet editions in addition to a number of other languages and is distributed free of charge. Its editorial perspective and its news values are robustly in opposition to the CCP and the activities of Falungong are reported favourably and in far more detail than in any other newspaper. Li Hongzhi has acknowledged that it was established to further the interests of Falungong adherents but the paper hotly denies that it simply acts as a mouthpiece for the organisation.

After Li Hongzhi moved to the United States, the public security authorities proceeded to suppress the organisation ruthlessly. Following the mass demonstrations in Beijing in April 1999, Falungong was banned and formally designated as a heterodox cult (*xiejiao*). Large quantities of its publications were seized and destroyed and leading figures in the movement were arrested and imprisoned, which seriously restricted its ability to organise. Falungong remains a popular organisation in China but there are fewer demonstrations and it is no longer a major source of public controversy on the mainland, although it maintains a powerful voice in Chinese communities abroad.

Ethnic minorities

The social position of many of the ethnic minority groups in China is closely linked to their religious beliefs and traditions, but they also have their own secular cultures, customs and in most cases languages, and they are subject to the minority policies of the CCP. Previous governments had policies on minorities but these were not well thought out and were not founded on direct and thorough knowledge of the minority groups. In 1924, Sun Yat-sen, who is claimed as a formative political influence by both the CCP and the GMD, set out his position on minorities as follows:

> Although there are a little over ten million non-Chinese in China, including Mongols, Manchus, Tibetans and Tartars, their number is small compared with the purely Chinese population, four hundred million in number, which has a common racial heredity, common religion and common tradition and customs. It is one nationality![24]

On the surface, the people of China today might appear to be one single ethnic group, or one nationality in the wishful thinking of Sun Yat-sen, the father of the Chinese Republic. China's 1.3 billion citizens are no longer dressed in almost identical clothes as they were portrayed in the days of the Cultural Revolution, but they all seem to speak the same language and have a common culture. Dig a little deeper, however, and this facade of conformity and uniformity swiftly evaporates. China is a multiethnic, multilingual and multicultural society. It is true that the language and culture of the Han Chinese people dominate, especially in the public arena, but even among the Han themselves there are considerable cultural and linguistic differences. Spoken Mandarin and Cantonese are as different from each other as is Portuguese from Romanian, even though they are both sometimes referred to as 'dialects' of Chinese.

Beyond the Han, China is home to a variety of ethnic groups, who are categorised as 'minority nationalities' (*shaoshu minzu*), a term derived from the system of ethnic classification that was used in the Soviet Union during the Stalin period. In most cases their languages, cultures and religions have very little in common with those of the Han.

Minority people are found everywhere in China, including in Beijing and the other major cities, and they may work in the same kind of employment and live in the same areas as the Han. The distinctiveness of their communities is most apparent in their traditional homelands, some of which have been designated autonomous regions by the government of the People's Republic. The majority of these homelands are on, or close to, frontiers, notably China's western borders with Central Asia, but there are also many in the southwest, particularly in the province of Yunnan.

Numbers

The Chinese state formally recognises the existence of fifty-five different minority nationalities: the people most recently acknowledged as comprising a distinct ethnic group are the Jinuo of Yunnan, who were granted nationality status in 1979. The largest group is the Zhuang of Guangxi in southern China, which has a population of sixteen million. The smallest is the Lhoba of Tibet, of whom there are fewer than 3,000. The minorities number more than 106 million, comprise 8.4 per cent of the total population of China but occupy 60 per cent of China's territory. The fact that minorities only amount to roughly 8 per cent of the population is often used by the government or by some Han people to reduce or even dismiss the significance of the minority communities, many of which exercise an influence far greater than their relatively small numbers would suggest. This is due to the fact that they are often the majority communities in their home areas and because these areas are mainly in strategic border locations.

Key ethnic groups

Some ethnic groups have played a more prominent role in Chinese history and society than others.

The 5.8 million Mongols who live mainly in Inner Mongolia and the northeast (Manchuria) are closely related to the Mongols of (Outer) Mongolia, and more distantly to the Buryat Mongols of Russia. They are united by their language and culture, their nomadic heritage and their devotion to Tibetan Buddhism. Today's Mongols are the ancestors of the warriors of Chinggis Khan and Khubilai Khan who conquered China, most of Central Asia and much of the Middle East during the thirteenth and early fourteenth centuries. They ruled China as the Yuan dynasty but then lost power and retreated to the steppes.

During the Cultural Revolution, many of the Buddhist monasteries of Inner Mongolia were destroyed by the Red Guards or fell into disuse. Some have become museums but others are being restored. There is an active underground movement in support of an independent Inner Mongolia, or southern Mongolia as its supporters prefer to call it, but any public expression of this movement in newspapers and organisations has been ruthlessly suppressed by the Chinese authorities.

The 10.6 million Manchus, originally from the northeast and the origin of that region's former name of Manchuria, were also tribal nomads but, when the Ming dynasty was on the point of collapse in 1644, they invaded China and put their own emperor on the Dragon Throne. The Manchus ruled China as the Qing dynasty until 1911 when they were replaced by a predominantly Han Chinese Republican government.

Although they ruled in a coalition with Mongol bannermen and a small number of nobles and officials from the Han Chinese elite, the Manchus were the dominant group and Manchu garrisons were established throughout China. The Manchu language, which is completely unrelated to Chinese but has close connections with Mongolian, gradually died out as a spoken vernacular but continued to play a role as a language of the records of the imperial court until the end of the dynasty. The Xibo (or Sibe) people of Xinjiang, who are descendants of Manchu troops sent to the region in the eighteenth century, speak a form of Manchu to this day.

Many Tibetans would be uncomfortable to be classified as a *Chinese* ethnic minority and some, possibly the majority, would prefer to be citizens of an independent Tibet. There are 5.4 million Tibetans living within the borders of the PRC, not only in the Tibetan Autonomous Region which is ruled by Beijing from its administrative centre, Lhasa, but also in the provinces of Gansu, Qinghai and Sichuan, parts of which belonged to old Tibet which was independent between 1911 and the creation of the PRC in 1949. Tibetan Buddhism with its distinctive hierarchy of monasteries and lamas functions quite separately from Buddhism as it is practised by Buddhists of Han Chinese origin. Its scriptures and liturgy are in the Tibetan language which uses a writing system derived from one of the scripts of ancient India, probably one of the early systems of writing used for the classical language, Sanskrit; it does not use classical Chinese, which is the language of translated Buddhist sutras in China.

The 8.4 million Uyghurs of Xinjiang are a Muslim Turkic people and their language, religion and culture have far more in common with the Uzbeks and also the Kazakhs and Kyrgyz people in former Soviet Central Asia than with the Han Chinese. The Uyghurs as a community are frequently referred to as 'restive', and have been collectively stigmatised as terrorists by the Chinese authorities since 2001 with very little justification; they struggle to maintain their cultural and religious identity in a state that is determined to assimilate them to Han norms.

The Hui are an interesting hybrid group in that they are Muslims of Central Asian and Middle Eastern ancestry but their normal language at home and in their communities is one of the regional varieties of Chinese. They number about ten million and have settled all over China, but they have had the greatest impact, both in terms of numbers and culture, in the northwest, particularly in Gansu province and in Ningxia which is formally designated a Hui Autonomous Region. They speak the Chinese of their home region but this is augmented by Arabic and Persian terms which have been incorporated into their discourse for centuries to convey religious and cultural meanings and to mark them out from the Han.

Yunnan province which lies on China's border with Burma and Vietnam has the most complex ethnic mix of any part of China. The numerous groups including the Dai, the Yao and the Nakhi (Naxi) are relatively small and widely dispersed. They speak languages related to Thai, Vietnamese and to other languages of Southeast Asia. Unlike the minorities in the northern and northwestern border areas, no single group dominates the province. CCP officials attempting to classify the different cultures tended to regard them as primitive, and indeed their economic level and social organisation do in many cases resemble patterns found in Asia many centuries ago.

Government policy, inequality and discrimination

The CCP's policy on ethnic minorities was based on the practice of the Soviet Union, but also drew on its own historical contacts with minority groups during the Long March at a time when it was consciously seeking to distance itself from the policies of the GMD Nationalists, who had to a large extent neglected the ethnic minorities. It was on the Long March that many CCP members came into contact with some of these communities for the first time.

On paper, the Party's policies are designed to give equality to minority groups and to ensure that they enjoy at least a token representation in bodies such as the CPPCC, the national advisory body. In practice, ethnic minorities and their cultures have suffered considerable discrimination, especially during periods of Maoist radicalism such as the Great Leap Forward and the Cultural Revolution. There is little sympathy among the majority Han population for expressions of minority ethnic identity and even less for demands for political independence by some Uyghurs and Tibetans.[25] The complex histories of the ethnic groups of Tibet and Xinjiang and their relationship with China are discussed in greater detail in Chapters 17 and 18.

13 Gender and modernisation

All of the economic, social and political changes that have taken place in China have been experienced by men and women of all classes, but they have not necessarily been experienced equally or in the same way. According to the popular political cliché, women 'hold up half the sky' but it is very unlikely that most Chinese women would consider that they were treated as genuinely equal to men.

Three obediences

Any reasonable comparison between the lives of women in traditional China and their position in China today cannot fail to acknowledge the vast improvement in their status and, for many, their opportunities in life and work. For centuries, the unquestioned assumption was that women were simply inferior to men. In this, China was no different from the other traditional peasant societies of Asia. Although there were philosophical attempts, drawing on Daoism, to emphasise the benefits of a complementary relationship between the male *yang* and the female *yin*, there is no doubt that this was a profoundly unequal relationship. More revealing were the 'three obediences' (*san cong*) which defined the relationships of women with the men in their families at different stages of their lives; it was of course assumed that they would not have any association with men outside their families. This manner of expressing social position was typical of the hierarchical attitude to society that is usually referred to for simplicity as Confucian: as a child, a woman would obey her father; on marriage, she would obey her husband; and when she produced a son (her primary social function), she would be obliged to comply with his wishes, at least once he had become an adult and certainly if she were widowed. Chinese society, however, was as complex and as muddled as any other, in spite of the attempts by the Confucian *literati* to impose a moral and social order: by no means all families followed this prescription but it was always there as a model for how women should behave.

Marriage

For a woman, marriage meant leaving the family home and moving into a new household with her husband. Indeed the normal Chinese word for marriage when applied to a woman is *chujia*, 'to leave the family'. The new household belonged to her husband's parents and was typically dominated by her mother-in-law. For many women in traditional China this relationship, and not the relationship with their husband, was the most important in their lives: a good relationship with the mother-in-law could lead to a relatively happy and fulfilled life (albeit a severely restricted one), whereas a poor relationship could lead to desperation.

Social position made a great deal of difference: the majority of Chinese women, who were from farming families, were fated to spend their lives either in agricultural or domestic labour. For wealthier women, there was status and prosperity but the price for rank was seclusion and social restriction. Chinese women of high social status, like women in other traditional Asian societies, were confined to the home and its immediate environs, a condition similar to the arrangement that was referred to as *purdah* in the Indian subcontinent and as the *harem* in the Muslim Middle East. This system had purportedly evolved to ensure the virtue of the women of the family, which was highly valued socially, and to demonstrate the wealth and status of the head of the household and his family.

In addition to wives, for men of means could take more than one wife, some women – concubines – had a relationship with men which was of a lower social status and did not formally entitle them to the same privileges and benefits of full family membership. Personality, intellect and opportunity made it possible for some women to transcend these social boundaries (as some women, notably celebrated courtesans, demonstrated in Europe). At the bottom of the social scale were women without husbands or families, some of whom made such a living as they could through prostitution. China was no different from any other pre-modern society in its snobberies and hypocrisy and this applied to the status of women as much as to other aspects of the social order.

Bound feet

One custom which distinguished the position of Chinese women from all other societies was the practice of binding feet. Many, if not most, traditional societies exhibit or have exhibited some form of physical restraint on women, whether it be relatively minor ones such as corseting or fundamental and brutal ones such as the range of practices that are grouped under the misleadingly mild term 'female circumcision'. The socially approved foot fetish appears to have been unique to China. The bound foot, or 'lily foot', which is reputed to have been both aesthetically and erotically stimulating for Chinese men, was created by bending a young girl's foot while the bones were still malleable and binding the foot with cloth so that the toes were forced underneath. The foot grew to be deformed and much smaller than an unbound foot: the small foot, the Golden Lotus, which ideally was supposed to be not more than three inches in length, was prized by both women and men. Naturally this practice severely restricted the mobility of those Chinese women who were subjected to it.

Some groups, notably the Hakka, have never practised the binding of feet. The practice was criticised by Western missionaries and was outlawed in 1902 under the Qing dynasty but this was during its final years when it lacked the authority to enforce the prohibition; it was also strongly opposed by the government of the Republic. Sun Yat-sen supported legislation prohibiting the binding of feet in 1912, during his brief Presidency. However, it persisted in the more remote rural areas and it was still possible to see elderly women with bound feet towards the end of the twentieth century.

Seeking alternatives

It would be wrong to suggest that all Chinese women were completely confined and inhibited by the restrictive Confucian system. Some women were able to find an alternative life through membership of religious or quasi-religious secret societies, including the Boxers who rebelled in 1899. Western Christian missionaries who had been horrified by the practice of binding feet tried to ban it within their congregations and European and American ideas about the position of women in society spread throughout the educated middle class in the early twentieth century. Women became aware of the possibility of new roles that they could play, but this was largely an urban phenomenon.

The legacy of subservience, mutilation and restriction motivated a new generation of women to seek equality. In the 1920s and 1930s many of them were attracted to radical movements, including the Chinese Communist Party (CCP), which actively recruited women and considered *funu gongzuo* (woman-work), to be one of the Party's most important tasks. Woman-friendly policies were developed, both before and after the CCP took power in 1949, and both the motivations for and the outcomes of these policies are still widely, and hotly, debated in China today.

Women in the People's Republic of China

The most significant piece of legislation directed towards the condition of women in the early years of the PRC was the *Marriage Reform Law* of 1950. It was enacted to reject traditional 'feudal' marriage arrangements by outlawing all forced arranged marriages and the betrothal of children before they had reached the age at which they could reasonably be expected to understand what was being planned in their name. Both of these practices had been common, especially in rural communities. The new law did not outlaw all arranged marriages; it did, however, insist that there should be informed consent on both sides. The freedom of marriage and of divorce was set out in the legislation but because of the persistence of conservative notions concerning the roles of women and the family (by women as well as men), the reality took longer to achieve.

During the years of Mao Zedong's chairmanship of the CCP, it was argued that women had achieved formal and official equality with men. This extended to work: women laboured in the fields and in the factories alongside men and in theory earned equal wages. Westerners visiting China for the first time were frequently surprised to see women in labouring gangs on the roads and on building sites. A large number of women were appointed as Party cadres and government officials, although it did not require particularly keen observation to discern that the vast majority of women cadres occupied relatively minor positions in the Party, in the communes or in the street committees of China's towns and cities. Nevertheless, since there had been very few opportunities for women to participate in government at any level before 1949 and virtually none at all before 1911, this can be considered as a major advance for women. Women also flourished in the professions of medicine, science and education, thanks in large part to the example of the Soviet Union where many women had become teachers and doctors.

Reform period

The introduction of economic reforms under Deng Xiaoping was a mixed blessing for women. Like men, they were in danger of losing their secure state employment following the collapse of the 'iron rice bowl' that had virtually guaranteed jobs for life and many were forced into the private sector. Some took to this new life with enthusiasm and assurance and there are many examples of successful women entrepreneurs. The class of professional women, building on the experience of doctors, teachers and scientists, also began to grown in size and influence and many were able to remain in official positions. The demands of the new society which provided these new career opportunities also created tensions in families and the rate of divorce increased.

The application of market principles to the labour force has, on balance, had a detrimental effect on the employment prospects of women. In the rush for growth and competitiveness many employers have ignored the legislation that protected the recruitment of women. As a result many more women are in low-paid employment or are obliged to work for lower wages than men in the same jobs. The enrolment of girls and women in education has also declined. This is particularly the case in the poorer and most underdeveloped parts of China but there are fewer girls than boys in primary education in general. At university level, fewer women are succeeding in gaining admission. This state of affairs is due partly to open discrimination by universities and colleges and partly to the re-emergence of traditional prejudices against the education of girls.

For women in the countryside, the choice has often been to stay in their village with little or no work or to travel, often great distances, in search of work. Many moved to the boom areas of the southeast to work in factories, some of them no better than sweat shops, where they endured conditions that were similar to those that had been experienced by their grandmothers' generation in the 1920s – poor wages, unhygienic and dangerous working conditions and in some cases physical restriction to the accommodation provided by their employers.

As the need for agricultural labour declined, some women who remained in the countryside were able to move into handicraft production, food processing and other small-scale industries. There were a number of government initiatives to assist in the creation of employment opportunities: local branches of the All-China Women's Federation encouraged the development of family smallholdings and the production of craft goods such as baskets, cushions and mats which could be sold in local markets. The Federation had been set up in 1949 as one of the mass organisations under the control of the CCP and was given the task of promoting and protecting the rights of women. During the 1990s it revised its view of its role and has claimed that it is now a non-governmental organisation.

In the 1980s, for the first time in decades, reports began to appear of the abduction of women and children in the countryside for sale as brides (or, presumably in some cases, into prostitution). The break-up of the communes had liberated women from agricultural work but alternatives were not always available. Although there is no reliable data on the trafficking of women and girls, this trade was given a new impetus in the 1990s when 'snakehead' gangs began to mastermind the emigration of large numbers of women, many of whom found their way into the sex trade in other countries.

Gender balance

For all women, but for rural women in particular, there was the added pressure of the one-child policy, which is discussed in more detail in Chapter 9. Not only has this policy had a profound effect on the lives of individuals and families, it has contributed to a startling gender imbalance in the country as a whole. As a result of the age-old preference for boy children, there has been a significant increase in the abortion of female foetuses and female infanticide. These practices have been common knowledge since the 1980s but they have become more widespread with the advent of ultrasound scanning technology and selective induced abortion, services that have been provided illegally by some doctors for fees of as much as RMB 1,000.

The whole process of scans and abortions is shrouded in secrecy and it varies from region to region, but the impact on the gender ratio has been obvious and dramatic. The United Nations recommends a male to female ratio of no greater than 107:100 but the figure for China was 116:100 in 2000 and 119:100 in 2005, according to figures issued by the Chinese Family Planning Association. In practical terms, this means that men will find it increasingly more difficult to find wives. When this is combined with the phenomenon of an aging population it raises the spectre of a new social problem: the likelihood of many single children having to support both of their parents and some of their grandparents for many years on a single salary.[1]

14 Environment

China, and this cannot be repeated often enough, is a developing country which is undergoing rapid economic and social change. These developments are comparable with the transformation that took place in Europe during the industrial revolutions of the eighteenth and nineteenth centuries and in the United States at a slightly later date. As an almost entirely agricultural society, traditional China was generally free from industrial pollution although accounts of the porcelain centre of Jingdezhen in the Ming dynasty refer to the constant smoke and flames emitted by the potteries and the noisy and dirty atmosphere that this created. Coal and tin mining have existed for centuries but the extraction of minerals was not on a scale comparable to that found in the West until relatively recently.

China has a great variety of landforms, from desert and grassland in the north to paddy rice field in the south and different regions of the country use land differently.

Remnants of traditional methods of hunting and gathering, agriculture and nomadic pastoralism are still practised alongside more modern forms of farming and industrialisation. Land use is also modified according to local customs and the mores of different ethnic groups.

In so far as it is possible to speak of one single traditional Chinese view of the environment and of humanity's relationship to the environment, the best example would be the concept of harmonisation with nature, of running with rather than against nature – an approach which is most closely associated with Daoism.

Since 1949 China's main priority has been industrialisation along the lines suggested by the model adopted in the Soviet Union and Eastern Europe with which China was at least formally allied in the 1950s. China under Mao also wished to catch up economically with the West, which had partially colonised it in the nineteenth and early twentieth centuries, and with Japan which had occupied a large amount of its territory between 1931 and 1945. This drive for economic development was associated with the assertion of a Chinese national identity and a reaction to what Chinese nationalists and patriots, including the Chinese Communist Party (CCP), conceived of as a century of national humiliation.

The CCP did not express any real concerns about environmental problems in the early years of its administration. It concentrated on the development of heavy industry, particularly iron and steel plants and the oilfields of the northeast. Although the construction of these plants created a severe environmental burden, this was virtually ignored during the 1960s and 1970s. The environmental costs of industrialisation were also ignored or downplayed in the Soviet Union and its allies and in Western Europe and the United States in the same period. Environmental concerns developed slowly. As China opened up to visitors in the 1970s and 1980s, journalists, academics and business travellers began to reach the industrialised areas of China and reports of disturbing levels of pollution gradually reached the West. At the same time Chinese officials, and later academics and students, began to travel abroad and they took back with them ideas of environmentalism that were becoming prevalent in the West.

Major environmental issues

The different geographical regions of China have suffered from varying forms of environmental depredation but some problems are more significant and widespread than others. One of these is the spread of acid rain caused by the sulphur dioxide that is emitted by factories and power plants and that has affected much of China's land mass: according to a report from the Standing Committee of the National People's Congress (NPC), it has at times been so serious that it has posed a threat to the safety of the food supply. According to the report more than half of the 696 cities and counties monitored had suffered from the effects of acid rain, in some cases on a daily basis. Sheng Huaren, Deputy Chairman of the NPC Standing Committee, argued that 'Increased sulphur dioxide emissions meant that one third of China's territory was affected by acid rain, posing a major threat to soil and food safety'. Sulphur dioxide emissions rose by 27 per cent between 2000 and 2005, largely because of the waste products of coal-burning power stations and coking plants, making China one of the principal originators of the chemical in the entire world. The pollutant was emitted at a rate that was double the acceptable environmental limit and it affected 40 per cent of Chinese cities. China has subsequently put in place plans to reduce the sulphur emissions in its coal-burning power plants as part of a drive to improve air quality. In the run-up to the 2008 Olympics there was particular concern about problems of pollution in Beijing and its environs on account of the effect of smog on athletes.[1] Atmospheric pollution, particularly in the urban areas, has been exacerbated by the exponential growth in the numbers of motor vehicles on China's roads.

There is also general concern about increased water pollution, including the discharge of untreated sewage and chemical waste products and the use of the rivers and the seas of China's coastlines for discarding waste products.

This has had a deleterious effect on fish, prawns and other forms of marine life, many of which form an important part of the national diet. Industrial plants along the Yangzi River became the target of government investigations as they were considered to be particularly serious polluters and a number, including three factories in Anhui province, were closed after intervention by the State Environmental Protection Agency. The agency was attempting to raise its profile after its deficiencies were revealed publicly in the case of the pollution of the Songhua River in November 2005 (see below).[2]

Deforestation has also been a major concern: in the early days of industrialisation, trees were cut down in considerable quantities for building programmes with little thought given to the need for replanting. Logging has had a serious impact on wildlife in some areas and the impact of soil erosion and creeping desertification is visible along hundreds of miles of railway track in northern China where the trees that held back the desert have been cut down. Netting is used to hold down the sand dunes and encourage the growth of plants that will bind them together. The erosion of soil from the hillsides and the expansion of the desert have also led to the silting up of rivers and a consequent increase in flooding.

Nuclear testing

The environmental impact of the testing of nuclear devices has also been a matter of great concern, especially among the Uyghurs of Xinjiang because the region around Lop Nor in central Xinjiang has been the site of nuclear tests since the 1960s. For decades there have been reports about the effects of radioactive contamination and pollution on the local population. Human rights activists from Xinjiang have assembled portfolios of photographs which present evidence of birth defects and other medical problems that appear to have been caused by nuclear testing and have attempted, unsuccessfully, to have the testing abandoned in their homeland. The nuclear industry, and in particular the testing of nuclear weapons, is covered by the strictest secrecy. It is highly problematic even to initiate discussions on these sensitive matters with government officials.

Environmental case study 1: Three Gorges Dam

Judging by the degree of environmental concern that it has generated, both within China and internationally, the development of the Three Gorges Dam has been the single most controversial of all the projects that have been initiated in contemporary China. The essence of the scheme is the creation of a large dam on the Yangzi River at Sandouping, in Yichang in the central region of Hubei province, which will provide electricity for China's development and will also assist in the control of flooding. When completed, the Three Gorges Dam will be the largest hydroelectric project in the world when measured by its potential output of 18,200 megawatts, but it has been dogged by controversy: critics, both domestic and international, have focused on the environmental costs to what is one of China's outstanding areas of natural beauty and also the human costs for displaced communities.

The idea of damming the Yangzi at this point is not a new one. It was raised by Sun Yat-sen as part of his comprehensive plan for developing China's economy as early as 1919 and initial surveys were carried out in the 1930s but it was not until the establishment of the People's Republic of China (PRC) that a project on this grand scale became practicable: several feasibility studies were commissioned in the 1980s after the State Council's formal endorsement of the project in 1979.

Construction of the dam commenced with great optimism in 1994 and in 2003 the process was sufficiently far advanced to allow the water to begin to flow. By

May 2006, the bulk of the work on the dam had been finished, with the completion of the main wall, but it is not expected to begin to generate electricity until 2009 when buildings to house its twenty-six turbines, a two-way lock (which became operational in 2004) and a one-step ship lift are finally completed. The total cost of the project has been put at US$25 billion by the PRC official press releases. This is within the parameters of the government's stated budget limit, but critics in China have estimated that the real cost is much higher and figures in excess of US$100 billion have been mentioned.

Criticism of the project falls into three categories: cost effectiveness, environmental degradation and involuntary migration:

1 Because government statistics in China are not available for independent scrutiny, it is not possible to ascertain the genuine cost of the project. Opponents of the dam have argued that not only is the real cost much higher than the publicly quoted costs suggest, but that there has been corruption on a grand scale throughout the whole process, with contractors bribing the development corporation responsible for the project. It is also alleged that the potential output of the dam will be much less than claimed by the government. It had argued that by 2009 it would be capable of supplying some 10 per cent of China's total electricity requirements. In addition there is considerable resentment in China because the dam is designed to supply electricity to the eastern and southeastern provinces, which are already the most highly developed regions, and it will contribute very little to the economic development of its own hinterland.

2 The issue of pollution is more complicated. It is possible to argue that in the longer term, whatever the immediate problems, the dam will reduce China's dependency on fossil fuels – that is, coal, gas and oil. However, in the short term there is concern about potential damage to local ecosystems and in particular to vulnerable species of wildlife, such as the Chinese river dolphin, which are threatened by the degradation of their habitat.

3 The construction also has serious implications for communities living in the immediate area of the dam because the inhabitants of many local villages have been, or will be, relocated to other parts of China. Over a million people have already been moved and some 1,200 towns and villages will have to be abandoned to make way for the dam. The resettlement is being managed by a Three Gorges Resettlement Bureau which, like other aspects of the project, has been accused of operating corruptly.

The environmental and other problems associated with the Three Gorges Dam are not peculiar to China and similar issues have been raised in the case of other large power-generation projects in developing countries. In September 2007, there were renewed warnings about the possibility of the construction of the dam triggering an environmental catastrophe. What made these warnings unusual and compelling was that they came from senior officials responsible for the construction.

The director of the State Council Three Gorges Construction Committee,

Wang Xiaofeng, in a report published by the official Xinhua News Agency after a discussion forum in Wuhan, raised concerns about inappropriate and unwise development in the region which, he contended, could lead to major ecological problems including soil erosion that might result in landslides on the steep hills that surround the dam. Landslips into the river had already caused unusually high waves that had damaged the river banks. The flow of the Yangzi had slowed above the dam, silting was becoming more acute and water pollution, especially reduction in the quality of drinking water for local people, was also causing concern. Wang and a senior engineer, Huang Xuebin, who had responsibility for the control of geological problems associated with the construction, also expressed their disquiet at the impact that the development was having on the lives of local residents. This level of public concern would once have been unusual but it reflects concern at a national level about the relationship between development and environmental problems. Wang was echoing concerns expressed publicly by Premier Wen Jiabao that China was in danger of sacrificing long-term environmental stability for short-term economic growth. In March 2007, when he was still deputy director of the Three Gorges committee, Wang had rejected allegations that the dam was causing major environmental problems and argued that the situation was stable. The change in his emphasis suggests a shift in the balance of environmental concerns in political circles at the national level.[3]

Environmental case study 2: Harbin water pollution

A chemical spillage in November 2005 in the city of Jilin that polluted the Songhua River with benzene and threatened the quality of drinking water supplies to Harbin in neighbouring Heilongjiang province has significant implications for environmental policy, crisis management and openness in the Chinese media.

After the disquiet over China's handling of the SARS crisis, the way that different bodies handled the Harbin water pollution emergency sheds light on the effectiveness of China's crisis management systems. It also raises important questions about the degree of transparency in media reporting and how far an order made in September 2005 which lifted reporting restrictions on natural disasters has genuinely changed attitudes in the press and broadcasting.

A series of explosions (a total of fifteen over a period of five hours) which began at 1:45 p.m. on 13 November destroyed the New Aniline Unit of the PetroChina petrochemical plant in Jilin. Five people were killed, over seventy were injured and the flames were so intense that they could not be extinguished until 4 a.m. the following day. Water from the fire-fighting efforts contributed to the contamination of the Songhua River which flows through Jilin and on to Harbin before running into the Heilong (Amur) River at the border with the Russian Federation, turning what had been a local pollution problem into an international incident.

Managing the crisis involved many different national agencies including the Chinese National Petroleum Corporation (PetroChina) itself; the State Environmental Protection Agency and its political master, the State Council; the provincial governments of Jilin and Heilongjiang; the city administrations of

Jilin and Harbin; the military; and the Foreign Ministry, which had to apologise to Moscow for the impending pollution of the Amur River. China has different levels of contingency plans for emergencies – at the enterprise, county, regional, city, provincial, inter-province and national levels - and these plans were put into effect immediately.

Reports in the official press which are confirmed by informal intelligence from the region suggest that the practical response to the crisis was impressive. Perhaps this is not surprising since water conservancy and hydraulic engineering are the backgrounds of many senior party leaders, including President Hu Jintao, under the 'double-load' system of technical and political training for CCP and government high-fliers that has operated for decades in China. Drilling teams from the Daqing oil field were deployed to dig deep ground-water wells to provide alternative supplies of water. Bottled water was donated by organisations around the country until supplies outstripped demand. Heilongjiang province set aside funds of RMB 10 million to deal with the emergency, with half of that sum being allocated to create new water supplies in residential areas. The People's Liberation Army Air Force sent fire engines and personnel trained to deal with deep wells and the army supplied water to hospitals and old people's homes. There has been no criticism of the speed or effectiveness of the aid and support to Harbin.

The handling of information about the crisis was less impressive. The immediate response of the Jilin authorities was the tried and tested one of saying nothing. When the Harbin municipal government discovered that the Songhua River had been polluted on 21 November, it initially covered up the problem, apparently on the instructions of central government, by claiming that the water had been cut off to allow maintenance work to go ahead. The degree of contamination was not acknowledged until the following day. Reporting of the incident in the Heilongjiang local press was restricted by the local bureaucracy. *People's Daily* in its domestic edition followed suit and information was released very slowly and restricted to pages 4 and 5. The overseas edition of *People's Daily*, which is not aimed at a domestic readership, although it is available in some parts of China, covered the crisis more fully as did its online English-language edition. *China Daily*, which is published only in English and has a tiny readership among Chinese citizens, covered the story in much more detail and on the front page, which could have given the impression to foreign observers that there was far more openness than was actually the case.

The story was gradually taken up by the *China Youth Daily* and the *China Economic Times*, both of which have a track record of publishing more challenging material. Both voiced criticism of a cover-up and the dangers of 'irresponsible lies' by officials and this was repeated in a *China Daily* editorial entitled 'Commentary: cover-up can't hide murky water truth' on 27 November, the day that water supplies to parts of Harbin were due to be restored.

Wen Jiabao, the Premier and (as the Chinese sources always point out) a member of the Standing Committee of the CCP Politburo, played a key role in the crisis. Without announcing his intentions in advance, he visited Harbin on Saturday 26 November to observe the level of water pollution and called for a full enquiry into the incident. This visit was seen as encouragement for local officials and staff in their relief efforts but was also intended as a warning to local governments that they should act decisively on environmental matters. Significantly, he also called for the timely release of information when crises occurred.

Wen, who is a geologist and engineer by training, has made clear his own position that environmental protection should be given far greater priority in the rush for economic growth. He made a speech on scientific sustainable development at the 21st Century Forum in Beijing in September 2005 and, on 23 November, just before travelling to Harbin, he had presided over an executive meeting of the State Council which was sitting to set medium-term targets for environmental protection.

Ironically, as the crisis was unfolding in the northeast, the First National Symposium on Inland Lakes was being held in the Jiangxi provincial capital of Nanchang. This conference heard that 70 per cent of China's rivers were contaminated and that this was affecting lakes and swampland. The causes of this, according to Chen Bangzhu who speaks on population, resources and environment for the advisory Chinese People's Political Consultative Conference, are the economic boom, the expansion of population and irrational development, but also inadequate legislation and surveillance and insufficient media coverage of environmental issues. The environment is the one area in which the CCP has allowed a relatively uncontrolled political debate. Environmental non-government organisations have been allowed to operate with relatively little interference and the support they have received created the first independent grassroots movement that has been tolerated since the CCP came to power in 1949.[4]

This crisis also had an international dimension as the contaminated water flowed towards the Amur River and eventually to the Khabarovsk region of the Russian Far East. China apologised to the government of Russia but Moscow will require assurances that everything possible has been done to prevent a recurrence of such pollution.

Questions have been asked about the causes of such a massive explosion in a strategically important industry but also about the way in which the incident was reported. The relative openness in that section of the press that is aimed at an overseas readership could be extended to the domestic media, although that has not yet happened. Premier Wen Jiabao undoubtedly used the ensuing debate to enhance his environmental credentials and to increase his political support in the northeast.

The immediate impact for the administrations of Jilin and Heilongjiang was the arrival of an inspection team sent from Beijing to inquire into the contamination and to ascertain whether local authorities were remiss in not intervening earlier. The general manager of the Jilin Petrochemical plant was dismissed, as were two of the plant managers who were judged to have been directly responsible for the initial explosions. Finally, in what was widely seen as an attempt by the government to demonstrate its commitment to accountability at the highest level, the director of the State Environmental Protection Administration (SEPA), Xie Zhenhua, submitted his resignation and it was accepted at the beginning of December 2005. SEPA was accused of having underestimated the seriousness of the explosions and their possible environmental and political impact.[5]

Environmental problems and multinational corporations

A particularly complex and politically sensitive issue is the question of the contribution made to China's environmental problems by foreign multinational companies. Concerns have been raised in China about the policies of some multinationals which are alleged to be exporting environmentally hazardous procedures to China where the regulatory framework and the enforcement regime are still underdeveloped in comparison with the West.

In October 2006, Pan Yue, who is Deputy Director of China's Environmental Protection Agency and of Deputy Minister rank, published an essay entitled 'On socialist ecological civilisation'. The title has a disconcerting Maoist ring about it, but the main thrust of his argument is important.

> With the rise of globalisation, developed countries have transferred their industry to developing nations as a form of environmental colonialism. In China, pollution has been moved from east to west and from the city to the rural areas. The rich consume and the poor suffer the pollution. The economic and environmental inequalities caused by a flawed understanding of growth and political achievement, held by some officials, have gone against the basic aims of socialism and abandoned the achievements of Chinese socialism.[6]

Other critics within China have gone further and have accused specific multinational companies of pursuing a policy of 'eco-colonialism', focusing their attention particularly on the transfer of waste processing and waste disposal projects to China, while some Western commentators have accused China of blaming the multinationals for what is essentially a domestic problem caused by the expansion of China's economy.[7]

Part IV

Politics and international relations

15 Government and politics

The formal structure of China's government in the early years of the People's Republic (PRC) closely followed the model of the Soviet Union which was a one-party state. Only one political party, the Chinese Communist Party (CCP), wielded any real political power; in the same way that the Communist Party of the Soviet Union was the only political authority in the USSR. In China there are also eight minor parties, known collectively as the Democratic Parties: the continuing existence of these political groupings reflects alliances that the Communist Party had made during the closing years of the Civil War in the 1940s. They played an important role in the early 1950s but their influence declined, especially after the Anti-Rightist campaign of 1957, and is now negligible.

In practice China was, and still is, governed under a dual Party–state system in which organs of government are shadowed by CCP monitoring bodies. This parallel system of checks and controls stretches from the very top of the central administration right down to the lowest level of the state, the government of the townships. There is, however, considerable overlap between personnel in the government and Party bodies and also with members of the armed forces, the People's Liberation Army.

Formal government has frequently been overshadowed and undermined by mass political campaigns which were a regular feature of China's political culture in the first thirty years of the PRC and were particularly associated with Mao's distinctive brand of revolutionary romanticism. The campaigns were a symbol of Mao's determination to press forward with the Revolution and to destabilise institutions, even those that had been set up by the CCP itself, if they were in danger of becoming entrenched and ossified. The culture of political campaigns has not completely died out but campaigns are now directed at very specific policy targets and are used in a more sophisticated and focused way.

Constitutions of the People's Republic

The first constitution, or more properly proto-constitution, of the PRC was the *Common Programme* that was adopted in 1949 by a broad range of parties under the guidance of the CCP. By 1954, after the end of the Korean War and the conclusion of the most violent phase of the political campaigns that the CCP used to consolidate its power, the PRC was ready to move towards the adoption of a full constitution. The first constitution proper was adopted by the first National People's Congress on 20 September 1954. It was drafted by a constitutional committee and drew heavily on the 1936 Constitution of the Soviet Union. It enshrined the principle that the PRC would be led by the working class, which effectively guaranteed that the CCP, which viewed itself as the representative of the working class, would dominate China for the foreseeable future.

The Constitution outlined the structure of the Chinese government, known at the time as the Central People's Government, and its major organs of state. The highest authority was to be a quasi-parliamentary body, the National People's Congress (NPC) (*Quanguo renmin daibiao dahui*) and the State Council (*Guowuyuan*), headed by the Premier, was created as the executive body of the state. Local People's Congresses at provincial and local level were also established, creating a hierarchy of bodies in which, formally at least, the lower levels selected representatives to attend the higher. The Constitution also outlined the rights and duties of citizens and established the national flag: a red flag with five stars and the national emblem – Tian'anmen, the southern gate of the Forbidden City, under the light of five stars in the centre, surrounded by ears of grain and a cogwheel at the base.[1] The flag was chosen as the result of a competition and represented the political symbolism of the time. The red background was intended to represent 'revolutionary enthusiasm' but also had echoes of Ming imperial red, the colour of the last Han Chinese dynasty; the large star represented the Communist Party and the four smaller ones the four classes of 'the people' that were in alliance with the CCP in the period of New Democracy: the national bourgeoisie, the petty bourgeoisie, the working class and the peasantry. It is also oddly resonant of the flag of the Guomindang's Republic of China and the Nationalist concept of the five nations of China: Han, Manchu, Mongol, Tibetan and Muslim. There is some confusion in China today about the symbolism of the stars; many accounts avoid the issue and simply say that the stars represent the relationship between the CCP and the people of China.

Although the Constitution is couched in democratic terms with many references to elections, it does not require very close reading to discern the considerable power wielded by the Standing Committee of the NPC and the State Chairman (President). Control of these positions meant control of the government. Elections did take place, but the electoral processes, which were set out in separate legislation, made it possible for the CCP to control the nomination of candidates to the elections at all levels and thus to control the entire process. The term 'Central People's Government' gradually fell into disuse but the executive arm of the government of China is still known as the State Council.

This Constitution was revised and simplified during the Cultural Revolution and the revised version that was published in 1975 contained a great deal of Maoist rhetoric. A third version was promulgated in 1978 shortly after the death of Mao, but the Constitution that is currently in force is the version that was drawn up in 1982 at the beginning of the 'reform and opening' period. It reinstated the position of State Chairman (President), which had been removed during the Cultural Revolution. This is a role distinct from that of Party Chairman although both posts have been held, and continue to be held, by the same individual. The new version also restored clauses on the role of courts of law, which had been expunged from the previous version. It has been in operation since 1982 but has been amended several times: the version currently in force is the text that was amended at the Tenth National People's Congress on 14 March 2004 and includes clauses on human rights, the mixed economy and private property.

National People's Congress

Under the Constitution, the highest authority of the state is the NPC, which is a body of representatives elected by the provinces, autonomous regions and the largest cities. It stands at the apex of a nationwide hierarchical network of people's congresses. Members of the NPC serve for a term of five years, and the full NPC meets annually, normally for two weeks in Beijing in the first quarter of each year (that is, during the spring), and has the authority to amend the Constitution, to enact legislation, to elect a Premier (who is nominated by the State Chairman) and the heads of the Supreme People's Court and the Procuratorate (the state prosecution service), and to rule on economic plans. When the NPC is not in session, its functions are exercised by a Standing Committee, which has very wide powers, including the authority to conduct elections, to convene its own sessions, to interpret legislation enacted by the full Congress and to supervise other state bodies including the State Council and the courts.

The NPC elects the Chairman of the PRC, the equivalent of a President in many republics, who has the power to nominate a Premier and senior ministers and officials and has the supreme authority to act in relations with foreign countries. The NPC also elects the Chairman of the powerful Military Affairs Commission and the President of the Supreme Court. It maintains eight permanent special committees which have responsibility for drawing up legislation on key domestic and foreign policy areas: finance and economics; education, science, culture and public health; ethnic minorities; foreign affairs; overseas Chinese; internal and judicial affairs; legal matters; and the environment.[2] The operation of the NPC and its Standing Committee is governed by two documents, the *Organic Law* of the NPC and the *Procedural Rules* of the NPC, which were revised in 1982 and 1989 respectively.

The degree of formality and tradition that this entails may suggest that the functions and status of the NPC are equivalent to those of a parliament in a Western-style democracy, but this is not the case. It has approximately 3,000 members and this makes it too cumbersome to function effectively as a debating body. Many of its powers are delegated to the Standing Committee which has 153 members (2006 figure – the number can vary slightly) and meets on a bi-monthly basis. Although the NPC formally approves new legislation, it does not in general initiate it. Most legislation is originated by CCP bodies and passed to the NPC, in which the CCP has in any case a substantial built-in majority – over two-thirds.

During the 1990s, the NPC began to flex its muscles and for a time appeared to be able to exercise a degree of independent judgement on some technical aspects of legislation, including tax laws. Increased attention has been paid to the meetings of the NPCs in recent years because they are now more open. In addition to the work reports that the President, Premier and other senior figures have always presented in public, press conferences are now held and foreign print and media journalists are permitted to attend.

NPCs since 1949 and their Chairmen

1 September 1954	Liu Shaoqi
2 April 1959	Zhu De
3 December 1964	Zhu De
4 January 1975	Zhu De
6 March 1978	Ye Jianying
6 June 1983	Peng Zhen
7 March 1988	Wan Li
8 March 1993	Qiao Shi
9 March 2003	Wu Bangguo

State Council

The State Council (*Guowuyuan*) was created as the executive body of the state, under the Premier and with ministries and commissions subordinate to it. It is formally responsible to the NPC, or to the Standing Committee of the NPC when the NPC is not in session, but it has far more authority than that might suggest. It functions in a manner similar to that of a cabinet in a Western parliamentary system and its members, who include the Premier, Vice-Premiers, members of the State Council and the Secretary-General of the State Council, are the most senior political figures in China's government. One of its most significant functions has always been the creation of the Five-Year Plans under which China's economy is still managed, but it also has broad responsibilities for law and order and supervises the work of China's ministries and specialist commissions. The State Council has monthly meetings but has a Standing Committee which meets at least once a week.

Chinese People's Political Consultative Conference

This government body, which has the most cumbersome and unpronounceable English title of all Chinese political organs, is usually referred to in English by its abbreviation, the CPPCC. It is a remnant of the attempts by the CCP in 1949 to create broad-based support for its policies in a united front, a term drawn from the Soviet Union under Stalin. This nod in the direction of inclusiveness did not last long but the CPPCC remained in place and includes delegates from ethnic minority groups, religious organisations and the small number of legal non-CCP political organisations. It is useful to the CCP as a sounding board for the impact of its policies on minority groups and meets annually in Beijing in the spring, at the same time as the NPC.

Chinese Communist Party

In 2007, the membership of the CCP (*Zhongguo gongchandang*) stood at seventy-three million, which almost certainly makes it the largest single political party anywhere in the world. The great majority of its members are male (83 per cent) and most are over thirty-five years of age (78 per cent). Government officials, military officers and carefully selected model employees from the state sector have traditionally been the most important component of the membership. In 2002, when reforms were introduced by Jiang Zemin to encourage previously unaligned businessmen and more women, scientists, academics, writers and artists to join the Party, it became clear that the CCP was no longer (if it ever had been, since 1949 at least) the preserve of political militants and Marxist idealists. A report issued by the CCP's Organisation Department just before the Party's Seventeenth Congress in October 2007 showed that, between 2002 and 2007, the size of the membership had increased by over six million: there were noticeable increases in the recruitment of women and people from the 'new social strata' – that is, the business and managerial classes.[3]

The CCP provides the body of men and women on whom the state can draw for political, social and economic leadership at all levels of society. It is a tightly disciplined, self-selecting elite group that is part of the career ladder for young Chinese people who aspire to important roles in government and society. Young aspirants can only become members after years of preparatory work, comprehensive tests and the support of senior members of their local Party branch. The benefits of membership are considerable: in addition to the support that the Party provides for careers in public organisations, members have always enjoyed access to superior housing, better education for their children and privileged sources of information which are denied to the majority of the population. In a society where *guanxi* (connections) are supremely important, the *guanxi* provided by the CCP are second to none. The CCP controls its membership by the Leninist principle of democratic centralism. In theory, this means that policy is decided on by mass democratic debate and, once decided on, is adhered to by all the members. In practice, in China as in the former Soviet Union, the centralism has always taken priority and the democracy was, and remains, difficult to discern.

The CCP has a top-down structure in which the lower level units are required to subordinate themselves to the higher, and ultimately to the central bodies in Beijing: the more junior members subordinate themselves to the more senior. This to some extent explains the continued influence during the 1980s and 1990s of Party elders who frequently restricted political developments and blocked policy changes long after they had retired from their formal positions. Deng Xiaoping, whose opinions were deferred to long after his retirement, and Jiang Zemin, who attempted to cling on to control of the Central Military Commission and then to manipulate the central Party organisations through his Shanghai faction, are the two highest profile examples of this. Retired senior Party officials are accorded special privileges and in many cases their sons and daughters are able to take advantage of the positions of their parents to secure political advantage or, alternatively, to advance their careers including, in an increasing number of cases, successful business careers.

The CCP is rather like grandfather's axe. Since its formation in 1921, it has had several new heads and countless new hafts to replace the broken ones, but it is still perceived as one organisation with a continuous existence, in spite of the internecine factional disputes that have often threatened to tear it apart and which are acknowledged in the copious accounts of Party history that have been published.

The longevity and tenaciousness of the Party are testimony to an underlying characteristic that has often been obscured by the political rhetoric of the day. Underneath the veneer of Marxism or Maoism (officially Marxism-Leninism, Mao Zedong Thought), there has been a constant emphasis on the national interests of China and the glory of the Chinese nation, past as well as present. After the death of Mao Zedong in 1976 and the implementation of Deng Xiaoping's reform programme in the 1980s, a dramatic shift in policy which appeared to dispense with or at least to reverse the entire previous economic policy of the CCP, it was to a large extent this patriotism or nationalism that enabled the Party to retain its dominant political position in China.

Since the beginning of the reform period there has been an attempt to broaden the base of the Party: the decision by Jiang Zemin to take active measures to recruit men and women from the world of business was controversial in China and caused raised eyebrows among international observers. This move reflected the changing role of ideology in the Party. What began as an imitation of Soviet-style Marxism-Leninism and an adaptation to Chinese conditions led to the emergence of Mao Zedong Thought in the early 1960s. Since the death of Mao, the role of ideology has diminished, gradually at first when radical economic reforms were launched under cover of a degree of ideological window dressing, and then dramatically. The CCP now appears to be a pragmatic and patriotic governing party but the announcement of the death of ideology in China may be premature: the domestic Chinese-language editions of *People's Daily* and other publications aimed primarily at Party and government officials are still couched in the old bureaucratic Marxist terms.

The CCP maintains its own internal training and ideological programme, at the head of which is the Central Party School, an elite body which has the responsibility of training the next generation of the Party leadership. There is a provincial network of Party Schools subordinate to the central body. The Party also guards its secret historical archives with great care and has an academic department, the Party History Research Centre, and its own publishing house: they are the authorised specialists in Party history and publish books on the current approved version of past controversies.

At the base of the Party structure are the local branches, which can be found in villages, towns and cities, but more significantly in all enterprises, including schools, factories, large shops and offices and military units. This penetration to the grassroots level has been one of the strengths of the CCP and one of the reasons for its ability to survive. The Party branches are not only the power base for the CCP in that locality and a reservoir to draw on when government officials are required, but they have also been used as a powerful tool for the local implementation of national policies, whether they were economic plans or delicate matters of social engineering such as the one-child policy.

The government-run news agency, Xinhua, revealed in July 2007 that as many as three million members of the CCP are employed by private firms – a considerable growth in recent years. It has been argued that this gives private businesses a voice in the corridors of CCP power, but it also gives the CCP a remarkable source of information on the internal workings of private businesses. During the 1950s when the CCP, newly arrived in the cities after the Civil War, was implementing its policy of nationalising private firms, members of the CCP branches who were working in these firms were put on to the boards of directors of their companies as a prelude to the state's taking control. In the twenty-first century this is not likely to be the function of CCP members in private industry, but the Party will certainly use them to monitor the management of firms and to ensure their compliance with government policy.[4]

Chinese Communist Party Congresses

According to the Constitution of the CCP, the National Party Congress (Conference) is the supreme policy-making body.[5] It is supposed to meet regularly – every five years – although that was honoured more in the breach than in the observance throughout the chaotic days of the Cultural Revolution and during Mao Zedong's final years in power. The number of delegates varies but is usually in the region of 2,000. All have been elected by Party members in their constituencies but it is an open secret that there is rarely, if ever, any choice of delegates and the election is rather a selection from an approved list of Party members. In practice, far from functioning as the supreme authority in the CCP, the National Congress gives formal and public approval to policies that have already been determined by those Party bodies that exercise genuine power, the Central Committee and the Politburo. The Sixteenth Party Congress met in November 2002 and the Seventeenth convened on 16 October 2007.

Central Committee and Politburo

Supreme political power resides, therefore, not in the Party Conference but in the two smaller bodies which are notionally subordinate to it, the Central Committee and the Politburo. The members of the Central Committee (200 full members and 150 alternate members) are formally elected by the Party Congress but this is not an open election and the names of candidates are approved in advance from a *nomenklatura* list in line with long-standing Chinese, and before that Soviet, practice.

The Politburo (the standard Russian abbreviation for Political Bureau, *zhengzhi ju*) which consists of twenty-two people is the centre of power in the CCP. The Politburo is selected from the Central Committee and is therefore the elite of the elite. It includes the most powerful faction leaders and also regional and provincial CCP secretaries.

There is an even smaller and more powerful group, the Standing Committee of the Politburo, which meets on a more regular basis. At the time of writing, it consists of nine people although there have been seven members in the recent past and sometimes as few as five, and it is effectively the group that runs China on a day-to-day basis. The most senior Party and government leaders – including the Secretary-General of the CCP, the Chairman of the NPC and the Chairman of the Central Discipline Inspection Commission – are all members of the Standing Committee. The deliberations and even the times of the meetings of the Standing Committee are not made public and there are no formal minutes openly available but there is sufficient anecdotal evidence to indicate that its meetings have often been very difficult, that 'struggle' (*douzheng*) is more common than discussion and that when a consensus or a majority decision is finally reached, this has often been after long and bitter dispute. Politburo Standing Committee members in December 2006 were: Hu Jintao, Wu Bangguo, Wen Jiabao, Jia Qinglin, Zeng Qinghong, Huang Ju, Wu Guanzheng, Li Changchun and Luo Gan.

After the Seventeenth Communist Party Congress, held in October 2007, the membership of the Standing Committee remained at nine. The new membership, in order of formal precedence and with their portfolios as known at the time, consists of: Hu Jintao (President of the PRC, Secretary-General of the CCP and Chairman of the Central Military Commission), Wu Bangguo (Chairman of the Standing Committee of the NPC), Wen Jiabao (Premier of the State Council), Jia Qinglin (Chairman of the CPPCC), Li Changchun (propaganda supremo), Xi Jinping (Head of the CCP Secretariat), Li Keqiang, He Guoqiang (Head of the CCP Organisation Department) and Zhou Yongkang (Minister of Public Security). Of the 2006 membership, Huang Ju had died during the year and Zeng Qinghong's resignation, which had not been widely expected outside the inner circles of the CCP, was accepted. Zeng had been Jiang Zemin's chief supporter within the higher echelons of the CCP and, although it is said that he asked to resign as he was approaching retirement age, he was clearly forced out.

Secretariat

The Secretariat is the administrative arm of the Politburo and exercises considerable political influence in terms of access to the most senior leaders. Most of its importance can be attributed to the fact that it is the political power base and the tool of the Secretary-General of the CCP.

Organisation Department

The Organisation Department is the bureaucratic heart of the CCP. It maintains a vast and comprehensive filing system, monitors the careers of all Party officials, assesses their performance and collects evidence for promotions. Its authority extends to the thousands of officials who are appointed to provincial and lower government bodies.

Central Discipline Commission

The Central Discipline Commission is the highest body in the network of Party discipline committees which monitor the management of the Party and adherence to policy. From time to time it is also charged with rooting out corruption among the most senior officials. The discipline inspection commissions have access to their own network of moles and informers and have been known to wield power ruthlessly. Ensuring the compliance of Party members with current policy decisions is their main role but they are also used in factional disputes and even the most senior leaders are not immune from their investigation. In 1998, the former Secretary of the Beijing CCP, Chen Xitong, was investigated by the Central Discipline Commission and sentenced to sixteen years imprisonment after having been found guilty of corruption in what was seen as part of an internal power struggle. In 2000, Cheng Kejie, who had served as Deputy Chairman of the NPC, was executed after having been accused of accepting bribes to a total value of US$5 million but this was an exceptional case.

Chinese Communist Youth League

As its name suggests, the Communist Youth League (CYL) (*Gongchanzhuyi qingnian tuan*) is the junior branch of the CCP. It was originally modelled on the *Komsomol* of the Soviet Union and serves as one of the most important conduits for recruiting potential Party members. Its influence extends far beyond that role and former members of the CYL have become one of the most important factional groupings within the Party. It has its own newspaper, *China Youth Daily*, which has acquired a well-deserved reputation for independence, radical journalism and attacks on corruption.

Factions within the Chinese Communist Party

There is no open recognition of the existence of political factions within the CCP, although they do exist and play a crucial role in intra-party discussion and conflict and in the careers of individuals. They are not necessarily factions in the sense that they are groups fighting for a clear political agenda within the Party. A more accurate term might be 'personal networks': individual members of the Party who seek promotion or preference will attach themselves to a more senior member with whom they can claim, or can develop, political *guanxi*.[6] In the early days of the PRC, these personal factions were often associated with the particular military unit to which individuals had been attached in the Civil War. In contemporary China, they are more likely to be the powerful political machines established in China's most prosperous regions. The Shanghai faction, which brought Jiang Xemin to power as President and still exercises considerable influence within the Party and the government, is the best known of these. Another faction is based on former members of the CYL, which is the power base on which Hu Jintao build his candidacy. These are only the tip of the iceberg since the entire

Party apparatus is riddled with factions and interest groups, most of which do not have a name or an individual leader who is well known outside the corridors of power in Beijing.

Some reformers have been calling for a recognition of the existence of internal Party factions as part of a commitment to a more open and democratic structure. This has been resisted as it is inimical to the fundamental principle of democratic centralism, which insists that the CCP should always present itself as one body with one mind and one will.

The political transition from Jiang Zemin to Hu Jintao was noteworthy because it was accomplished without factional disputes spilling over into public conflict. The Great Leap Forward and the Cultural Revolution can be understood partly as precisely that and the current leadership is taking pains to avoid the chaos that was produced by these tactics. As a result of Jiang Zemin's Three Represents[7] policy, which encouraged entrepreneurs to join the CCP, the potential for the proliferation of new factions has increased greatly. It remains to be seen whether these can be contained within the CCP and whether there will be pressure from the newer members, either for their factions to be recognised publicly or for the creation of new political bodies.

Minority 'democratic' parties

There is a group of political parties, left over from the negotiations that took place at the time of the foundation of the PRC in 1949, which broadly agreed with the then programme of the CCP and have been allowed to remain in existence. They are the Revolutionary Committee of the Guomindang, a left-wing splinter group of the main Nationalist Party; China Democratic League; China Democratic National Construction Association; China Association for the Promotion of Democracy; Chinese Peasants' and Workers' Democratic Party; Chinese Party for Public Interest (*Zhigongdang*); September Third Society and the Taiwan Democratic Self-Government League.

The democratic parties have been retained as they provided evidence of the CCP's willingness to engage in united front politics and to consult a wider constituency than their own members. They were consulted in the early days of the PRC but, like other non-CCP organisations, they fell foul of the intellectual repression of the Hundred Flowers and Anti-Rightist campaigns in the mid-1950s. The democratic parties had provided much of the trenchant criticism of CCP practices that was published during the Hundred Flowers period but, at the end of the movement, members of these parties who were most sympathetic to the CCP or who even had dual membership were given the task of identifying and denouncing 'rightists' in their own ranks and these names were handed over to the Public Security Bureau during August and September 1957. As a result of these acts of betrayal, perhaps as many as 12,000 members of the democratic parties were identified as rightists, dismissed from their posts and sent to the countryside or to industrial complexes for re-education through labour. Any vestige of genuine political influence that these parties had exercised was destroyed in this campaign.

They were unable to attract new members and they became completely irrelevant to the political process although they remain in formal existence to this day.

Illegal and underground political parties

There are no legal opposition parties in China – the 'democratic' parties described above cannot be described as being in opposition to the CCP – and it has been almost impossible for dissidents, or anyone who wishes to express an alternative political voice, to organise themselves in any open manner. During the chaotic days of the Cultural Revolution when many normal forms of political control were removed or relaxed, there were attempts to do so. Some of the Red Guard factions that emerged in response to Mao's call to rebel began to look like political parties and they were soon curbed as the CCP sought to rebuild itself after 1969. The most interesting of these was the leftist umbrella grouping in Hunan province that went by the name of *Shengwulian*, an abbreviation for Hunan Province Revolutionary Great Alliance Committee. *Shengwulian* issued a manifesto, *Whither China?*, in March 1968 which attacked Mao and his supporters as a new type of bureaucratic ruling class and called for a social revolution against them led by the workers and peasants. It proposed the establishment of a national version of the People's Communes as a form of mass democracy. This idea was swiftly denounced by Party leaders at a mass rally in the Hunan capital of Changsha. The political organisation that would be used to control China in the late 1960s and 1970s was the system of Revolutionary Committees, controlled by the military, which the CCP used to bring the Cultural Revolution to an end and not organs modelled on the mass democracy of the Paris Commune.

During the Cultural Revolution, there were also attempts to form political parties in the ethnic minority border regions. Inner Mongolians began to associate themselves into a movement for an independent southern Mongolia and, in Xinjiang, the Eastern Turkestan People's Party was launched with covert assistance from the Soviet Union. These organisations were short-lived and were swiftly crushed when the authority of the CCP and its government was re-established at the end of the Cultural Revolution.

Perhaps the only real opposition movement of any significance to emerge since the Cultural Revolution was the China Democratic Party, which argued for the democratic reform of the Chinese political system. This party can be traced back to the 'democracy wall' activists of the late 1970s who argued for genuine democracy in the years immediately after the death of Mao Zedong and, in its most recent incarnation, to the democracy movement of 1989 which was suppressed by the military on 4 June. The organisation was declared illegal in China – the fact that its name was identical to one belonging to an organisation created in Taiwan during the period of martial law did not help – and its best known activist, Xu Wenli, spent over sixteen years in prison for his political activities. Nonetheless it has continued to exist in exile in Europe and in the United States.

There have been reports of a number of initiatives to establish opposition parties since, with the most recent being the announcement in December 2007 of the formation of a New Democracy Party by Guo Quan, a former academic at the Nanjing Normal University (Teachers' College). The New Democracy Party advocates the abolition of the single-party dictatorship that is exercised by the CCP and its replacement by a multi-party system. The name of the new group, New Democracy, harks back to the more inclusive and broader-based politics of the early 1950s. The authorities are unlikely to allow this party to operate openly and Guo's home has already been searched by police. He claims that his party has hundreds of supporters and the tacit support of thousands more.[8]

People's Liberation Army

The roots of the modern People's Liberation Army (PLA) lie in the armed defence units created by the CCP during the uprisings of 1927 that were precipitated by the breakdown of the party's political alliance with the Guomindang (GMD). These units were known as the Workers' and Peasants' Red Army (*Gongnong hongjun*) and 1 August, the date of the formal creation of this Red Army in the Jiangxi city of Nanchang, is still celebrated as Army Day in the PRC. Throughout the second period of cooperation (Second United Front) between the CCP and the GMD during the Japanese Occupation that lasted from 1937 to 1945, the Red Army units did not use their own titles but went under names such as Eighth Route Army and New Fourth Army to suggest that they were part of a single national military organisation: in fact, they functioned to a large extent as independent units with their own command structures and political commissars. The independence of these units was re-asserted at the beginning of the Civil War that followed the capitulation of the occupying Japanese army in August 1945 and the CCP forces were re-designated the Chinese People's Liberation Army (*Zhongguo renmin jiefang jun*) on 1 May 1946.

Power did grow out of the barrel of a gun. If it had not been for the victory of its armed units during the Civil War, the CCP could not have formed the government of the PRC in 1949. After the Civil War, the PLA established its position in China through the military campaigns to bring the outlying territories, including Tibet and Xinjiang, under the control of Beijing. It enhanced its prestige greatly during the Korean War when, under the flag of the Chinese People's Volunteers, it was pitted against the technically superior forces of the United States which headed a United Nations coalition. More controversial was its role in the fighting with Soviet troops at the Ussuri River, on the border with the Russian Far Eastern region, in 1989 and China's military invasion of Vietnam in 1979.

The relationship between the PLA and the CCP has been close and symbiotic. Although the institutions have remained formally separate, it was often difficult to distinguish between the senior personnel of the two during the war years and, since 1949, PLA officers have served in Party organs. There is also a CCP structure within the PLA which ensures that the military remain fully informed of CCP policies. Notwithstanding Mao's dictum that 'the Party always commands the gun: the gun shall never command the Party', the military and its ethos have played a significant and at times dominant role in the political direction of the CCP. During the final chaotic months of the Cultural Revolution, the military dominated the political structures to such an extent that much of China was effectively under martial law. Service in the PLA was regarded as proof of loyalty, discipline and patriotism and therefore became a useful step on the road to Party membership. Many former soldiers returned to their villages with the prestige, authority and ideological training that would set them on the road to a Party and government career, even if only at the local level. Since the end of the Cultural Revolution, the role of the PLA in politics has been downgraded. With increased professionalism came a separation from national politics and there is no longer a representative of the army on the Standing Committee of the Politburo, the key decision-making body in China. During the 1980s the military was allowed, and even encouraged, to develop business interests: for some individuals, these were extremely lucrative. This policy was curbed during Jiang Zemin's presidency because of the prevalence of corruption and the fear that the army was losing its focus on defence, and the size of the military was drastically reduced.

The formal link between the army and the Party is the CCP's Central Military Affairs Commission (CMAC), which exercises political control over the military and is the body from which Deng Xiaoping and Jiang Zemin were, in turn, reluctant to resign as Chairman. This gives an indication of the authority of that committee. Technically there are two Military Affairs Commissions, the second being a government body that is operated under the auspices of the NPC. It is the CCP's CMAC that exercises real authority over the armed forces and, because the membership of the two bodies overlaps, they function to all intents and purposes as one organisation. At the time when all CCP leaders had at least some military experience, as was the case in the first twenty or thirty years of the PRC, there were direct and informal personal and individual relationships between the Party and the military. In contemporary China, few of the most senior political figures have a military background (many of them being university-trained engineers and technologists who have also had a thorough political education within the CCP) and the military has developed its own separate professionally trained cadre of officers, so the formal institutional relationship has become more important.

The CMAC normally has a membership of eleven, most of whom are senior military officers of general rank. However, the Chairman and Deputy Chairman are always from the highest echelons of the CCP and the Chairman of the CCP automatically becomes the Chairman of the CMAC, although this is formally subject to ratification by the NPC. The remit of the CMAC is the oversight of all matters military: this includes the appointment of senior officers, budget allocations, the size of the PLA and the deployment of its military units.

The CMAC also controls the People's Armed Police (PAP), which is a strategic paramilitary police unit (paralleled to some extent by the Gendarmerie in France or the Carabinieri in Italy) that was established in 1983 and is deployed in riot control and in the most politically delicate situations, such as operations against pro-independence groups in Tibet and Xinjiang. The PAP is also charged with the duty of guarding senior members of the government and the CCP and with protecting the most significant state installations, including Zhongnanhai, the walled area to the west of the Imperial Palace (Forbidden City) in Beijing, which is where the senior leadership live and work – China's Kremlin. There is a clear boundary between the PAP, which is part of the military and recruits many former soldiers, and the civilian police authorities, the *Gong'anju*, which are the responsibility of the Ministry of Public Security (*Gong'anbu*).

In March 2003, the NPC was presented with a budget for increasing military expenditure by 9.6 per cent, the lowest increase for over a decade. China has increased its expenditure on the PLA each year, although it is widely assumed that the publicly announced budget represents only perhaps a quarter of the real total expenditure once the costs of the purchase of armaments and research and development are included.[9]

The PLA has also played a part in economic development, particularly in the outlying areas, and has been called upon for support by the civil authorities in times of natural disasters – for example, during the great earthquake which devastated the Tangshan region in 1976 and in the many episodes of severe flooding in southern China. The PLA played a major part in the rescue and relief effort after both the Sichuan earthquake and the floods of 2008.

Conscription and volunteers

Although all citizens of the PRC are formally required to be available for military service, in peacetime this is entirely voluntary and there is generally no shortage of recruits, who traditionally came from the rural areas. Service in the PLA still confers status and not only is it a way for young peasants to leave their home villages and travel around China but it is also a sound basis for securing a government job later in life. At the age of eighteen, everyone has to register with the government authorities unless they have a place at a university, in which case they will be required to undertake a programme of military training at the beginning of their course.

The PLA conducts its nationwide recruitment exercise once a year during the winter and the formal basis for recruitment and conscription is the *Military Service Law* of 1984 which provides for compulsory and voluntary elements of military service and for the operation of a militia in addition to the regular armed forces. All citizens between the ages of eighteen and twenty-two are technically eligible for military service. They become eligible on 31 December of the year in which they reach their eighteenth birthday, are required to register before 30 September of that year and then remain eligible for conscription until they are twenty-two years of age. The assumption is that most recruits will be men but women are also enlisted. No one who is the sole breadwinner for their family or is a full-time student can be required to enlist.

Out of almost ten million men who reach military age in any given year, fewer than 10 per cent are in fact recruited into the army and the number of women who are recruited annually is small. During the 1980s the PLA modified its conscription policies in an attempt to increase the quality of recruits. The higher educational standards that have been required since then went some way to counter the previous dominance of rural recruits and there is now significant recruitment from the towns and cities.[10] The PLA recruitment office issued two interim regulations in 2006, requiring that all applicants for the armed forces should take psychological tests. This was in response to concerns that had been expressed by senior military officers about the suitability of recruits in the past.[11]

Although the existence of a CCP organisation within the military and a strong sense of common interest bind the Party and the army together, it cannot be assumed that the views of the CCP and the PLA are identical. There is evidence that the PLA are far more hawkish on certain key issues of international relations than the main body of the CCP and that, in certain foreign policy debates, there is considerable tension between the two groups. Members of the PLA, and in particular its officer corps, are deeply imbued with a powerful sense of what they would regard as patriotism, but outsiders might view as nationalism, in their determination to protect the motherland (*zuguo* – a more accurate translation would be something like 'ancestral homeland'). In particular, many senior and middle-ranking officers in the military are deeply attached to what they perceive as their highest patriotic duty – the recovery of Taiwan for the PRC.

The PLA celebrated its eightieth anniversary on 1 August 2007. To mark this milestone, a sizeable and well-attended exhibition was mounted by the Military Museum of the Chinese People's Revolution, which is on Fuxing Road in the Haidian district of Beijing and is dedicated to the history of the PLA. The aim of the exhibition was to demonstrate not only the longevity of the PLA and its central role in the construction of the PRC – and thus the legitimacy of its contemporary political influence – but also its transformation from a highly politicised peasant army into a modern professional force. The twenty-first-century Chinese military machine is equipped with advanced weaponry, including nuclear weapons, and is determined to extend its global reach with its fleet of five long-range type 094 Jin class nuclear ballistic missile submarines and, in the longer term, aircraft carriers.[12]

The PLA is dominated by senior officers of the land forces but the navy and the air force play significant roles and the role of the navy in particular is likely to become more vital to China's Pacific defence strategy in the future.

Political campaigns

A list of the formal decision-making bodies within the CCP or the Chinese government gives only a partial, and in a sense misleading, picture of the way that politics has dominated China since 1949. A series of dramatic mass political movements or campaigns (*yundong*), designed to persuade or coerce the populace into accepting the policy or political trend current at the time, began in the 1950s and lasted until after the Cultural Revolution. These movements began with a series of mainly urban political campaigns in the 1950s, of which the most important were the Suppression of Counter-Revolutionaries, Three-Anti and Five-Anti campaigns. They followed on from each other and to some extent overlapped and they took place at a time of great international tension – the outbreak of the Korean War – during which the isolation of the PRC became almost complete.

The first targets of the campaigns for suppressing counter-revolutionaries were individuals who were deemed to have been active opponents of the CCP, but as the campaign unfolded it drew in thousands of minor officials who had worked for the Nationalist Guomindang or had simply been associated with its government and their past conduct was investigated in detail. Many were exonerated but others were convicted and imprisoned or executed. The campaign was carried out in part through the courts, but it was also a mass movement which is said to have involved 80 per cent of the population. There were mass meetings at which alleged counter-revolutionaries were denounced before they were executed and individuals were forced to betray people they knew had been involved with the previous regime.

The Three-Anti, or Sanfan, campaign was publicised as a mass movement to counter corruption, waste and the culture of bureaucracy. It was aimed primarily at officials who were employed in government departments that were responsible for financial and economic affairs and who were suspected of being implicated in corruption through official contacts with the old commercial and banking elite.

At the same time as the Three-Anti campaign, a parallel campaign was being mounted against another set of evils, this time five in number: bribery, tax evasion, fraud, theft of government property and the leakage of state secrets. This was the Five-Anti (Wufan) movement and it was directed against the 'national bourgeoisie', the industrialists and powerful merchants who had until then been treated as allies, since those who had not collaborated with the Japanese could be included in that category.

Hundred Flowers and Anti-Rightist campaigns

A campaign to bring educated Chinese into line with CCP policies was framed around the celebrated call to 'let a hundred flowers bloom and a hundred schools of thought contend' (*baihua qifang, baijia zhengming*), a phrase that had echoes of the glorious days of ancient Chinese philosophy. The slogan was vague enough to allow for a range of interpretations but the message it was intended to convey was that there was room for a plurality of views. The fact that it was conveyed with a classical slogan was intended to reassure traditional scholars and the older professionals and to bolster the idea that this was a Chinese way of solving the problem. The implication was that there would now be greater intellectual freedom and also that it would be possible for the educated classes to criticise the bureaucracy. In practice, it led to the denigration and isolation of much of China's educated class and this was formalised in the subsequent Anti-Rightist campaign which stigmatised and punished tens of thousands of professionals who had been identified as opponents of Mao. The damaging effect of this campaign on the families and careers of people accused of being 'rightists' lasted for decades.

Great Leap Forward

In the late 1950s and early 1960s, the Great Leap Forward dominated the press and newsreel film in China as well as the nascent television industry. There were constant images of the mass mobilisation of people from all walks of life, leaving their routine jobs and delighting in voluntary labour in the service of the state to complete some essential public works project. The drab and uniform clothing that men and women wore at the time – approximating to military battledress in blue, or sometimes green or grey, denim – gave rise to the notion that China was a nation of an 'army of blue ants' on the move. The images of labour mobilisation were accompanied by overt political slogans and with increasing frequency by portraits of Mao Zedong, an illustration of the growing 'cult of the personality' on the model that Mao and his supporters had borrowed from Stalin. The Great Leap Forward ended in catastrophe, with famine stalking the countryside and millions dead from hunger and disease.

Cultural Revolution and after

The Cultural Revolution can be seen as the last of the major campaigns associated with Mao's ideas of continuous revolution. The campaign for converting bourgeois art into proletarian art which began the movement rapidly degenerated into a major factional conflict with violent clashes between Red Guard groups and the collapse of political order. The Cultural Revolution did not, however, see the end of political campaigns. The campaign against Lin Biao and Confucius of the early 1970s was actually part of a factional battle aimed specifically at Zhou Enlai.

Bourgeois liberalisation

The final political mobilisation that was organised in the old-fashioned Stalinist manner was the campaign against bourgeois liberalisation (*zichanjieji ziyouhua*), which took place in 1985–87. It was launched by conservatives in the Party hierarchy, notably Chen Yun, Peng Zhen and Hu Qiaomu, who were opposed to the pace of the reform programme but particularly to what they perceived as excessive Westernisation and democratisation that accompanied the reforms. The conservatives believed that the increasing influence of the West was a genuine threat to the 'four cardinal principles' that Deng Xiaoping had emphasised as a counterbalance to the reform movement and, in particular, that it undermined the leadership of the CCP. The principal target of the campaign was Hu Yaobang, who had in many ways been ahead of his time in his views on democratisation and political pluralism.

The campaign was to some extent prompted by the appearance in China of very limited examples of Western culture, which appeared to enrage the older generation. Colourful clothes, new hairstyles, beauty parlours and rock music all made their first appearance: the pop group Wham played to a youthful audience of 15,000 in the People's Gymnasium in Beijing in April 1985. However, it was the movement for democracy which began with demonstrations in Hefei, led by the astrophysicist and dissident Fang Lizhi, that prompted the campaign. Bourgeois liberalisation had been identified as an evil by the CCP Central Committee in 1986 and in January 1987 an authoritative article criticising this iniquitous deviation appeared in *People's Daily*. Hu Yaobang was forced to resign as Secretary-General of the CCP and many renowned intellectuals, including Fang Lizhi, were expelled from the CCP and sought refuge abroad.

These political campaigns have more or less died out but they were a powerful and pernicious presence in Chinese society from the 1950s to the 1970s and the after-effects still linger on: people learned how to cope with them but they were always looking over their shoulders waiting for the next salvo. In addition to the losses of family members to prison or sometimes to execution and the damage to careers, there was also (and still is, even if to a lesser extent) a protective culture of self-censorship that has stifled debate and creativity. Whatever criticisms Chinese citizens today might have about the political system under which they have to live in the twenty-first century, they have reason to be grateful for the absence of these campaigns.

Village committees: democracy from below?

Outbreaks of rural disorder beginning in 2004, and especially the violent suppression of the demonstrations in Guangdong province, have raised the question of the role of village committees in the minds of Chinese political leaders and thinkers as well as international observers.

The Chinese government has been promoting the development of directly elected village committees since the early 1980s and serious attempts to introduce direct elections began in 1987. Rural unrest escalated in the 1990s and Beijing considered strengthening these committees as a way of creating bodies that would resolve conflict and assure its control over the countryside. How effective and how democratic they are is a moot point, but the impetus has been to ensure the consolidation of state power rather than the spreading of democracy for its own sake.

When the People's Communes were dismantled in 1978 at the beginning of the reform era, this was not only the end of collective agriculture but the end of a system of rural local government that had been in operation for twenty years. The idea of village committees, or more correctly 'villager committees' (*cunmin weiyuanhui*), was introduced to fill the vacuum. These committees are subordinate to the Ministry of Civil Affairs (*minzheng bu*) but they operate below the lowest level of the formal government structure, the township. The relationship between the committees and the township is evolving but has not been precisely defined.

The 1982 Constitution of the PRC included provisions for the direct election of committees by residents of the villages. This was strengthened by the draft version of the *Organic Law on Villager Committees*, which was provisionally adopted by the National People's Congress in November 1987, and which set out detailed regulations for the organisation and role of the committees and the procedures to be adopted in elections. During the trial period that followed, twenty-five provinces established committees. Many observers were highly sceptical about the election process. The government claimed that the election procedures were independent of the CCP and should be seen as a shining example of rural democracy. However, in many cases it was simply a case of the CCP providing a slate of candidates for the village residents to approve. In some elections independently minded candidates did secure election and this posed a challenge to the supremacy of the Party in the countryside. There was considerable opposition to the law within the CCP and there was a significant body of opinion that saw it as a threat by Western-style ideas of democracy to China's political system and to the power of the CCP, but in November 1998, an amended version of the legislation was passed by the NPC.

Typically, the village committee consists of between three and seven villagers elected for a three-year term. It has a wide range of administrative responsibilities, which includes taxation and the management of budgets, public property and services, public order, social welfare and the resolution of local disputes. This gives the committee a considerable degree of local power but it is overseen by a village representative assembly which is supposed to be able to check abuses.

During the 1990s rural China experienced a serious social crisis which was in part caused by budgetary decentralisation, the decline in funding from central government and the search by local authorities to find new ways of generating revenue. Peasant families that had expected to receive land were dispossessed as wealthier families acquired large landholdings. Many were impoverished by the high taxes set by local government, often illegally. Resistance to these taxes and protests against corruption by local officials led to thousands of incidents of serious disorder in the countryside. These were aggravated by conflicts between farmers over land ownership. More recently the forced, and some claim illegal, seizure of land by local officials and businessmen for the construction of non-agricultural enterprises has exacerbated the situation further. This is particularly the case in the rural areas on the outskirts of major urban centres.

During these conflicts and protests, a new generation of peasant activists has started to acquire political and organisational experience. There has been a proliferation of autonomous organisations with names such as the Peasant Burden Reduction Group and Peasant Rights Preservation Committee. The CCP has never been comfortable with independent political organisations and has sought to incorporate them into structures that they were able to control or to suppress them. At the same time they have been obliged to accept that the peasants represented by these organisations had genuine grievances that it was necessary to address.

It was hoped that the revised 1998 *Organic Law on Village Committees* which made provision for them to be run democratically and to be financially accountable would solve some of these problems. The law required:

- the open nomination of candidates by individuals rather than a Party slate
- more than one candidate for each position
- secret ballots in private voting booths
- a public count
- the immediate announcement of the result
- a recall procedure if the electors were not satisfied with the performance of the committee members.

In spite of this formally democratic system, the CCP has not abandoned its attempt to control the process. It continues to provide its own candidates and in some cases has talent-spotted able and popular village activists and recruited them to the Party. However, it does genuinely appear to be supporting the development of village elections as a way of regulating conflict among farmers over land and assuring social stability.

The committees are also seen as a method for legitimising the Party in the rural areas and this is particularly important for its power base. The roots of the modern CCP were in the peasant movement of northern China in the 1930s and 1940s and the leadership are keenly aware of the potential power of that peasantry. They recognise that they need to keep the rural poor on their side rather than risk the development of independent organisations led by intellectuals from the countryside. It is important to note that, however open and democratic the village committee elections are, the CCP secretary in the village is not elected but is appointed by more senior Party bodies. There have been many reports of conflict between elected village heads and appointed Party secretaries: in the final analysis, the Party secretaries can override other bodies because they are able to call on more powerful support from higher CCP organisations.

The village committees do not automatically represent the interests of the peasants. In many cases they have taken the side of developers and local officials and this has given rise to the demonstrations and disorder seen recently in Guangdong province. There have also been concerns that the committees are being taken over by rural groups based on extended families or clans that operate outside the law and in some cases by criminal gangs and mafia-style organisations. On its own, the strengthening of village committees is unlikely to solve the problems of rural unrest. A genuinely independent judicial system would help as this would give poor farmers a legitimate outlet for their grievances but it seems unlikely at present. In the wake of recent protests, the few independent lawyers who have been willing to represent peasants have been barred from the courts.

There is an urgent need for clarification of the legal rights of peasants. Theoretically all land still belongs to collectives but it is parcelled out to families who have the right and responsibility to farm it. The state is effectively the real owner but it is the new generation of landlords who have real power in the villages. They are involved in increasingly complex land disputes and the poorer peasants are excluded from ownership and political power.

Some Chinese scholars have argued for the reintroduction of Peasant Associations. These were organisations used by the CCP in its campaigns for rent reduction and land redistribution from the 1920s to the 1940s. They were abandoned when the Party came to power and were effectively replaced by cooperatives and subsequently the People's Communes. While their historical role was as revolutionary organisations, it is now being argued that they could function as representative organisations for peasants and play an important role in social integration in the countryside. It is interesting that one major outbreak of rural disorder in 2006 took place in Dongzhou and Shanwei, which are only a few miles from Haifeng and Lufeng, the centres of the first Peasant Association movement in China in 1922.[13]

Central state, local state

The village committee experiment reflects general problems of governance faced by the Party-state in the reform period. It has been argued that as the CCP has reduced its control over the economy it has also lost its authority over the regions. The relationship between the central state – the Party committees and government ministries in Beijing – and the local state – the town and district councils – is an intriguing and evolving process.

Although it is not possible for central government to manage all aspects of the operation of local government directly, this is an issue that has absorbed many politicians in Beijing since the early years of the reform programme. Overall control of policy and style of government is achieved by exhortation and political persuasion but also by a systematic programme of cadre evaluation. Local cadres are trained and evaluated and rotated between lower- and higher-level posts in an effort to ensure continuity and consistency in the interpretation and implementation of policy. The cadre evaluation system is not new but it has been overhauled and strengthened to take into account the demands of economic and fiscal decentralisation and the devolution of decision-making to the regions.

Cases in which this system has failed tend to be highlighted, notably when there is local corruption or when political problems lead to disturbances. In general, it appears that the system has enabled the central state to retain a great degree of control over the actions of local officials.

The Mao problem

Assessing the role of Mao Zedong in the political history of China has always been problematic, both within China and among outside observers and analysts. As the leader of the most successful CCP grouping, hailed as the victor in the Civil War and as the founding Chairman of the PRC, Mao was the dominant figure on the mainland from 1949 until his death in September 1976.

His shadow continues to hang over contemporary China. His portrait still hangs just above the southern entrance to the old Forbidden City, just below the rostrum on Tian'anmen Gate from where he proclaimed the establishment of the PRC on 1 October 1949, and overlooking Tian'anmen Square which lies to the south. His likeness also remains on China's banknotes even though his economic policies were rejected long ago. Although Mao memorabilia are for the most part now sold to curious Westerners, he is still if not revered then at least respected by many ordinary Chinese.[14]

On 8 September 2006, the eve of the thirtieth anniversary of his death, the Chinese-language website of the official newspaper of the CCP, *People's Daily*, led with photographs from 1965 to 1974 showing Mao with world leaders and other prominent figures including President Richard Nixon, the British Prime Minister

Edward Heath, King Sihanouk of Cambodia and the Malaysian Prime Minister Mahathir Mohammed. The accompanying commentary was a reassessment of Mao's international influence and by no means a negative one, emphasising his role as an international statesman and the part that he had played in putting China on the world map.[15]

Assessments of his contribution to China's modernisation and his own character are many and varied. Was he simply China's Stalin, a replica of the Soviet autocrat, or was there something different about him, something that could be called peculiarly Chinese? Was he a new-style version of the traditional Chinese emperors?

During the 1970s, Mao and Maoism had attracted the attention of radical Third World movements and a body of left-wing intellectuals, primarily in Europe. Third World radicals were attracted by Mao's approach as they saw the success of the peasant-based CCP as a model for their own political aspirations. Many peasant movements in Asia and Latin America declared themselves to be followers of Mao, or at least to have been influenced by his analysis of the potential of peasant revolution. What attracted many was the simplistic version of this analysis which was popularised, at first in the PLA and then in China at large, by Lin Biao who was at the time designated as Mao's 'close comrade in arms' and was his heir presumptive. Much of the image of Mao that the West perceived in the 1960s and 1970s was manipulated and popularised by Lin, a spin-doctor before the concept had been invented. Lin's vision postulated the encirclement of the cities of the world by the countryside of the world in the same way that the CCP, it was argued, had encircled China's cities from its rural bases.[16] In an era when there was widespread support and sympathy, particularly on the left, for peasant movements of national liberation, this appealing but unsophisticated argument won many devotees.

Time has not been kind to either these ideas or the movements that espoused them, but even in the early twenty-first century, when there are few Maoists in China, there are groups declaring themselves to be Maoists in Asia and Latin America. In India, the Naxalite insurrection of 1967 in the district of Naxalbari in West Bengal was inspired by Maoism and, in spite of severe government repression which almost eradicated them in the 1970s, their ideas live on and the Communist Party of India (Maoist) can maintain, with considerable justification, that it has the support of large numbers of the poor and dispossessed. Maoist ideas are particularly influential in the regions inhabited by groups that are usually thought of as ethnic minorities but are known in India by the quaint term 'tribals', with all its archaic echoes of the British Raj.[17] Maoist rebels attacked a freight train at Latehar in the northeastern Indian state of Jharkhand on 26 June 2007, destroyed railway tracks and abducted the driver and the guard of the train. They also called for an economic blockade in the region to protest against the development of special economic zones, arguing that these would further impoverish many poor villagers. Similar attacks were reported in the state of Bihar, from which Jharkand was carved in 2000.[18]

In Nepal, a Maoist insurgency had challenged the troubled monarchy of that Himalayan kingdom for decades until the government took steps to try to bring them into the political mainstream in April 2006. By May 2008 the Maoists dominated the Constituent Assembly and had achieved one of their key aims, the abolition of the monarchy. In Peru, a major guerrilla movement which, like many of the radical groups in South America, is largely supported by indigenous or minority peoples is known as the *Sendero Luminoso* (Shining Path) and declares its allegiance to Mao and Maoism.

In Europe, the *événements* of May 1968 in Paris and the radical student and worker movement that accompanied them were contemporaneous with the most dramatic period of the Cultural Revolution; some European radical thinkers and activists, notably Jean-Paul Sartre, sought to ally themselves with Maoism. Most of those who did so had little direct knowledge or experience of Mao Zedong's policies or the Cultural Revolution in China, which was hardly surprising since China was off-limits to most outsiders at that time. There was no real understanding of the authoritarian and Stalinist nature of Mao's regime and some young Western radicals were attracted to the libertarian and anti-bureaucratic rhetoric that was emanating from the Red Guard movement.

The publication of *Mao: The Unknown Story* in 2005 brought a contentious and highly publicised version of Mao's life before the English-speaking general public for the first time.[19] This polemical and sensationalist work was published by a commercial firm rather than a serious academic press and the authors claimed to have used sources that had been neglected by previous biographers, including documents from archives in Russia that had been previously unavailable. The book focuses on the negative qualities of Mao and his unpleasant personal characteristics and habits and it has planted in the collective consciousness of the non-specialist public the idea that Mao, personally, was responsible for as many of seventy million deaths in China during the period of his rule.

Scholars of the Mao period and specialists in Mao's writings and activities have taken issue with this biography, not in any spirit of sympathising with Mao or support for his policies, but because the citations do not add up. Many sources which could have been used have been omitted. Individuals who knew Mao well were not interviewed, including foreigners who had worked with him closely and had acted as his translators or interpreters. Many of the sources that have been chosen are partial and in some cases highly suspect. Is it sensible to believe that documents written by members of the Soviet government, the Communist Party of the Soviet Union and the former Soviet security services, which are lodged in the archives in Moscow and Leningrad, are accurate and factual because they show China and Mao in a negative light, when during the Cold War years they would have been regarded with the deepest suspicion?

Clearly Mao was not the sort of person to be invited to dinner parties and it may not have been advisable to introduce one's daughter or favourite niece to him, but was he a monster? He was almost certainly an egomaniac of the highest order, a man who had no compunction about blighting the career of anyone who opposed him and had very little regard for the sanctity of human life, especially the lives of the peasants whose cause he was supposed to espouse. However, there is a problem in trying to match the image of Mao that has been purveyed in the

West – that of a sadistic monster who had no education or ideas of his own – with what appears to have been the genuine reverence shown to him by huge numbers of Chinese people including some of the most highly educated. He continues to be regarded with a great deal of pride as the leader, albeit a highly flawed leader, who made it possible for China to 'stand up'. The good old days of Mao are looked back on with a degree of nostalgia as people contend that, in spite of the poverty that everyone suffered from then, there was no corruption and that social problems such as prostitution and drug abuse were unknown. This view through rose-tinted spectacles, however short-sighted and ill-informed it might be, is still widespread. There is sufficient evidence of if not corruption then at least the abuse of privilege among senior Party and government officials that goes back decades, but it was not public knowledge at the time and the opportunities for financial corruption were in any case small since there was very little money available.

People who knew Mao in his early days, including some who suffered under his regime, still contend that he was most comfortable with peasants and liked and respected them. He had his finger on the pulse of rural China and he clearly had a talent for framing policies and ideas in a way that peasants would respond to positively; in his speeches and writings he mixed idioms from several Chinese traditions, including Daoism and Buddhism, with a veneer of Marxism. To a large extent, Mao (and many of his supporters in the CCP) retained a narrow-minded outlook. Mao had travelled very little. He was not an enthusiast for sophisticated urban culture, even less for foreign society and he seemed most at home in the peasant heartlands of China. He never made the transition from revolutionary political heavyweight to international statesman and he did not transcend his romantic attachment to the tradition and legends of rural peasant rebels.[20]

16 Fourth- and fifth-generation leadership

When the Central Committee of the Chinese Communist Party (CCP) was due to meet in full session between 9 and 11 October 2000, the published agenda indicated that it would be concentrating on the Tenth Five-Year Plan for the development of the national economy and, in particular, the Western Development programme, the grand plan for developing the impoverished western regions of the country. (For details of this programme, see Chapter 21.)

In reality, the meeting was at least as concerned to establish the basis for a smooth transition from the generation of leaders led by Jiang Zemin to what would become known as the fourth-generation (*di sidai*) leadership of the People's Republic of China (PRC). The impending retirement of President Jiang Zemin, Premier Zhu Rongji, and the Chairman of the National People's Congress (NPC), Li Peng, within two years was confirmed and the names of the men who were to lead the new generation were given new prominence: they were Hu Jintao as Vice-President, Wen Jiabao as Vice-Premier and Zeng Qinghong, promoted to be the head of the CCP's Organisation Department.

The new generation of leaders that finally emerged after the Sixteenth Congress of the CCP in November 2002 showed the Party in flux, still fully committed to economic modernisation but also unswervingly dedicated to maintaining its own central and unchallengeable role in preserving the stability of the state. It also marked the beginning of the decline of the Shanghai faction in Party politics, a decline that was finally confirmed by the forced resignation of Zeng Qinghong in October 2007.

First three generations of leadership in the PRC

The concept of generations of leadership in the Communist Party and the PRC emerged in the public discourse in the 1990s during the final years of Deng Xiaoping's life. The issues of succession and the balance of change and continuity were always in the minds of the Party hierarchy and its collective memory in the Secretariat. Once the concept of a 'fourth generation' had become commonplace, it became necessary to be more precise in reclassifying the earlier leadership into three predecessor generations.

First generation

The key figures of the first generation, although that term was never used at the time, were Mao Zedong, Liu Shaoqi, Peng Dehuai, Lin Biao and Zhou Enlai. They were the founding generation of the CCP in power and brought with them the legacy of the Long March; the revolutionary struggle in the countryside; the guerrilla resistance to the Japanese Occupation; and the battlefields of the Civil War on which they defeated the armies of the Nationalists. They also carried with them the baggage of factional, political and personal differences which were to bedevil China's domestic politics during the 1950s and which came to a head in the Cultural Revolution.

Second generation

The second generation were Deng Xiaoping and the group of veteran Party leaders (often designated simplistically as 'moderate' or 'conservative') who came to power following the death of Mao Zedong in 1976 and the elimination of his political supporters, notably the Gang of Four. The major contribution of the second generation to the political development of the country was their willingness to tackle the thorny problem of economic reform as China emerged from the years of the Cultural Revolution.

Among the key members of this group were Chen Yun, respected as the Party's economics supremo, and Hu Yaobang and Zhao Ziyang, who both became Premier, one after the other. This particular coalition came to grief after the military suppression of the Democracy Movement in Beijing on 4 June 1989.

The demise of the Soviet Union and the Communist states of Eastern Europe had been on the mind of Deng and his colleagues of the second generation and the lessons they took from this included the ideas of ensuring the legitimacy of the CCP by creating strong economic growth and maintaining close Party links to the growing business sector while at the same time consolidating the Party's authority over the military apparatus. This combination was far from the liberal regime that some Western observers were looking for but the pragmatism that Deng and his supporters demonstrated ensured the stability and continuation of the regime, which was above all else the main aim of the CCP. According to their own lights, they were successful.

Third generation

Jiang Zemin, who succeeded Deng, was widely regarded as a nondescript caretaker Chairman of the Party. His administration followed Deng's prescription for stability and growth but he will be remembered above all for his initiative in admitting senior people from the business community to the Party. At the end of his term of office, Jiang seemed unusually reluctant to relinquish the authority and influence of his position, unusual even for a CCP leader. This was assuaged somewhat by the possibility that his ideas would be preserved for posterity, partly as a result of a strange biography which was written by an American investment banker, Robert

Kuhn, but approved by the Chinese authorities, which tried to present Jiang, in the eponymous title, as *The Man Who Changed China*. This was followed in 2006 by a multi-volume compilation of his speeches and writings in a *Selected Works* that ran to 654 pages in length.[1]

Far more significant in the long term than Jiang was his Premier, Zhu Rongji. Zhu, like Jiang, was a former Mayor of Shanghai and was renowned for the bluntness of his manner and the shortness of his temper, but also highly respected for his competent management of China's transition to a semi-market economy. He was largely responsible for the technical aspects of China's successful application to join the World Trade Organisation (WTO).

Fourth generation

The two most prominent fourth-generation figures in the Politburo Standing Committee are President Hu Jintao and Premier Wen Jiabao. The Vice-President, Zeng Qinghong, who is part of the powerful Shanghai faction associated with former President Jiang Zemin, had a much lower profile but he is known to have exercised considerable influence and had the reputation of being a shrewd political operator. He was also widely assumed to have seen himself as Hu's successor as President until his retirement at the Seventeenth CCP Congress in October 2007, which put paid to any ambitions he might have harboured. There had been much speculation on whether a Hu–Zeng axis was emerging, which would eventually eliminate Wen Jiabao, or whether Wen was successfully consolidating his own position by embracing populist causes such as the reduction of poverty, opposition to political corruption and environmental protection. By the end of the Seventeenth CCP Congress which was held in the autumn of 2007, Hu and Wen were still in post but Zeng had retired.

Hu Jintao was born in Anhui province in southern China in 1942. He studied hydroelectric engineering at Qinghua (Tsinghua) University in Beijing and joined the CCP while he was a student in 1964. He is a classic product of the 'double burden' system under which China's future potential leaders were simultaneously educated in technology and trained as politicians. His early career was in the Ministry of Water Conservancy and Power, an unexciting post but one in which he was dealing with some of the fundamental issues in the development of China's economy.

Hu Jintao's political history is often described as obscure but this is mainly because some of the important but low-profile positions he has occupied were in the west of China and out of the political limelight. He is best known for the authoritarian style with which he ruled Gansu, the poor and remote province in the northwest, in the 1970s and 1980s and for his role as CCP Secretary in Tibet in the 1980s and 1990s, when he imposed martial law. He was also head of the Central Party School. One of his power bases is a group of former members of the Communist Youth League (CYL), of which he was First Secretary in 1984–85. He was recalled to Beijing in 1992 as a member of the all-powerful Standing Committee of the Politburo under Deng Xiaoping. When he became President of

China in 2003, he brought with him to Beijing a number of officials from the CYL and promoted them to key positions.

Like previous leaders of the CCP, Hu Jintao realised that he needed to ensure that the military remained firmly under the control of the Party and to guarantee their support for him personally in order to consolidate his power. When Jiang Zemin retired, somewhat reluctantly, from the post of Chairman of the Central Military Commission on 19 September 2004, Hu Jintao moved rapidly to strengthen his personal relationship with senior military officers. He was responsible for promoting several key officers, including members of the CMC, to the rank of general and appeared publicly at PLA functions and exercises. He has also made a point of being photographed with senior officers while wearing the *zhongshan zhuang* (often called the 'Mao jacket') in military green rather than his usual trademark Western-style suit, collar and tie.[2]

Hu Jintao has also strengthened the CCP's links to the increasingly important business sector, continuing the process that was begun by Jiang Zemin. His 2006 New Year broadcast address focused on his commitment to 'peaceful development', the consensus term for China's non-aggressive rise to power and multilateralism. However, he also made a point of stressing his continuing support for the 'one China principle' and the active promotion of the peaceful reunification of Taiwan and opposition to Taiwanese secessionists (that is, the Democratic Progressive Party of Chen Shui-bian), the cause dearest to the heart of the military. His priority is to maintain the legitimacy and longevity of the CCP and all other matters are subordinate to that. He is seen as a cautious but determined politician, a steady hand on the tiller and someone who is not easily rattled. He is prepared to tolerate administrative reforms but is unlikely to countenance any fundamental political change.

Premier Wen Jiabao's image is of a meticulous, perhaps even dull, functionary who is more concerned about results than political slogans. He was trained as a geologist and worked in Gansu province and during China's long drawn-out period of applying to join the WTO he was given the crucial task of developing policies on agriculture, finance and the environment. He had previously worked with Hu Yaobang, Zhao Ziyang and Jiang Zemin when they were successively Party Chairmen and in June 1989 he accompanied Zhao Ziyang when he made his celebrated visit to the students who were on hunger strike in Tian'anmen Square. Unlike Zhao, who was sacked and placed under house arrest, Wen's political career survived.

Since his appointment as Premier, Wen Jiabao has identified himself publicly with popular causes, especially the environment, openness, decreasing the wealth gap and attacks on corruption. Wen visited Harbin on 26 November 2005 to observe the recovery work after the pollution of the Songhua River. He admonished local officials for not having acted quickly enough and warned them against any attempt at a cover-up. He has stressed the need for putting the protection of the environment ahead of the push for economic growth at any cost. On the eve of New Year 2006, he visited the cities of Jiujiang and Ruichang in the northeast of Jiangxi province which had been devastated by an earthquake on 26 November.

The quake cost the lives of thirteen people and left over 100,000 homeless and Wen emphasised the need for reconstruction, not only of housing but also of schools which had been damaged or destroyed. He is himself from a humble family background and has acquired the reputation of having genuine concern for the lot of the common people, although, as with all CCP leaders, it is difficult to know to what extent these are his genuine views.[3]

The third member of the ruling triumvirate and the person seen until 2007 as the heir apparent to Hu Jintao was Zeng Qinghong. He is the son of Zeng Shan, a Civil War veteran who became Deputy Mayor of Shanghai after the victory of the CCP in 1949 and later served as Minister of Internal Affairs. Zeng Qinghong was educated as an engineer, joined the CCP in 1960 and became a member of the powerful Shanghai faction in the Party. His position in the faction was consolidated in the 1980s when he worked for the then CCP Secretary in Shanghai, Jiang Zemin. When Jiang succeeded Zhao Ziyang as Secretary-General of the CCP after 4 June 1989, Zeng Qinghong moved to Beijing with him. Respected for his political acumen but not popular, Zeng is regarded as having been Jiang's hatchet man and thus responsible for removing Jiang's political opponents. Since the final retirement of Jiang from politics, Zeng acted as his master's voice in the Politburo Standing Committee and was the effective head of the Shanghai faction in the government. In 1999 he became head of the CCP's powerful Organisation Department, which has administrative responsibility for appointments and promotions within the Party. Although like any successful Chinese machine politician Zeng Qinghong played his cards close to his chest, some insiders believe that he was the most liberal or at least the most open-minded of the ruling triumvirate. His retirement was announced before the opening of the Seventeenth CCP Congress in October 2007.

Political anniversaries

The way that the CCP treats the anniversaries of the deaths of its former leaders can reveal a great deal about its internal balance of power at any given time. The commemorations of the deaths of both Hu Yaobang and Zhao Ziyang pointed to interesting tensions within the ruling triumvirate in the Politburo Standing Committee.

In the final months of 2005 there was considerable debate behind the scenes in Beijing on how to mark what would have been the ninetieth birthday of Hu Yaobang, who died in 1989, and the first anniversary of the death of Zhao Ziyang. In CCP terms, Hu, whose death provided the focus for the Democracy Movement which was crushed on 4 June 1989, and Zhao were both considered to have been liberal reformers ahead of their time: attitudes to their legacy give an indication of the state of internal Party politics in 2005 and 2006.

A commemoration of the ninetieth anniversary of Hu Yaobang's birth was held in the Great Hall of the People on Friday 18 November. It was a low-key affair, described as a 'symposium' by *People's Daily*, and attended by three members of the Politburo Standing Committee, including Wen Jiabao and Zeng Qinghong. Hu Jintao did not attend although he had been behind the original decision to hold the memorial meeting. This was perhaps surprising, as Hu Jintao had been appointed head of the CYL by Hu Yaobang in the 1980s and continued to associate himself with the more liberal and tolerant ethos that his mentor encouraged.[4] Hu Yaobang was Secretary-General of the CCP in the mid-1980s and not only was he seen as liberal minded but he was personally responsible for the rehabilitation of political figures who had lost their posts during the Cultural Revolution. He was dismissed as Premier in 1987 after a series of demonstrations by students which began as protests against the increasing involvement of Japanese business in the Chinese economy but went on to attack corruption and demand greater democracy.

Zhao Ziyang died on 17 January 2005 but there were no public ceremonies to mark the first anniversary of his death, which should have been standard practice. Instead it was commemorated by a small gathering of family and friends; campaigners for democracy were firmly discouraged from attending. The former Premier is honoured for his role in extending the market reforms that he had developed in Sichuan province to the whole of China in the 1980s, but his role in the 1989 crackdown, when he appeared to side with the demonstrating students, led to his house arrest for fifteen years and made him a powerful symbol for reformers within the CCP. Rumours persist that he left behind a manuscript giving his version of the bitter political battles behind the scenes that led to the unleashing of units of the PLA on unarmed demonstrators on 4 June 1989.[5]

The thirtieth anniversary of the death of Zhou Enlai on 8 January 1976 was commemorated by the publication of a substantial memorial volume, *Pictorial Biography of Zhou Enlai (Zhou Enlai hua zhuan)*. The book was launched at a symposium which was held in the Zhou Enlai Memorial Chamber in the Mao Zedong Memorial Hall, and was presided over by the Deputy Chairwoman of the Standing Committee of the NPC, Gu Xiulian. The former Premier is still venerated as a great revolutionary and many Chinese believe, rightly or wrongly, that he ameliorated some of the harshest policies of the Cultural Revolution.

In different ways, Hu Jintao and Wen Jiabao are both followers of the Hu Yaobang and Zhao Ziyang style of government. Zeng Qinghong, as the protégé of Jiang Zemin who succeeded Zhao, did not have the same loyalty to their memory. The subdued commemoration of the two former leaders suggests a determination to keep alive their legacy without seriously disturbing the delicate factional balance within the Party. The legacy of Zhou Enlai is less divisive but tends to benefit the reformers.

Hu and Wen function as part of a team as well as being rivals. It is tempting to see them as respectively a hardliner and a liberal, but that would be simplistic. Wen has succeeded in enhancing his authority by his championing of popular causes. Zeng's influence was believed to be considerable because of his leadership of the Shanghai faction and his close connections with former President Jiang Zemin. In fact, he was at one time thought to be a serious candidate for the post of President himself but this prospect vanished with his retirement at the Seventeenth CCP Congress.

Preparations for the Seventeenth Congress

On 12 November 2006, the CCP announced the programme for electing delegates to the Seventeenth CCP Congress which was scheduled to meet in the autumn of 2007. The seventy million members of the Party would elect a total of 2,220 delegates in thirty-eight electoral units throughout the country. This was an increase of about one hundred in the number of delegates compared with those who were elected to the Sixteenth Congress, which met in 2002 when Hu Jintao was confirmed as CCP Chairman. The Party also decreed that at least 30 per cent of the delegates should be from the grassroots, which means that they should be farmers and industrial workers rather than existing Party officials and that women and members of the ethnic minorities should be better represented. It was argued that these changes were necessary to accommodate the six million new members who had joined the CCP since the Sixteenth Congress.[6]

Fifth generation

As the Seventeenth Congress of the CCP loomed in October 2007, the talk was of a new generation of leaders, the fifth generation, to succeed Hu and Wen. During the preparatory period insiders canvassed several names but there was considerable interest in the fact that Hu Jintao was presumed not to have the authority that his predecessors could wield to anoint a specific successor and a suspicion that the new leadership would only emerge after a long period of horse-trading and might result from the growing influence of provincial Party leaders. Initial leaks from the plenary meeting of the Central Committee which preceded the conference pointed to a collective leadership with no individuals specifically named as potential successors to the most senior posts, but with the advancement of two rising stars, Li Keqiang of Liaoning province and Xi Jinping from Shanghai. At the end of the Congress, Xi came onto the congress platform ahead of Li and this was taken as evidence that he is being groomed as the successor to Hu Jintao.

17 Tibet

The status of Tibet and its relationship with China has become one of the most intractable and emotive issues in Asian, and indeed, world politics. The official Chinese stance is that Tibet, which it insists on calling Chinese Tibet (*Zhongguo Xizang*), has always been an integral part of China and that it always should be. Supporters of self-determination for Tibet point to its *de facto* independence between the collapse of the Chinese empire in 1911 and the controversial Seventeen Point Agreement signed in 1951 between the Tibetan government and representatives of the newly victorious Chinese Communist Party (CCP). Many also argue that this independent status in fact has had a much longer history and that Tibet was an autonomous and genuinely self-governing entity for centuries. In other words, there is an assumption that Tibet was independent until 1951 and that it has suffered under an unlawful occupation by the Chinese thereafter.

This view is also broadly speaking the position taken by the members and supporters of the Dalai Lama's government-in-exile in the Indian city of Dharamsala. The existence of this alternative focus of loyalty and authority has been a source of great solace for Tibetans inside and outside China and simultaneously a source of great irritation and anger for the Chinese authorities who have worked tirelessly to attempt to ensure that the Dalai Lama is not accepted as a major religious or political figure on the international stage.

The conflict has been highlighted by a number of prestigious and glamorous media and Hollywood figures who have rallied to the defence of Tibetan culture, and also by Western adherents of Buddhism. Whether this cause has been taken up because of genuine spiritual conviction, deep knowledge of the religion, language and culture of Tibet or for reasons of political fashion must of course be a matter for individuals to judge.[1]

Tibet and Qing China

The influence of the Qing dynasty in Tibet declined in the nineteenth century as the Manchus became preoccupied with the challenge of Western incursions on the coast and the domestic rebellions of the Taiping, the Nian and the Hui Muslims that broke out in inland China and which were much closer to their capital, Beijing, than was Tibet. By the middle of the century, the authority of the Manchus in Tibet had decreased to the point where the suzerainty that the dynasty was supposed to exercise had become to a large extent symbolic. This autonomy increased as the century wore on and the thirteenth Dalai Lama (1876–1933) became known as the Great Thirteenth, not solely because of the extraordinary authority that he exercised, even for a Dalai Lama, but because it was during his rule that Tibet emerged from under firm and direct Chinese control.

After the expedition under the command of Sir Francis Younghusband in 1903 turned into a full-scale invasion of Tibet by the forces of British India, the thirteenth Dalai Lama left Lhasa, the Tibetan capital, and took refuge in Urga, the capital of Mongolia which was also a bastion of Tibetan Buddhism – Urga was renamed Ulanbaatar (Ulan Bator) after the Mongolian Revolution. The Dalai Lama arrived in Urga in October 1904 and, in his absence, the Chinese government declared that he had been deposed. Tensions arose between the Dalai Lama and the Jebtsundamba Khutukhtu, the highest Mongolian spiritual authority, and the Dalai Lama returned to Tibet and attempted to arrive at an agreement with the Chinese government.

The Anglo-Chinese Convention of 1906 effectively repudiated the gains made by Younghusband's adventure and reaffirmed the Qing dynasty's suzerainty over Tibet. In 1908 Zhao Erfeng was charged by the Qing government with the mission of bringing the eastern province of Kham, and eventually the whole of Tibet, more firmly under Chinese control and assimilating its institutions into the Chinese empire. Troops under Zhao's command began to arrive in Lhasa in February 1910 and the Dalai Lama, believing that the Chinese government had reneged on an agreement with his officials, fled again, but on this occasion to Darjeeling in India.

Independence after 1911

When the news of the Chinese Revolution of 1911 reached Lhasa, the Tibetans rose against their Chinese masters, directed by a special group that the Dalai Lama had established in India.

> By April 1912, the Tibetans had prevailed: about three thousand Chinese troops and officers surrendered and were permitted to leave Tibet via India. In the fifth Tibetan month of the Water-Mouse year (1912), the Dalai Lama returned to Tibet, staying first in Chumbi and then, in January 1913, finally entering a Lhasa free of Chinese troops and officials for the first time since the eighteenth century.[2]

Although the new President of the Republic of China, Yuan Shikai, attempted to mend fences with the Dalai Lama by restoring his former titles, the Dalai Lama insisted that in future he would exercise both spiritual and temporal authority in Tibet and 'cut even the symbolic tie with China'.[3]

The position of Tibet in the years following the collapse of Qing rule has been described as 'static and non-changing, living in splendid isolation and illusionary independence'.[4] Its independence may have been an illusion; it was, however, without doubt a period of genuine political separation from China that lasted until 1951 and, ever since that date, the *de facto* autonomy of the period has fired the aspirations of Tibetans who have sought to create an independent state.

The political and legal status of Tibet has been a matter of international controversy since the middle of the twentieth century when what had primarily been a long-standing but local question of borders and sovereignty achieved international prominence as one of the disputes of the Cold War between the United States and China. It is worth repeating the entrenched positions that have been taken up in this dispute. To many Tibetans, the position is simple: Tibet is and always has been an independent state that was occupied illegally by the Chinese in 1951. For the present government of the People's Republic of China (PRC), the position is equally simple: Tibet has always been and always will be part of China. The legal justification for this claim is extremely dubious but that is the premise on which Beijing's actions in Tibet are based. What is incontestable is that from the fall of the Qing dynasty in 1911 until the People's Liberation Army (PLA) marched into Tibet in 1951, Tibet functioned *de facto* as a fully independent state, ruled by a combination of secular and lamaist bureaucracies.[5] The situation is complicated further by the fact that the Tibetan Autonomous Region as it is constituted today is only the core region of what was Tibet before 1951 and substantial parts of the territories of old Tibet, or 'ethnographic Tibet' as it is sometimes called, have been transferred to the Chinese provinces of Qinghai, Sichuan and Gansu.

Tibet incorporated into the People's Republic of China

When the CCP was victorious in the Civil War which ended in 1949, Tibet became part of the PRC, as did Xinjiang in a similar manner. The intention was that this would happen by means of a process that was known as 'peaceful liberation' (*heping jiefang*). This was achieved in Xinjiang to a certain extent but Mao and the CCP acknowledged that the position of Tibet was different because of its isolation and because of the absence of a sizeable settled Han Chinese community there. In December 1949, judging that Tibet could only be 'liberated' by military action, Beijing began to make preparations for an invasion of the eastern provinces of Tibet, particularly Chamdo, while at the same time opening negotiations with the Tibetan government. The Tibetans failed to send a delegation to Beijing for these talks and on 7 October 1950, the PLA Eighteenth Army crossed the frontier into Chamdo with the intention of rendering inoperative the Tibetan army units based there and cutting off Lhasa. The poorly led, and frankly somewhat amateurish, Tibetan forces were no match for their battle-hardened counterparts in the PLA and the entire Tibetan army was defeated within two weeks. The PLA could have moved directly to take control of Lhasa as there were no significant military obstacles preventing it from doing so, but Mao's preferred strategy was to hold Chamdo and to try for a negotiated settlement that would win the approval of the Dalai Lama and thus the majority of the population of Tibet.

The Tibetans appealed to the United Nations asking that the independent status of their country be recognised but this was rejected after Britain and India vetoed any discussion on the issue. Britain believed that any demand for China to withdraw from Tibet would be unenforceable and India was reluctant to compromise the close relationships that, at the time, it was hoping to develop with the PRC.

Reluctantly, the Tibetan government decided to send a delegation to negotiate with its new masters in Beijing and the result was the Seventeen Point Agreement, signed in Beijing on 23 May 1951, which gave the Tibetan authorities limited autonomy within the PRC in return for agreeing to assist the PLA in its occupation of Tibet and ceding to Beijing the right to conduct foreign relations on its behalf. On 16 October, PLA troops moved to garrison Lhasa under the terms of the agreement. The circumstances under which this agreement was signed remain controversial but it was clearly signed under duress. The Dalai Lama did not take part in the negotiations. He had moved from the Potala Palace in Lhasa to the small town of Yadong, a Tibetan community close to Sikkim on the border with India, in preparation for a swift withdrawal should the PLA march on Lhasa. He returned to Lhasa in August 1951 and agreed to lend his support to the Seventeen Point Agreement in a telegram which was sent to Mao Zedong on 24 October. The Seventeen Point Agreement preserved most of the traditional political and religious structures of Tibet, including the unique role of the Dalai Lama, in exchange for the acknowledgement of Chinese suzerainty over the country. Beijing's strategy during this early period of the PRC was moderate and *laissez-faire* in comparison with later policies and the feudal and monastic economy remained intact – there was no confiscation of land from either the secular feudal landlords or the monasteries.

The agreement applied only to the Tibetan Autonomous Region – that is, the area around the capital Lhasa and Shigatse, the site of the Tashilunpo Monastery, and westwards into the high plains and the mountains. It did not apply to the Tibetan-speaking communities in Gansu, Sichuan and Qinghai, and when land reform and collectivisation policies were carried out in these areas they provoked great hostility from the Tibetan minorities and there were large-scale migrations westwards into central Tibet. In the mid-1950s, the radical collectivisation programmes finally reached central Tibet and resistance to Chinese rule, largely organised by ethnic Tibetan refugees from outside the Tibetan Autonomous Region, was growing apace. Mao tried to reassure the Dalai Lama that Tibet would be protected from the radical reforms that were tearing apart the old rural society in the rest of China, but the resistance movement proved too powerful and the Dalai Lama found himself on the sidelines.

Tibetan insurgency

In March 1959 the attention of the leadership in Beijing was diverted from its factional disputes and the ill-tempered internal debates over the Great Leap and the Communes by news from the far west of China that an armed revolt had broken out in Tibet against the administration that the CCP had established there in 1951. This was seen by Beijing as a serious assault on the integrity of the PRC, and the leadership of the CCP decided that it required an immediate and determined response.

The Tibetan revolt broke out on 10 March 1959 when the headquarters of the PLA and the Chinese government in Lhasa were surrounded by demonstrators. Forces loyal to the Tibetan government turned on the PLA garrison in the Tibetan capital on 19 March. The rising had little chance of succeeding and assistance from the Central Intelligence Agency that some Tibetans believed they had been promised did not materialise in time. Over the next four days, the PLA suppressed the revolt, both in Lhasa and elsewhere in Tibet. The Dalai Lama had left Lhasa two days previously and crossed the border into India on 31 March, renouncing the Seventeen Point Agreement. The Tibetan government was dissolved and a preparatory committee was set up to establish a new Tibetan Autonomous Region government. The Chinese also decided that the Seventeen Point Agreement no longer applied and moved against the monastic and landed elites, confiscating the largest landholdings and closing down monasteries. The Dalai Lama established a government of his own in exile and the Panchen Lama, who was based at the Tashilunpo Monastery in Shigatse, became the highest ranking spiritual leader within Tibet. Historically, incarnations of the Panchen Lama have played an important role as a link between China and the Tibetans. The Panchen Lama was appointed Chairman of the preparatory committee for the Tibetan Autonomous Region on 28 March 1959 on the interesting but specious grounds that the Dalai Lama was being held by rebels against his will.

The Dalai Lama fled into exile in Dharamsala (a hill station in the northern Indian state of Himachal Pradesh). Tibet was designated an Autonomous Region of the PRC on 9 September 1965. The Dalai Lama and his senior religious and political officials remained in Dharamsala, depriving Tibet of the spiritual leadership that most of the population recognised.[6] The Prime Minister of India, Jawaharlal Nehru, formally invited the Dalai Lama to establish his government-in-exile in Dharamsala, an area that although predominantly Hindu had a tradition of Tibetan Buddhism that can be traced back to the eighth century. Dharamsala, and especially the part of Upper Dharamsala which is known as McLeod Ganj, has become a large community of Tibetans in exile. The name McLeod Ganj (market) is a reminder of the history of the area as a nineteenth-century hill station of the British Raj, when it was popular as a summer escape for expatriate members of the Indian Civil Service working in Delhi.

The Cultural Revolution of 1966–76 increased the scale of the political attacks on Tibetan Buddhism and its material culture that had begun during the suppression of the 1959 rising.[7] The death of Mao Zedong in September 1976 led to a period of relative liberalisation and in the mid-1980s, influenced by CCP Secretary-General Hu Yaobang (whose premature death in 1989 precipitated the Democracy Movement and the demonstrations in Tian'anmen Square that were crushed on 4 June). The number of Tibetans participating in local government in Tibet increased and the status of the Tibetan language and Tibetan culture in government and education was enhanced.[8] Hu Yaobang visited Tibet in 1980 on the twenty-ninth anniversary of the Seventeen Point Agreement and was openly critical of the condescending and, in many cases, frankly racist policies and attitudes of Han Chinese cadres in Tibet.[9]

In October 1987, partly in response to a major international diplomatic initiative by Dharamsala to try to procure a settlement to the Tibet question, a wave of demonstrations began in Tibet, led by monks and nuns who supported the creation of an independent Tibet under the Dalai Lama. The first demonstrations were led by monks of Drepung Monastery, which is to the west of Lhasa and is the senior monastery in the Gelug or Yellow Hat tradition. They carried out religious circumambulations of Lhasa and were arrested when they marched on government offices. The protests became violent after demonstrators were arrested and assaulted and police fired on the crowds, killing some of the protestors.

Demonstrations continued, once more led by monks and nuns, whose courage and fortitude in the face of alleged brutality was recognised internationally. A further demonstration took place in 1988 when the Panchen Lama (who was to die unexpectedly shortly afterwards on 28 January 1989) visited Tibet from Beijing in an attempt to ensure the success of the Great Prayer Festival that is traditionally held to accompany celebrations of the Tibetan New Year. Many monks felt that their festival had been hijacked by the CCP and a minor *contretemps* exploded into riots that were followed by mass arrests and a political and religious clampdown. A nationalist Tibetan Buddhist movement had been formed, stimulated by, but isolated from and essentially independent of, the leadership in Dharamsala.[10]

The death of the tenth Panchen Lama in January 1989 and the search for his reincarnation, who would become the eleventh, precipitated another crisis. The Panchen Lama is second only to the Dalai Lama in the Tibetan spiritual hierarchy and some Buddhists in Tibet even place his spiritual authority ahead of that of the Dalai Lama. In the twentieth century, successive Panchen Lamas were generally closer to governments in Beijing than any other high lamas and this resulted in divisions and disagreements over spiritual and political precedence. Beijing tried to take control of the selection process but the choice of a new Panchen incarnation also requires the confirmation of the Dalai Lama. The Dalai Lama announced the name of his candidate, Gedhun Choeki Nyima, on 14 May 1995 but in November of the same year Beijing endorsed a different contender, Gyaltsen Norbu, and the whole process collapsed in complete disarray.[11]

Conflict between the Tibetan religious leadership and Beijing concerning the succession of the Panchen Lama was highlighted when the Abbot of Kumbun Monastery, which is in the province of Qinghai, part of old Tibet, was expelled from the Chinese People's Political Consultative Conference in June 2000 after leaving China for the United States in 1998. Agyo Lobsangtubdain Gyurma had been a member of the committee established by the Chinese that was entrusted with locating the reincarnation of the Panchen Lama but he spoke out in support of the Dalai Lama and rejected the Chinese choice of Gyaltsen Norbu.[12]

The Dalai Lama gave an interview to the journal *Asiaweek* in 2000, in which he reflected on the effect that his death would have on Tibetan people. He said '... if I passed away, the reincarnation would logically come outside Tibet, in a free country. But China will choose a boy as the next Dalai Lama, though in reality he is not.' He added that Tibetans would reject any Panchen Lama who was nominated by Beijing.[13]

Reports of ill-treatment and brutality continued to emerge from Tibet and monks and nuns, the standard-bearers of Tibetan national and religious identity, were frequently the targets. Five nuns, arrested after demonstrations in May 1998, were interrogated in Drapchi Prison and beaten with belts and electric batons after calling out Tibetan nationalist slogans when they were ordered to sing Chinese patriotic songs. They committed suicide.[14]

A young lama, virtually unknown outside the Tibetan community, left Tibet in December 1999 to join the Dalai Lama in Dharamsala. The seventeenth Karmapa Lama who was fourteen years old at the time left the Tsurphu Monastery to the northeast of Lhasa, saying that he was going abroad to buy musical instruments and black hats worn by previous incarnations of the Karmapa. Unusually, the Karmapa Lama, Ugyen Trinley Dorge, who was the son of nomads, had been recognised in 1992 by both Beijing and the Dalai Lama as a reincarnation of the previous head of the Kagyu sect.[15]

The flight of the Karmapa Lama embarrassed the authorities and was followed by an additional political offensive against monasteries in Tibet. Thirty monks were expelled from the Jokhang Temple in Lhasa in June 2000 and the government threatened reprisals against anyone who had taken part in pilgrimages during the festival of Sagadawa. Children were told that they would be expelled from school, officials that they would be dismissed and pensioners that their pensions would be stopped. There were also reports of houses being raided and the seizure of religious objects and photographs of the Dalai Lama. Members of the CCP and teachers who had photographs of the Dalai Lama in their possession were fined.[16]

In September 2000, the Tibetan government-in-exile published a report, *China's Current Policy in Tibet*, in which it claimed that Beijing was aiming at the 'total destruction' of Tibetan culture. The report also argued that the Dalai Lama had moderated the more extreme elements of Tibetan nationalism and that China's refusal to have any contact with him could lead to more violent expressions of dissent.[17]

Qinghai–Tibet railway

Tibet's isolation has been a decisive factor in the development of its distinctive culture. It is physically isolated from China by distance and by the difficulty of developing land transport links from the lowlands to the high plateau. It is isolated from its near neighbour, India, to which it owes its historic Buddhist tradition, by the Himalayas. For some passionate supporters of the culture of Tibetan Buddhism this seclusion has been wholly positive and there are those who will argue that it is precisely Tibet's contact with the outside world that threatens its ancient religious culture. Others, including many thoughtful Tibetans, have concluded that, on the contrary, this isolation has been at the root of Tibet's problems at least since the early part of the twentieth century.

This being the case, the construction of a railway link between China proper and Tibet could never be discussed simply in terms of transport and communications. The railway, which links Xining, the capital city of Qinghai province, to the Tibetan capital Lhasa, had been in the minds of Chinese government planners for generations. It is regarded as an indispensable infrastructural project, without which the economic development of Tibet and its integration into China could not be guaranteed. It took so long to come to fruition largely because of the difficult terrain it would have to cross and the altitude problems that affect not only travellers but also engineers and labourers working on the roof of the world. Track, engines and carriages all required special design to be enable them to operate successfully at high altitude and the coaches had to be equipped with an oxygen supply for passengers.

The Qingzang Railway (Qing and Zang are the standard abbreviations for Qinghai and Tibet, respectively), which is mooted as the world's highest railway, runs for a total of 1,220 miles: the stretch from Xining to the city of Golmud has been operating since 1984 but the final section taking the railway to Tibet was not completed until it became part of the Western Development plan (see Chapter 21). Golmud is the principal city of the Haixi Mongol, Tibetan and Kazakh Autonomous Prefecture, the name of which gives an indication of the complex ethnic mix of this mountainous region. Construction of the key final stage from Golmud to Lhasa began in 2001 and was complete by the autumn of 2005. The formal opening ceremony took place on 1 July 2006 after months of testing of both track and rolling stock.

Services using this line include long-distance trains which run to Lhasa from Beijing, Chengdu, Chongqing, Xining and Lanzhou. The journey from Beijing to Lhasa takes almost forty-eight hours and even the section from Xining to Lhasa takes twenty-six hours, in spite of journey speeds which are fast in comparison with much of the rest of China's railway system.

Critics of the construction project argue that, far from improving the lives of Tibetans, the new rail link will serve to strengthen China's control over Tibet and will encourage the migration of young Tibetans away from their homeland in search of employment. Further, it will promote the migration to Tibet from the east of Han Chinese who are likely to obtain preferential treatment in employment opportunities. There are also concerns about the potential environmental impact of the increased flow of tourists and traders to the Tibetan plateau. The Qinghai–Tibet highway which also brings in trade and migrants has not experienced the same high-level criticism. Because the opening of the railway line was turned into a high-profile event by the Chinese government, it became a symbol for the entire economic and political relationship between Beijing and Tibet.

Talks on the future of Tibet between Beijing and the Dalai Lama's representatives continue behind the scenes, although this is not at all apparent from the rancorous rhetoric that is used by both sides in public, especially in statements emanating from Beijing. In October 2007, the Dalai Lama was awarded the Congressional Medal of Freedom by the President of the United States, George W. Bush. This was applauded by many Westerners as a sign of American support for religious freedom. Beijing was predictably outraged at what it could argue was outside interference in its own domestic affairs; when demonstrations to celebrate the award of the medal took place in Tibet, they were crushed with some force by the Chinese authorities.

18 Xinjiang

As the Xinjiang Uyghur Autonomous Region marked its fiftieth anniversary in 2005, Beijing was deploying both the carrot of economic development and the stick of political and religious repression to maintain its control of the region.

In the past, Xinjiang has been described as both the 'pivot of Asia' and a pawn of the Soviet Union. Today it is the only part of Islamic Central Asia controlled by China, and it is China's land bridge to Eurasia. It is both oil-rich and politically unstable because of separatist sentiment among the indigenous Muslim and Turkic-speaking Uyghurs, many of whom would like a return to an independent Eastern Turkestan, a state which existed briefly in the 1940s.

In Xinjiang, the Islamic traditions of Central Asia and China overlap although they maintain a largely separate existence and the mosques of the Chinese-speaking Hui communities are quite separate from Uyghur mosques.[1]

The network of mosques across Xinjiang provides the framework for the complex system of worship, education and law that dominated the region before it came under the control of the Chinese Communist Party (CCP) in 1949. It is difficult to obtain credible statistics on the total number of mosques but one estimate suggests that in 1949 there were 29,545 mosques in the whole of Xinjiang. By the start of the Cultural Revolution (roughly 1966–76) this had been reduced to 14,119; many had fallen into disrepair, some had been requisitioned by the government and others had been demolished or closed down during anti-religious and other campaigns such as the movement for land reform. During the chaos of the Cultural Revolution, there were said to be only 1,400 active mosques, but by 1990 the number had risen again to over 17,000 and there were more than 43,000 other 'places of religious activity', presumably shrines and *madrasas*.[2]

Mazars: Sufi tomb culture

While mosques in Xinjiang are found in most villages, towns and cities, the *mazar* tombs of the Sufi *shaykhs* (or *sheikhs*) and the religious complexes that have grown up around them are usually in isolated rural settings.[3]

The tombs are the homes of the mystical Sufi orders (predominantly the Jahriyya and Khufiyya branches of the Naqshbandiyya). Members of the orders make pilgrimages to the tombs on the anniversary of the death of the founding *shaykh* and on major religious festivals. These pilgrimages have on occasion attracted crowds of such a size that the authorities have banned or restricted them. The *mazar* culture is viewed by the Chinese state as a serious threat to its authority and has been the subject of frequent repression by the authorities; it has also been attacked by conservative Muslims and by Islamic reformers influenced directly or indirectly by Wahhabi teachings that have spread to Xinjiang from Saudi Arabia.

It is impossible to estimate with any confidence how many active *mazars* there are in Xinjiang, but a serious and authoritative study by an Uyghur scholar lists seventy-three major sites.[4] Because of the Uyghurs' dislike of the regulation of mosques by the government, this parallel Islam is becoming more popular. The fact that these sects are part of a trans-national Islamic movement (in particular, the highly political Naqshbandiyya) is also attractive to the isolated Turkic-speaking Muslims of Xinjiang but troubles the Chinese authorities.[5]

Demonstrations and resistance in Xinjiang

Antagonism between Uyghur Muslims and the Chinese authorities had persisted since the suppression of the insurrections of the 1950s, but the conflict became more acute and more visible in the 1980s. It was most intense in two areas of Xinjiang: the southwest which is dominated by the great Uyghur cultural and Islamic centre of Kashghar and the Yining/Ghulja region in the northwest which is close to the border between China and Kazakhstan.[6]

Major disturbances began in April 1980 with riots in the town of Aksu, which is midway between Urumqi and Kashghar, following clashes between local Uyghur people and members of the quasi-military Xinjiang Production and Construction Corps (XPCC) and groups of demobilised Red Guards, who were predominantly Han. This led to similar disturbances in Kashghar, student protests in Urumqi and demonstrations by Uyghurs studying in the Central Nationalities Institute in Beijing who protested against racial and religious insults against Muslims. Generalised disaffection at Chinese rule was gradually evolving into a broad opposition movement.

On 5 April 1990 in the town of Baren, which lies close to Kashghar, the regular prayers at a mosque turned into demonstrations against the CCP's policies towards ethnic minorities. Some protesters called for a *jihad* against the unbelievers and there were demands for the establishment of an Eastern Turkestan state. The demonstrators were able to ward off the police and it took the intervention of units of the People's Armed Police and regular troops from the Kashghar garrison to subdue them. The Baren Uprising was not simply a spontaneous act of defiance: it was the result of a carefully planned and organised operation by a group which identified itself as the Eastern Turkestan Islamic Party and explicitly linked politicised Islam with the call for the independence of Xinjiang. The rebels attacked military vehicles and launched an assault on the town hall, which was the local symbol of Chinese administration. Police, troops and the militia of the XPCC put down the uprising after an early morning counterattack on 6 April. The incident revealed the depth of anti-Chinese feeling, the degree of organisation of the rebels and the Islamisation of the independence struggle. There were bomb attacks by separatist units on a bus in Urumqi in 1992 and on government buildings in the city of Kashghar in 1993.

The focus of opposition moved to the town in the Ili region which is known as Yining to the Chinese and Ghulja to the Uyghurs. It is an important symbol to many Uyghurs as it was the seat of an independent East Turkestan government in the 1940s. Unrest in the spring of 1995 began with demonstrations calling for an end to Chinese rule in the region and police stations and local government offices were attacked and looted. There were also verbal, and occasionally physical, assaults on imams who were considered to be compromised by their cooperation with the Chinese authorities. The government mobilised 20,000 troops under the command of the Lanzhou Military Region to put down the insurrection. Its parallel political response was to launch a nationwide 'Strike Hard' campaign, ostensibly against organised crime and hooliganism but, in the ethnic minority areas including Xinjiang, also designed to strike at the roots of opposition to Beijing's rule.

The Strike Hard campaign in Xinjiang led to harsh and sustained repression during 1996 and there were public trials of large numbers of Uyghurs who were accused of serious criminal offences but who were also alleged to be linked to the separatist movement; many were executed. There were also persistent reports of secret executions of separatists without trial. In this atmosphere of repression and anger, young Uyghurs took to the streets of Yining/Ghulja on 5 February 1997, attacking Han Chinese residents of the city. Police action to stop the violence led to an escalation of the protests and the following day there were further attacks on Han residents and their property. The Yining Uprising has become notorious for the violence with which it was suppressed. Official figures claim that fewer than 200 people were killed by the police and military, but eyewitness reports suggest that the death toll was much higher and may have run into the thousands. The violence continued sporadically until 9 February and there were bomb attacks by separatist groups in Urumqi on 25 February and, unusually, in Beijing on 7 March. Public security organisations were placed on the highest alert nationwide and launched a major crackdown in Xinjiang, arresting thousands of people in what was essentially an intensification of the Strike Hard campaign. The authorities also embarked on campaigns of political education utilising the theme of national unity.[7]

CCP policy and the Religious Affairs Bureau

The CCP has sought to regulate all religions, including Islam, through the Religious Affairs Bureau which was established by the State Council in 1954 and its successor organisation, the State Administration for Religious Affairs, established in 1998. It created the Chinese Islamic Association with which all mosques, *madrasas* and other Muslim organisations are legally obliged to register. Many groups, including some of the Sufi organisations, have refused to register on the grounds that an atheist state should have no authority over their doctrines and forms of worship.

This has created a conflict, not only between unregistered Muslim organisations and the government but also between registered and unregistered Muslim groups. The Chinese Islamic Association fell into abeyance during the Cultural Revolution but was resurrected after Deng Xiaoping came to power in 1978. New mosques were built and older ones that had been damaged during the Cultural Revolution were restored or even extended and worship became more open and relaxed.

When the rise of political and ethnic dissent began to alarm the authorities in the 1990s, the situation changed abruptly. The confidential internal *Document No. 7*, issued by the CCP in 1996, identified separatism in Xinjiang as the greatest threat to the region and to the nation as a whole. *Inter alia* it demanded a crackdown on illegal *madrasas*, a restriction on the construction of new mosques and an end to independent classes in martial arts and Qur'an study sessions which were suspected of being used as cover for separatist activities. It called for a purge of Party cadres who were also devout Muslims and who had refused to give up their beliefs in spite of years of CCP ideological indoctrination.[8]

Religious restrictions in Xinjiang

State control over Muslims in Xinjiang was reinforced after the publication of *Document No. 7* and further intensified after the uprising in Yining/Ghulja in February 1997. The attacks by Al Qaeda on New York and Washington in September 2001 reinforced China's fears of the links between separatism and political Islam, but the repression in Xinjiang had already been in place for five years.

Under the new restrictions, children under the age of eighteen were prohibited from entering mosques and the wearing of the *hijab* and other forms of Islamic dress was strictly forbidden in schools. Members of the CCP and the Communist Youth League and employees of government organisations, including retired members of staff, were forbidden to enter mosques and notices outlining these restrictions appeared in Uyghur at the entrances to all mosques. Mosques were also barred from any involvement in disputes over marriage and family planning and there was a specific prohibition on reading out the Islamic marriage contract, the *nikah*, in the mosque before a couple getting married had been issued with a valid civil marriage certificate. The aim of these restrictions was to assert the primacy of civil laws over Islamic law and to restrict the authority of the local *qadi* judges. Printed or taped materials which related to anything deemed to be religious extremism or separatism were also explicitly banned and the teaching of religion anywhere other than in a registered mosque was also outlawed. The new restrictions limited the sale of religious literature in general and a list of banned books was issued to booksellers.

The training of 'patriotic religious personnel'

It has been estimated that there were 54,575 imams or more senior religious leaders in Xinjiang in 1949 but that, as a result of the campaigns of the 1950s, this had been reduced to 27,000 by the start of the Cultural Revolution in 1966. Officially, few were active during the Cultural Revolution but in reality imams simply continued to operate without the knowledge of the Chinese authorities.

The only organisation for training imams from the whole of China, including Xinjiang, in the 1950s and 1960s was the Chinese Islamic Academy in Beijing. In 1987 an Islamic Academy was established in Urumqi specifically to cater for imams from Xinjiang and the first graduates left the academy in 1992 to staff the mosques of the region. The Qur'an was also published in an Uyghur translation to cater for those whose grasp of Arabic was poor. The Religious Affairs Bureau exercised considerable control over the training and curriculum of Islamic education.[9]

During 2001, 8,000 imams from the mosques of Xinjiang were compelled to take part in a 'patriotic education campaign'. This was organised by a special work team under the control of the central government in Beijing and ran from 15 March to 23 December. Imams were required to attend seminars during which they were instructed in the CCP's thinking on legal, political and religious topics and they were ordered to avoid any involvement with mosques or other groups that were deemed to be involved in separatist activities. This campaign was designed to strengthen government control over the registered mosques and to increase the gulf between these official bodies and those that refused to register.

There were no serious outbreaks of violence associated with separatists or with political Islam between 1997 and 2008, but Xinjiang remained tense and Uyghur Muslims continued to be subjected to severe and ongoing surveillance and repression, especially at work and in schools and colleges.

The present-day government in Beijing emphasises the growing modernisation and economic prosperity of its northwest frontier province of Xinjiang but constantly draws attention to what it perceives as a real threat from extremist Islamist and separatist activists.

The preparations for the fiftieth anniversary of the foundation of the Xinjiang Uyghur Autonomous Region, which was celebrated on 1 October 2005, were accompanied by an increase in the rhetoric of political repression as Beijing warned of threats that were posed to the unity and stability of China by armed insurgents, allegedly linked to Al Qaeda. In reality, there was little change in the level of repression experienced by Uyghurs in Xinjiang. The surveillance and the restriction on religious activities and religious education has been severe and relentless since 1996, and, apart from a temporary period of tension, did not increase appreciably as a result of the 11 September 2001 attacks on New York and Washington. Beyond the rhetoric, Beijing is genuinely concerned that a combination of Eastern Turkestan nationalism and political Islam will continue to destabilise the region and that a long-term climate of discontent could erupt into a popular movement that it would feel obliged to suppress with overwhelming military force. These concerns were aired most dramatically in the Politburo's internal *Document No. 7*, which was published confidentially in 1996 but has been leaked in both Chinese and Uyghur versions. The rise of the Taliban in Afghanistan, the civil war in Tajikistan and unrest in Uzbekistan and Kyrgyzstan all persuaded analysts in Beijing that Central Asian Islam is a serious long-term threat to China's stability.

Economic reform in Xinjiang

Beijing's strategy in dealing with the problem of ethnic separatism in Xinjiang since the early 1990s has been twofold. On the one hand, there has been ruthless repression of any unofficial religious activity and any political or cultural activities that could be classified as separatist. On the other hand, the CCP has embarked on an ambitious programme of economic reform, on the assumption that the principal underlying reason for the disaffection of the Uyghurs is not ethnic nationalism but poverty and underdevelopment. The decision was made to confront the problem of the relative underdevelopment of China's western provinces as a whole and the policy of the Great Development of the Western Regions (*Xibu da kaifa*), the Go West policy, was launched in 2000 in Chengdu, the capital of Sichuan province (see Chapter 21).

The development of the energy resources of Xinjiang has been one of the notable consequences of the Go West policy. An oil pipeline which links the region with Kazakhstan and another pipeline which transports much-needed natural gas to fuel the industrial and commercial development of Shanghai are two of the most important enterprises, although the impetus for both projects predates the announcement of the Go West policy. Both are major infrastructure projects which are designed to ensure that Xinjiang's vast natural resources are deployed to support the overall development of China's economy. Both have been financed through partnerships with foreign corporations, although China has retained overall control of the process.

There has also been substantial investment in the oilfields of northern Xinjiang, which has enjoyed far greater development than the predominantly agricultural south of the region. This has been achieved in part by the import of modern technology, technical expertise and labour, in some cases from abroad but mainly from the east of China. The expertise and labour is provided by predominantly Han Chinese engineers, technicians and workers and their presence in the region in well-paid and high-status occupations has increased the anxiety of Uyghurs, who are usually less well educated and less competent in the Chinese language, that they are being marginalised in their own land.

In spite of the undoubted improvements in the economy of much of Xinjiang over the past five years, ethnic and political tensions remain unresolved. For the government of the People's Republic of China (PRC), the preservation of Xinjiang as an integral part of the PRC is non-negotiable: it is seen as a vital source of China's escalating energy requirements and is essential to the security of China's Inner Asian borders, especially since the establishment of US bases in Central Asia. It is also a matter of national pride that no part of the existing territory of China should be lost.

Although there have been no serious disturbances in Xinjiang since the late 1990s or associated acts of political terror, the problem has not disappeared.

Some of the armed insurgent groups that existed within Xinjiang have been forced out, first to Kyrgyzstan and subsequently to Afghanistan and the Tribal Areas on Pakistan's border with Afghanistan. If they have been renewed or replaced, the new organisations have so far kept a very low profile. However, support for independence, or at least loathing of Chinese control, remains as strong as ever and could re-emerge at any time as was shown by bomb attacks in Kashghar and Kuqa in August 2008.

19   Hong Kong

Hong Kong became a British possession at the end of the Opium War (1839–42). The island of Hong Kong was ceded to the British Crown in perpetuity under the Treaty of Nanjing which was concluded in 1842 and which marked the formal end of the war. The Kowloon peninsula, which is on the mainland, was acquired in 1860 and in 1898 Britain was given a ninety-nine-year lease to the New Territories which lie to the north of Hong Kong on the border with Guangdong province. This lease expired in 1997 and consequently 1997 was the date set for the return of the colony to China. In theory, Hong Kong island could have been retained by Britain but in practice, it could not have functioned independently without resources and labour from the mainland parts of the colony.

Between 1842 and 1997, Hong Kong was run as a Crown colony with a British governor and a civil administration that was dominated by expatriate British officials. It developed as a trading and manufacturing centre and became one of the most important ports and financial centres of Asia. No attempt was made to create a system of political democracy: Hong Kong under the British was an unequal society with most of its Chinese inhabitants, who were the majority of the population, taking no part in the running of the territory in which they lived. Nevertheless it was an economic success story from which much of the population benefited. The Second World War and the post-war mood for decolonisation changed it significantly and set it on the long slow road to its eventual return to China on 1 July 1997.

Japanese Occupation

The occupation of Hong Kong by the Imperial Japanese Army during the Second World War lasted from the surrender of the British garrison by the Governor Sir Mark Young on 25 December 1941 to the capitulation of Japan in August 1945. This difficult and uncomfortable period is known to many Hong Kong residents simply as 'the three years and eight months'. The colony was ruled under martial law, thousands of British servicemen and women and civilians were imprisoned in internment camps and there were widespread food shortages which led to malnutrition, the spread of disease and the consequent loss of life. Conditions were much harsher for the majority of the population of the colony, the Chinese, than for the Europeans. Japanese troops behaved towards the Chinese with at best callousness and at worst brutality, as they had in the rest of occupied China. Although some sections of the population, including elements of the business class of Indian origin, were initially seduced by the Japanese claim that they would liberate fellow Asians from the racist rule of European colonialists, this illusion did not last long and reality soon set in. Some members of the local business community, irrespective of ethnic background, cooperated with the Japanese occupiers as they had in other parts of China. There was also resistance but it was in vain.

Japan established its own colonial administration and Japanese specialists were brought in to occupy the most senior government and administrative posts, with Chinese employees remaining in subordinate positions.

Return of the British

In August 1945, after the unconditional surrender of the Japanese government and the collapse of Japan's dreams of empire, plans for the reoccupation of the colony were put into effect almost immediately and a British naval task force entered Hong Kong harbour on 30 August 1945. Rear Admiral C. H. J. Harcourt, the commander of the task force, sailed into Hong Kong on board the cruiser *HMS Swiftsure* to re-establish the British government's control over the colony. A British military administrative office was set up in Victoria on Hong Kong island on 1 September and on 16 September the new administration accepted the formal surrender of the Japanese garrison in the colony at Government House.[1]

The reoccupation was effected by means of a certain diplomatic sleight of hand because it did not entirely meet with the approval of Chiang Kai-shek. Chiang assumed that his Guomindang (GMD) government was going to resume its control over the whole of China – control that had been so rudely interrupted by the Japanese attack on Nanjing in 1937. As nationalists, the GMD were opposed to the occupation of Hong Kong by the British and wished it to be returned to China. Chiang had made it clear that he wished the surrender of the Japanese forces in Hong Kong to be taken by his own Nationalist troops, but circumstances obliged him to compromise and the surrender was in fact taken by the British but under his nominal authority as a courtesy. Sir Mark Young returned as governor for a year but he was replaced by Sir Alexander Grantham in July 1947.

Even at this early stage, the shadow of the eventual handover had fallen over Hong Kong and a division was beginning to emerge between those who thought they could somehow avoid the inevitability by economic and political reform and those who accepted it and tried to work towards the best possible outcome. In both cases, there was an agreement that the priority for Hong Kong should be economic development. The assumption was that prosperity would reduce demands from the Chinese population of Hong Kong for the return of the colony to China. It was also hoped that Hong Kong would be so valuable to China as an intermediary during the period of China's isolation after the Korean War, and later as a financial services centre with international connections and credibility, that Beijing would not wish to exert overwhelming pressure on the colony. Many in the administration and the populace in general simply avoided the issue and went about their normal business.

The British presented the new post-war administration as simply a case of carrying on where they had left off after a brief, ill-mannered, interruption by the Japanese Occupation. In reality, the character of Hong Kong society was never to be the same again: it changed subtly but profoundly. Some of the changes came about as a result of legislation: strict regulations on the Chinese-language press were rescinded and the exclusive residential areas of the Peak were no longer limited by law to Europeans. More significantly for long-term social change in the colony, there was a drive to recruit additional Chinese employees into government service at all levels. The colonial apparatus remained but it was being opened up to the local majority population.

Hong Kong and the PRC

As the Civil War in China came to an end in 1948–49 and it became clear that the Chinese Communist Party (CCP) was going to form the next government, what had been a gradual flow of refugees moving south turned into a mass migration and thousands of Chinese citizens headed towards the colony. Most of the migrants were farmers who settled in the New Territories, the largest area of land in Hong Kong: it is in the north of the colony and is geographically part of the mainland. The farmers were able to rent small parcels of land – market gardens – and grew vegetables for which there was an increasing demand in the urban areas of Hong Kong. This new market-oriented economy disrupted the older rice-growing economy of the New Territories, which faced collapse. Emigration to the United Kingdom from Hong Kong began in this period as many farming families chose to migrate rather than find different ways of earning a living in Hong Kong.[2]

The political and personnel changes that occurred in the People's Republic of China (PRC) in the 1970s made it easier for progress to be made in its relations with Hong Kong. After the death of Lin Biao in 1971, Zhou Enlai's more intelligent and conciliatory foreign policy permitted high-level contacts with the United States and other Western governments. Mao Zedong died in 1976 and the 'reform and opening' policy agenda of Deng Xiaoping incorporated an awareness of the need for China to engage with the wider world.

At the same time, the new Governor of the colony, Sir Murray Maclehose, who had been appointed in 1971, took a practical and positive approach to contacts with Beijing. He broke with all precedents by developing a cordial working relationship with the Xinhua (New China) News Agency office in Hong Kong. Xinhua is the official news agency of the PRC and its office in Hong Kong was for many years the only form of representation that Beijing had in the colony: it acted both as an unofficial embassy and as an important conduit for information and for informal and, in many cases, unacknowledged negotiations.

Preparing for the handover

The Governor, Sir Murray Maclehose, made an official visit to China in 1979 to discuss an improvement in trade between Hong Kong and China and, in particular, to take part in discussions with the government of the PRC on how the colony could assist in China's ambitious programme of economic modernisation. Although this was not the beginning of formal negotiations about the terms and timetable for the formal handover of Hong Kong to China, it was a useful reconnaissance mission and enabled the Governor and his closest colleagues to form an opinion of the attitudes of the new reform-minded leadership in Beijing on the Hong Kong issue.[3] One of Governor Maclehose's significant domestic policy initiatives was the establishment in 1974 of the Independent Commission Against Corruption (ICAC), which attempted to stamp out what was perceived to be an unacceptable level of corruption in the civil service and the police and was an issue that had to be resolved before the handover.

The task of initiating the formal negotiations on the future of Hong Kong with Beijing fell to Lord Maclehose's successor as Governor, Sir Edward Youde, who took office in 1982 and these negotiations took place the same year, both before and during the visit to China of the British Prime Minister, Margaret Thatcher. Mrs Thatcher took an uncompromising stance on the continuation of a British presence in Hong Kong after what she regarded as her success in the Falklands War. However, the Chinese under Deng Xiaoping were equally, if not more, intransigent and were insisting on the return of Hong Kong to Chinese control. In theory, there was a difference between the legal status of the island of Hong Kong which had been ceded to Britain in perpetuity in 1842 and the New Territories, which were British by virtue of a ninety-nine-year lease that was due to expire in 1997. In practice, there was common consent that the two parts of the colony were not viable separately and would have to be treated as a whole. An accommodation between Britain and China was therefore essential for Hong Kong's continued economic success and social stability.

Negotiations between Britain and China continued until September 1984, by which time it was clear to the British negotiators that Beijing was not going to give way in its determination that Hong Kong would return to China. Britain had hoped to be able to continue administering Hong Kong after the transfer of sovereignty, but this was completely unacceptable to the Chinese side. The Sino–British Joint Declaration on Hong Kong was agreed and initialled in Beijing on 26 September 1984 by Sir Richard Evans, Britain's ambassador to the PRC, and Zhou Nan, the Chinese Deputy Minister of Foreign Affairs. The formal signing ceremony by Mrs Thatcher and the Chinese Premier, Zhou Enlai, took place in Beijing on 19 December and, after a period of formal ratification, the agreement became effective from May 1985.

Joint Agreement

Under the terms of the Joint Agreement, it was agreed that the sovereignty of the entire territory of Hong Kong would be transferred to China on 1 July 1997. Britain would continue to be responsible for administering the territory in the interim and the PRC would cooperate in this. China agreed that it would create a Special Administrative Region (SAR) to govern Hong Kong and allowed that the SAR would enjoy a considerable degree of autonomy in all questions with the exception of foreign policy and matters connected with defence. A SAR was a new concept, although Special Economic Regions, including Hong Kong's immediate neighbour Shenzhen within the PRC, were already in existence.

The Joint Agreement provided for a Chief Executive to be nominated by China in place of the Governor but accepted that existing personnel, including foreign nationals, would be able to remain in post. Existing social and economic practices, the legal system and the rights and freedoms that the colony had traditionally enjoyed would be respected. It was also announced that a *Basic Law* would be drawn up and that this would be enacted and ratified by the National People's Congress (NPC) in Beijing. This law would guarantee the status quo in Hong Kong for fifty years under a formula that went by the name of 'one country, two systems'. In other words, although Hong Kong would be deemed to be a constituent part of the PRC, it would be governed according to the long-established capitalist system and in a manner that would take into account the distinctive way of life that prevailed there rather than the state-dominated economic system of the mainland. There had been great apprehension in Hong Kong about the outcome of these negotiations and, although there was still concern and lack of confidence in the willingness and ability of China to act on the basis of the Joint Agreement, the feeling overall was one of relief and an acknowledgement that things could have been much worse.

Basic Law

The *Basic Law* was drafted by a joint committee which included members from both Hong Kong and the PRC. There was considerable public consultation in Hong Kong and rather less on the mainland. It was adopted by the Seventh NPC on 4 April 1990 and became effective on the day of the handover, 1 July 1997. The text of the *Basic Law* covered the autonomy of the SAR: the maintenance of the status quo for fifty years and the preservation of the existing system of legislation, including protection from arbitrary detention or imprisonment and freedom of speech, the press and assembly. A number of issues remained contentious, notably the question of the right to abode of mainland residents who might wish to settle in Hong Kong; the possibility of a move towards complete universal suffrage; and the length of the term of office of future Chief Executives.

Democracy in Hong Kong?

When the Joint Agreement became effective in May 1985, Hong Kong entered a period of uncharted waters. An issue that had concerned both residents and foreign observers for decades but had been largely avoided by the administration, Hong Kong's lack of democracy, suddenly acquired greater importance in this transitional period. It has been argued that the absence of democracy in Hong Kong in the post-war period was due to the lack of grassroots demand and a popular perception that, at least in economic terms, the government was delivering the goods. However, there was a long-established core of activists who had argued for redressing the democratic deficit. The spilling over of the Cultural Revolution into Hong Kong in 1967 certainly did not help the cause of democracy and the demonstrations provoked more alarm than sympathy. The colonial government did use the opportunity this presented to increase the degree of public participation in the processes of government and the positive response that this generated suggests that democratisation was long overdue.[4]

Hong Kong did not have a democratically elected parliament. The legislative body of Hong Kong, the Legislative Council (Legco) was created in 1843 by the British colonial administration under the terms of the *Charter of Hong Kong, Letters Patent of Queen Victoria*. The members of Legco were not democratically elected but were appointed to advise the Governor, who alone had the authority to enact legislation. When the 1843 *Charter* was replaced in 1917, the wording of the new *Letters Patent* was altered to clarify the relationship between the Governor and Legco by stressing that Legco was not merely an advisory body but that its consent was required for legislation. Membership of Legco was increased from time to time until, by 1976, it had twenty-three official and twenty-three unofficial members (the unofficial members did not have government posts and were in large part drawn from the business community). The first elections to Legco did not take place until 1985 and the number of unofficial members was increased so that it exceeded the number of official members. In 1995 the final Legco before the handover included twenty of its membership who had been returned by direct elections. Legco had evolved very slowly from an advisory to a legislative body but resistance to the idea of elections by full universal suffrage continued to the very end.

The final colonial Governor, Chris Patten, was a British conservative politician who had lost his seat in the constituency of Bath in the 1992 elections. His governorship was controversial because of his abrasive manner towards officials in Beijing and the changes he made to the functional constituencies from which the unofficial members of Legco were elected. These changes effectively extended the franchise in the last elections before the handover, apparently against the understanding that had been reached in the negotiations and were against the wishes of Beijing. The final Legco of the colonial era was dissolved after the handover and replaced by a provisional body. The new Legislative Council of the Hong Kong SAR with eighty members was elected in May 1998.[5] Patten's reforms attracted a great deal of support within Hong Kong, especially but not exclusively among the expatriate community, and some considered that he had taken an important stand against Beijing.

The formal handover of power to the PRC took place on 1 July 1997 in a ceremony which was attended by Prince Charles, the heir to the British Crown. After the ceremony he and the last Governor departed from the last colony on the royal yacht, *Britannia*.

The governance of Hong Kong was assumed by the first Chief Executive,

Tung Chee-hwa, a businessman with close ties to the government in Beijing. He was succeeded in 2005 by a former civil servant, Donald Tsang, who had served as the colony's Financial Secretary from 1995. Currently, the Chief Executive is not directly elected, but in December 2007, pressure from Hong Kong led to an agreement by the Standing Committee of the NPC in Beijing that direct elections could be considered from 2017 and that Legco could be elected by universal suffrage by 2020. This was a disappointment to many, who had hoped that direct elections would be introduced in 2012.[6]

The Portuguese colony of Macao, Hong Kong's near neighbour, agreed to revert to Chinese rule under similar conditions in 1999.

20 Taiwan

The relationship between Taiwan and the People's Republic of China (PRC) remains an enigma to outsiders. The existence of two separate Chinese states, neither of which recognises the other, is one of the more bizarre political hangovers from the Cold War. The situation makes no sense without some understanding of the historical process by which this situation arose in the 1940s and 1950s.

The government of the Republic of China on Taiwan chose to regard itself as Free China throughout the Cold War period, in spite of the fact that it was a one-party state (as was the PRC), that it ruled Taiwan under martial law for thirty-eight years and that it was largely a regime staffed by supporters of the Guomindang (GMD)[1] Nationalists, imported from the mainland, who governed the indigenous Taiwanese and aboriginal populations often against their will.

Economy of post-war Taiwan

From 1945 the economy of Taiwan grew at an unprecedented rate. Supporters of the Free China concept choose to attribute this either to the superiority of the GMD's policies over their Communist rivals on the mainland or to the greater capacity of the island's population for hard work and creativity. However, the economic development and prosperity of Taiwan in the 1950s could not have been achieved without the generous financial support of successive United States administrations, initially by means of aid packages as part of the US economic support for its Cold War allies and, when these were withdrawn in 1965, as a financial arrangement that acknowledged Taiwan's role in the provision of supplies for the US forces during the Vietnam War.

The government in Taipei implemented a programme of Land Reform at the same time that the Chinese Communist Party (CCP) was carrying out its own policies of confiscation and redistribution of agricultural land on the mainland. For the GMD, this programme of rural reconstruction was not a socialist policy as such but a practical realisation of Sun Yat-sen's policies of 'land to the tiller'. It was a three-stage programme which began with an overall reduction in the rent paid by tenant farmers; continued with the sale to farmers of publicly owned land that had originally been retained by the Japanese colonial administration to encourage immigration from Japan; and was completed with a compulsory purchase programme under which the government acquired land from large land holdings and resold it to farmers at cost plus interest. Agricultural productivity and the rural standard of living increased as a result of these policies.

Taiwan's industrialisation was even more successful than its agricultural transformation. A period of post-war reconstruction was followed by a four-year economic plan which provided investment for small and medium-sized enterprises. By 1956, the number of factories and factory workers and their per capita income had risen dramatically. During the 1960s, Taiwan gradually moved towards a policy of encouraging the production of consumer durables for the export trade and established itself as a major participant in international export markets.[2]

Taiwanese and mainlanders

Since 1949, Taiwan (or Formosa, as it continued to be known in the West for many years, retaining the name *Ilha Formosa* (Beautiful Island), that had been given to it by Portuguese traders) has been presented in contrasting political guises. To many Westerners, and to the government of Chiang Kai-shek during what it believed was its temporary exile on the island, it was Free China. The government, and its allies overseas, continued to regard Chiang's administration as the legitimate government of the whole of China and assumed that it would one day resume its rightful position and govern the mainland once more from its capital in Nanjing. To the newly established government of the PRC in Beijing, Taiwan was a bastion of the defeated Nationalist GMD where they had been able to find short-term refuge. Beijing believed that in due course the Nationalist rebels would be crushed and the island would return to being a province of China and would submit to the authority of the CCP's government.

The Cold War in Asia, exacerbated by the Korean War, ensured that these two positions became firmly entrenched. For the people who lived in Taiwan, it was never as simple as these arguments suggest. The group of military officers and civilian administrators, who had crossed to the island, both in advance of and accompanying the retreating Nationalist government during the Civil War of the late 1940s, gradually established themselves, not as members of a transitory administration but as a new ruling elite for the island. They displaced the colonial administration that had been controlled by Japan and replaced it with a Chinese government, but this was not a government of Taiwanese but one of mainlanders who spoke Mandarin and brought with them the cultural attitudes and political networks of the mainland.

The indigenous Taiwanese, the descendants of a much earlier generation of migrants from Fujian, who spoke the language of that southeastern province of China in a modified Taiwanese form, were effectively excluded from power. Their language is often called 'Taiwanese' but that name is unhelpful as it suggests that it is only spoken on the island. Linguistic specialists know it as *Minnan*, which is also spoken in the southern part of Fujian province on the mainland. *Min* is the traditional single-character name for Fujian and *nan* means south.

The ethnic and political conflict between these two groups has affected every aspect of the development of Taiwan's history from the 1940s until the present day but, for most of that time, it is a conflict that has been obscured, and was rarely referred to and little understood by outsiders. If the confrontation with the CCP was the GMD's major overseas challenge in the years after the Second World War, its confrontation with the movement for Taiwanese self-government was its greatest domestic challenge.

Taiwan gradually evolved into a one-party state, a mirror image of its Communist adversary on the mainland: the GMD was the only political party legally permitted to exist until 1986 and martial law, which had been imposed in 1947, remained in force until 1987.

Movement for democracy in Taiwan

The beginnings of a movement for a democratic Taiwan can be traced to the periodical, *Free China (Ziyou Zhongguo)*. In its inaugural edition in November 1949, the prominent liberal intellectual, Hu Shi, set out the journal's twin objectives of supporting the idea of a free and independent China based on Taiwan and opposition to Communism. Initially the outlook of *Free China* chimed with the views of the GMD, which was on the point of taking power on the island. However, when the Korean War broke out and Taiwan began to receive aid from the United States which strengthened its political position, the GMD no longer felt able to tolerate the discordant voices of the liberal intelligentsia, began a rectification campaign and arrested dissidents. *Free China* responded by attacking the economic and social policies of the GMD administration in articles and editorials, including a special edition criticising Chiang Kai-shek on the occasion of his seventieth birthday. It grew more and more unsympathetic to the government and in 1960 opposed a proposal that Chiang Kai-shek should be appointed to a third term in office. The Constitution of the Republic of China specified that a President should be elected for a term of six years and that this could be extended for a second term but not a third. The National Assembly voted to suspend this constitutional requirement in February 1960, in the light of the tension between Taiwan and the mainland, and on 21 March Chiang was elected for a third term in office as President. He subsequently served a fourth and a fifth term. *Free China* also called on the government to abandon the idea of a counterattack on the mainland and proposed the establishment of a separate Democratic Republic of Chinese Taiwan to oppose the PRC. A group associated with *Free China* formed a political party, the China Democratic Party, to contest elections but, on the eve of the party's launch in September 1960, the leaders were arrested by the troops of the Taiwan garrison headquarters on suspicion of involvement in an armed rebellion and the party was strangled at birth. *Free China* was outlawed and ceased publication that year.

The repression was so severe that an open and organised opposition did not reappear until the 1970s, by which time Taiwanese society was undergoing great changes as a result of the industrialisation of the island and the emergence of a new middle class. In the early 1970s, the periodical *University Review (Daxue zazhi*) took on the role of the government's main critic although it did not actively engage in politics. It was joined by *Taiwan Political Commentary* (*Taiwan zhenglun*) in 1975.

The Extra-Party (*Dangwai*) movement which developed in the 1970s became the major focus for dissidents. The term *Dangwai* (literally 'outside the party') had originally meant anyone who was not a member of the GMD but it became used more widely for members of the opposition movement who did not necessarily belong to any political grouping. This group was coalescing into an influential movement. When issue No. 5 of *Taiwan Political Commentary* was banned in 1977, a number of opposition activists who were associated with it stood in elections. Some were elected and the movement benefited from a higher profile and a more organised presence throughout the island.

Taiwanese politics after Chiang Kai-shek

Chiang Kai-shek died in 1975, having been effectively President of Taiwan for life, although he had never been acknowledged as such. On 6 April, he was succeeded by C. K. Yen (Yen Chia-kang) who had been his Vice-President, this succession being in accordance with the provisions of the Constitution. However, this was a presidential appointment in name only. Chiang Ching-kuo, Chiang Kai-shek's son, became Chairman of the GMD in 1975 and it was he who exercised real power. In 1978 Chiang Ching-kuo formally succeeded Yen as President and he was elected to serve for a second term as President in 1984. His Vice-President in this second term was Lee Teng-hui, who was not a member of the mainlander elite but a Taiwan-born politician who had been Mayor of Taipei and Governor of Taiwan and who had been educated at Cornell University in the United States, where he had completed a PhD in agricultural economics. Lee Teng-hui was the most significant of the group of native-born Taiwanese protégés of Chiang Ching-kuo, who had been strongly in favour of advancing the political careers of non-mainlanders who showed promise.

Now that there was no longer the powerful guiding or restraining hand of Chiang Kai-shek, divisions began to emerge within the GMD between factions that can be characterised broadly as the old guard and the modernisers, although like all factional descriptions these are oversimplified. The GMD had been transformed from a revolutionary party with a strong link to the military into a mainstream political organisation concerned with policy and with the minutiae of the day-to-day running of an administration. It became a more bureaucratic organisation and this reduced the requirement for unquestioning loyalty, so the existence of a range of political views became more acceptable.

Formosa (Kaohsiung) incident

In August 1979 a group of political dissidents who were opposed to the GMD's monopoly of power, many of them lawyers, and others who had been part of the *Dangwai* movement, launched a new journal. Its Chinese name was *Meili dao*, a literal translation of the Portuguese name *Ilha Formosa* (Beautiful Island) by which Taiwan had been known until the mid-twentieth century, and it is generally known in English as *Formosa*. During the autumn of 1979, it established fifteen branch offices throughout Taiwan, effectively the branches of an embryonic political party, albeit one without a name (*meiyou dangming de dang*) or an openly acknowledged existence; political parties other than the GMD remained illegal under the martial law regime.

The magazine was harried by supporters of the GMD, the police and military intelligence and this campaign of harassment culminated in simultaneous attacks on the home of the publisher in Taipei and the offices of the magazine in the cities of Kaohsiung and Pingtung on 29 November 1979.

On 10 December, opposition politicians organised a demonstration in Kaohsiung, a major industrial city, port and naval base in southwestern Taiwan, in association with *Formosa* magazine to mark International Human Rights Day. What had begun as a peaceful demonstration turned into a serious disturbance after the intervention of police and undercover agents of the security services and a number of the organisers were arrested. Among those arrested were Annette Lu, who was later to become Vice-President of the Republic of China, and other opposition activists who were later to occupy senior positions in the Democratic Progressive Party.

Reforms of 1986

In March 1986 a commission that had been appointed by President Chiang Ching-kuo and consisted of twelve members of the Central Committee of the GMD was convened to make recommendations on six major reform proposals. These were the repeal of the *Emergency Decree on Martial Law* which by 1986 had been in force for thirty-eight years; the legalisation of new political parties, some of which had already been operating illegally for years; the reinforcement of local sovereignty; the creation of a parliamentary system; the internal reform of the GMD; and an onslaught on crime and corruption.

On 28 September 1986 six organisations applied to be registered formally as political parties. The biggest of these, the Democratic Progressive Party (DPP) went on to capture eleven seats in the National Assembly and twelve seats in the Legislative Yuan in the elections that were held in December 1986. This election victory was a turning point in the political history of Taiwan and, for the first time, it introduced to the legislature politicians who were openly in favour of a genuinely independent Taiwan with no claim to rule the mainland.

Martial law was finally lifted on 15 July 1987 and in November of the same year residents of Taiwan were permitted to visit relatives across the Taiwan Straits in the PRC for the first time since 1949.

Lee Teng-hui era

Chiang Ching-kuo had been in poor health for some time and he died on 13 January 1988. His protégé, Lee Teng-hui, was sworn in as President and, at the Thirteenth

Congress of the GMD in July 1988, he was also confirmed as party Chairman, a notable achievement for a native Taiwanese. At the same meeting, many Taiwan-born politicians were elected into key posts in the new leadership. Of the thirty-one members of the Standing Committee of the party, sixteen were Taiwanese in origin and Lee Teng-hui's first cabinet brought eight Taiwanese politicians into government.

The Thirteenth Congress had also agreed on a number of measures to improve relations with the mainland and to enable personal, family, cultural and business exchanges between Taiwan and the PRC. The only proviso was that none of these exchanges should in any way suggest any recognition of the PRC or endanger Taiwan's security. There was no question that transactions between the two sides of the Taiwan Strait could be carried out on the basis of equal relations between two independent states. The government in Taipei, in common with the government in Beijing, remained formally committed to the idea of a reunified China at some point in the future and was not prepared to compromise on this fundamental principle.

However, in July 1999 President Lee Teng-hui issued a statement in which he argued that future contacts between China and Taiwan should be on the basis of 'special state-to-state relations'. This was much closer to asserting Taiwan's formal independence and was viewed by many commentators as dangerous brinkmanship which was bound to provoke the wrath of the government in Beijing. Lee was becoming detached from mainstream GMD politics and was already planning his retirement at this time. Both of these factors were used to limit the damage that his remarks were believed to have caused and to reduce cross-straits tension which had escalated as a result of his statement. He was subsequently expelled from the GMD in September 2001 when he broke party discipline by publicly endorsing election candidates from another political party, the Taiwan Solidarity Union (TSU). This new party had been formed in August 2001 by defectors from the GMD, many of whom were personal supporters of Lee Teng-hui. The TSU was the first political party to use the name Taiwan in its official title and this was a deliberate move to emphasise its pro-independence credentials at a time when the DPP was being criticised by many supporters of complete independence for being too willing to reach an agreement with Beijing.

Chen Shui-bian's presidency

Chen Shui-bian, the leader of the DPP, was elected President in March 2000 in a historic election that brought to an end fifty years of unbroken rule by the GMD. Chen Shui-bian was born into a poor farming family in the south of Taiwan, the heartland of the independence movement. He practised law and was drawn into pro-independence politics when he represented several of the defendants in the *Formosa* incident in 1979. He became active in the *Dangwai* opposition movement and served on the Taipei city council where he became mayor in 1994. His style is populist and he is often referred to by the familiar soubriquet of A-bian, which can be either affectionate or slightly disdainful, depending on the context.

Although he had been a vociferous supporter of the idea of an independent

Taiwan, he moderated his calls for immediate formal independence in order not to provoke a military response from Beijing. The DPP was one of the new parties that first registered in 1986 and it has been by far the most successful of the pro-independence groups. In the 2000 election President Chen defeated the GMD candidate Lien Chan, a protégé of former president Lee Teng-hui and an independent contender, James Soong, but his government still did not have a majority in parliament. In the December 2001 parliamentary elections, the GMD lost its parliamentary majority for the first time since 1949. The DPP secured eighty-seven seats in the legislature, the GMD had sixty-eight members and other parties had seventy between them.

China–Taiwan relations and the 1992 consensus

On 24 January 2001, Vice-Premier Qian Qichen of the PRC, who had been a widely respected former Foreign Minister, called on the Taiwan authorities to accept the 1992 consensus on the principle of One China.

This consensus was the result of a meeting between the two organisations established in China and Taiwan to manage cross-straits relations. The Association for Relations Across the Taiwan Straits (ARATS –PRC) and the Straits Exchanges Foundation (SEF – Taiwan) met in Hong Kong in 1992. The consensus, which was that both sides should abide by the One China principle, may not have been a consensus at all as the Taiwan side rejected it, but since the rejection came after the election of the pro-independence DPP, the status of this consensus is disputed.[3]

Political relations between China and Taiwan remain strained but economic relations have developed in a way that belies the degree of cross-straits tension that appears to exist. Taiwanese firms have invested heavily in the mainland economy and in 2002 there were at least 50,000 businesses based in the island operating in the PRC.[4] In Shanghai, there is a resident Taiwanese community that is at least 300,000 strong and runs its own schools and a newspaper. At the same time, however, direct trade, transport and communications are banned, although there have been moves to relax these restrictions. The economies of China on both sides of the Taiwan Strait are linked closely together but closer economic integration is hampered by the lack of a political accommodation.

The role of the Guomindang (GMD) has changed significantly since it went into opposition. In spite of the historical antipathy between the GMD and the CCP, the GMD was prepared to enter into discussions with Beijing and continued to insist on a policy of reunification in the long term in the face of the growing wave of sentiment in favour of independence. However, at a GMD congress that was held in the city of Taoyuan in June 2007, major changes were made to the Constitution of the party, enabling it to concentrate on the island of Taiwan and the 'people's welfare' (the old reformist term used by Sun Yat-sen) rather than having reunification as its main objective. The party leader, Ma Ying-jeou, who was the GMD's candidate in the presidential elections which were held in 2008, indicated that he would be willing to conclude a peace agreement with the PRC. These moves reflect the party's willingness to bow to the contemporary political reality of Taiwan's *de facto* independence rather than the historical commitment to one China which has both united and divided the GMD and the CCP since the 1920s.[5]

The tacit acceptance of the status quo for all practical purposes does not mean that Taiwan has abandoned all prospects of retaining its former position in international organisations. There has been continuous low-level diplomatic pressure by Taipei and its supporters, particularly in the United States, ever since the PRC replaced it in the United Nations (UN) in 1971. However, Beijing has maintained the upper hand and has far more supporters in the UN that does Taipei. On 20 July 2007 an application for Taiwan's membership of the UN, signed by President Chen Shui-bian, was sent to the Secretary-General, Ban Ki-moon. In contrast to previous attempts to rejoin either the full UN or its subsidiary organisations (for example, the UN Convention on the Elimination of All Forms of Discrimination Against Women – CEDAW – in March 2007 and the World Health Organisation in April 2007), all of which had been submitted under the name of the Republic of China, this application was in the name of Taiwan. This did not placate the PRC, which immediately responded that it would resolutely oppose the application as it considered it to be yet another attempt to split China that was destined to fail. Not surprisingly, this attempt to overturn the decision of the UN to recognise the PRC in its resolution of 1971 was firmly and swiftly rejected by the UN. In spite of this clear rejection, the Taiwan government was not prepared to abandon plans to organise a ballot calling for the island to be admitted to the UN. A referendum was planned to take place in conjunction with presidential and parliamentary elections that are scheduled for 2008.[6]

In July 2007, supporters of a formal declaration of independence for Taiwan celebrated the twentieth anniversary of the ending of martial law. The name of the Chiang Kai-shek Memorial Hall, established in 1980, was formally changed to the National Taiwan Democracy Memorial Hall earlier in the year but campaigners were demanding that the bulky statue of Chiang Kai-shek which still dominates the complex be removed to signify both a complete break with the past and a rejection of the psychology of the martial law era.[7]

Constitutional change and the elections of 2008

The National Assembly, Taiwan's parliament, was elected on the mainland in 1947 on the basis of nationwide constituencies and moved to Taiwan after the GMD's defeat in the Civil War. Members of the Assembly continued to hold their seats representing constituencies on the mainland, although after 1949 there were naturally no elections. The perpetuation of this system, which claimed to represent the people of the mainland, was widely regarded as absurd and, in 1991, a reformed parliament, the second National Assembly, was elected on the basis of direct elections in Taiwan only. It was this second National Assembly that approved the constitutional amendments that made possible direct elections to the presidency and vice-presidency in 1996. The Assembly then withdrew from political decision-making and gradually devolved its authority to the Legislative Yuan (*lifayuan*).

In 2005 the National Assembly voted to abolish itself. The Legislative Yuan thus became the only parliamentary body and is often referred to as the parliament (*guohui*), although it can be argued that, constitutionally, it is not a genuine independent parliament but the legislative branch of a presidential system.

The Legislative Yuan is a body that has also existed since 1947 and is one of the six Yuans that together make up the administration of the Republic of China in a system that had its origins in the political thinking of Sun Yat-sen.[8] The Legislative Yuan is, as its name suggests, the main body for creating legislation but until 2005 it was overshadowed by the National Assembly; the Executive Yuan is the cabinet and the President serves as the head of that body; the Control Yuan is a monitoring body with particular responsibility for investigating allegations of corruption; the Judicial Yuan administers the courts and the justice system; and the Examination Yuan is responsible for the recruitment to the civil service through competitive examinations.

Politics in Taiwan in the early years of the twenty-first century is complicated and confusing, not surprisingly for a political system in transition. The main political parties have been the DPP, which is openly in favour of an independent Taiwan and the GMD, which has an interesting position in that it is in favour of one China (Taiwan and the mainland under one rule) while maintaining its absolute opposition to the CCP. However, because of its adherence to the idea of one China, it has been able to negotiate with Beijing more easily than has the overly pro-independence DPP. There have been rifts and alliances and smaller parties have also played a role and it has become common to discuss Taiwanese politics in terms of a Pan-Blue coalition around the GMD and a Pan-Green coalition based on the DPP. To a large extent, differences over policies have been overshadowed by allegations of corruption against leading members of both political camps, which have often led to lengthy court cases.

In the elections to the Legislative Yuan that took place in January 2008, the voters overwhelmingly elected representatives of the GMD which had been in opposition since 2000. The GMD secured eighty-one out of a total of 113 seats in the parliament. The DDP, the party of the incumbent President Chen Shui-bian, was only able to take twenty-seven seats, with the remainder going to minority parties. Chen Shui-bian responded to this defeat by resigning as leader of the DDP although remaining as President. The presidential elections in March 2008 were won by Ma Ying-jeou, the Guomindang candidate. Although the Guomindang had been bitter rivals of the Communist Party for control of China, their return to power has resulted in greatly improved relations between Beijing and Taipei. High level visits between the leader of both parties led to announcements that restrictions on cross-straits air travel and currency exchange regulations would be relaxed. The first of a series of regular direct passenger air services across the Taiwan Strait took place on July 4th 2008, with a flight from Guangzhou to Taipei.

21 Western Development programme

The strategy of embarking on the long-term development of the western region of the People's Republic of China (PRC) emerged in 1999. It is legitimised as having been part of Deng Xiaoping's analysis of the 'two overall situations' (*liang ge daju*) which envisaged the economic development of the coastal regions as the priority, followed by the inland territories of China's west, regions that are remote from the centre of power and predominantly poor and backward. Development began under Jiang Zemin and his 'third-generation' leadership but, after the Sixteenth National Congress of the Chinese Communist Party (CCP) in 2002, although Hu Jintao and the 'fourth generation' continued to implement the policy of economic development in the region, there was far less rhetoric about 'western development' as a programme.

For the purposes of the Western Development policy (*Xibu da kaifa*), the western regions were identified as the autonomous regions of Tibet, Xinjiang, Inner Mongolia, Ningxia and Guangxi, the provinces of Sichuan, Guizhou, Yunnan, Shaanxi, Gansu and Qinghai and the municipality of Chongqing. This classification immediately suggests a number of problems: while some of these administrative units, notably Guizhou and parts of Xinjiang, contain some of the most deprived communities within the PRC, the same clearly cannot be said for Sichuan, which has been an economic success story for decades, and in particular the city of Chongqing, which, after a deft recalculation of the area under its administrative authority, overtook Shanghai as China's largest city in 1997.

The Western Development policy is also contentious in that it entails a significant transfer of resources and personnel from the east of China, and that has raised concerns about the repopulation of ethnic minority areas by a mass resettlement programme of Han Chinese. Li Guantong, the Director of Regional Development for the State Council's Development Research Centre, issued a statement rebutting what he believed were inaccurate reports in the foreign media of a large-scale resettlement project and the aim of converting China's western regions into a 'container' for the increasing population of China as a whole, a total planned transfer of 300 million people. Li was attending an international symposium on the development of China's western regions in Chongqing, which had been designated as the lead city in the development programme. At the same symposium, Cai Fang, Director of the Institute of Population Science at the Chinese Academy of Social

Sciences, made it clear that he was not in favour of a mass transfer of population but he believed that the flow of people between the east and west should be allowed to develop naturally and regulate itself according to the market. Policies that were being adopted to permit the temporary migration of skilled workers to the west of China would, it was said, mean that these migrants would be able to retain all of their formal connections and registrations in the east and could return freely whenever they wished.[1]

Implementation in 2000

The year 2000 was designated as the date for implementing the plans that had been generated in 1999. The responsibility for implementation was given to a 'leading group for the development of the western region' under the overall direction of the State Council, and it was agreed that specific plans for the west should be included in the national Tenth Five-Year Plan. The planners drew attention to the need for careful planning and explicitly warned against adventurist policies such as those carried out during the 1958 Great leap Forward. They also acknowledged the 'backwardness of the western region in economic and social development' and concluded that, since this backwardness was the result of a long process of historical development, it was reasonable to expect that it would also require a long process to change it.

For it to have any chance of success, the plan required the cooperation of a number of different agencies: the question of coordination was therefore vital. For example, to deal with ecological issues alone would involve government departments of forestry, water conservancy, agriculture and land. Overall, planning would have to include a dozen provincial, municipal and autonomous regions as well as the quasi-autonomous Xinjiang Production and Construction Corps. Cooperation would also involve local government in neighbouring provinces and the planners warned of the dangers of 'localism' which could impede the progress of the project.[2]

West China Forum 2004

On 18 November 2004, the West China Forum met in Nanning, the capital of the Guangxi Zhuang Autonomous Region. The forum is sponsored by the West China Development Office of the State Council, the State Development and Reform Commission, the Ministry of Commerce, the Information Office of the State Council and the regional government of Guangxi. Over 300 participants represented the twelve western provinces and regions that are directly involved in the Western Development programme and also the Xinjiang Production and Construction Corps (XPCC). The inclusion of the XPCC is a reflection of its unusual status as it is considered to be equivalent in rank to a provincial-level administration.

The keynote speech was given by Zeng Peiyan, member of the CCP Politburo and Vice-Premier of the State Council. He reiterated the influence of 'Deng

Xiaoping theory' on the Western Development programme and emphasised the role of strategy in the state's coordinated plan for modernisation and the development of regional economies. He pointed to five key tasks in the programme which were later taken up in more detail by Premier Wen Jiabao (see below), but singled out two major developments, the Qinghai–Tibet Railway and the construction of tarmac roads in every rural county, as being of particular significance.

Wen Jiabao on five years of Western Development

In February 2005, Wen Jiabao, the Premier, put his own personal imprimatur on the Western Development project in formal 'written instructions' issued under the less than snappy title: *Blaze New Trails in a Pioneering Spirit and Do Solid Work to Continuously Bring about a New Situation in the Large-scale Development of the Western Region.* Reaffirming that the underlying reason for the programme was the need to bridge the gap between the increasingly prosperous east and the underdeveloped west, he ordered that priority be given to agriculture and related rural issues but also to the protection of the environment of the western regions. The gap between east and west, which has widened dramatically since the inception of the 'reform and opening' strategy of 1978–79, is illustrated by that fact that approximately two-thirds of Chinese citizens living below the poverty line (defined as having an annual income of less than RMB 625 or US$75) live in the rural areas of western China.[3]

The introduction to this lengthy document was essentially a progress report on the first five years of the Western Development project. The priority of the state has been macro-level development with the emphasis on planning guidance, major construction projects and the allocation of substantial amounts of funding. According to Premier Wen, the central government had committed RMB 460 billion for construction and RMB 500 billion in respect of transfer payments and special subsidies. As a result, the growth of the economy in the western regions had accelerated. Total output value had increased by 8.5 per cent, 8.8 per cent, 10 per cent, 11.3 per cent and 12 per cent in 2000, 2001, 2002, 2003 and 2004 respectively and these reported growth rates were higher than those claimed for previous years.

The development and modernisation of the infrastructure, a fundamental requirement evident to even the most casual visitor to the region, has been a major priority. Wen Jiabao claimed that state investment in fixed assets in the west had experienced an annual increase of more than 20 per cent on average, a figure that is substantially higher than for China as a whole. Work started on sixty key construction projects for which the total investment has been RMB 850 billion. These include projects to improve major road and rail communications, water control and the transmission of electricity and natural gas from the west to the east. Whether this last item is of significant benefit to the western regions is a moot point but it does indicate one of the key underlying reasons for the strategy: the integration of the economy of the west into the national economy to secure resources that are essential to China's economic development as a whole.

Priority was also given to the protection of the environment of the west, a particular concern of Wen Jiabao, with emphasis on the return to forest conditions of land that had been previously cleared for agriculture and the reafforestation of barren mountain sides and wasteland. These projects are all designed to have wider benefits, including control over the dust storms from the north and west that regularly plague Beijing and Tianjin, conservation of farming land and reduction in water pollution in the area around the Three Gorges Dam and in the headwaters of China's major rivers. There has also been an attempt to transfer scientific facilities to the west and in this way to improve educational and medical provision in the region.

Wen Jiabao also stressed the collateral benefits of the Western Development strategy. Equipment and technology required for the construction of major projects in the west had to be sourced in eastern China. Conversely, as has already been noted, energy and both raw and processed materials have been transferred from the west to the east. The net result is the strengthening of economic interdependence between the west and the east of China which the CCP regard as an essential prerequisite for the maintenance of social and political integration and stability. In Wen's own words, the project has 'made it possible for people of various ethnic groups across the country, especially the people in the western region, to see the hopes and prospects for the development of the western region'. However, he went on to acknowledge that 'we should also soberly note that the development of the western region is faced with many difficulties and problems and that the tasks are still very arduous'. Among these problems he listed the weakness of the existing infrastructure, environmental degradation and the serious shortage of water resources, education and cultural backwardness and the shortage of trained and qualified personnel. Overall the tone is bland and optimistic and Wen avoids specific details but he does acknowledge the difficulties faced.

Wen Jiabao presented the development of the west as a *sine qua non* for the development of China as a whole. He drew attention to the fact that the population of the west of China (as defined for the purposes of this project) was 30 per cent of China's total but that its GDP per capita has been only 40 per cent of the level achieved in the east. Net income in the rural west is approximately 50 per cent of that in the east and, of China's rural poor, over 60 per cent are to be found in the west. In the west there are still twenty million people who 'have yet to solve the problem of food and clothing'. It is this inequality and the potential dangers for China's overall development and stability that have prompted the central authorities to place such a great emphasis on, and devote such a high level of resource to, the development of the west. 'There will be no well-off life in the country without a well-off life in the western regions, and there will be no modernisation in the country without modernisation in the western region', Wen continued. He pointed to the potentially powerful combination of the advantages possessed by the west in terms of market resources and labour with the east's advantages in capital, technology and skilled personnel or 'talented people'.

He stated explicitly that the 'large-scale development of the western region will constitute an important guarantee for the lasting political stability of the whole country'. Drawing attention to the complexity of the ethnic make-up of the region (fifty of China's recognised ethnic minorities have a significant presence in the west) and its strategic position on China's land borders with a total of fourteen states, he articulated the importance of gradually narrowing the 'development gap between the regions' and consolidating 'the favourable situation featuring ethnic solidarity, social stability and border security'. He did not single out any particular region in the west but it should be noted that in 1996, a key policy paper, *Document No. 7*, identified Xinjiang as the region in which stability was most under threat and called for economic development and an improvement in the lives of the people as an important component of the policies of combating instability.[4]

In this February 2005 speech, Wen Jiabao identified five 'major tasks' for the Western Development programme.

1   Resolving the three rural issues (*san nong*): that is peasants (*nongmin*), agriculture (*nongye*) and rural areas (*nongqu*). This is an issue that applies throughout China and not just in the underdeveloped western region, but rural problems are particularly acute in the west. He argued that priority should be given to farming and to raising the income of peasants by increasing efficiency, moderating the tax burden and enabling them to earn more as migrant workers or in non-agricultural occupations. Wen set 2007 as the target date for alleviating basic poverty.

2   Improving the environment, primarily by returning agricultural land to forest and grassland, while preserving and improving the living standards of peasants and herdsmen in these areas.

3   Improving infrastructure, with an emphasis on water conservancy and transport, notably the construction of the western section of the national highway network.

4   Developing local competitive economies 'with distinctive local features'. He highlighted energy, mining, tourism and specialised agriculture including the growing and processing of plants for Chinese medicine but also pointed to the need for developing new high-technology industries in the area.

5   Implementing social programmes, including education and public health. He argued that high priority should be given to making the standard system of nine-year education compulsory throughout the region and eliminating illiteracy, which was still a major problem among the young and middle-aged. This presumably refers to literacy in Chinese rather than, say, Tibetan or Uyghur. He also called for mechanisms to attract and retain able and well-qualified personnel from outside the region, which would of course increase the westward migration of Han Chinese people and could deny employment to members of local ethnic minorities.[5]

This final issue highlights crucial omissions from Wen's speech and indeed from most discussions of the Western Development programme. The western region is treated as a unit, with no real account taken of the ethnic make-up of its components and potential ethnic conflicts in the region.

Economic development and migration

Although the greatest internal migration of China's population has been from the underdeveloped west to the prosperous and rapidly industrialising coastal areas of the south and southeast, there has also been a smaller but significant movement of population in the other direction, towards the northwest and particularly to the most northwesterly region of China, Xinjiang. Indeed, unlike the southwards migration which began relatively recently and is still increasing, the migration to Xinjiang has continued, virtually without interruption, since 1949 and has historical antecedents that go back thousands of years.[6]

There has been migration from the prosperous east to the underdeveloped west for centuries but, until recently, it has been on a relatively small scale. The question of large-scale migration raises the question of whether the economic development of China's west can ever be merely a neutral device for the alleviation of poverty or whether it is necessarily a conscious political tool, designed to stabilise the western regions, which are on China's sensitive borders with Mongolia, Kazakhstan, Kyrgyzstan, Takijistan, Afghanistan and the Indian subcontinent. Stabilisation necessarily means the suppression, by political or military means, of any social or political movements that demand autonomy or independence. Foreign capital will not be attracted to China's western regions if there is a constant danger of riots, demonstrations or sabotage in the areas that are being developed. In the long term, Beijing hopes that economic development will guarantee stability, but in the short term, this stability may have to be imposed and that is likely to lead to repression and possibly even to bloodshed.

One of the greatest fears of the non-Han populations living in the western regions is that their societies, languages and cultures will be threatened and eventually extinguished by the migration of educated and better-qualified Han 'pioneers' from China proper. This type of migration is not new: Chinese were allowed to move into southern Xinjiang to open up new land for cultivation as early as 1831 and there was large-scale migration and settlement by demobilised troops after the region came under the control of the PRC in 1949. However, the scale of the proposed developments suggests that they cannot be carried out without the transfer of at least hundreds of thousands more people from eastern China, where there is already a floating migrant population of perhaps 120 million people from farming backgrounds who have been forced off the land and are looking for employment.

A social and ethnic transformation of the western regions on this scale will be resented and resisted by the local people. They will struggle to protect their languages, whether these are Turkic – such as Uyghur written in the Arabic script – and other related languages spoken by their neighbours even further west in Central Asia, or Tibetan, related to Chinese only distantly and written in characters derived from a script that was devised to write the Sanskrit of ancient northern India. They will also struggle to protect their religions – Islam in the case of Xinjiang and the Hui Muslims of Ningxia and Lama Buddhism in Tibet, both of which were suppressed during the Cultural Revolution of the 1960s but have proved extremely resilient and have enjoyed a popular revival since the

1980s. Migration from China proper would also be likely to expand the existing educated middle class, predominantly Han, and further deepen the conflict with ethnic minority groups unless measures were adopted to spread employment to the minority communities.

What appears on the surface to be a laudable policy of developing a backward region and reducing poverty has a hidden agenda and this could lead to further conflict between Han and non-Han rather than the stability it is designed to produce. An earlier scheme to resettle subsistence farmers from other provinces to Qinghai, which was to be funded by the World Bank, collapsed in July 2000 when it was pointed out that the plan involved the resettlement of Han Chinese on land that is now in a Chinese province but was part of old Tibet and formerly known as Amdo. After concerns were expressed about the possible dilution of Tibetan culture in the region and allegations of cultural genocide, the World Bank attached new conditions which China rejected.

There have been similar plans to relocate farmers from the land around the Three Gorges Dam to the southern Xinjiang city of Kashghar, where almost the entire population is ethnic Uyghur, and to move poor Hui Muslims away from the farmlands which contain the tombs of the *shaykhs* who founded the Sufi orders to which they belong. These policies show deep insensitivity to cultural and religious differences and are likely to increase, rather than reduce, the risks of inter-ethnic conflict.

Migration and Xinjiang

Although the Western Development project is targeted at the west of China in general, with no real discrimination between the constituent parts, the impact on various areas is likely to differ considerably, depending on the ethnic make-up of the particular region and the relationship between non-Han and Han peoples who live there. In the case of Xinjiang, there is already considerable disquiet and resentment at the preferential treatment that appears to be given to Han migrants in employment.[7]

The policy of the CCP's government after 1949 followed very closely the imperial policy of garrisoning the frontiers with soldier-farmers to protect the borders. Quasi-military, administrative and production organisations were set up with the approval of the central government and the region attracted large numbers of migrants from a variety of backgrounds.

The pattern of migrating groups into Xinjiang since 1949 is quite clear and falls into a number of discrete types, although they overlap to some extent. The first group were ex-servicemen who were demobilised or transferred to civilian employment and resettled in Xinjiang from the 1950s onwards. Because they were predominantly Han and because of their connections with the People's Liberation Army (PLA) and frequently with the CCP, they have become the backbone of Chinese society in Xinjiang and Beijing has often taken their loyalty for granted. When PLA General Wang Zhen took control of Xinjiang in September 1949, he had at least 89,000 troops under his command and this was increased by a further

80,000 when the Nationalist GMD forces under Tao Zhiyue surrendered and put themselves under his command. Agricultural production in Xinjiang was barely adequate for the indigenous population, let alone for an occupying force, so the soldiers of the PLA were required to produce their own food supplies. During the early 1950s there were over 100,000 troops engaged in agriculture and related occupations while still retaining their defence capability. This was the origin of the Xinjiang Production and Construction Corps. During the 1950s the original military colonists were reinforced by demobilised troops from other areas, including the northeast: these were often specialists with technical knowledge that was relevant to the key tasks of border protection and cultivation.

As Sino–Soviet relations grew more tense during the late 1950s and early 1960s, border security became an even higher priority and more troops, specialist cadres and demobilised ex-servicemen from central China were deployed on the frontiers including Xinjiang. This trend continued throughout the Cultural Revolution period and into the 1980s, and many brought their families and settled more or less permanently in the region. During the 1950s, military transfers amounted to perhaps 10,000 a year but this number reduced to 1,000 a year in the 1960s and slowed down even further in the 1970s and 1980s. Nevertheless, the total migration of military and military-related personnel to Xinjiang over the past fifty years is approximately 300,000. They also found themselves in the most powerful and influential positions in Xinjiang society and acquired a reputation for being both 'red' and tough.

The second group consists of criminals, who were brought into Xinjiang for 'reform through labour' (*laogai*), and political prisoners. As part of their sentence, they were required to work in the prisons or on the *laogai* farms for little or no wages, both during and after their sentences, and this provided a source of cheap labour for Xinjiang although these labourers were far less reliable politically than the demobilised troops. This type of migration began as early as May 1951 when the Xinjiang Military Region accepted 10,766 prisoners from central China. In 1954 a total of 27,643 criminals and 7,116 who had finished serving their sentences were allocated to the farms run by the XPCC (the *bingtuan*). This figure rose to 97,673 in 1956, 123,000 in 1975 and, during the campaign against hooliganism in 1983, many serious criminals from the cities of eastern China were transferred to Xinjiang.

The supply of labour provided by demobilised soldiers and criminals was inadequate for the needs of the developing border region and plans were drawn up to transfer more people. A campaign in the mid-1950s to 'assist the border regions and protect the motherland' was followed by a central directive issued in August 1958 at the height of the Great Leap Forward to encourage the voluntary migration of young people to the borders and the minority areas to reduce the population pressure on the densely populated regions of Anhui, Jiangsu, Hubei and the Shanghai area. It was estimated that two million young people would move and hundreds of thousands did indeed migrate in the late 1950s and early 1960s; the migrants were mostly peasants but they also included students, workers and unemployed people from the towns and cities. Many of the migrants, particularly those who came from the rural areas, were members of the CCP or the Communist Youth League (CYL). This flood of enthusiastic and patriotic 'educated youth' (*zhishi qingnian*) and 'youth supporting the border regions' (*zhibian qingnian*) continued until the mid-1960s when it was subsumed into the nationwide *xiafang* campaign of transferring urban young people to the countryside – a process which continued during the Cultural Revolution.

In addition to those who moved westwards under official government programmes, there were thousands of *mangliu* or migrants who entered Xinjiang without government sanction. Statistics for what were essentially illegal migrants are necessarily unreliable, but *Xinjiang Daily* reported that there were at least 10,000 in Urumqi alone in July 1957 and the numbers increased dramatically as a result of the Great Leap Forward, with peasants moving west to escape the collectivisation or the famines. Xinjiang, and particularly the Xinjiang Production and Construction Corps, was largely shielded from both the famine and collectivisation because of its special position.

The successors to these *mangliu* were the non-local labour (*wailai gong*) who were recruited to work in the west of China from the beginning of the reform and opening period in 1979–80. However, they now had official sanction since government policy had changed. There was a desperate need for new blood: most of the original demobilised military and ex-prisoners had reached retirement age and, in many cases, their children did not want to follow in their footsteps and continue to farm and open new land. Although far more attention has been paid to the migration of *wailai gong* labour from the central provinces to the southeast, where the economic boom has been most apparent, the exodus towards the northwest has also been extremely important in this period.

In 1983 the non-resident population, usually classified as 'mobile' or 'floating' population (*liudong renkou*) in Xinjiang was 179,100 and between 1981 and 1989 625,800 people are recorded as having moved there from other provinces, an average annual entry of 78,000, many of them finding work in the service sector including low-level repair and maintenance jobs. In the 1990s there was an upsurge in migration to Xinjiang. At the same time the demand for labour changed and migrants found work in other sectors. These included agriculture (including the farms run by the Xinjiang Production and Construction Corps), mining and the oil industry, but also construction, handicrafts and trade at all levels. As many as 500,000 migrants were travelling to Xinjiang each year: of these perhaps 100,000 would become long-term residents, while the remaining 400,000 were typically short-term workers for picking cotton and other seasonal jobs and many are employed by the XPCC. Although the work is arduous and working conditions far from ideal, the potential income is sufficient to attract such large numbers of mainly rural people seeking work.

Other forms of relocation have included migration for marriage and family reasons, including the directed transfer of large numbers of young women from central China in the 1950s to redress the negative female–male balance of population in Xinjiang. There have also been transfers of cadres and specialist scientific and technical staff to assist in the development of the region and some overseas Chinese who have 'returned' to China from Indonesia, Malaysia, Vietnam and elsewhere, either as voluntary migrants or refugees, have been settled in Xinjiang.[8]

Migration to Xinjiang and indeed to other border and minority regions is therefore far from being a new phenomenon. The migration that is being encouraged under the Western Development programme represents a modification of the existing pattern rather than a new initiative. However, the crude migration statistics obscure the important issue of the impact of migration on the ethnic composition of Xinjiang. Although there are no precise figures on the ethnic origin of the migrants, by common consensus they are overwhelmingly Han, as would be expected from their provinces of origin. The impact of this migration over the years since 1949 was to increase the Han population of Xinjiang to a total of at least five million by 1982. In percentage terms, the proportion of Han in Xinjiang has risen from 6.7 per cent in 1949 to 10 per cent in 1954, 28 per cent in 1960, and 40 per cent in 1970 – a level at which it remained for some years, partly because Uyghurs and other ethnic minority communities were exempt from the strict application of the one-child policy. The impact on the ethnic composition of Xinjiang has been significant, although it has not been homogeneous. Migration has been greatest to the areas of greatest industrialisation, such as the oilfields in the north of the region, and much of southern Xinjiang has received a relatively low level of Han immigration.

Oil and gas pipelines

As the Chinese economy continues to develop, energy, always a key component, has begun to loom even larger in the equation. China became a net importer of oil in 1993, and in 2003 it became the second largest country in terms of energy consumption, ranking after only the United States. The availability and security of its energy supply has preoccupied economic planners for decades. In the 1960s, the northeast was the major source of oil, but hopes are now pinned on what are believed to be colossal oil and natural gas resources in the Tarim Basin in Xinjiang, some of which have already been tapped. These reserves, above all other consider-ations, are the reason why Beijing is not willing to countenance any suggestion of independence for Xinjiang and why it has clamped down on any hints of an Uyghur independence movement. To ensure security of supply, it must maintain political control over the region and that requires a degree of social stability.

The importance of this factor is illustrated by the troubled history of the West–East Pipeline project, a major undertaking that was planned and executed by Chinese and foreign companies. This complex venture began in July 2002 with a total investment of over RMB 140 billion (US$16.9 billion) in a plan to transport natural gas from the Tarim Basin in western Xinjiang and the Changqing gas field in Shaanxi province to Shanghai, the nerve centre of China's developing economy and a gas-guzzler of a city. The pipeline runs from Xinjiang through Gansu, Ningxia, Shaanxi and Shanxi, which contain some of China's most challenging terrain, and onwards through Henan, Anhui and Jiangsu to Shanghai and parts of Zhejiang province. When fully operational, the pipeline will supply twelve billion cubic metres of gas to the Shanghai region. The Changqing gas field in

Shaanxi was initially the main source of supply and this eastern section of the project was completed in October 2003 when trial operations were inaugurated. Supplies from Changqing were due to be replaced by gas from the Tarim Basin on 1 December 2004 and this western section, which runs from Lunnan in Xinjiang to Jingbian in Shaanxi, was able to begin transmission of gas on 6 September 2004. The formal opening of the pipeline was marked by Jiang Zemin, the President of China, on 1 October 2004, China's National Day, when he pressed a button at the gas compression facility in Jingbian to open valves controlling both the western and eastern sections of the pipeline, symbolising the full operation of the project. The intention was that commercial supplies of gas would be flowing by 1 January 2005. In his speech, Jiang Zemin declared that the opening of the pipeline would be a boon for both the east and the west of China. The east, which is desperate for energy, would get the supplies of gas that it needed while the project would also be a boost to the economic development of the west, as that region would be able to supply gas which would otherwise have to be purchased elsewhere.[9]

On 27 December 2004, the National Development and Reform Commission announced that commercial operations would in fact begin on 30 December.[10] By this time, the joint venture between PetroChina and the foreign companies with which it had been working on the creation of the pipeline had been dissolved, as the two sides were unable to reach agreement on an investment strategy that was acceptable to all parties. Although the details of the disagreement have not been made public, among the issues at stake were the distribution of gas reserves and the length of the joint-venture contract. PetroChina had brought in foreign specialists in 2001 because, at the time, it wished to share the costs of investment in the project and the risks involved in what was one of the largest and strategically most sensitive projects of the reform period. However, by late 2004 it had come to the conclusion that there was no longer any need to employ either foreign capital or foreign expertise, possibly because the scale of recent finds of gas reserves in northwestern China had given them confidence that they could go it alone. The companies that led the two foreign consortiums, Royal Dutch Shell and Exxon Mobil, were notified of the termination of the agreement on 2 August 2004.[11] Members of the foreign consortia were disappointed that they had been cut out of the deal at such short notice and at such a late stage, after they had contributed to the planning and the engineering for several years. They had also contributed to programmes to alleviate poverty in China's west and environmental improvement work as part of what they conceived as their corporate and social responsibility.

The importance of this project, both for its economic and strategic value and for its role as a symbol of national development, can be adduced from the fact that the announcement was made on China's National Day. Although it was a grave disappointment for the foreign partners, it is perhaps hardly surprising that such a strategically important project, which is central to China's energy security and which has profound implications for China's economic development, should be brought entirely under the control of the government at a time when national sentiment is rising in China.

Regional autonomy and the ethnic dimension

Official statements on the Western Development policy have in general ignored or played down the ethnic dimension. However, *Regional Autonomy for Ethnic Minorities in China*, a White Paper issued by the Information Office of the State Council on 28 February 2005, indicated clearly that the government was still planning to rely on the existing structures of regional autonomy to manage this issue. The document reiterates the standard argument that of the fifty-six ethnic groups identified in China, the fifty-five other than the Han are 'relatively small, so they are customarily referred to as "ethnic minorities"'. It quotes the fifth national census carried out in 2000 in which the total population of the fifty-five ethnic minority groups was recorded as 104.49 million, which is 8.41 per cent of the total population of the PRC. Regional autonomy, it goes on to say, is 'critical to enhancing the relationship of equality, unity and mutual assistance among different ethnic groups, to upholding national unification, and to accelerating the development of places where regional autonomy is practised and promoting their progress'. The White Paper draws on the history of customary rule by non-Han communities during the imperial period and specifically mentions the system in Xinjiang under which local *begs*, leaders of Uyghur communities, were responsible for local government. It also praises Hui and Inner Mongolian resistance to the Japanese invasion while castigating the separatists of Eastern Turkestan, Tibet and Manzhouguo, thus clearly defining those who are inside and those who are outside the project of national unity represented by the CCP and the PRC. It acknowledges that 'the level of economic and social development in these regions [ethnic minority regions] is relatively backward' and argues that:

> Regional autonomy for ethnic minorities enables them to bring into play their regional advantages and promote exchanges and cooperation between minority areas and other areas and consequently quickens the pace of modernisation both in the minority areas and the country as a whole and helps achieve the common development of all regions and prosperity for all ethnic groups.[12]

The development of ethnic autonomous areas is linked explicitly with the Western Development strategy.

> To accelerate the development of China's western regions and ethnic autonomous areas, the Chinese government launched a grand strategy for the development of western China in 2000, which covers five autonomous regions, 27 autonomous prefectures and 83 of the 120 autonomous counties (banners). In addition, three other autonomous prefectures are allowed to enjoy the preferential policies the state has adopted for the western regions.[13]

This reinforces the impression that the development of the economies of minority areas and the promotion of prosperity of all ethnic groups are seen as key priorities for the state and the White Paper proceeds to list a series of ten key measures designed to achieve these objectives:

1 *Speeding up development in ethnic minority areas.* The Western Development strategy is clearly the most significant example of this.

2 *Infrastructure projects.* Notable among these are the West–East Gas Pipeline, the West–East Power Transmission Project and the Qinghai–Tibet Railway. Projects in Tibet and transport projects in general were singled out for special emphasis.

3 *Financial support for autonomous areas.* Subsidies and special funding for minority areas have been in place since 1955 and were maintained after the financial reforms of 1994, with additional funding being made available to minority areas in 1995.

4 *Environmental protection measures.* Environmental concerns are one of the major platforms of Premier Wen Jiabao.

5 *Educational projects.* Universal nine-year compulsory education remains a key target rather than a reality for many communities in the ethnic autonomous areas and this is the responsibility of the Compulsory Education Project for Impoverished Areas. Special provision has been made to increase the number of ethnic minority students in universities and colleges by positive discrimination, including the acceptance of lower entrance requirements.

6 *Poverty alleviation.* The desperate need for action on poverty in the ethnic minority regions is indicated by the decision of the state to establish the Food and Clothing Fund for Impoverished Ethnic Minority Areas in 1990 and the seven-year 'Programme for Delivering Eighty Million People from Poverty' that was launched in 1994. The 'More Prosperous Frontiers and Better-of People' programme designed to address the problems of poor infrastructure and food and clothing supplies in the impoverished minority regions was initiated in 2000.

7 *Social welfare.* The state invested RMB 1.37 billion in public health and related projects in the minority areas. Radio and television coverage was also extended to these regions as and when electricity became available.

8 *External relations.* Wider access to trade with both neighbouring countries across the borders and neighbouring counties within China was encouraged by decentralising decision-making to local enterprises.

9 *Twinning.* Developing regions are twinned with more developed regions in a practice that dates back to the late 1970s. Western regions received aid from the more advanced east.

10 *Preferential fiscal policies.* Preferential policies on loans and taxation for ethnic minority businesses were introduced in June 1997.

The official position is that the 'system and practice of China's regional ethnic autonomy have been immensely successful'. The White Paper rehearses statistics which demonstrate that the autonomous areas have enjoyed rapid economic growth. Living standards, as measured by per capita net income and housing conditions, have improved. The infrastructure has improved. Traditional cultures have been protected and promoted – a claim supported by the publication of books in ethnic minority languages, by the creation of computer software for use with these languages and by the establishment of research institutes specialising in the art, literature and other cultural relics of the minorities. The level of education in the minority areas is said to have been raised significantly with increased enrolment. Similarly health services have been improved. Foreign trade and tourism are also at an all-time high in the minority areas.

The evidence adduced is impressive and it is clear that many improvements have been made in the infrastructure of the western regions, with the most obvious being the construction of roads and the development of facilities for transporting water to the arid zones. However, the statistics are not supported by independent studies. It is also significant that the issue of ethnic minority culture is at the very end of the White Paper, giving the impression that it has been added as an afterthought.

Western Development, nation-building and ethnicity

The Western Development programme contributes to the ongoing nation-building project of the CCP by addressing the economic base rather than the cultural and ethnic superstructure. The assumption, usually unspoken, is that if the western region of China can be developed and brought up to an economic level that is the same as, or close to, that of the east and southeast, then the problems of social unrest and ethnic separatism will either disappear or become insignificant.

The programme itself concentrates almost entirely on the economic benefits of integrating the underdeveloped west and the developed east, on the assumption that the development will benefit all citizens of China, whereas there is considerable evidence that not only are the benefits greater for the east but that the western populations are aware of this and resent it. It makes passing mention of the ethnic differences of large parts of the western region, but the very definition of the west, to include Sichuan and Shaanxi provinces and the city of Chongqing, indicates that there has been an attempt to dilute ethnic and cultural differences by subsuming them in a wider economic model. The particular problems of the border regions of Tibet, Xinjiang and Inner Mongolia, where there are real or potential movements of cultural and ethnic nationalism, are not completely ignored but are minimised by this approach.

The tried and tested system of creating autonomous regions, prefectures, counties and banners has been relied on to deal with these problems. It can be argued that these have been remarkably successful from the point of view of the central government in Beijing. All of the border regions have remained within the PRC since 1949; the revolts in Tibet in 1959 and the insurgency in Xinjiang since 1980 have been defeated and contained respectively; Inner Mongolian nationalism remains relatively passive. The system has created a political elite which includes members of the ethnic minorities, usually subordinate to their more senior Han Chinese colleagues, educated and trained by the CCP and owing their careers to the Party. This elite has managed the difficult relations between the border regions and Beijing with some success.

However the autonomous areas were created during the era of a tightly controlled political structure and a centralised and planned economy that was subject to rigid state planning. It is not at all clear whether they can meet the challenges of an economy that is opening up and allowing the creation of a new private sector and an urban middle class. The Beijing-trained ethnic minority elites are in many cases coming under considerable pressure to choose between loyalty to the CCP and allegiance to their own communities.

The success or failure of the Western Development programme will depend on whether it can manage the growing ethnic tensions that are becoming apparent as the economy of the west develops and its people have more and more contact with both the rest of China and neighbouring countries. At present the indications are that, although the economic development is showing signs of success, it is not addressing the ethnic issues but is ignoring them in the hope and expectation that, as they become prosperous, minority communities will be less concerned about their cultural and national identities and aspirations.

22 China and the world 1

Strategic relationships

International relations and the legacy of history

There is no country more conscious of it history than China. The record of China's economic domination by the West and Japan from the middle of the nineteenth century to the middle of the twentieth is taught to all school children and it is a central part of the discourse on China's national identity, whether at the formal or informal level. This was the period of China's 'national humiliation' (*guochi*): an important source of the legitimacy of the Chinese Communist Party is its ability to demonstrate that it freed China from that humiliating state of being, as Mao Zedong would have put it, a 'semi-colony'. China was of course never completely colonised and the degree of colonisation was much less that the process by which large parts of Africa, Latin America, South Asia and South-East Asia were brought under the economic and political control of European powers in the nineteenth century, but this has not made the resentment any less intense. Neither should the CCP take all the credit for liberating China from the influence of the West and from the Japanese occupation in the 1940s, but it does.

The 'unequal treaties', beginning with the Treaty of Nanjing, which was signed in 1842 at the end of the Opium War, were the initial focus of this resentment. Chinese thinkers of a patriotic or nationalist turn of mind insisted, not without justification, that the series of treaties concluded with Western powers from the end of that war onwards had been signed under duress: the repeal of these treaties became an important rallying cry for nationalists. The unequal treaties were eventually repealed in 1943 under the Guomindang's wartime administration, by which time they had become largely irrelevant in practical terms. The military occupation of their native soil by Japan was the main concern of most Chinese in that period. However, it was not until the return of Hong Kong to China in 1997 that many Chinese, and not solely those sympathetic to the CCP, could feel that the dishonour had been erased. These memories of subservience and humiliation have informed, and it can be argued that to some extent they have also hindered, China's development of a modern approach to foreign policy.

China was a member of the Communist bloc from 1949 until the collapse of the Soviet Union in 1991, but it was never an acquiescent member meekly following the political orders of Moscow. A Treaty of Friendship, Alliance and

Mutual Assistance that was signed in Moscow on 14 February 1950 presented a picture of the People's Republic of China (PRC) and the Soviet Union united in a common purpose but there were great strains from the outset. Mao Zedong's determination to be independent increased after the death of Stalin in 1953, when he could claim to be the senior world Communist leader, and by 1956 there was a considerable divergence between the approach of China and the USSR to domestic and international policy. These differences escalated when Mao launched the ill-fated Great Leap Forward in 1958 and in 1960 the USSR withdrew all technical assistance from China. The Sino–Soviet dispute became common knowledge in 1963, deteriorated even further during the Cultural Revolution and was never resolved. By the time that Soviet power finally collapsed in 1991, China was fully capable of acting alone and was doing so.

The Chinese alternative to Moscow's policies of confrontation under Stalin and peaceful coexistence during Khrushchev's regime was 'revolutionary diplomacy', a concept that was attributed to Mao Zedong, as most major policy decisions were, but was probably at least as much the product of Lin Biao's military approach and strategic thinking. In broad terms, 'revolutionary diplomacy' envisaged the encirclement of the capitalist nations (the cities of the world) by the developing peasant countries of the Third World, a strategy that mirrored the historical experience of Mao's CCP in rural China during the 1930s and 1940s. This is very revealing of the very limited awareness that the CCP had of international affairs at the time. The practical consequence of this view of the world was the cultivation by Beijing of national liberation and other radical movements in the Third World, often in opposition to similar bodies sponsored by Moscow. Most of this 'revolutionary diplomacy' involved little more than rhetoric and the amount of useful support in terms of finance or weaponry that was given to revolutionary organisations outside China was limited.

'Revolutionary diplomacy' came to an end with the death in a mysterious aircraft accident of Lin Biao and members of his family in September 1971. Lin had been nominated as Mao Zedong's heir apparent in 1969 but Mao was afraid that Lin was trying to oust him and it is possible that preparations were being made for an attempted *coup d'état* against Mao by Lin and members of his family. Lin had been adamantly opposed to any idea of a rapprochement with the United States, which to Mao suddenly seemed worthy of consideration because the Sino–Soviet dispute had escalated to the point where there were serious military clashes in the border areas of northeastern China.

Zhou Enlai, the most experienced and sophisticated international political actor in the CCP leadership, regained his formal power, protected the Foreign Ministry from the worst of the depredations of the Red Guards and oversaw the return to more conventional diplomatic relations with other states in 1971 and 1972. The highlights of this 'normalisation', as it was called, and the dramatic indication that China was coming in from the cold were Beijing's accession to the United Nations (UN) seat that had been occupied by Taiwan since 1949 and the visit to China by the President of the United States, Richard M. Nixon. Although radical rhetoric continued for some years, this often served to obscure the real intention of China, which was to play a key role in international organisations and to replace Taiwan as the international voice of China.

Since the 'reform and opening' era that developed on Deng Xiaoping's watch in the late 1970s, China has steadily expanded its role in international organisations, especially in the UN and its subsidiary bodies. One of the most significant developments was the long-drawn-out and eventually successful negotiations for membership of the World Trade Organisation (WTO), which China was finally able to join in 2001. China's position in these organisations has evolved from that of an outsider, more concerned with rhetoric than reality, to a seasoned player with highly professional diplomats operating at all levels and determined to be taken seriously.

Since its entry into the UN in 1971, China has concentrated on developing a network of diplomatic and economic relations, both with the major international players, including the United States and Japan, and with less powerful states. At the dawn of the twenty-first century, approaches were made to Latin America and Africa, primarily for economic reasons as China sought both raw materials and low-cost labour. Whether these will become key partners for China in the long term remains to be seen. The collapse of the Soviet Union in 1991 compelled Beijing to establish new economic and diplomatic relationships with its immediate neighbours to the west in the great land mass of Central Asia and then with the Muslim states of the Middle East and these are discussed in the following chapter.

Ambassador Sha Zukang's interviews

An extraordinarily forthright and no-holds-barred broadcast interview that was given to the BBC in August 2006 by China's Ambassador to the United Nations in Geneva, Sha Zukang, was either alarming or refreshing, according to the point of view of the listener.

> All the time I feel great. I always feel proud of my country. I don't have that kind of mentality of inferiority to anyone. I am so proud as a Chinese national and as Chinese Ambassador: I am not inferior to anyone in the world...China's military build-up is not threatening anyone. It is for legitimate defence. So, we are not fighting anywhere; we are not killing innocent people in the world today anywhere and we have to be careful, careful to make sure no one in the world can harm China. We are determined to defend our country with [a] little bit [of a] military increase. They are trying to make a huge story about it... China's population is six times or five times that of the United States. Why blame China? No! Forget it! It's high time to shut up. It is the US's sovereign right to do whatever they deem good for them, but, don't tell us what is good for China!'[1]

Ambassador Sha's breathtakingly undiplomatic diplomacy, his heart-on-sleeve patriotism and his impassioned defence of the right of his country to defend itself may have startled those observers who chose to believe that China's move towards a market economy necessarily predicated a 'peaceful rise' and that it was becoming more and more like the West in its attitudes. To anyone who had heard the same views in conversations with Chinese thinkers as well as the man in the street, it was refreshing to hear them again, in English, in public, and from a senior diplomat: the realisation that these views are widely held, if not always expressed so candidly, may make possible a more realistic analysis of China's international position and role.

China and the United States

The relationship between the United States and the newly created PRC got off to a bad start in the 1940s and slowly worsened – sometimes not so slowly. Although the United States had been a key player in the international efforts to mediate in the Chinese Civil War that broke out almost immediately after the defeat of Japan in 1945, its political loyalties were not in any doubt. In spite of the fact that US diplomats were engaged in negotiating for a coalition government and that many experienced American 'old China hands' were at best highly critical of Chiang Kai-shek's regime, when negotiations failed and it came to a choice, the United States supported the Guomindang (GMD).

The GMD was forced off the mainland by its defeat in the Civil War and re-established its administration on Taiwan. The formation of the PRC was announced on 1 October 1949 and, by that time, Mao Zedong had already declared that China must 'lean to one side' and ally itself with the USSR. The expulsion of Western missionaries and the takeover by the Chinese state of foreign, including American, businesses exacerbated relations further but it was the Korean War, and the experience of conflict between Chinese troops and the Americans – who led the coalition with South Korea and other members states of the UN – that effectively prevented the establishment of normal diplomatic and commercial relations. The war and the 'loss of China', as it was perceived in the United States, created problems for both sides. On the one hand, China endeavoured to exclude American influence; on the other, the United States, during its McCarthy period, forbade commercial dealings with the PRC and banned its citizens from travelling to China. McCarthyism dominated the US domestic political scene between 1950 and 1955. It was a period of anti-Communist paranoia that created the impression that America was under immediate and serious threat of internal subversion by agents of the Soviet Union and, increasingly, China. Distinguished American China specialists such as Owen Lattimore and John Service were excluded from their academic and government posts and many 'old China hands' were accused of being sympathetic to Communism – a shameful case of guilt by association.

There were few contacts between the United States and the PRC in the 1950s and 1960s. Washington devoted its efforts to shoring up the Chiang Kai-shek regime in Taiwan and the Central Intelligence Agency (CIA) mounted ineffectual and often incompetent attempts at subverting the new administration, such as the parachuting of Tibetan exiles back into their homeland – from where they were never heard of again.

During the Cultural Revolution, the United States was condemned by China for its imperialist policies and Beijing consistently articulated its fears that it was being surrounded by American forces or at least by forces sympathetic to the United States. This was not purely a case if political paranoia: in addition to Taiwan and Japan, which were firm allies of the United States, American forces were present in large numbers in South Korea. The United States was also prosecuting its interests in Vietnam, fighting against both the North Vietnamese government in Hanoi, which was supported by Moscow and Beijing, and the guerrillas of the National Liberation Front (NLF). The NLF, the Viet Cong to the American military, was a coalition of nationalists and Buddhists, dominated by the Communists, which was active in the south of the country where it was attempting to destabilise and overthrow the government of America's allies in the capital, Saigon.

As the Cultural Revolution began to run out of steam in 1969 and 1970, Mao Zedong and the most influential leaders of the CCP and the People's Liberation Army (PLA) began to reassess their view of various threats to their long-term survival. During the Cultural Revolution, they had already launched a barrage of vitriolic abuse against their erstwhile ally, the Soviet Union, in the press, referring to the Moscow leadership as the 'New Tsars' and characterising their policies as 'social imperialism'.

Richard Milhous Nixon became President of the United States in 1969. His track record gave no hint of the changes that he was about to bring to Sino–American relations. He had established a reputation as a tough, indeed ruthless, right-wing lawyer who had played a key role in the anti-Communist witch hunt of the McCarthy period. However, once in office his priority in foreign affairs was to disengage from overseas involvements and from Asia in particular; to downgrade the overseas military commitments of the United States; and to avoid becoming enmeshed in future major military entanglements after the quagmire of the Vietnam War. The war was becoming increasingly unpopular among the American public at the same time that it was becoming impossible for the United States to achieve a military victory. The 'Nixon Doctrine', as his disengagement policy became known, was the basis for a reassessment of America's policy in East Asia and it was the conjuncture with a similar reassessment being carried out in Beijing that made such profound change possible.

Nixon visited Beijing in 1972 but the ground had been prepared by his Secretary of State, Henry Kissinger, in secret meetings and shuttle diplomacy throughout the previous year. The visit permitted the opening of negotiations for the normalisation of diplomatic relations. A US diplomatic liaison office was established in 1973, although the formal appointment of an ambassadors was not ratified until 1976. The long-drawn-out negotiations were dogged by the issue of Taiwan.

Since the normalisation of diplomatic relations, the main emphasis of both sides has been on economic relations, primarily trade: there have also been increasingly acrimonious disputes about the relative value of the *renminbi* (RMB) and the US dollar. A series of political crises has indicated clearly how serious are the tensions that remain between China and the United States. The three most potentially dangerous of these crises have been the North Atlantic Treaty

Organisation (NATO) bombing of the Chinese embassy in Belgrade in May 1999; the collision between a US navy reconnaissance aircraft and a Chinese fighter over Hainan island in April 2001; and allegations in 1999 that a Chinese-born American scientist had been passing nuclear secrets to Beijing.

In May 1999, during NATO operations in Yugoslavia, which was in a state of civil war before its eventual collapse, the Chinese embassy in the capital Belgrade was struck by bombs. The building was badly damaged and three Chinese citizens, all journalists, were killed. The CIA took responsibility for the attack, and maintained that it had been at fault because it was using an old map that was out of date. However, rumours spread in China that the bombing had been deliberate because the embassy was being used to assist the Yugoslav army in its radio communications. In China, students demonstrated outside foreign embassies and on some university campuses foreign students were the target of verbal abuse in an atmosphere that became extremely threatening. Relations between the United States and China improved towards the end of the year and the two parties came to an understanding on the payment of compensation to the families of the victims and recompense for the damage to the embassy. This did not finally resolve the matter, especially in the eyes of many Chinese who persist in believing that the attack was deliberate: rumours continue to circulate about possible reasons for the bombing.

On 1 April 2001, a Lockheed EP-3E Aries II signals reconnaissance aircraft, operated by the US Navy, was patrolling close to Hainan, a large island which lies off the southern coast of China. US sources claimed that it had been operating legitimately in international airspace but Shenyang J-8 fighters of the PLA air force intercepted it on the grounds that it was within Chinese airspace and was on an espionage mission. The wing tip of one of the fighters touched the reconnaissance aircraft, the fighter crashed and the pilot is presumed to have been killed although his body has never been found; the US aircraft was able to effect an emergency landing on Hainan. US diplomats were hurriedly dispatched to Hainan to negotiate for the release of their crew, all of whom had survived, and the men were released ten days later. However, the Chinese authorities did not release the EP-3E for several weeks, presumably so that they could assess or even remove any advanced technology with which the aircraft was equipped.

The fact that the aircraft was intercepted was an indication of the tension between the Chinese and American military on the borders with Chinese airspace: the speed with which a negotiated settlement was reached is a mark of the importance attached by the two governments to maintaining diplomatic relations.

A number of ethnic Chinese working in the United States have fallen foul of either American or Chinese accusations of spying. In December 1999, Wen Ho Lee, who was born in Taiwan but is a US citizen and worked at the Los Alamos National Laboratory, was arrested on suspicion of having passed classified information about US nuclear weapons to the PRC. These allegations were subsequently dropped, although Dr Lee pleaded guilty to a less serious technical charge of downloading restricted data, but the length of time that he had been held, in solitary confinement and without charge, made his case a *cause célèbre*.

China and Japan

The 'normalisation' of Sino–Japanese relations did not take place until after the thaw between China and the United States, as befitted Japan's status as a junior partner in the historical anti-Communist alliance in Asia. The San Francisco Peace Treaty that had been signed on 28 April 1952 at the formal close of the post-war occupation by the allies and the US–Japan Mutual Security Treaty that was concluded in 1960 committed Japan to the American cause: Tokyo also signed a peace treaty with the Nationalist government on Taiwan. In practice, Japan operated an informal and undeclared 'two China' policy as it contrived to keep its economic relations and political alliances separate. Japan traded with the PRC, signed non-governmental agreements on commerce and fisheries and became involved in what the Chinese side termed 'people's diplomacy', primarily the exchange of cultural delegations. Between 1958 and 1971 Beijing made regular formal protests at the military alliance that it believed had been created against China by the relationship between Japan and the United States and particularly by the stationing of American troops in Japan.

Once the Nixon visit had unblocked diplomatic relations, Japan was in a position to regularise its own relations with China. The Chinese Premier Zhou Enlai and his Japanese counterpart Tanaka Kakuei came to an agreement in 1972 (the Zhou–Tanaka statement) that formed the basis for progress towards full normalisation. However, it was not until 1978, again in line with the timetable established for US–China relations, that China and Japan concluded their Treaty of Peace and Friendship.

Economic relations

The relationship with Japan was to prove vital for China's economic modernisation during the 1980s when economic issues predominated and political differences were set aside, albeit temporarily. The two states signed a long-term trade agreement in 1978 which resulted in a substantial increase in the volume of trade between them, and, as a close neighbour and a highly developed economy, Japan was well placed to invest in China's newly modernising industries and also to transfer advanced technology. It imported iron and steel from China and in return exported electrical goods and other consumer durables.

One of the firms that benefited from substantial Japanese investment was the Baoshan steel complex in Shanghai and the history of this company illustrates many of the problems that were faced by Sino–Japanese joint enterprises. A contract for investment and technology transfer to enable the creation of the plant was signed with Nippon Steel in December 1978 but financial retrenchment by the Chinese government led to the Japanese taking heavy losses. The scale and cost of the project came under fire at the meeting of the Chinese Fifth National People's Congress (NPC) in 1980 and construction of the plant was halted. It was restarted in 1981 and the furnaces were finally lit in 1985 but it operated with a lower output than had originally been planned.

On the political level, Japan was beginning to emerge from the cloud that it had been under since the Second World War: Tokyo began to enjoy a higher profile internationally and came under pressure to take a more active role in regional diplomacy and defence. Japan's reluctance to do so was matched by the opposition of other regional powers, especially China, Korea and other countries that had been occupied by the Japanese military during the Second World War and were deeply suspicious of Tokyo's motives.

Political differences between China and Japan came to a head in the 1980s, although initially they were still inextricably linked with economic relations. In 1985 and 1986, Chinese students demonstrated in Beijing against what was described by some commentators in the PRC as Japan's economic invasion of the mainland. The demonstrations spread to other major cities including Xi'an, Chengdu and Wuhan. It was clear to anyone travelling in China in the mid-1980s that Japanese products, particularly electrical and electronic goods, had suddenly begun to appear in Chinese shops in vast quantities. They were expensive but they were also popular because the quality and reliability were far greater than that of equivalent Chinese goods at the time – this was above all the case with radio cassette recorders and cameras. The Chinese government devalued its currency by 13.6 per cent in July 1986 in a move designed to stem the flow of imports from Japan and promote Chinese exports: the value of the RMB dropped by 40 per cent against the Japanese *yen* in the course of a year.

Talking about the war

The major political conflicts between China and Japan were in the context of visits by Japanese politicians to the Yasukuni Shrine and school textbooks. On the face of it, both of these issues appeared peripheral and inconsequential in terms of normal diplomatic relations, but for China they were regarded as a test of Japan's willingness to distance itself from the attitudes that had led to war and the occupation of China in the 1930s.

On 12 August 1985, on the fortieth anniversary of VJ Day (Victory Japan Day, the date of Japan's unconditional surrender in 1945), the Japanese Prime Minister Nakasone Yasuhiro visited the Yasakuni Shrine in Tokyo. The shrine is a war memorial and Shinto religious complex that was established in 1869 to commemorate all those who had fallen in the conflict to defeat the Tokugawa Shogunate and establish the government of the Meiji Restoration in 1868, which marked the beginning of Japan's great advance to modernisation. It was also created to provide a permanent resting place for the spirits of the war dead, in accordance with the tradition of Shinto, Japan's traditional religion. This was not in itself controversial but soldiers, sailors and airmen who died in subsequent conflicts, up to and including the Second World War, were also commemorated at the shrine. In 1979 it was revealed that, without any public announcement, the names of fourteen individuals who had been convicted at the Tokyo War Crime Tribunal of Class A war crimes during the Second World War had been included in the list of those to be commemorated. This provoked outrage in China and Korea, the two countries which had arguably suffered most from the Japanese Occupation, and visits by Japanese Prime Ministers to the Yasukuni Shrine have been a source of considerable friction ever since. In 1986, such was the furore that Mr Nakasone did not make a planned visit to the shrine in August. This shrine has also been the focus of political conflict within Japan, as ultra-nationalist groups intent on defending Japan's war record protest if Prime Ministers do not make annual visits.

A parallel source of conflict was the publication in Japan of history textbooks for schools in which the invasion of China by Japan was played down or even justified. Textbooks play a far greater role in teaching methodology in Japan than they do in the West. In the 1980s the word of an adopted textbook was law and the teacher would not feel able to deviate from it in the classroom. In a memorable but far from atypical geography lesson in a secondary school in Toyota 1984, the teacher had the textbook in front of him, as did the pupils: he then wrote out a passage from the book on the blackboard, and then read the same passage aloud to the class. There was no discussion.[2]

China argued that unless the Japanese corrected the false impression that there had been no invasion, their good faith would be in doubt. At the same time, the ultra-nationalists in Japan insisted that there should be no about-face on the textbooks or on the Yasukuni issue. Right-wing militants who tour the cities in garishly decorated loudspeaker vans are adamant that it was not only the Japanese who were militarily aggressive in the 1930s.

Other related issues were the rights claimed by both Taiwan and China to a student hostel that had been set up for Chinese students who were studying in Japan; the vandalism of a memorial to Zhou Enlai by ultra-nationalists in 1987; and the firing of shots at China's consulate in Fukuoka in 1988. China established a museum at Lugouqiao (Marco Polo Bridge), which is just outside Beijing at the location where the 1937 invasion of China began, and a memorial in Nanjing to the victims of the massacre that took place there later the same year.

These political differences have not been conclusively resolved but it is a mark of the closeness between the two countries, and particularly the perceived mutual economic interest, that after the suppression of the Democracy Movement in Beijing in June 1989 and the flight of foreign businesses fearing that a civil war was about to break out, Japanese business interests were the first to return. Since 1989 this rapprochement has continued. Japanese business continues to play an important role in the economic development of China. Relations between the governments are on the whole stable, with occasional crises that still reflect China's unease about Japan's attitude to its role in the Second World War.

In 2007, the seventieth anniversary of the 1937 Rape of Nanjing was commemorated by the formal opening of an extended memorial hall in the city of Nanjing dedicated to the victims of the massacre. Until recently, the tone of Chinese discussions of the war, including the documentation in the memorial hall, has been relentlessly negative but the tenor of the exhibits in the new hall highlights the need for looking forward as well as backwards and emphasises the development of peaceful relations between Beijing and Tokyo. The most senior Chinese leaders avoided the commemoration in Nanjing and this was seen as a gesture of reconciliation by Japan.[3]

In December 2007, the Japanese Prime Minister, Yasuo Fukuda, who had taken office the previous September, held talks with the Chinese Premier, Wen Jiabao, during his first visit to Beijing. Although the meeting was amicable and emphasised increased bilateral cooperation, it was noted that there was no resolution of one of the major current areas of disagreement between China and Japan, the rights to natural gas fields which are located in the East China Sea between the two countries and are the subject of a dispute over maritime borders. However, in an important gesture to China, Prime Minister Fukuda indicated that he would not visit the Yasukuni Shrine during his term of office. His predecessor, Koizumi Junichiro, had visited the shrine during his time in office and those visits had led to restrictions on contacts at the highest levels.[4] The visit demonstrated a determination to maintain cordial relationships in spite of some serious differences of opinion.

China and North Korea

By the end of the twentieth century, China had become North Korea's only long-term ally but this alliance was never an easy one. The first formal diplomatic agreement between the two states was a treaty signed on 11 July 1961 in Beijing by Zhou Enlai and the North Korean leader, Kim Il-sung. It provided for economic cooperation; for either side to come to the assistance of the other in the event of a military attack by an outside power or powers; and it enshrined the aspiration of reunifying Korea in a peaceful and democratic manner.[5] This treaty is still in existence and there have been other, undisclosed agreements but the degree of cooperation between North Korea and China has varied considerably over the years.

Economic collapse

As the North Korean economy deteriorated in the 1990s, the country became increasingly reliant on outside food aid to stave off the threat of famine. China was a major contributor along with South Korea, Japan and the two largest donors, the United States and the European Union. The constant threat of a confrontation between Pyongyang and the United States over allegations concerning the production of nuclear weapons and the testing of missile warheads alienated much of the international community and increased North Korea's isolation and its dependence on China.

North Korea has suffered from severe food shortages since the catastrophic natural disasters and famine of 1995. In the spring of 2002 the World Food Programme, run by the United Nations' Food and Agriculture Organisation, was predicting that the country had only three months supply of food remaining and appealed to the international community for increased donations.[6] Pyongyang relaxed the state-controlled system of rationing grain, probably at the prompting of its Chinese advisers, and allowed the introduction of a limited market in some areas in an attempt to alleviate the shortages of rice.

By 2005 China's contribution to food aid for North Korea – wheat, flour and other grains – had increased dramatically and Pyongyang had been able to dispense with aid from other sources. International aid agencies were compelled to leave North Korea and the work of the World Food Programme was severely restricted, in spite of the fact that there were credible reports of another impending famine following in the wake of typhoons and large-scale floods.[7] Pyongyang's dependence on China increased pressure on China by the international community, primarily the United States, to use its influence to persuade the government of Kim Jong-Il, who had succeeded his late father Kim Il-sung in 1994, that it should not proceed with its nuclear power and nuclear weapons programme.

Historical ties

The extent and effectiveness of Beijing's influence on Pyongyang has, however, always been difficult to determine. Some sections of the Korean Party of Labour, the Communist Party that runs North Korea, operated closely with the CCP as early as the 1920s and 1930s and the close relationship between Beijing and Pyongyang, likened in a classical Chinese analogy to that between the lips and the teeth, was particularly strong during the Korean War. Although a close relationship, it was a fraught one. China was railroaded into the Korean War by a combination of sleight of hand by Kim Il-sung and Stalin's bullying, and the Chinese People's Volunteers (CPV) who fought in Korea suffered enormous losses, estimated at 900,000 killed and injured. Mao Zedong's son, Mao Anying, died in a US bombing raid on the CPV headquarters in December 1950 and as he had been placed by Mao under the personal protection of the leading Chinese field commander, Marshal Peng Dehuai, this was to sour relations between the two men for years to come and was one of the personal causes of the bitter factional disputes within the CCP that led to the Cultural Revolution.

China and North Korea were not defeated in the war, which ended in a stalemate that over fifty years later has still not been formally resolved by a peace treaty. However, both regimes suffered greatly in terms of diplomatic representation and economic investment. China was branded an aggressor and effectively isolated for thirty years. As part of the truce agreement, a demilitarised zone was established between the North and the South and the United States continues to maintain 35,000 troops in South Korea.

China's attitude to North Korea is akin to that of someone dealing with a difficult and embarrassing friend or relative. The historical ties between the two make it impossible for China to abandon its neighbour and ally, but Beijing insiders who deal with Pyongyang are quite scathing about how demanding and manipulative they find Kim Jong-Il, who came to power when his father Kim Il-sung died in July 1994, and his entourage. Kim Jong-Il has never possessed the authority or power that his father was able to wield and, although he took formal control over the armed forces on the death of his father, the delay in his appointment as state President and General Secretary of the Korean Workers' Party (he was not formally given this post until October 1997) was universally understood to be an indication of the weakness of his position in the Pyongyang elite. Long-standing rumours of a bitter power struggle within the elite were largely substantiated when a senior political theorist, Huang Jang-yop, defected to the South Korean embassy in Beijing in February 1997.

Beijing continues to encourage Kim Jong-Il to take the path of economic reform that China has followed so successfully and has organised high-profile guided tours of the most dramatic developments in the Shanghai region, such as Pudong, for him and his senior colleagues[8]. However, apart from limited market reforms in the food supply system, Kim and his officials have been reluctant to take that step.[9]

Crisis 2003

A new phase in the confrontation over Pyongyang's nuclear programme began in October 2002 when the United States accused the North Korean government of having begun the processing of enriched uranium in contravention of an agreement that had been reached in 1994. North Korea claimed (or admitted) that it had a previously undeclared nuclear weapons programme, although there was considerable doubt over whether it actually possessed any functioning nuclear weapons. In reprisal the United States led a boycott of the supply of oil to North Korea in November 2002. In December of the same year, Pyongyang expelled two inspectors from the International Atomic Energy Authority (IAEA – the UN regulatory body) and in January 2003 announced its decision to withdraw from the Nuclear Non-Proliferation Treaty. It was announced in February 2003 that the Yongbyon five-megawatt nuclear power reactor, the main North Korean nuclear plant, and its plutonium reprocessing facility had been reactivated and upgraded.[10]

Since April 2003, Pyongyang has consistently demanded direct talks with Washington to resolve the crisis rather than the six-nation talks process that is preferred by the West because they include the regional powers most directly affected by the North's nuclear programme.[11]

At the end of August 2003, the parliamentary body of North Korea, the Supreme People's Assembly, formally approved a statement by its Foreign Ministry that Pyongyang had no option but to pursue its policy of developing a nuclear deterrent to defend itself against possible pre-emptive nuclear strikes by the United States. However, other sources in Pyongyang indicated that there was still the possibility of negotiation and, as usual with North Korea, the genuine policy direction remained shrouded in mystery. China responded to the increased tension by transferring responsibility for the security of its border with North Korea from the police to the PLA; reports that Beijing had deployed as many as 150,000 troops along the border were nevertheless treated with some scepticism. The United States upgraded its Patriot anti-missile defence system which is based at the Suwon Air Base south of Seoul in South Korea – the Patriot system is designed to target and destroy incoming ballistic missiles, cruise missiles and aircraft.[12]

On 19 September 2003, the IAEA passed a resolution strongly advising North Korea to abandon its nuclear deterrence policy but a statement from KCNA, the official news agency in Pyongyang, rejected this contemptuously and maintained that it was under no compulsion to comply with the IAEA's instructions since it had withdrawn from the Nuclear Non-Proliferation Treaty in January 2003.[13]

On 13 August 2003, as plans were being finalised for a six-nation conference on the nuclear crisis, the Ministry of Foreign Affairs in Pyongyang issued a statement renewing its demands for a non-aggression pact with the United States as a precondition for relinquishing its nuclear ambitions.[14] The conference, with delegates representing North and South Korea, Russia, China, Japan and the United States, met on 26 and 27 August in the Diaoyutai State Guest House in Beijing, which had been the venue for many high-level diplomatic negotiations since the establishment of the PRC. The meeting was presided over by the Chinese Foreign Minister, Wang Yi, and the pessimistic mood that had prevailed during the preparatory meeting was clearly justified when the meeting concluded without a joint statement and a North Korean spokesman rejected the idea of a further round of meetings.[15]

Continuing confrontation 2006

A six-party meeting in July 2006 proved as inconclusive as the previous meetings and there were also signs of further strains in relations between China and North Korea. There have been persistent rumours about North Korea's involvement in money laundering and, more recently, in the counterfeiting of foreign currencies including the US dollar and possibly the Chinese *renminbi*. After US authorities took action against the Banco Delta Asia, a bank based in Macau which held substantial deposits of money belonging to Pyongyang, Beijing took the unusual step of following suit and froze North Korean bank accounts which were reported to have contained millions of dollars.[16]

Delegates to the thirteenth meeting of the ASEAN Regional Forum (ARF), which was convened in Kuala Lumpur, Malaysia, on 28 July 2006, were hoping to arrange a parallel meeting at this forum during which they would be able to discuss Pyongyang's nuclear plans. However, the North Korean Foreign Minister, Paek Nam-sun, warned that his delegation would walk out if there were any hint of condemnation of Pyongyang's missile tests by ASEAN members. Another spokesman for Pyongyang, Jong Song-il, made it clear that the financial sanctions that had been imposed on North Korea were the main obstacle to discussions at that stage.[17]

On 9 October 2006, North Korea announced that it had carried out a nuclear test. Although there was scepticism in specialist scientific circles about the nature and magnitude of the explosion, it was taken seriously by international bodies. Pressure on China to curb the excesses of its neighbour (and alleged friend and ally) increased. Beijing imposed additional financial restrictions on Pyongyang after the test and the threat of cutting off oil supplies to North Korea was also mooted. China had apparently only been given twenty minutes advance warning of the test.

Wen Jiabao, the Chinese Premier, insisted that diplomacy and dialogue were the only appropriate means to resolve the crisis and President Hu Jintao despatched a high-level delegation to Pyongyang, led by Tang Jiaxuan, a former Minister of Foreign Affairs and an experienced and respected diplomat. Although there was no detailed communiqué of the results of this mission, Kim Jong-Il is reported to have agreed that North Korea would not test any further nuclear devices; some sources even suggested that he had expressed regret about the consequences of the test to the Chinese team. However, it was also reported that there had been a mass rally of over 100,000 North Koreans in Pyongyang to give support to the nuclear test.[18] Eventually North Korea did agree to resume its participation in the six-party talks and the consensus is that this was almost entirely due to China's insistence.[19]

In December 2006, the US government made Pyongyang an offer of economic assistance in exchange for an agreement that North Korea would cease its programme of developing nuclear technology. The offer followed meetings that took place once again in the Diaoyutai State Guesthouse in Beijing and involved the US Assistant Secretary of State, Christopher Hill, and the Deputy Foreign Minister of North Korea, Kim Kye-gwan, in addition to Chinese officials. These proposals, which were far more detailed than previous offers from Washington, included commitments by the USA, Japan and South Korea to supply further food aid, an agreement on mechanisms for removing the restrictions on North Korean funds that were deposited abroad and assistance in developing Pyongyang's non-nuclear energy sector.[20]

Koreans in China: minorities and refugees

One factor in relations between North Korea and China that is often overlooked is the existence of an ethnic Korean population living within the borders of the PRC: the existence of a Korean minority in China is hardly surprising given that the two countries have a common border. The ethnic Korean population of China is approximately two million: most live within the Yanbian Korean Autonomous Prefecture which borders on North Korea, but there are also Koreans living in other parts of China, including Beijing which is home to a thriving Korean community and has many excellent Korean restaurants. Since the onset of the North Korean famine, steadily increasing numbers of Koreans have been attempting to leave the North and move to China, where, in some cases, they have relatives.

North Koreans who cross the border into the PRC to flee economic hardship and political persecution are considered by the Chinese authorities to be economic migrants: they are treated as illegal immigrants and are under constant threat of deportation. Although China has obligations to refugees under the UN Refugee Convention and Protocol, it claims that these obligations are superseded by an agreement that it has with the government of North Korea in Pyongyang. The contents of this agreement are confidential but it has been suggested that procedures adopted by Beijing and Pyongyang to deal with cross-border migrations date back to informal attempts to deal with Chinese fleeing into North Korea during the famines that followed the Great Leap Forward in China in 1958. A protocol on border security, signed by the two sides in 1986 but never made public, obliges China to repatriate North Koreans rather than treat them as refugees.[21]

Consequently, China does not permit the UN High Commission for Refugees (UNHCR) and other agencies to have access to North Koreans living within the borders of China. UNHCR, which has maintained an office in Beijing since 1995, argues that many migrants from North Korea are genuine refugees and should be treated as such but Chinese officials insist that this is an internal problem and UNHCR has complained that it has been obstructed in attempts to treat these people as refugees.[22]

In spite of these difficulties, the pressure on North Koreans to risk the border crossing into China grew as economic conditions in North Korea deteriorated dramatically, especially in the 1990s when there was severe famine in the rural areas and the country became dependent on foreign aid. It is difficult to quantify the scale of the migration of refugees from North Korea into China because, for political reasons, and motivated by national pride, neither side wishes to admit to the numbers involved but refugee agencies describe it as a mass exodus. According to a report from the Brookings Institution, a research and policy think-tank based in Washington, DC, the Chinese government claims that there are 10,000 North Koreans living within the borders of the PRC, whereas the US State Department works on a figure of 30,000–50,000. Even this figure is believed to be a considerable underestimate by non-government organisations with a special interest in refugees and some of these organisations have put the figure as high as 300,000. China deports refugees back to North Korea on a regular basis, possibly as many as 10,000 annually.[23]

This migration has been complicated by the involvement of South Korean Christians who have assisted in smuggling people across the border and there have been a number of high-profile cases of North Koreans demanding political asylum in foreign embassies, in particular the Japanese embassy in Beijing. There is a sizeable, and generally disadvantaged, Korean community in Japan which dates back to Japan's colonial adventure in Korea at the beginning of the twentieth century and the migration of Korean labour to Japan. Most of these Japanese Koreans (*zainichi*) were originally from what was then the northern part of colonial Korea and many of them retain ties with their family members in North Korea.

The authorities in Beijing were so concerned about the possibility of divided loyalties among the Korean community in the northeast of China that they launched an ideological education campaign in September 2003 to remind Koreans living in the Yanbian Korean Autonomous Prefecture that 'their motherland is China'. This was in response to legislation being drafted in South Korea which aimed to extend the rights of Korean nationality to all those who were 'Korean by blood' – a policy which Beijing regarded as a direct attempt to undermine the status of Yanbian Koreans as a Chinese national minority. This is taken seriously by Beijing because there are concerns that, if the North Korean regime collapses or suffers a military defeat, or if there is an agreement on the peaceful unification of Korea (however unlikely that might seem in the light of the history of conflict between the two Koreas), Korean nationalist opinion might demand the inclusion of Yanbian in an enlarged Korea.[24]

Rapprochement 2007–8

In early August 2007, it was announced that the leaders of North and South Korea would meet in Pyongyang from 28 to 30 August. This was unusual but not unprecedented since in 2000 Kim Jong-Il had met Kim Dae-jung, who, as President of South Korea at the time, was pursing a 'sunshine policy' of rapprochement towards his northern neighbour. The 2007 meeting followed protracted confidential negotiations between the two sides and an international agreement that had been reached to provide aid for North Korea in exchange for disarmament and which had resulted in the closure of the Yongbyon reactor in July 2007. Cynics suggested that one reason for the meeting was an attempt to bolster the chances of the South Korean President Roh Moo-hyun in elections which were due in December 2007. President Roh was nearing the end of his first term of office as President and polls indicated that he was running second to the opposition Grand National Party which has a hard-line approach to North Korea.

After the three-day meeting, the two sides issued a declaration in which they called for an international conference which would conclude with a treaty to take the place of the armistice, still the only formal conclusion to the Korean War. Parallel negotiations included discussions on continued nuclear decommissioning, cross-border freight transport and fishing in the disputed western maritime borders. Although the summit was greeted with relief and a degree of enthusiasm, it was not at all clear whether any substantive changes had taken place.[25]

At the end of November 2007, there was more optimism about the reduction of tensions between North Korea and the United States than there had been for many years. There were reports that a US diplomat had established an office in Pyongyang to act as liaison officer between the two governments and that arrangements were being made for others to join him in preparation for the anticipated normalisation of diplomatic relations.[26] There were also rumours that changes in the government of North Korea were imminent. Intelligence from Pyongyang suggested that Jang Song-taek, the brother-in-law of the Dear Leader Kim Jong-il, had been appointed head of Pyongyang's security service. Korean analysts view Mr Jang as less narrow-minded and more outward-looking than most of the Pyongyang leadership and this is attributed to his extensive overseas experience. He has a reputation as an economic reformer, one of a minority within the North Korean elite, and was reported to have been directing a project to create a Chinese-style special economic zone close to the country's border with the PRC.[27]

Regular rail links between North and South Korea began on 12 December 2007: initially these only involved freight trains and, although there were hopes that people would be able to cross the border by rail in the future, there were no announcements of immediate plans to resume passenger services. The economies of both Koreas stand to gain considerably from this traffic.[28]

By the end of 2007, it was beginning to be assumed that, after decades of recurrent crises, the normalisation of relations between North Korea and its former adversaries was finally becoming a reality. In early December, the President of the United States, George W. Bush, wrote a personal letter to Kim Jong-Il urging the North Korean government to honour undertakings that it had made in the six-party negotiations and reveal full details of their nuclear programmes. A positive reply was received by the White House. This was a verbal rather than a written response and it was not immediately clear whether it had come from Kim personally, but this unprecedented direct contact was treated as further evidence of normalisation.[29] In January 2008, Pyongyang missed a crucial deadline for declaring details of its nuclear programme and it appeared that it was business as usual.

However, by the summer of 2008, Pyongyang had released data on its nuclear programme to China and the cooling tower at the Yongbyon plant had been demolished to demonstrate that its nuclear weapons enterprise was being dismantled. Food supplies from the UN and the USA began to flow into North Korea after UN officials had obtained unprecedented access to the rural areas.[30]

Overseas Chinese: the politics of diaspora

Ethnic Chinese communities outside China, from southeast Asia to Europe and the Americas, have played an important role in the development of China's relations with the rest of the world. This role has often been unreported and unrecognised and it has not always been positive, either for China or for the communities of the Chinese diaspora.

The most common modern Chinese term for individuals and communities of ethnic Chinese origin who are resident outside of China is *huaqiao*. It is sometimes considered to be a reference to a bridge between two cultures, as the character for *qiao* is similar to the character for 'bridge'. This is, however, rather fanciful and the *qiao* in *huaqiao* actually refers to an inn or the place of rest for Chinese sojourners who were temporarily away from their native villages for trade or for work – although temporary became permanent in the case of many of these communities. The usual English translation is 'overseas Chinese' although some prefer 'Chinese overseas'. The term was not usually applied in the PRC to people resident in Hong Kong and Macau before those territories returned to China and it is not used for the residents of Taiwan. The preferred term in these cases is *tongbao* (literally, 'born of the same parents' and, by extension, 'compatriots').

It has been estimated that the total population of overseas Chinese is something of the order of thirty million. Some 80 per cent of these live in Southeast Asia, in both the mainland (Vietnam, Cambodia, Laos and Thailand) and the island states (Philippines, Indonesia and Malaysia). There are also significant communities of Chinese origin in the Caribbean, Peru, India, Australia, Canada, the United States and Europe, including Eastern Europe where the Chinese-speaking population increased dramatically following the collapse of the Soviet Union in 1991.

The majority of Chinese who live in states such as Malaysia and Indonesia have been settled in their countries of domicile for several generations and have usually taken the nationality of that country. That is also true in North America and much of Europe, but other communities have not yet reached that stage of development.

The majority of the people of the Chinese diaspora trace their origins to the southern coastal provinces of Fujian, Guangdong, Guangxi and the island of Hainan (now also a province). Their languages and cultures are those of the south rather than the Mandarin-speaking north, and the *lingua franca* in Chinese communities outside China tends to be Cantonese although many people, especially in Singapore, Malaysia and Indonesia, speak Hokkien (Fujianese) or Hakka. There has been emigration in every historical period but it was during the nineteenth and early twentieth centuries that economic pressures and military and political crises in China (notably the Taiping Rebellion and its suppression by the Qing armies) precipitated the large-scale emigration of young men.

Many of these travelled initially to the regions that are now part of the states of Malaysia and Indonesia and settled in towns rather than in the farming areas which were already occupied by local people (known in the Malay language as the *bumiputra*, 'sons of the soil'). Chinese settlers established themselves in industry and commerce rather than agriculture, although they did occasionally become involved in specialist farming enterprises such as the production of rubber or pineapple growing. Distinctive Chinatowns also began to appear. Denied access to most agricultural trades, many Chinese settlers earned their living as itinerant pedlars or village shopkeepers and, over time, they acquired a reputation for business acumen. Their success in business and the wealth and status that it brought them did not always assist them in their relations with the indigenous population; rivalry and envy often led to racial tensions and, at times, to intercommunal violence. Initially Chinese settlers in Southeast Asia did not assimilate well. In common with other diaspora communities, the earliest arrivals saw themselves as sojourners who assumed that they would return to China once they had made their fortunes. They maintained their own Chinese languages, brought Chinese women over from their home villages to marry (although this was at a later stage in the migration process) and, if they could, they educated their children in Chinese-language schools.

Second- and third-generation settlers began to assimilate; they took local names, became proficient in the local tongues (principally the widespread language of administration and commerce which is today known as either *Bahasa Indonesia* or *Bahasa Malaysia* – two national versions of the Malay language) and sent their sons and daughters to local schools where they mixed with the non-Chinese population. When China acquired a Communist government in 1949, the position of the overseas Chinese communities became more troubled and complicated. The mentality of the Cold War created a climate of suspicion and encouraged searches for 'Reds under the bed'. Chinese in Malaysia and Indonesia were suspected of being sympathetic to Beijing and therefore to the CCP. Some were indeed prominent in the Communist Party in Malaysia but even those who were not involved in any political activity were suspect and frequently discriminated against. In Malaysia, there were transfers to special village reservations. In Indonesia, anti-Chinese pogroms as late as 1998 resulted in many deaths and the destruction of Chinese careers and businesses. After riots and the fall of the Indonesian President Suharto, who was suspected of having used inter-communal tensions to bolster his regime, legislation that had discriminated against Chinese Indonesians, especially their use of the written Chinese language, was repealed.

The reform period provided new economic opportunities on the mainland for Chinese entrepreneurs from outside China. Their capital and business prowess were welcomed by the new order that emerged after the death of Mao and overseas

Chinese businesses have been involved in the major economic development projects of the last two decades.

China and India

China and India share the distinction of being the nations that are tipped to be the twin economic powerhouses of the twenty-first century. They are also the world's most populous countries: India has a population of 1.1 billion which may catch up with or even overtake China's 1.3 billion. Both are predominantly rural societies that are making great strides in their progress towards industrialisation and modernisation. Historically China owes a major debt to India as the source of one of its core religions, Buddhism. They do not, however, have much in common in terms of political structure or culture and relations between the two have been difficult since the foundation of the two modern states in the aftermath of the Second World War.

The two states have a common border but much of it is mountainous, and it includes the Himalayas which are a formidable barrier to communication of any kind, although there are traversable passes and there is a long history of trade and religious pilgrimage across the mountains. The small independent states of Nepal and Bhutan also lie on this border. There are serious disagreements over the demarcation of the borders, the most significant for Sino–Indian relations being two long-standing disputes relating to Aksai Chin in the Jammu and Kashmir region in the west and Arunachal Pradesh (south Tibet to the Chinese) in the northeast of India, close to Assam, which was part of the North East Frontier Agency under the British Raj.

In the 1950s, during the Cold War and the movement for decolonisation, China and India cooperated successfully and a popular slogan of the time was *Hindi Chini bhai bhai* (India and China are brothers). What became known as the Five Principles of Peaceful Cooexistence (*panch shila*, also written *panchsheel*) were agreed during negotiations between Zhou Enlai and the Indian Prime Minister Jawaharlal Nehru for the Sino–Indian treaty which was signed in 1954. The essential points of this agreement were peaceful coexistence in spite of different ideological positions, equality, mutual respect, non-aggression and refraining from interference in the internal affairs of each other's country. These idealistic principles were popular and in tune with the spirit of the time and were widely used in negotiations between other Third World countries.

However, China and India also competed for leadership of the Non-Aligned Third World, notably during the conference of developing nations that was held in 1955 in the Indonesian city of Bandung. The term 'non-aligned' can only be applied very loosely in this period: the Third World was not exempt from the divisions of the Cold War and India drew close to Moscow while its regional rival Pakistan became an ally of the United States. As the Sino–Soviet dispute unfolded around 1960, China also formed a strategic alliance with Pakistan to counter the influence of the Soviet Union in Delhi, in spite of Pakistan's close relations with the United States.

From the 1950s to the 1970s, China and India were held up as models for the alternative routes that developing countries could take: Indian democracy or Chinese dictatorship. The differences between the economies of the two states were never as great as their political differences might have suggested: India, like China, had a planned economy with an important role for the state. However, India did implement a multiparty democracy which China never even attempted.

The simmering border disputes erupted into full-scale conflict in 1962 after complaints by both sides over military incursions into what each considered to be their own sovereign territory in northern India, close to Tibet and Xinjiang. Heavy fighting began in early October of that year but the armed conflict, although bitterly fought, was short-lived and it came to an end when the Chinese side announced a unilateral ceasefire at the end of November. As a result of its military advances, China had retained its control over Aksai Chin but it did not take all of the territory that it claimed as its own in the northeast of India. It concluded an agreement with Pakistan, India's rival, on border demarcation and the war came to an end. Since the ceasefire there have been numerous minor skirmishes in the border region but there has been no fighting on the scale of the 1962 conflict.[31]

Although the main border disputes are about Aksai Chin and Arunachal Pradesh, the issue of Tibet has been a major obstacle to the achievement of satisfactory Sino–Indian relations. After China's suppression of the Tibetan uprising of 1959, the Dalai Lama had been given asylum in Dharamsala, a town in the northwestern Indian state of Himachal Pradesh. The Dalai Lama intended to return to Tibet in due course and a Tibetan government-in-exile was created in Dharamsala: this was regarded by the government of the PRC as unacceptable interference in China's internal affairs and therefore a breach of the Five Principles of Peaceful Coexistance. (For further discussion of the Tibet issue, see Chapter 17.)

In spite of all these unresolved issues, relations between the two Asian giants have improved gradually and there have been constant discussions on trade and cooperation. The border dispute remains a hard nut to crack: there is still no joint agreement on the implications for border demarcation of the ceasefire line of 1962, although tensions have been reduced since interim agreements were signed in 1993 and 1996. Both sides continue to claim that the other is still occupying territory illegally. India's nuclear tests in May 1998 temporarily destabilised diplomatic relations with Beijing, not least because the Hindu Nationalist Bharatiya Janata Party (BJP) government in New Delhi claimed that the tests were motivated by fears of a nuclear threat from China. The Indian Foreign Minister, George Fernandes, called China 'India's enemy number one'.[32]

When conflict erupted between India and Pakistan over Kashmir in May 1999, both sides appealed to China for support but China remained neutral in public and appears to have supported international demands for a peaceful solution to a conflict that was potentially perilous since both sides are nuclear states. High-level political and diplomatic visits by Chinese and Indian politicians have continued and relations have warmed.

Sonia Gandhi, the President of the Indian National Congress, which was the dominant party in India's post-BJP ruling coalition, visited China in October 2007 at the invitation of the CCP and its Chairman Hu Jintao and arrived in Beijing just after the CCP's Seventeenth National Congress. Mrs Gandhi, the widow of former Prime Minister Rajiv Gandhi who was assassinated in 1991, made positive comments about the social and economic development of China during a visit that was intended to strengthen bilateral relations in general in addition to links between the two political parties. Although published accounts of the meetings between the two sides did not go beyond the usual platitudes, there were reports that their discussions had broached some of the more intransigent issues in Sino–Indian relations, including the border disputes.[33]

Meetings between the Chinese Premier Wen Jiabao and his Indian counterpart Manmohan Singh in December 2005 and January 2008 were productive and there have also been joint military manoeuvres. China and India have concluded agreements on trade and economic cooperation in fields such as construction, financial services, education and tourism. Trade is likely to be the key to the relationship between the two states, and fierce competition can be expected as well as strategic cooperation. In 2006 it was estimated that the total value of bilateral trade was of the order of US$20 billion and this figure is set to rise significantly.[34]

China and Africa

As China's domestic economy expanded in the 1980s and 1990s, the government began to search for new overseas partners. The PRC required additional markets for its manufactured goods but it also needed inexpensive supplies of raw materials and, above all, energy. Commercial relations were developed with a number of other Third World regions including the countries of ASEAN and Latin America but the most interesting and, in many ways, the most controversial have been China's relations with African states.

China does not have a record of an imperial past in Africa and this might put it at an advantage in comparison with those Western nations which were former colonial powers on the continent. However, there is a long history of Chinese contact with Africa. The naval squadrons of the Chinese Muslim Admiral Zhenghe, who explored the Indian Ocean between 1405 and 1433 during the reign of the Yongle Emperor of the Ming dynasty, reached as far as the coast of East Africa. Although these missions were discontinued, trade between China and Africa persisted as is attested by finds of datable Chinese porcelain at various sites on the Swahili coast. Chinese men were recruited to work as indentured labourers in the gold fields of the Transvaal during the early years of the twentieth century. These early migrants were the basis for the modern Chinese community in South Africa, although it has been augmented by more recent arrivals, some from the PRC but many from Taiwan, including entrepreneurs who set up small businesses. Taiwan and South Africa sustained a diplomatic relationship during the period when South Africa was ostracised by most of the developed world because of its apartheid policies; Taiwan was excluded from the UN in 1971 and was constantly searching for political and economic allies.

Tanzania and Zambia Railway

The more recent involvement of China in Africa began in the 1960s and was essentially part of the PRC's rivalries with both the USSR and Taiwan for political influence on the continent. In 1970 construction began on a railway to link the port of Dar-es Salaam, the largest city in Tanzania and at the time its capital, to the Zambian border where it would connect with the Zambian railway network.[35] This was a considerable foreign aid project for China, particularly in view of the fact that at the time it was itself a very underdeveloped country. For Tanzania, it provided a much-needed link to the economy of Zambia which was developing on the basis of vast resources of copper until the price of the metal dropped in the 1970s. The most significant gain for newly independent Zambia was that it would no longer be economically dependent on the regimes of Rhodesia and South Africa, both of which were dominated by elites of European origin. The Tanzam Railway, which in due course also became known as the TAZARA (Tanzania and Zambia Railway Authority) or the Uhuru (freedom) Railway, went into operation in 1975. Its economic value has been questioned but there is no doubt that it had a political value for Beijing as an emblem of China's support for the movement against colonialism in the 1970s.

Oil and construction

By the 1990s the rhetoric of anti-colonialism and Third World solidarity had given way to hard-headed commercial considerations. Thousands of Chinese workers and managers, mainly in the construction and energy industries, moved to work in African countries such as Angola, Sudan, Zimbabwe and Zambia in that decade. An oversimplified, but not entirely inaccurate, analysis of the relationship is that China acquired valuable raw materials – oil in the case of Sudan and Angola and valuable minerals elsewhere – and in return, the Africans benefited from the construction or improvement of their infrastructure which was desperately inadequate. Many Western companies had been reluctant to become involved in development projects in these states, partly because of concerns about human rights and corruption and partly because of real or perceived risks in regions where there were ongoing insurgencies or countries that have only recently emerged from long and brutal civil wars.

Chinese companies, mostly state owned, do not have to answer to the same demands for corporate social responsibility that face their counterparts in the West. Life is not easy for the new expatriates, many of whom experience a substantial culture shock in Africa, as did earlier generations of Chinese who came to the continent as diplomats or bearing foreign aid. In many cases the new Chinese expatriate existence is made tolerable by the creation of residential and social compounds for Chinese engineers and labourers where they can use their own Chinese language, eat their own Chinese dishes and have their own Chinese entertainment.[36]

Chinese businesses in Africa rarely employ local workers. Not only are almost all managers sent from China, but the vast majority of the workforce are also brought in. This has created conflict with local communities and there have been complaints that Chinese companies do not make a sufficient contribution to the local economies and in particular to the problems of unemployment that many African countries face.

The similarities between this lifestyle and the concessions created by Westerners in China in the late nineteenth century are striking, but some Chinese expatriates tend to regard themselves almost as commercial aid workers rather than new colonialists. More formally, Li Anshan, a historian of Africa at Beijing University, argues that 'both China and Africa have suffered the ill-effects of the colonial era. This shared experience underlies the ideas of equality and respect for sovereignty that each highlight in their approach to international relations.'[37] This policy of non-interference is far from being a new one and dates back to the Five Principles of Peaceful Coexistence that were agreed at the Bandung conference in 1955 as the basis for China's relationship with other Third World countries. It is an important part of Beijing's justification for working with regimes that many in the West criticise as dictatorial.[38]

Beijing Forum on China–Africa cooperation

A government White Paper, *China's African Policy*, was published by the Ministry of Foreign Affairs in Beijing in January 2006. As part of its strategy of formalising relations between China and the various African states with which it had economic relations, China organised a Forum on China–Africa cooperation in Beijing in November 2006. Representatives of forty-eight African countries attended and trade agreements that were reported to be worth over £1 billion sterling were signed: in addition, preferential loans and export credits were promised by President Hu Jintao in his address to the conference. The following year, Hu made official visits to Cameroon, Liberia, Sudan, Zambia, Namibia, South Africa, Mozambique and the Seychelles to strengthen China's political and economic relationships with those countries.

Darfur

China has been severely criticised for its close relationship with the Khartoum government in the light of the serious and persistent human rights abuses that have occurred in the Darfur region of Sudan during the civil war that began in 2003. In November 2007, 135 members of the Chinese armed forces were deployed to Dafur as part of a joint peace-keeping mission that had been mounted by the African Union and the UN.[39] Rebel forces, that is armed groups opposed to the Khartoum government, declared that they would not regard the Chinese contingent as neutrals but as supporters of the regime in Khartoum.

China is the largest customer for Sudan's oil and has been at least since 1999; in return it has exported, among other commodities, weapons to Sudan and has also contributed to building the infrastructure of the oil industry by developing its exploration, production and refining technologies. This close relationship is alleged to have been responsible for China's refusal to support international sanctions against the Khartoum government. According to Li Anshan, whose academic analysis is in line with the thinking of the Chinese government on Africa, 'China has consistently opposed economic sanctions in Sudan. China believes the Darfur issue is an issue related to development, where sanctions would only bring more trouble to the region...the international community has to give Sudan some time to solve this problem'. He also argued that Chinese aid was tackling the root of the problem, poverty. Representatives of the rebel forces opposed to the Khartoum government did not see it that way and threatened to attack both Chinese military contingents and Chinese companies operating in the region. The influence that China can bring to bear on the Khartoum government is probably overestimated. Beijing is determined to maintain the principle of non-interference in Sudan's internal affairs and has maintained that it is supplying far fewer armaments than has been alleged.[40]

It remains to be seen whether China can develop economic relations with African countries without turning into a colonial or quasi-colonial power. The prospects are not good; the United States initiated its international relations strategy in the nineteenth and twentieth centuries as a counter to European colonialism, only to become an neo-colonial power in its own right. Japan's attempt to create a Greater East Asia Co-prosperity Sphere, partly on the basis of a promise to drive out the Europeans and Americans, also developed into a colonial system – albeit a short-lived one.

China's international status has evolved rapidly and in December 2007, the World Bank entered into a new relationship with China in connection with its work in Africa. China was previously a major client of the bank, from which it had received significant aid, but following a significant donation by the Export–Import Bank of China, the major international banking arm of the Chinese state, to the World Bank's International Development Association which targets the poorest communities in the world, China is now treated as a major donor rather than a recipient.[41]

23 China and the world 2

New neighbours to the west

China's relations with its immediate neighbours to the west, and to a certain extent with the states of the Islamic Middle East with which those states have close cultural and religious ties, were rekindled in the 1990s after the fall of the Soviet Union. Strictly speaking the states on the other side of the inner Asian frontier were not new neighbours because they had always been there, but during the Cold War and the Sino–Soviet dispute, China's contact with them was so limited that when the borders reopened in the 1990s, diplomatic relationships had to be rebuilt almost from first principles.

Central Asia and Xinjiang

China's closest neighbours on its western and northwestern borders are the Central Asian states of the former Soviet Union. The collapse of the Union of Soviet Socialist Republics in 1991 and the creation of the new independent sovereign states of Kazakhstan, Kyrgyzstan and Uzbekistan produced significant changes in political relations across China's inner Asian frontiers. It was essential for China to forge diplomatic relations with the new states, and discussions on long-standing border demarcation issues and troop reduction began almost immediately. Commercial and political relations developed swiftly and the impact on the Xinjiang Uyghur Autonomous Region, which is that part of China nearest to Central Asia (or alternatively, that part of Central Asia currently under Chinese rule), was particularly dramatic. The border routes across the mountains were opened to trade for the first time in over thirty years; informally they opened at once but officially they were authorised from 1992 onwards. Families and communities, which had enjoyed little contact for many years, renewed their acquaintance and trade developed at a rapid pace.

The new links were not restricted to commerce. Religious – that is, Islamic – connections were also renewed and there were exchanges of political ideas. The emergence of independent Turkic Islamic states in the vicinity was immensely attractive to Uyghurs who looked to them for assistance in their own bid for independence. Initially there appears to have been serious and genuine support for an independent East Turkestan from other Turkic states, including Turkey, but as China's confidence in dealing with its Central Asian neighbours grew,

Beijing made it perfectly clear that this support would be treated as unwarranted interference in China's internal affairs and would not be tolerated. Beijing negotiated with the stick of its overwhelming military superiority and the carrot of lucrative trade and energy deals, and persuaded the Central Asian states that they should curb any political activities by their own Uyghur communities, which were particularly important in Kyrgyzstan and Kazakhstan, on behalf of Uyghurs in China. The new Central Asian governments complied readily, partly because they were concerned about the threat to their own stability from political Islamist movements (particularly in Uzbekistan and Kyrgyzstan). The demise of Communist regimes in Central Asia had led not to the hoped-for democratisation of the region but to the emergence of authoritarian governments based partly on pre-Soviet clan and regional ties and partly on Soviet political culture. Although there was still distrust of China, they shared many common values and a common political idiom.

Nevertheless, these changes fuelled expectations in Xinjiang that the establishment of an independent East Turkestan state was imminent and incidents of rioting and violent attacks on institutions associated with the Chinese state took place throughout the region. These included bus bombings in Urumqi in 1992, an explosion in Kashghar in 1993 and, in 1995 and 1997, serious disturbances in Yining/Ghulja, the site of the government of the Eastern Turkestan Republic of the 1940s. The 1997 disturbances were serious and many lives were lost when police and the military suppressed them: this was the last insurrection on such a scale to date.[1]

Beijing's response to this deepening conflict was to launch a 'Strike Hard' campaign in 1996. This campaign was a national one and was targeted at crime in general throughout the whole of China, but in ethnic minority areas, the priority was clearly to suppress any manifestation of separatism. Mass arrests, short- and long-term administrative detention, the seizure of unauthorised Islamic printed or recorded materials and a clampdown on unregistered and therefore illegal mosques and *madrasas* were all employed in order to root out separatism. Although this had the desired effect of curbing overt manifestations of separatist or Islamist protest, it did not extinguish the sentiment which gave rise to them. Attacks on police and military bases continued by a small number of paramilitary separatist units which operated clandestinely. Political re-education campaigns were used to persuade Islamic clerics that they should be more active in supporting the Chinese Communist Party's (CCP's) policy on religion and to give support to registered mosques and imams and isolate unregistered radical groups. As part of this drive to suppress separatist movements, Beijing also put pressure on the governments of neighbouring Central Asian states to compel them to prevent any separatist activity that could be construed as anti-Chinese from taking place within their borders. The governments of Kazakhstan and Kyrgyzstan both complied, partly because of political and economic pressure from China but also because they perceived a common menace from Islamist political movements. Some Uyghur activists in their territories were returned to China for arrest and trial and severe restrictions were placed on the press and political activities in the Uyghur minority communities in Kazakhstan and Kyrgyzstan. This awkward alliance formed the basis for the Shanghai Cooperation Organisation (see below).

The Kazakhs and Kyrgyz of Xinjiang are from the same ethnic background as their counterparts in Kazakhstan and Kyrgyzstan. There are sizeable minority Uyghur communities in both of these former Soviet Central Asian republics: the Uyghurs are closely related to the Uzbeks of Uzbekistan and there are Uzbek communities in other parts of Central Asia, including Xinjiang. The Uyghur and Uzbek languages are extremely close (effectively two forms of the same language) and the two peoples share a common literary and cultural tradition. Many independent scholars consider that they are essentially the same people although both Uyghurs and Uzbeks prefer to maintain the distinction between their languages and communities.

Although Xinjiang is firmly under the administrative control of China, it is therefore not surprising that the most important social and cultural bonds of the Uyghurs are with the Turkic peoples to the north and west in former Soviet Central Asia. These bonds were severed during the Sino–Soviet dispute which began in the early 1960s. The mass migration of Kazakhs, Uyghurs and others from northwestern Xinjiang into Kazakhstan in 1962 prompted China to seal its borders and contact between China and its western neighbours was minimal for decades. Mikhail Gorbachev's ill-fated visit to Beijing during the protests in Beijing by students and citizens that were suppressed by the People's Liberation Army (PLA) on 4 June 1989 was supposed to repair this rift but it was not until the collapse of Soviet power in 1991 that the borders were reopened and the divided communities began to communicate with each other.

Shanghai Cooperation Organisation

As China developed new forms of political relations with its Central Asian neighbours, bilateral meetings on border and trade issues were found to be inadequate to deal with the rapidly changing geopolitical environment. Political Islam became more and more influential in Afghanistan and Tajikistan and the new governments of Uzbekistan and Kyrgyzstan considered that it posed a serious threat to their authority. All of the regional powers perceived that in spite of great differences between them, they had a common interest in combating this new force which all saw as a threat to the stability of the region.

The first meeting of what was to become a major regional grouping took place in Shanghai in 1996 when the foreign ministers of China, Russia, Kazakhstan, Kyrgyzstan and Tajikistan met to discuss common concerns. An agenda was constructed around the issues of border security and ways of combating insurgent Islamic forces and the smuggling of Islamic literature, weapons and narcotics. The grouping which planned to meet on a regular basis became known as the Shanghai Five but was renamed the Shanghai Cooperation Organisation in June 2001 when Uzbekistan was admitted. The new name was sufficiently flexible to allow for the admission of other members. Pakistan, the only other state being seriously considered for membership, was not permitted to join as there were serious doubts about the government's relationship with political Islamist groups.

Western Development

Beijing's strategy in dealing with the problem of ethnic separation in Xinjiang since the early 1990s has been twofold. On the one hand, there has been the severest repression of any unofficial religious activity and any political activity that could be classified as separatist. On the other, there has been a recognition that poverty and underdevelopment lie at the root of the region's social problems and programmes to alleviate this poverty have been initiated from time to time.

The decision to tackle the problem of the relative underdevelopment in the whole of China's western provinces led to the policy of the Great Development of the Western Regions (*Xibu da kaifa*), which was launched in 2000 in Chengdu, the capital of Sichuan province. The Western Development policy was targeted at the whole of the west of China, not just Xinjiang, and this includes Ningxia, Gansu, Qinghai, Sichuan and also Tibet. The Western Development policy is dealt with in more detail in Chapter 21.

11 September 2001

China reacted to the attacks on New York and Washington by restricting the access of foreigners to Xinjiang, which has a seventy-kilometre border with Afghanistan, and by declaring that separatism in Xinjiang was a terrorist phenomenon that China should be given *carte blanche* to deal with as the authorities saw fit. This provoked international concern in human rights circles, including the office of the United Nations High Commissioner for Human Rights, Mary Robinson, and although the anti-terrorist rhetoric has remained, China has done very little new to suppress separatism but has continued the policies it began in 1996 with the Strike Hard campaign. When the war in Afghanistan is finally over, the coalition led by the United States may not remain in place and China may once again be faced with the need to demonstrate to Muslim states that it is not using the cover of the 'war against terrorism' to clamp down on Islam *per se* in Xinjiang.

More difficult to assess is the long-term impact of the presence of US troops in Central Asia. During the Cold War this was completely unthinkable as it was under the absolute control of the Soviet Union. Since 1991, Russia has taken the view that it is the one outside power with a legitimate interest in the region and this has been recognised by its inclusion in the Shanghai Cooperative Organisation. Central Asian states were initially reluctant to accept US and allied troops on their territory in the war against the Taleban and it will be interesting to see whether in the long term some limited military contact will remain as part of Uzbekistan and Kyrgyzstan's resistance to the rise of political Islam in the Ferghana Valley.

After the 11 September 2001 attacks on New York and Washington, the administration of George W. Bush embarked on an unusual bout of diplomatic activity with the aim of establishing military bases for the first time ever in a number of the countries of former Soviet Central Asia. The Central Asian states are situated just to the north of Afghanistan, close to those areas in which the remnants of the Al Qaeda organisation are believed to have gone to ground. Mounting operations from the north avoids the political difficulties associated with basing US military forces inside Pakistan, where there is still considerable sympathy for the ousted Taleban and its Al Qaeda allies among the poorer sections of the rural population.

This unprecedented move by the US government and military has profound implications for regional stability in an area where post-Soviet dictatorships and radical Islamist movements seem to be the only political options available to communities searching for national identities and economic stability.

In particular, the US presence in Central Asia poses a challenge for China, which has come to regard the region as its own backyard, and in which it has exerted a considerable influence in the last decade. China has never had any concrete conflict of interest with the United States in Central Asia in the past and the outcome is difficult to predict. The status of Russia, which was formerly the regional overlord and retained a *primus inter pares* role among the governments of Central Asia even after they became independent, is also called into question.

US bases in Kyrgyzstan

The first Deputy Interior Minister of Kyrgyzstan welcomed the presence of US troops in his country when they were allowed to use Manas airport and suggested that members of the coalition might have a long-term future in Kyrgyzstan 'if the situation in the region deteriorates'.[2] Two hundred US servicemen had arrived at Manas by 25 December 2001 and were preparing to establish a more permanent base in Kyrgyzstan.[3] It had been agreed that airfield security would be the joint responsibility of US and Kyrgyz forces, with US troops guarding the outer perimeter.[4] The Kyrgyz Defence and Foreign Ministers visited the base on 14 January 2002.[5] A high-level delegation of US senators, led by the senior Democrat Thomas Daschle, visited Bishkek for discussions on the situation in Afghanistan and the future of US–Kyrgyz relations and inspected US troops stationed at the airfield.[6] Although the initial agreement for the US presence was for one year, local commentators suggested at the time that it was likely to last much longer than this.[7]

The first ever programme of US–Kyrgyz joint military exercise, code-named Black Knight, began on 5 February in the Chonkurchak district which is about thirty kilometres outside the Kyrgyzstan capital, Bishkek. The US military provided ten instructors, presumably from detachments of special forces troops. Key units of the Kyrgyz armed forces including 'special subdivisions of the Kyrgyz Defence Ministry and the National Guard' and the National Border Service underwent specialist training in counter-terrorist operations and mountain warfare. This included landing in combat zones, surveillance and reconnaissance, ambush tactics and the evacuation of wounded personnel, and training was carried out in poor mountain weather conditions. Specific counter-terrorist training included combat operations in populated areas, dealing with the taking of hostages and techniques for clearing buildings. Although the Kyrgyz armed forces are generally regarded as poorly trained and inexperienced in comparison with their US counterparts, these units included troops with combat experience against armed groups associated with the Islamic Movement of Uzbekistan, which had penetrated the Batken region of southern Kyrgyzstan in 1999 and 2000. US officers were highly critical of the lack of organisation of the Kyrgyz units and their Kyrgyz counterparts felt that they had learned to be more professional as a result of the exercises.[8]

A radio station in Bishkek announced on 25 February that the first stage of the exercises had ended and by March 2002 it was estimated that approximately 1,500 US or coalition troops were based at an airfield outside Bishkek.[9] Visiting journalists pointed out that the level of US investment in the infrastructure and the potential economic benefits to Kyrgyzstan were indicative of planning for a long-term US presence in the region.[10]

Kazakhstan

Discussions on the establishment of a US military presence on Kazakhstan also began in January 2002.[11] Kazakhstan is less useful as a forward base for operations against Al Qaeda as it does not share a common frontier with Afghanistan and its military airfields are reported to have deteriorated severely since independence. However, it is the largest Central Asian state and it is both politically stable and the most Westernised, or more accurately Russified, of all the Central Asian countries. It is not involved in the same kind of conflict with radical Islamist movements that affects Kyrgyzstan and Uzbekistan. The degree of US military involvement in Kazakhstan remains somewhat shrouded in mystery but *The Times* reported that a special forces unit of the US army had been training soldiers of the Kazakh Mountain Chasseur battalion in counter-terrorist techniques since February.[12]

China and the Middle East

Connections between the Middle East and China date back at least to the sixth century AD. Traders and diplomats from what is usually referred to as Arabia, but almost certainly included the Persian-speaking world, appeared in China as early as the Tang Dynasty (618–907), entering the country by two main routes, overland across Central Asia by what was later to become known as the Silk Route and by sea into southeastern China, now sometimes called the Spice Route as most of its travellers were merchants seeking spices from the islands of southeast Asia. Some of these traders settled in the port cities of the southeastern coast, in particular Quanzhou, Changzhou and Guangzhou (Canton), which all became important commercial centres. In the Muslim cemetery in Quanzhou, it is still possible to see gravestones with inscriptions in Arabic, Persian and Chinese, commemorating settlers from the Yemen, Persia and Central Asia who died and were buried there.[13] The Tang dynasty capital, Chang'an, known today as Xi'an, had a resident community of diplomats and merchants from the Middle East and Central Asia.

The composition of China's population was profoundly affected by the political and social changes brought about by the Mongol conquests of East and Central Asia in the thirteenth century. On their expeditions westward to conquer Central Asia, the armies of Chinggis Khan and his successors sacked major Islamic centres including Bukhara and Samarkand and transported sections of the population including skilled armourers, craftsmen and enslaved women and children back to China, where they were settled as servants of Mongol aristocrats. When the Mongols established their Yuan dynasty (1271–1368) to rule China, they used Central Asians as border guards, tax collectors and administrators, finding them more loyal than the Chinese population they had conquered. In the Mongol perception of society in China, Mongols were the elite, but the Muslims from the steppes of Central Asia came next in the hierarchy and were considered superior to both the Chinese population and the non-Chinese minorities who lived in south China.

The gradual penetration of Islam into China which reached a high point in the sixteenth and seventeenth centuries, created communities of Muslims, especially in Xinjiang and the northwestern and southwestern regions of China proper. Unlike the rest of the population of China, they had a natural interest in the Middle East, their spiritual home, and maintained a connection with the region through the *hajj*, whenever this was possible. The distance from Mecca, the difficult terrain and the cost made the pilgrimage difficult for Muslims from China and political constraints have added to their isolation, both under the empire and in modern times.

The People's Republic of China (PRC) was born during the wave of nationalism and decolonisation that followed the Second World War and the new government of China shared many of the concerns and problems of other Third World states. Although the PRC was initially aligned with the Soviet Union and the rest of the Communist bloc, political, doctrinal and personal conflicts that had led to a split between the two were never resolved during the lifetime of the Soviet Union. Consequently China's search for allies steered it towards the Third World and, because of its size and cultural confidence, it gradually came to see itself as a natural leader of those states. This includes relations with the Muslim states of the Middle East, Central and South Asia.

New Great Games in Central Asia

The opening-up of Central Asia after the collapse and fragmentation of the Soviet Union in 1991 gave rise to intense competition by Turkey, Iran, Saudi Arabia and to a lesser extent (at least initially) Pakistan, for political, economic and spiritual influence in the region. Because Beijing encouraged these mainly Muslim countries to invest or trade with China, it has therefore felt it necessary to demonstrate its tolerance of Islam and to show that its Muslim population was able to live and worship in ways that were acceptable to the rest of the world of Islam. While Turkey, as a modernising Muslim nation with a secular government, might be seen as its most natural ally, the potential threat of pan-Turkism led China to turn also to the radical Islamic state of Iran as a countervailing force.

In the nineteenth century, the Great Game was the competition between the expanding empires of Russia and Great Britain for hegemony in the heart of Asia. In the late twentieth century the new Great Game had new players and new prizes, both secular and spiritual.

Turkey

Turkey has continued normal diplomatic relations with China, including discussions about economic cooperation, but, conscious of domestic support for pan-Turkism and the potential benefits of a wider Turkic-speaking community, successive governments have shown a particular interest in Turkic minorities in China. Isa Yusuf Alptekin, the most prominent Uyghur *émigré* leader, whose influence in Xinjiang was feared by Beijing in spite of his advanced age, met Turkey's Prime Minister Suleyman Demirel and other senior political figures on a number of occasions. In 1991, Prime Minister Demirel was reported by *émigré* Uyghurs as having said that he would 'not allow the Chinese to assimilate their ethnic brothers in Eastern Turkestan' and would make representations to the United Nations.[14] Alptekin was received by President Turgut Ozal in 1992, and in an emotional meeting presented the President with a traditional Uyghur coat and cap and an Eastern Turkestani flag, symbolising his handover of the Eastern Turkestani cause to the Turkish President because, at ninety-one, he was too old to continue himself. President Ozal is reported to have said, 'I declare that I have taken delivery of the Eastern Turkestani cause. The Turkic republics under former Soviet rule have all declared their independence. Now it is Eastern Turkestan's turn. It is our desire to see the ancient homeland of the Turkic peoples a free country.'[15] Some of the accounts of these meetings are from *émigré* Uyghur sources which would obviously wish to emphasise the importance of their organisations, but the Chinese response suggests that they took the exiles very seriously.

Alptekin met government leaders again in Ankara on 22 and 23 December 1992, to ask them to bring the issue of increased Han Chinese immigration in Xinjiang to the United Nations (UN) and the Turkish parliament was also asked to send a mission to Xinjiang to investigate alleged human rights abuses and to report on its findings to the UN Commission on Human Rights.[16] In response, an article in *People's Daily* in November 1992 claimed that the Turkish President Turgut Ozal and Prime Minister Suleyman Demirel had openly accepted that there should be a Turkic homeland extending 'from the Great Wall of China to the Balkans' and treated Isa Yusuf Alptekin as President-in-exile of East Turkestan.[17] Alptekin died in 1995 at the age of ninety-three, having 'lived out his last days in Istanbul, in a modest flat overlooking the railway line once used by the Orient Express'.[18]

In 1993 Qiao Shi, who was Chairman of the Standing Committee of the National People's Congress (NPC), and China's most powerful security chief at the time, met Turkish visitors including Dorgan Gures (Chief of General Staff) and Nevzat Ayaz (Defence Minister) to discuss defence links.[19] Qiao Shi visited Turkey again in November 1996, and, during talks in Ankara with his opposite number Mustafa Kalemli, made it abundantly clear to the Turkish authorities that the Chinese government was implacably opposed to the activities of separatist movements based in foreign countries, including Turkey. He addressed the Turkish National Assembly on 7 November and praised the Turkish government for its non-interference in China's internal affairs and for restricting the activities of Uyghur separatist organisations in Turkey.[20] The following month, according to reports circulating in Taiwan, Turkey and China signed an agreement on military cooperation, under which Turkey would be able to buy surface-to-surface missiles from China and would acquire a licence to produce them in Turkey with technology transferred from China.[21] Turkish governments have had to perform a delicate balancing act to deal with the incompatible demands of pan-Turkism and trade with China.

In the immediate aftermath of the collapse of the Soviet Union, many Central Asians were interested in the possibility of following a Turkish model of development. The Presidents of both Uzbekistan and Kazakhstan declared their intentions of taking 'the Turkish route'. Turkey capitalised on this good will and significant resources were invested in linking the newly emerging former Soviet states with Turkey. Turkish Airlines was one of the first foreign carriers to establish air links with Almaty, the capital of Kazakhstan, and the capitals of the other Central Asian states. Turkey provided moral support to the nascent states and offered to educate students from Central Asia and Turkish television was beamed to the region. Ankara established an agency specifically to coordinate Turkish aid to Central Asia, although in reality that aid was severely restricted by Turkey's relative lack of financial resources. The Turkish President, Turgut Ozal, organised a summit of the Turkic nations in October 1992 but political and cultural differences between the states and the degree of Russification that had taken place in Central Asia over the previous century-and-a-half made relations and even basic communication far more difficult than either side had expected.[22]

In 1994 the importance attached to relations with Turkey was immediately apparent to visitors to Almaty. Many academics and government officials were either in Turkey or were about to visit Turkey.[23] The Deputy Prime Minister of Turkey, Bulent Ecevit, after spending a week in China in June 1998, expressed a strong interest in developing economic ties, including joint ventures, and announced that Turkey had established a trade and information centre in Shanghai.[24] Reports from the Taiwanese central news agency at the same time claimed that Turkey had granted permanent residence status to about 1,000 Uyghurs who had recently arrived there from Xinjiang to join the 50,000 already in the country.[25]

A previously unknown directive from the office of the Turkish Prime Minister was publicised in February 1999 by the popular Turkish newspaper *Hurriyet*. It had been distributed to government organisations at some point during the premiership of the Motherland Party politician, Mesut Yilmaz, in the 1990s. The burden of the document was to urge ministers and government officials not to take part in any political activities organised by East Turkestan and Uyghur organisations based in Turkey. This was in recognition of Xinjiang's status as part of the territory of the PRC and because the Turkish government conceded that *émigré* activities were creating difficulties in Turkey's relations with China.[26] The speaker of the

Turkish parliament, Hikmet Cetin, received Li Peng on 5 April 1999 when Mr Li visited Ankara in his capacity as Chairman of the Standing Committee of the NPC, a position seen to be broadly similar to that held by Cetin. The official Chinese news agency, Xinhua, reported that Mr Cetin reiterated Turkey's opposition to separatist activities, and this was reinforced in a meeting between Li Peng and Prime Minister Bulent Ecevit.[27]

Iran

Cooperation between Iran and China on atomic energy projects was confirmed in 1991[28] and a delegation from the Iranian Centre for Strategic Research visited China in November 1991.[29] Higher-level visits took place, by the speaker of the Iranian Majlis, the parliament, in December of the same year[30] and the Foreign Minister Ali Akbar Velayati in April 1992.[31] Arms sales by China to Iran have been controversial: Chinese official sources have consistently played them down or even denied that they took place at all, but there is general agreement that tanks, artillery, surface-to-air missiles, fighter aircraft and a nuclear reactor have been sold to Tehran.[32] It is widely assumed that Iran has bought Silkworm missiles from China and there have been regular reports of visits of high-ranking Iranian military officials to China. Qin Jiwei travelled to Tehran at the end of October 1992 on what was the first visit made by a Chinese Foreign Minister since the 1979 revolution in Iran. He had meetings with President Rafsanjani and the Iranian Minister of Defence.[33]

The Chinese government has repeatedly denied that it was providing missiles to Syria and Iran. A Foreign Ministry spokesman, Wu Jianmin, at a press conference on 4 February 1993, rejected US Defence Department claims that China was cooperating with Syria and Iran to develop cruise missiles.[34]

The Iranian President, Ali Akbar Hashemi Rafsanjani, visited China in September 1992 after the Non-Aligned Movement conference in Jakarta. After meeting central government leaders in Beijing and signing a nuclear cooperation agreement,[35] he met Tomur Dawamat, the Regional Government Chairman, in Urumqi for discussions on economic, commercial, scientific, technological and cultural exchanges, including talks on joint Xinjiang–Iran projects, rail links via Kyrgyzstan and Tajikistan and a new air route.[36] President Rafsanjani visited Kashghar on Friday 11 September and led afternoon prayers in the Etgar (Id Gah) Mosque. Crowds of Uyghur, Kazakh, Kyrgyz and Hui Muslims waited for him outside the mosque and when he walked briefly around the square after the service there was tremendous applause from the mainly Muslim onlookers in spite of a massive police presence.[37]

Controversy over China's arms sales to Iran was renewed in August 1993 when the 19,000-ton freighter, the *Yinhe*, en route from China to Dubai and under suspicion of carrying chemicals which could be used in the manufacture of nerve and mustard gas and similar chemical weapons, was shadowed by the US Navy destroyer *Chandler* through the Gulf of Hormuz. After initially refusing to allow the ship to be searched, the Chinese authorities changed their minds when it was refused permission to dock in Dubai, and the *Yinhe* changed course for Saudi Arabia.[38] The *Yinhe* was subsequently found not to have been carrying the chemicals alleged by the US authorities but Washington declined to pay the compensation demanded by Beijing in respect of the delay.

The Iranian newspaper *Jomhuriyat-e Eslami* (Islamic Republic) carried a report on the suppression of the Yining disturbances in February 1997 and criticised China's policies as an attempt to separate Xinjiang's Muslims from their co-religionists across the borders.[39]

As China's economy has developed, its energy needs have become increasingly important and this has influenced its political relationships with oil-producing countries, including Iran. An initial agreement on the supply of oil and gas by Iran to China valued at US$70 billion was concluded in October 2004 by the China Petroleum and Chemical Corporation, also known as Sinopec. Under the terms of this agreement, China agreed to invest in the development of the major Yaravan oil field in the southwest of Iran in return for guaranteed supplies of crude oil and liquefied natural gas. Towards the end of 2007 a further agreement worth a further US$2 billion was signed. China does not feel obliged to comply with sanctions against Iran that have been put in place by the United States and its allies.[40]

Pakistan

Relations between China and the individual states of South Asia have been complex. China has been in a constant state of tension with India since the India–China war of 1962 over territorial disputes, especially concerning the Aksai Chin region of Kashmir and parts of Arunachal Pradesh in northeastern India. These tensions have been further exacerbated by the question of Tibet and by India's willingness to provide a haven for the exiled Tibetan spiritual leader, the Dalai Lama, and his followers in Dharamsala. These considerations have led China into an alliance with India's main political rival since independence in 1947, Pakistan. During the Cold War this alliance was a strange one, since New Delhi was close to the Soviet Union and Pakistan had enjoyed reasonably amicable relations with the United States.

Pakistan and China agreed to open the Khunjerab Pass to border trade from 1 May 1993.[41] On 25 August 1993, the United States imposed sanctions on China and Pakistan after months of enquiries into allegations that China had supplied Pakistan with components for the M-11 missile in violation of international agreements, principally the Missile Technology Control Regime (MTCR). The cost to China of these sanctions was of the order of US$500 million. The M-11 missiles have a range of 300 miles and a payload of half a ton, which would have a serious effect on the balance of power in the region. Defence analysts believed that the missile would enable Pakistan to hit targets in India, Iran and the former Soviet Union, but there has been a difference of opinion within the US intelligence and defence establishment on the precise level of threat it poses. Both China and Pakistan initially denied that any transfer of missile technology had taken place, with Pakistan later claiming that the last shipment had been in February 1992. Technically, the missiles may be only just outside the parameters of the MTCR, which restricts the transfer of missiles with a range of over 187.5 miles, since the range of the M-11 is 190 miles. China's response to the sanctions was a firm rebuttal of the accusations. Deputy Foreign Minister Liu Huaqiu lodged a firm protest in a meeting with the US Ambassador Stapleton Roy and alleged that 'This naked hegemonic act has brutally violated the basic norms governing international relations'. He argued that China was not violating the terms of the international agreement but that US sanctions left China 'with no alternative but to reconsider its commitment to MTCR'.[42]

Washington announced on 25 August 1993 that sanctions in response to China's alleged arms sales would include a restriction on the transfer of satellite and other advanced technology for two years. China did not sign the agreement on MCTR, but had said early in 1992 that the guidelines would be respected as part of an agreement on the removal of earlier US sanctions that had been imposed after the crackdown on the democracy movement in June 1989. China denied that the arms sales to Pakistan break international rules as, according to defence analysts in Beijing, the missiles were only designed for short-range use. The PRC indicated that it felt a grave sense of injustice, contrasting its own arms sales policy to what it claimed was a grave threat to Chinese security when the United States sold 150 fighter aircraft to Taiwan in 1992. Arms sales are an important source of foreign currency for China, although they dropped from an estimated annual value of US$4.7 billion in 1987 to US$100 million in 1992.

This was the first action taken against China by the Clinton administration and the suspicion in Washington was that the decision had been based on domestic political considerations to demonstrate that the administration had a decisive foreign policy. American manufacturers of satellite-launching equipment resented the loss of sales for which they were not compensated.[43] However, the action had a certain logic in seeking to curb China's growing aerospace industry and as a way of retaliating for the alleged sale of chemical weapons to Iran in the case of the *Yinhe* which the US was unable to stop docking in Dubai.

China and Pakistan signed an agreement in Rawalpindi on 4 December 1993 under which China agreed to provide Pakistan with credit facilities for the procurement of defence equipment. At the same time, Li Ruihuan, a member of the Standing Committee of the Politburo of the CCP and Chairman of the advisory body, the Chinese People's Political Consultative Conference (CPPCC), visited Islamabad with a high-level delegation and stayed there for a week. General Zhang Wannian, Chief of the General Staff of the PLA, also toured the Afghan–Pakistan border and the Khyber Pass and reiterated China's habitual support for Pakistan.

Pakistan television, broadcasting from Islamabad on 3 July 1997, carried a response from the Pakistani Foreign Office to concerns raised about the deployment of Indian missiles on the border and the test of a Hatf missile. It claimed that nuclear cooperation between Pakistan and China was purely for peaceful civilian use of the technology and that there were no military implications. Reports from the United States, however, clearly indicated that the Central Intelligence Agency (CIA) still believed that China was providing considerable technical assistance to the nuclear weapons programmes of both Pakistan and Iran.[44]

The question of Xinjiang has rarely been raised publicly in discussions between political leaders of the two countries, even though there is a close trading connection between southern Xinjiang towns, such as Kashghar, and Pakistan via the Karakorum Highway. Pakistan is also one of the sources of copies of the Qur'an and other Islamic materials coming into Xinjiang, either directly or as a gateway for materials coming from Afghanistan or further west.

General Pervez Musharaff, at the time Chairman of the Joint Chiefs of Staff Committee of the Pakistan armed forces, but later to take over the government of Pakistan in a *coup d'état* and have himself designated Chief Executive, visited China in May 1999 as the guest of the Chief of the General Staff of the Chinese PLA, General Fu Quanyou. He also met President Jiang Zemin, who reaffirmed China's 'friendship in adversity' with Pakistan and stressed the importance of the military ties between the two countries. If the Xinjiang question was discussed at all, there was no hint of this in any of the official press statements.[45]

Pakistan's Prime Minister, Nawaz Sharif, also made a state visit to China in June 1999, but decided to return to Pakistan early in view of the growing tension between India and Pakistan over the Kashmir issue.[46] It was later revealed in the Urdu-language newspaper *Jang*, published in Rawalpindi, that during these talks, the Chinese government agreed to supply Pakistan with eighty F-7 PRC fighter aircraft as an emergency measure. The F-7 was one of the most up-to-date aircraft in China and had previously been used exclusively by the Chinese air force: the first examples were due to be delivered to the Pakistan air force in August 1999, during an official visit to Beijing by the Chief of Staff of the Pakistan air force[47]

The initial response of the authorities in Beijing to the 1999 military coup in Pakistan was to adopt a wait-and-see policy: there were diplomatic comments about maintaining stability in the subcontinent and the long-term prospects for improving trade between China and Pakistan. Stability is what matters to Beijing, rather than the nature of the regime in Islamabad or whether it is military or democratic, and that is consistent with Beijing's policy towards other Third World countries since 1949.

The added tension between India and Pakistan did not cause China any real problems and indeed made Pakistan a more reliable ally. A military government in Pakistan is also likely to be a positive asset in terms of weapons sales.

However, because separatism and unrest in Xinjiang have been major preoccupations of Beijing since the mid-1990s, there is serious concern that any kind of instability in Pakistan could cause an upsurge in support for political Islam there and a consequent boost for Islamic insurgents in Xinjiang.

The role of the Pakistani military in this is complex. On the one hand, there is considerable support for militant political Islam within its ranks and there has also been sympathy for the Taleban in Afghanistan, particularly from elements in Pakistan's military intelligence community. However, there is also a long-term commitment to a stable Pakistani state which could be threatened by Islamist militancy.

The Foreign Ministry in Beijing has lodged formal diplomatic protests with Islamabad over the alleged combat training by members of the Pakistani security forces of Uyghurs in Afghanistan. China claimed that it had extracted this information from a group of Uyghurs who had been arrested and interrogated by the Chinese police after they had crossed from Pakistan back into Xinjiang.

Afghan connection

There have been persistent rumours that the Chinese military sent a group of Uyghurs for combat training in Afghanistan as part of an alliance against the Soviet Union's offensive between 1979 and 1989, although it has not been possible to confirm this from independent sources. While it might have seemed a good idea to build up Chinese credibility in Islamic Central Asia during the Sino–Soviet dispute, if the Chinese did send this group, it must in retrospect have seemed a bad decision when Uyghur militancy began to develop in Xinjiang. In 1998, Chinese officials were reported as having said: 'We closely follow developments in Afghanistan where Islamic fundamentalism is strong. This is very dangerous for Xinjiang.'[48]

Ahmad Baghlan, the leader of a separatist group in Xinjiang, was reported to have escaped from Xinjiang in late November 1998 and to have reached Badakhshan in Afghanistan after travelling through the mountainous border region of Wakhan. His flight followed the arrest and brief detention of another separatist leader, Abdul Rasul, after he was due to give a press conference in Islamabad to protest against what he claimed was a decision not to allow Muslims from Xinjiang to participate in the *hajj* pilgrimage to Mecca.[49]

China and the Taleban, or its government, formerly known as the Islamic Emirate of Afghanistan, concluded a military agreement on 10 December 1998. China agreed to train military pilots and, in return, the Taleban allowed Chinese scientists to examine unexploded American cruise missiles that had landed in Afghanistan.[50] Both Washington and Moscow were opposed to this and tried to persuade China to cut its ties with the Taleban as a UN embargo on the sale of arms and in particular the monitoring of arms supplies from Pakistan, due to come into force in December 2000, was being prepared. China agreed not to veto this embargo and, in return, it has been suggested that American diplomats in Beijing had given information to Beijing about Uyghurs working with the Taleban and about drugs and weapons alleged to have been imported into Xinjiang from Afghanistan.[51]

In October 2001, following the invasion of Afghanistan by coalition forces led by the United States, reports began to emerge that a number of Uyghurs had been captured during the fighting, particularly in the operation by the Northern Alliance, a coalition opposed to the Taleban, to capture the city of Mazar-e Sharif with the support of US forces. It was alleged that these Uyghurs had been working with Al Qaeda or the Taleban, although no evidence was ever produced. It subsequently emerged that the United States was holding twenty-two Uyhgurs without charge in the Guantanamo Bay prison camp in Cuba.

In May 2006, five of those detained were cleared of any association with terrorist activities and released. Their release was delayed, in part because they could not be repatriated to China where they would almost certainly have faced the death penalty. After prolonged international negotiations, they were granted political asylum in Albania, a predominantly Muslim country.

24 China rising and a 'harmonious society'?

The fundamental question that underlies long-term developments in China is what the future has in store for the uneasy alliance between the Chinese Communist Party (CCP) and the state that it controls, and the market economy as this extends nationwide beyond the rapidly developing coastal regions. It is a question that could be posed to the CCP leadership, in terms of the classic Marxist analysis of conflict between the economic base and the social and cultural superstructure, but it rarely is.

The argument that was put by the Chinese leadership in the early phase of its drive for economic reform was that they were creating a specifically Chinese type of socialism, 'socialism with Chinese characteristics' in the official terminology, although on closer inspection this concept never amounted to much more than rhetoric. Political ideology, apart from patriotism or nationalism, is not a significant factor in twenty-first-century China and even the half-hearted attempts to invoke the spirit of Yan'an, the self-sacrificing soldier Lei Feng, or the model official Jiao Yulu that were revived during the 1990s appear to have disappeared completely below the horizon. The success of the economy is all-important and it is quite common when discussing problems of democracy with people in China to hear them say that they are not concerned whether China achieves political democracy as long as there is economic democracy. What matters to them is whether or not they can earn a reasonable living in the way that they choose.

Part of the reason for these changes in attitude is the emergence of new social groupings in China. Over the last few decades, an elite group of technocrats has emerged as the most important political force. Many of its members have been educated abroad and they are deeply committed to modernisation as the primary goal for China. These men and women are often, although by no means exclusively, the children of senior party, military and government officials. They are often highly sceptical of political theories, especially any that involve socialism or Marxism, and are more interested in Western management techniques and economic principles, although that has not prevented many of them from joining the CCP.

Since the 1980s another social group has also surfaced, the *nouveaux riches*, who were originally derided as the *getihu* (individual entrepreneurs), a group that was largely banned from operating their businesses during Mao's lifetime. Most started with small businesses, but many are now extremely wealthy, even by Western standards, and some are functioning in ways that are indistinguishable from their counterparts in the West. The relationship between the new business class and the existing party elite is still evolving, but it has been an important factor in the emergence of one of China's major problems – corruption.

Corruption

Financial corruption by officials, which was largely absent from political life during the periods of radical political rhetoric, has been one of the persistent problems of the reform period and is present on a vast scale and at all levels. Political demonstrations in 1986 and in the run-up to the 1989 democracy movement included passionate denunciations of nepotism and corrupt practices by government officials and senior Party members. It is difficult to quantify the level of corruption, and in many cases even to define with any degree of precision what practices are corrupt, but the effect of corruption on the wider society is clearly a matter of serious concern to the Chinese authorities.

There have been numerous public criticisms of corrupt officials by senior Party leaders and exemplary sentences have been handed down to those who have been found guilty in court. One of the most dramatic criticisms came in a speech by President and CCP Secretary-General Jiang Zemin that was published on 1 July 1993. The speech coincided with a suspended sentence of death that had been passed after the trial of a senior Chinese banker for his involvement in the illegal sale of bonds in return for bribes, a case in which a Deputy Minister was also arrested. The overheating economy and frozen official salaries during the 1990s encouraged this kind of behaviour and, although some of the most spectacular cases have involved central government and Party officials, corruption is particularly rife among local officials including those who serve in rural areas. County town officials have been accused of the worst excesses and were blamed by Jiang Zemin for not following central government guidelines. What marked out Jiang's speech in 1993 was his warning, unprecedented for a Chinese leader, that unless corruption was brought under control, the CCP could lose power. The formal attack on corruption continues under Hu Jintao and there have been many more high-profile convictions, including that of Chen Xitong, the Mayor of Beijing, who was sentenced to sixteen years imprisonment in 1998 and the execution of a number of corrupt senior officials. In June 2007, the former head of the State Food and Drug Administration, Zheng Xiaoyu, was executed after having been convicted of taking bribes of over RMB 6.5 million. The bribes were given by firms that manufacture medicines and which wished to avoid the normal licensing process: the case followed a series of scandals in which the use of unregistered products had caused illness and death. The execution of Zheng Xiaoyu was seen as a particularly harsh punishment but the Chinese government regarded it as an exemplary sentence that was justified in their campaign against rising levels of official corruption.[1]

Order and disorder

Like the Confucian emperors of old, what the cautious leadership in China today fears most is *luan* (disorder). There appears to be a remarkable consensus among both Chinese official spokesmen and Western observers from a business background that China has now completely abandoned its radical past and is on a stable path towards a capitalist, or at least a mixed, economy and that this will automatically lead to long-term stability.

There have, however, been many outbreaks of disorder, particularly in the rural areas, as has been demonstrated in earlier chapters, and some Chinese commentators have expressed concerns that a period of serious social disorder leading to nationwide unrest is a distinct possibility. This could be ignited by popular revulsion against official corruption, by land disputes, or by bankruptcies and strikes that may occur if the economy overheats.

If there is unrest on a significant scale, it is in the peasant heartland of China that it could spread most rapidly. In a report that he gave in 2004, Wan Li who was Chairman of China's quasi-parliamentary body, the National People's Congress (NPC), complained of the degree to which peasants were being exploited. At that time, they were being given IOUs, known as 'white slips', in lieu of payments that were due to them from the government. The families of peasants working on construction sites in south China and other boom areas were given 'green slips' as receipts for remittances sent by their relatives. These were handed over by the authorities instead of money payments, and the recipients found it extremely difficult to cash them.

When this withholding of cash is added to the problems that farmers were already facing – high taxation; a level of rural unemployment that may be as much as 50 per cent in some areas; and endemic corruption, especially over the sale of land for development – it is clear that conditions in many rural areas are becoming intolerable. Peasant farmers have been reported as saying that they need a new Chen Sheng and Wu Guang, referring to the leaders of the peasant revolt who helped to overthrow the authoritarian Qin dynasty in 206 BC. There have been persistent cases of farmers attacking officials and refusing to pay levies and taxes and influential local leaders are emerging in some rural areas. Widespread disturbances that, in certain circumstances, could have turned into peasant insurrections have been reported in the rural areas of the provinces of Sichuan, Henan and Guangzhou, among others, and there have also been well-documented accounts in legal journals and newspapers of the resurrection of secret societies which were officially wiped out in 1949. Analysts are hampered by limited knowledge of what is really happening in some of the more remote areas of the Chinese countryside. The sheer size of the rural areas, poor communications and the censorship of the official media all make it difficult to arrive at a precise assessment of the scale of the problem. From the 1990s into the twenty-first century, the number of disturbances over tax diminished as the government adjusted its policies and eventually abandoned the land tax, but these were replaced by disputes over the sale of farming land to developers in deals which also involved official corruption.

The last resort for the government in dealing with tax revolts or more serious disturbances would be the People's Liberation Army (PLA). It could once have been regarded as unswervingly loyal and it enjoyed great national prestige, but its efficiency and reliability have been put under considerable strain. During the 1980s there was a move to reduce the size of the PLA by one quarter, and many men and women in the services were moved to non-military duties, which included manufacturing and other business-related activities. Recruitment suffered because fit young peasants, the backbone of the army for forty years, preferred more profitable occupations such as private farming or establishing their own businesses. It is also widely believed that some sections of the PLA are unhappy about the image of the military after the suppression of the Tian'anmen demonstrations in 1989 and may be unwilling to act in the same way again. The Hong Kong news magazine *Zheng Ming*, which has always maintained connections with high-placed sources in Beijing, reported that army garrisons were reshuffled during the 1990s to avoid the threat of factional disputes at a senior level within the PLA and CCP about the nature of 'reform' within the military. The army has now been stripped of its business activities and has become more professional and this has probably reduced the level of discontent.

In the old days, whenever there were threats of disorder, the approach adopted by conservatives in the CCP hierarchy was to fall back on military training accompanied by political education and ideological pressure, using tired revolutionary models such as the soldier hero Lei Feng and the model official Jiao Yulu. The response of young Chinese today is even more unenthusiastic than it was in the past, and the military training for university students, which was introduced after the suppression of the 4 June demonstrations in 1989, lapsed fairly swiftly. Although there appears to be an acceptance that these measures failed and that China's problems can no longer be resolved by returning to the old authoritarian thinking of control, ideological education and military training, no viable political alternatives have been put forward by the central political leadership.

One notable feature of the reform decade has been a marked growth in the regionalisation of the economy, initially in the Special Economic Zones of the southern coastal provinces but also in the border areas of the northwest, the northeast, Tibet and the southwest, where the liberalisation of cross-border trade with Central Asia, India and Pakistan respectively brought local economic growth that was unprecedented in post-war China. Although there have been other periods of decentralisation, including the years of the Cultural Revolution, it is possible now to discern in the regions strong feelings of political and economic consciousness, even in the northwest border area which has long been regarded as one of the most backward in China. Where there is a conflict of interest between local financial needs and national requirements, as in the case of a celebrated dispute between Guangdong province and Beijing over the payment of taxes, it can no longer be assumed that Beijing will automatically get its way.

There are concerns about the possibility of division and disorder and no Chinese politicians wish to see a return to a divided China, such as the warlord period of the 1920s when the CCP was founded. Economic logic seems to be pushing China towards decentralisation and the growth of regional power centres, with a lesser role for a weakened political centre. The precise regional powers which might emerge are not yet fixed, but those most likely to succeed economically could be: the south of Guangdong province, including the original Shenzhen special economic zone in cooperation with Hong Kong; Fujian and Shanghai, which are increasingly cooperating with businesses in Taiwan; and the Beijing–Tianjin nexus. Other possibilities include the northeast in trading partnership with Korea and the Russian Far East; Xinjiang and the other regions of northwestern China; and Tibet – although the economic development of these last two regions is dependent on the satisfactory resolution of ethnic conflicts. The rapid development of the coastal regions has already raised a number of serious questions about the future of the poor interior, which is far less likely to attract capital and which the Western Development programme was designed to address. There are also concerns about the possibility of inter-regional conflict for scarce resources and the long-term effect on social stability of migration to provinces where there are greater job opportunities.

These regional issues are, as has been suggested, exacerbated by the question of inter-ethnic conflict in some of the border areas. Although the movement for Tibetan autonomy is the best known outside China it is not the only one, and the Beijing leadership is likely to face further demands for autonomy from the Uyghurs of Xinjiang and the Mongolians of Inner Mongolia – demands which seem somewhat less unrealistic since the dissolution of the Soviet Union and the opening of China's borders, which have encouraged contacts with related ethnic groups outside China.

It has long been an article of faith, both with the CCP and the Guomindang (GMD), that China must remain as a single unified state within the boundaries set by the Manchu Qing emperors in the eighteenth and nineteenth centuries and controlled by a single political authority. The centrifugal forces of regionalism pose an underlying threat to centralised power of this nature but it is difficult to say whether, and to what extent, they pose a genuine threat to the unity of China. A degree of decentralisation, if not actual political division, is likely to play a positive role in accelerating the economic and social modernisation of China, but it also poses a grave threat to the future of the CCP as the only ruling body.

Peaceful development and a harmonious society

On 22 December 2005 the Information Office of the State Council issued a White Paper on the future development of China. The watchwords of the document were 'peaceful development', 'harmony' and 'prosperity' and the authors attempted to systematise a debate that had been under way within the political elite of the People's Republic of China (PRC) for some years. Although it has echoes of both Nikita Khrushchev's policies of peaceful co-existence from the Soviet Union of the 1950s and Zhou Enlai's negotiations for the five principles of peaceful co-existence in China's relations with Third World countries of the same era, it is presented as a new and modern approach to China's development and its relationship with the outside world.[2]

Central to this approach is the successful development of the economy and the creation of a society that is described as *xiaokang*. This is a term that was not used in public in the PRC before the late 1990s but it is a concept that has a distinguished historical pedigree in traditional Confucian discourse: it was often used as a description of the type of society that would immediately precede the utopia of Datong (Great, or Universal, Harmony) in the Confucian schema of historical development. It was resurrected by Hu Jintao and Wen Jiabao and can be translated as 'comfortably off' – in other words, not necessarily very wealthy but certainly not poor. Perhaps the Chinese leadership have in mind the generally affluent and middle-class (as they see themselves) population of their economically successful, and fellow Confucian, neighbour, Japan. The *xiaokang* approach is the complete antithesis of the class conflict approach to social change that characterised the CCP under Mao Zedong.

President Hu Jintao, in a speech to leading members of the CCP at the Central Party School – the training ground for the next generation of the Party – on Monday 25 June 2007, reaffirmed his commitment to the spreading of wealth and tackling corruption as the main tasks for the CCP if it is to achieve this goal of a 'comfortably off' society by 2020. The extension of social services, particularly health and education, to the 800 million residents of rural China, many of whom are desperately poor, was identified as a crucial part of this strategy. Hu also accepted that the struggle against corruption was going to be a long haul and that the road to success would be extremely complex and fraught with difficulties.

In addition to senior figures from the Party centre, the meeting was attended by senior officers of the military and security services and by delegates from regional and provincial Party and government organisations. In keeping with his track record of caution on political reform, Hu warned that any reform of the political system would have to keep pace with economic and social development, which he once again identified as the highest priority for China in the twenty-first century. While conceding that participation in the decision-making process could be improved by opening up new channels for consultation and that the rule of law was essential, he insisted that the leading role of the CCP must be maintained and effectively ruled out political reform and the extension of Western-style democracy.

The session was not open to foreign journalists but it was reported in *People's Daily* the following day. Hu Jintao's speech was clearly intended to set the tone for political discussions in the run-up to the CCP's Seventeenth National Conference.[3] The congress which took place in October 2007, and was reported by the international media more widely and in more depth than any previous Party Congress, was notable for the complete absence of policy changes. The CCP emphasised its continuing commitment to economic growth but there was no mention of reforms to the political system.

The congress selected a small group of new leaders to join the Politburo. The names of two of them, Li Keqiang and Xi Jinping, had been widely canvassed in advance and when Xi took to the platform immediately after Hu Jintao and ahead of Li, this was generally taken as a signal that Xi Jinping was to be the future leader of China after Hu's scheduled retirement in 2012. The implications were clear: a planned and smooth change of leadership over the following five years, but continuity in policies and continuing rule by the CCP.

Glossary of selected Chinese terms

baihua qifang, baijia zhengming   let a hundred flowers bloom and a hundred schools of thought contend
baomu   maid, housemaid, au pair
Beijing wanbao   Beijing Evening News
Beijing tuhua   Beijing local dialect
Cankao xiaoxi   Reference News
Cankao ziliao   Reference Material
Changjiang   Yangzi or Yangze, literally 'long river'
chuanbo meijie   mass media
chujia   marriage when applied to a woman, literally 'to leave the family'
cunmin weiyuanhui   villager committees
da yuejin   Great Leap Forward
danwei   work unit, e.g. factory, office, hospital, school
Daoist   Taoist
dibao   urban minimum living standard guaranteed income
douzheng   struggle
fabi   legal currency, last currency of Nationalist regime
Falungong   a neo-Buddhist religious movement, literally 'exercise of the wheel of the law'
funü gongzuo   woman-work, Party work for and with women
gaige kaifang   reform and opening
getihu   small entrepreneurs, literally 'individual households'
Gong'anbu   Ministry of Public Security
Gong'anju   Bureau of Public Security, police
Gongchanzhuyi qingnian tuan   Communist Youth League
gongkai   open or public, in contrast to neibu
Gongnong hongjun   Workers' and Peasants' Red Army
Guangming Ribao   Guangming Daily, a national newspaper. Guangming means 'light' or 'bright' but the paper is invariably referred to by its Chinese name, even by foreigners
guanhua   official language, Mandarin, during the imperial era
guanxi   connections
Guiyidao   the Way of Returning to, or Following, the One – a Daoist organisation

guochi national humiliation
Guomindang Nationalist Party; Kuomintang is an older spelling
Guowuyuan State Council
guxiang ancestral home
Han the majority Chinese population
heping jiefang peaceful liberation
huang yellow, but covers a wider spectrum and includes light to medium browns
huaqiao overseas Chinese, members of the Chinese diaspora
hukou household registration system
Jiangnan southern China – that is, south (nan) of the Yangzi River (jiang)
Jidu jiao Protestant Christianity
jihua shengyu planned birth policy, the official name for the 'one-child' policy
juyou zhongguo tese de shehuizhuyi socialism with Chinese characteristics
Kuomintang see Guomindang
Kuo-yu (Guoyu) usual name in Taiwan for Standard Chinese, Putonghua
laobaixing the mass of the population, literally the 'old hundred names', used both affectionately and patronisingly
laogai reform through labour – labour camps
laojiao education through labour – labour camps for administrative detention without trial
Lifayuan Legislative Yuan (Taiwan legislative body)
madrasa (Arabic) Qur'anic schools
mangliu mobile or floating population
Minhang (abbreviation for Zhongguo minyong hangkong ju) CAAC, Civil Aviation Administration of China
Minnan Southern Min language spoken in the south of Fujian province and in Taiwan
minquan people's power
Minzheng bu Ministry of Civil Affairs
Nanfang Ribao Southern Daily, Guangdong provincial newspaper
neibu internal, the opposite of gongkai
nongcun shehuizhuyi gaochao high tide of socialism in the countryside
nongmin shengchan hezuoshe agricultural producers' cooperatives
nongye shengchan zeren zhi responsibility system for agricultural production
Putonghua Standard Chinese, Mandarin
qigong breathing exercises
qing dark blue, green or even nearly black
Quanguo renmin daibiao dahui National People's Congress
Renmin gongshe People's Communes
Renmin Ribao People's Daily
renminbi (RMB) people's currency; the basic unit is the yuan
renquan human rights
san cong three obediences of women – to father, husband and son

shangfang petition

shaoshu minzu minority nationalities

shaoxiandui Young Pioneers

Shengwulian Hunan Province Revolutionary Great Alliance Committee, Cultural Revolution organisation

shenzhou sacred territory, China

tianming mandate of heaven

Tianzhu jiao Roman Catholic Christianity

tie fanwan iron rice bowl –lifetime employment system

tongbao compatriot, Chinese living in Taiwan and Hong Kong

tudi gaige land reform

wailai gong migrant labour

xiahai cast into the sea of people forced into private employment or business

xiang township administrations

xiejiao heterodox beliefs, cults

xinfang letter of complaint and petition

Xinhua New China, New China News Agency

yin yang complementary male and female elements

Yiguandao Way of Pervading Unity – Daoist organisation

yundong mass political movements or campaigns

zhengzhi ju Politburo, standard Russian abbreviation for Political Bureau

zhibian qingnian young people supporting the border regions

Zhigongdang Chinese Party for Public Interest – legal minority party in the People's Republic of China

zhishi qingnian educated young people

zhixian magistrate

Zhongguo gongchandang Chinese Communist Party

Zhongguo minyong hangkong ju Civil Administration of China

Zhongguo renmin jiefang jun Chinese People's Liberation Army

Zhongguo renmin yinhang People's Bank of China

Zhongguo Xizang Chinese Tibet

Zhongnanhai walled area immediately to the west of the Imperial Palace (Forbidden City) in Beijing, where senior members of the Party and government live and work; China's Kremlin

zhongshan zhuang high-collared Sun Yat-sen jacket, often called the 'Mao jacket'

Zhou Enlai hua zhuan *Illustrated Biography of Zhou Enlai*

Zhu de huifu Lord's Recovery – independent Protestant church

zichanjieji ziyouhua bourgeois liberalisation – target of campaign in the 1980s

zuguo motherland or, more accurately, ancestral homeland

Biographical notes

Chen Boda (1904–89) Mao Zedong's political adviser, speech writer and editor from the Yan'an period. Member of CCP Politburo and editor of theoretical journal *Red Flag*. Leader of the Cultural Revolution group and ally of Lin Biao.

Chen Shui-bian (1950–) President of Republic of China (Taiwan), elected 2004, and leader of the pro-independence Democratic Progressive Party until January 2008.

Chen Yun (1905–95) CCP economic supremo and influential figure in the economic modernisation of China in the post-Mao period. A veteran of the Long March and an economic planner trained in the Soviet Union, he opposed China's move away from the planned economy.

Chiang Kai-shek (1887–1975) Leader of the Guomindang and President of the Republic of China on the mainland until 1949 and on Taiwan until his death. After being defeated in the Civil War of 1946–49, he presided over the beginnings of the Taiwanese economic miracle with financial support from the United States but ruled the island under conditions of martial law, never losing sight of his main political goal – the reconquest of the mainland.

Deng Xiaoping (1904–97) Secretary-General of the CCP in 1956, associated with the pragmatic and managerial policies of Liu Shaoqi rather than the revolutionary romantic approach of Mao, and purged during the Cultural Revolution. Returned as Deputy Premier after the Cultural Revolution but was forced to step down after the 1976 Tian'anmen incident. Returned to power after the fall of the Gang of Four and spearheaded the drive for economic reform.

Fei Xiaotong (1910–2005) Pioneer of social anthropology in China after training under Bronislaw Malinowski at the London School of Economics. His books *Peasant Life in China* and *Earthbound China* are classic accounts of rural life in China before the Second World War. He was also active in the Democratic League and a delegate to the CPPCC and held senior posts in the Chinese Academies of Sciences and Social Sciences.

Hu Jintao (1952–) President of PRC since 2003 and concurrently Chairman of CCP and Central Military Commission.

Hu Qiaomu (1912–92)   Editor of Mao Zedong's *Selected Works* and speech writer to the Chairman.

Hu Shi (1891–1962)   Scholar of Chinese literature and philosophy, May Fourth Movement activist and supporter of writing in the vernacular. Hu rejected Marxism in favour of a pragmatic liberal approach, gravitated towards the Guomindang and was the ambassador in Washington 1938–42. He settled in Taiwan and became head of Academia Sinica in 1958 but quarrelled with Chiang Kai-shek over censorship and democracy.

Hu Yaobang (1915–89)   Secretary-General of the CCP from 1982 to 1987. He was dismissed after student demonstrations and replaced by Zhao Ziyang. His death on 15 April 1989 generated further demonstrations by students, which led to the Democracy Movement.

Hua Guofeng (1921–2008)   Caretaker Chairman of the CCP after the death of Mao Zedong. He was closely associated with the ultra-leftists and, even though he ordered the arrest of the Gang of Four, he soon lost power to Deng Xiaoping.

Jiang Qing (1914–91)   Wife of Mao Zedong and leading member of the Gang of Four. With an acting background in the Shanghai film industry, she used her powerbase in the city to support Mao's leftist position during the Cultural Revolution and became a leading member of the Cultural Revolution group and the Politburo. Arrested in 1976, she was tried with the other members of the Gang of Four and sentenced to death in 1981 with a two-year stay of execution. She apparently committed suicide.

Jiang Zemin (1926–)   CCP General Secretary and Chairman in the third generation of leaders and President of the PRC from 1993 to 2003. He is remembered for his policy of encouraging entrepreneurs to join the CCP.

Jiao Yulu (1922–64)   A model county CCP secretary who was heroically devoted to the people and was the subject of a hagiographical film in 1990

Kang Sheng (1899–1975)   The CCP's internal security supremo for much of his career and closely associated with the Cultural Revolution group. He was posthumously stripped of all his Party posts and implicated in the deaths and persecution of many senior CCP members during the Cultural Revolution.

Lee Teng-hui (1923–)   President of Taiwan and previously Mayor of Taibei and Governor of Taiwan province. First native Taiwan-born politician to achieve high office under the GMD. Outspoken supporter of formal independence for Taiwan, retired from office and joined Taiwan Solidarity Union.

Lei Feng (1939–62)   Soldier and model Communist who died on duty when he was hit by a falling telegraph pole. His posthumously published diaries, improved by the PLA's propaganda department, were used to present him as a model young Communist.

Li Hongzhi (1951–)   Founder of Falungong. Reputed to have been a member of the PLA, he left China in 1996 to settle in the United States after the suppression of Falungung by the government.

Lin Biao (1901–71)   Marshal of the PLA and Minister of Defence in 1959 after dismissal of Peng Dehuai. Backed Mao in the Cultural Revolution and was designated Mao's successor after the Ninth Party Congress in 1969. Died mysteriously in an air crash in 1971 amid allegations that he had tried to stage a military coup to overthrow Mao.

Liu Binyan (1925–2005)   Campaigning journalist and dissident member of the CCP. He was exiled from China in 1989 and lived in the United States.

Liu Shaoqi (1898–1969)   Chairman of the PRC from 1959 to 1969 and 'top Party-person taking the capitalist road' during the Cultural Revolution. His machine politics and pragmatism contrasted with Mao's revolutionary romanticism and he died after prolonged ill-treatment by Party inquisitors.

Ma Ying-jeou (1950–)   Taiwan GMD chairman and successful candidate in 2008 presidential election.

Mao Zedong (1893–1976)   Most prominent leader of the CCP, Party Chairman from 1943 and the instigator of the Great Leap Forward and the Cultural Revolution. Mao was famed for his advocacy of guerrilla warfare and for his recognition of the importance of the peasantry for China's Revolution. In office, he was impatient with pragmatism and gradual change and he has been held responsible for millions of deaths that have been attributed directly or indirectly to his policies.

Panchen Lama   Senior Tibetan Lama considered by some to possess higher spiritual authority than the Dalai Lama, by others to be the second-highest ranking lama. Panchen Lamas have often been under the influence of the Chinese court. The tenth Panchen Lama, Choekyi Gyaltsen, lived in Beijing from 1959 until his early and unexpected death in 1989 and was accused by some Tibetans of having betrayed their cause. In a dispute over the eleventh incarnation, one candidate has been named by the Dalai Lama and one by the PRC religious authorities.

Peng Dehuai (1898–1974)   Minister of Defence from 1954 to 1959. Peng had spoken out courageously against the Great Leap Forward because of the threat to China's economic development and the future of the armed forces. Conflict with Mao Zedong came to a head at the Lushan Plenum of 1959 and he was purged. He was arrested during the Cultural Revolution and died in prison.

Sun Yat-sen (1866–1925)   Leading advocate of early Chinese Republic who served briefly as first President before being ousted by Yuan Shikai. His *Three People's Principles* (*Sanmin zhuyi*) remains influential among Nationalists and he is also acknowledged as the founding father of the Republic by the CCP.

Tang Jiaxuan (1938–)   Minister of Foreign Affairs 1998–2003, member of State Council and influential figure in China's diplomacy.

Tsang, Donald (1944–)   Chief Executive of Hong Kong SAR since 2005 and previously Financial Secretary before the handover and Chief Secretary in 2001.

Tung Chee-hwa (1937–)   Hong Kong businessman with close connections to Beijing and first Chief Executive of Hong Kong on its return to China in 1997. His regime was unpopular and he resigned in 2005 before the end of his second term of office and became a Deputy Chairman of the CPPCC.

Wang Hongwen (1935–92)   Former Shanghai cotton mill security guard and founder of the Shanghai Workers' Revolutionary General Headquarters during the Cultural Revolution. He became Vice-Chairman of the CCP in 1975 but fell from grace with the other members of the Gang of Four and was sentenced to life imprisonment.

Wen Jiabao (1942–)   Premier of the State Council since 2003. A trained geologist, with administrative experience in Gansu province, Wen is known for his approachable manner and interest in popular issues such as the environment, poverty and corruption.

Wu Han (1909–69)   Respected historian, writer and Deputy Mayor of Beijing, whose play *Hai Rui Dismissed* was the first target of the radicals in the Cultural Revolution. He died after severe ill-treatment in prison.

Wu Yi (1938–)   Deputy Premier of the State Council and the most senior female politician in China. She trained as an engineer and is respected for her economic competence and diplomacy.

Xi Jinping (1953–)   Emerged as member of the Standing Committee of the Politburo at the Seventeenth CCP Congress in 2007 and is widely believed to be the preferred successor to Hu Jintao as President in 2012.

Yao Wenyuan (1931–2005)   Shanghai radical and literary critic whose article on Wu Han's play initiated the debate that launched the Cultural Revolution. He was sentenced to twenty years imprisonment as one of the Gang of Four.

Zeng Qinghong (1939–)   Vice-President of the PRC and widely tipped as a successor to Hu Jintao as President until his retirement from the Central Committee in 2007. He was effectively the head of the Shanghai faction in the CCP after the retirement of Jiang Zemin.

Zhang Chunqiao (1917–2005)   Shanghai journalist and director of propaganda for the city's Party Committee in the 1960s. Supporter of Jiang Qing's drive to revolutionise opera and film and initiator of the Shanghai Commune. Chairman of the Shanghai Revolutionary Committee in 1967 and as one of the Gang of Four sentenced to death with a two-year stay of execution.

Zhao Ziyang (1919–2005) CCP Secretary General and Premier until his removal in 1989 after the suppression of democracy demonstrations in Tian'anmen Square on 4 June. Remained under house arrest until his death.

Zhou Enlai (1898–1976) First Premier of the PRC. Urbane but ruthless, he maintained his position in the hierarchy throughout the Cultural Revolution. Widely regarded as a pragmatist and a statesman, he acquired a reputation for having saved the lives and careers of many senior Party figures in the turmoil of the 1960s but he was also implicated in persecution.

Further reading

Publishing about China has become a growth industry since China became more accessible in the 1980s. The quality of books varies considerably and even the best date rapidly. Some suggestions for further reading are offered here.

Contemporary reporting and analysis

Stephanie Hemelryk Donald and Robert Benewick, *The State of China Atlas*, Berkeley: University of California Press, 2005.

Rob Gifford, *China Road: A Journey into the Future of a Rising Power*, London: Bloomsbury, 2007.

John Gittings, *The Changing Face of China: From Mao to Market*, Oxford: Oxford University Press, 2005.

Duncan Hewitt, *Getting Rich First: Life in a Changing China*, London: Vintage, 2007.

James Kynge, *China Shakes the World: The Rise of a Hungry Nation*, London: Phoenix, 2007.

Susan L. Shirk, *China: The Fragile Superpower*, Oxford: Oxford University Press, 2007.

Xinran, *The Good Women of China: Hidden Voices*, London: Vintage, 2003.

Economy

Stephen Green, *Reforming China's Economy: A Rough Guide*, London: Chatham House, RIIA, 2003.

He Kang (editor-in-chief) *China's Township and Village Enterprises*, Beijing: Foreign Languages Press, 2005.

Peter Nolan, *China at the Crossroads*, Cambridge: Polity, 2004.

Society

Chen Guidi and Wu Chuntao, *Will the Boat Sink the Water?: The Life of China's Peasants*, London: Public Affairs, 2006.

Pierre Haski, *Le Sang de la Chine: quand le silence tue*, Paris: Bernard Grasset, 2005.

Harry Hongda, Wu *Laogai: The Chinese Gulag*, Boulder: Westview, 1992.

Ian Johnson, *Wild Grass: China's Revolution from Below*, London: Penguin, 2004.

Colin Mackerras, *China's Ethnic Minorities and Globalisation*, London: RoutledgeCurzon, 2003.

Elizabeth J. Perry and Mark Selden (eds), *Chinese Society: Change, Conflict and Resistance*, London: Routledge, 2003.

Norman Stockman, *Understanding Chinese Society*, Cambridge: Polity, 2000.

Politics

Joseph Fewsmith, *China since Tiananmen: The Politics of Transition*, Cambridge: Cambridge University Press, 2001.

Willy Wo-Lap Lam, *Chinese Politics in the Hu Jintao Era: New Leaders, New Challenges*, New York: M. E. Sharpe, 2006.

Roderick MacFarquhar and Michael Schoenhals, *Mao's Last Revolution*, Cambridge: Belknap Press of Harvard University Press, 2006.

Tony Saich, *Governance and Politics of China*, Basingstoke: Palgrave Macmillan, 2004.

Philip Short, *Mao: A Life*, London: Hodder and Stoughton, 1999.

Michael Yahuda, *The International Politics of the Asia–Pacific 1945–1995*, London: RoutledgeCurzon, 1997.

Hong Kong and Taiwan

Christopher Hughes, *Taiwan and Chinese Nationalism: National Identity and Status in International Society*, London: Routledge, 1997.

Simon Long, *Taiwan: China's Last Frontier*, Basingstoke: Macmillan, 1991.

Tsang, Steve Yui-Sang, *A Modern History of Hong Kong*, London, New York: I. B. Tauris, 2004.

Tibet and Xinjiang

Patrick French, *Tibet, Tibet: A Personal History of a Lost Land*, London: HarperCollins, 2003.

Melvyn C. Goldstein, *The Snow Lion and the Dragon: China, Tibet and the Dalai Lama*, Berkeley: University of California Press, 1997.

Melvyn C. Goldstein, *A History of Modern Tibet, 1913–1951: The Demise of the Lamaist State*, Berkeley: University of California Press, 1989.

Dawa Norbu, *China's Tibet Policy*, Richmond: Curzon Press, 2001.

Tsering Shakya, *The Dragon in the Land of Snows: A History of Modern Tibet since 1947*, London: Pimlico, 1999.

Michael Dillon, *Xinjiang: China's Muslim Far Northwest*, London: RoutledgeCurzon, 2004.

S. Frederick Starr (ed.), *Xinjiang: China's Muslim Borderland*, New York: M. E. Sharpe, 2004.

Christian Tyler, *Wild West China: The Taming of Xinjiang*, London: John Murray, 2003.

Notes

Preface

1 This conundrum was posed, rather more pithily, in Lindsey Hilsum, 'The many sides of China', *Amnesty Magazine*, pp. 14–17 July/August 2007.

1 Land, people and culture

1 Central News Agency, Taipei, 15 November 2006.
2 The Chinese word *huang* covers a wider spectrum of colour than the English 'yellow' and includes light to medium browns. Similarly, the Chinese character for *qing* in Qinghai can be dark blue or green or even nearly black.
3 Written characters do have some elements which indicate phonetic values but these are not regular enough to be a reliable indication of the pronunciation of characters: pronunciation has to be learned separately for each character. Since a high level of literacy requires familiarity with thousands of characters, this is a demanding task.

2 China's past in the present

1 This assessment applies mainly to China proper, the regions where the Han are in the majority. The situation in Tibet, Xinjiang and Inner Mongolia was much more complicated.

3 Economic growth and the changing economy

1 *BBC News*, 12 October 2005.
2 *Financial Times*, 20 October 2006.
3 *Financial Times*, 20, 21–22 July 2007.
4 Rudolf Hommel, *China at Work: An Illustrated Record of the Primitive Industries of China's Masses, Whose Life Is Toil, and thus an Account of Chinese Civilization*, Cambridge, Mass: MIT Press, 1969 [1937].
5 Cheng Jin, *Chronology of the People's Republic of China 1949–1984*, Beijing: Foreign Language Press, 1986, pp. 2–3. The GAC functioned as the cabinet in the early 1950s.
6 Li Fuchun, 'Bianzhi diyi ge wunian jihua ying zhuyi de wenti' (Problems to be considered in drawing up the First Five-Year Plan) (15 September 1953), in *Jianguo yilai* Vol. 1, pp. 402–6.
7 Audrey Donnithorne 'Economic planning', in *China's Economic System*, London: Allen and Unwin, 1967, pp. 457–95.
8 National Development and Reform Commission website, http://en.ndrc.gov.cn
9 *Market News International*, Beijing.

4 Rural economy

1 Hsiao-Tung Fei (Fei Xiaotong), *Peasant Life in China*, London: Routledge and Kegan Paul, 1939.
2 Chu Li and Tien Chieh-yun, *Inside a People's Commune*, Beijing: Foreign Language Press, 1975, pp. 55–6.
3 *Beijing Review*, 3 May 1982.
4 *Xinhua*, 16 June 2007.
5 *Wall Street Journal*, 5 May 2006.
6 'Rural area development key to stability', *Xinhua*, 19 January 2006.
7 State Council, 19 January 2006.
8 'Zhongguo nongmin xinnian gaobie nongye shui', *Renmin Ribao* (overseas edition), 30 December 2005.
9 NPC plenary session, 1 April 2004.
10 *People's Daily*, 18 January 2006.
11 *Financial Times*, 8 November 2006.
12 He Kang (editor-in-chief), *China's Township and Village Enterprises*, Beijing: Foreign Languages Press, 2005.
13 International Labour Organisation report, 1998.

5 Urban and industrial economy

1 Peter Nolan makes this point powerfully in *China at the Crossroads*, Cambridge: Polity, 2004, pp. 156–67.
2 *Chinese Labour Bulletin*, 14 October 2005.
3 Huang Ju died on 2 June 2007, only days after he had been selected as a Shanghai representative to the Seventeenth CCP Congress due to be held in October 2007. He was only sixty-nine years old and there had been rumours about his health for some time but the manner in which his death was reported raised speculation that there was some mystery surrounding it.
4 *Xinhua*, 10 August 2007.

6 Banking, finance and foreign trade

1 These were, of course, based on the *valyuta* foreign currency shops of the Soviet Union.
2 For example in small shops and stalls in Kashghar in the 1990s.
3 Audrey Donnithorne, *China's Economic System*, London: Allen and Unwin, 1967 pp. 402–33.
4 Stephen Green, *Reforming China's Economy: A Rough Guide*, London: Chatham House, RIIA, 2003; *Financial Times*, 28 August 2003.
5 *Financial Times*, 17 December 1999.
6 *Financial Times*, 13 December 1999.
7 *Financial Times*, 28 August 2003.
8 Zhang Zhichao, 'China's foreign exchange policy in a time of change, *Durham East Asian Papers* No. 11, Durham: University of Durham, 2000; *Financial Times*, 20 October 2006.
9 *China Daily*, 9 November 2006; *BBC News*, 4 December 2006.
10 I am indebted to Yang Zhengming for information on the decline of joint-venture companies.
11 *BBC News*, 11 December 2006.
12 *Financial Times*, 28 June 2007.
13 *Financial Times*, 25–26 August 2007.

7 Tourism and transport

1 *Financial Times*, 12 October 2007.

8 Rural and urban social change

1 *Agrarian Reform Law of the People's Republic of China*, promulgated by the Central People's Government of 30 June 1950, Chinese text in *Jianguo yilai* Vol. 1, pp. 336–45.
2 Frederick C. Teiwes, 'Establishment and consolidation of the new regime', in Denis Twitchett and John K. Fairbank (general editors), *Cambridge History of China Volume 14: The People's Republic, Part 1: The Emergence of Revolutionary China 1949–1965*, Cambridge: Cambridge University Press, 1987, pp. 83–8. For detailed information on the evolution of land policies and their social consequences, see Chao Kuo-chun *The Agrarian Policy of the Chinese Communist Party 1921–1959*, 1960. Contemporary first-hand accounts of the movement in specific villages can be found in the classic *Fanshen* by William Hinton Harmondsworth, Penguin Books, 1972, and two books by Isabel and David Crook, *Revolution in a Chinese Village: Ten Mile Inn*, London: Routledge and Kegan Paul, 1959, and *Mass Movement in a Chinese Village: Ten Mile Inn*, London: Routledge and Kegan Paul, 1979.
3 Domes *Internal Politics of China 1949–1972*, pp. 97–9; Party History Research Centre, *Central Committee of the CCP History of the Chinese Communist Party: A Chronology of Events*, p. 273.
4 Domes *Internal Politics of China 1949–1972*, pp. 97–8.
5 Kam Wing Chan and Li Zhang, 'The *hukou* system and rural–urban migration in China: processes and changes', Department of Geography, University of Washington, c. 1996.

9 Education and health

1 R. F. Price, *Education in Modern China*, London: Routledge and Kegan Paul, 1979.
2 Peter Mauger *et al.* (eds), *Education in China*, London: Anglo-Chinese Educational Institute, 1974.
3 *People's Daily*, 2 June 2000.
4 Carrie Gracie, *BBC News*, 29 July 2006.
5 *Compulsory Education Law of the People's Republic of China*, China Education and Research Network, 2005.
6 Emily Hannum and Albert Park, *Educational Reform in China*, London: Routledge, 2007.
7 *People's Daily*, 29 June 2002.
8 *PKU* (Beijing University News), 10 November 2005.
9 Julia Kwong, 'The re-emergence of private schools in socialist China', *Comparative Education Review* Vol. 41, No. 3, August 1997, pp. 244–59.
10 Ministry of Education.
11 *BBC News*, 30 June 2006; Jonathan Watts, *Guardian*, 26 October 2006; *International Herald Tribune*, 30 November 2007.
12 *BBC News*, 'China's high-cost health care', 24 April 2003.
13 *People's Daily*, 6 November 1999; 'State Council – China's social security and its policy', *People's Daily*, 7 September 2004.
14 *South China Morning Post*, 13 November 2006; *BBC News*, 12 November 2006.
15 *People's Daily*, 14 November 2006.
16 *BBC News*, 29 June 2007.
17 *Financial Times*, 4 October 2007.

18 Pierre Haski, *Le Sang de la Chine: quand le silence tue*, Paris: Bernard Grasset, 2005. Haski's book is a remarkably detailed account based on the author's own investigations in the villages of Henan.
19 *BBC News*, 20 April 2007.
20 *People's Daily*, 30 December 2001.
21 *South China Morning Post*, 28 December 2002.
22 Jonathan Watts, 'Chinese villagers riot over "one child" policy', *Guardian*, 21 May 2007.
23 *BBC News*, 7 January 2008.

10 Law and human rights

1 S. van der Sprenkel, *Legal Institutions in Manchu China*, London: Athlone Press, 1962.
2 Henry McAleavy, 'The People's Courts in Communist China', *The American Journal of Comparative Law* Vol. 11, No. 1 (Winter 1962) pp. 52–65.
3 Jerome A. Cohen, 'China's legal system in transition', testimony to the United States Congressional Executive Commission on China, Tuesday 26 July 2005, and reprinted in an edited form in *China Daily*, is a clear and concise account of the current legal system in China and its shortcomings (www.cecc.gov/pages/hearings/072605/Cohen. php); see also 'A slow march to legal reform' by the same author *Far Eastern Economic Review*, October 2007, pp. 20–4 and Hu Juan, 'The development of the Chinese legal profession since 1978', *Durham East Asian Papers* 9, East Asian Studies, University of Durham.
4 Cohen, 'China's legal system in transition', 2005.
5 Cohen, 'China's legal system in transition', 2005.
6 Press Release of the United Nations Office of the High Commissioner for Human Rights, 22 August 2005, 2 December 2005; *BBC News Online*, 2 December 2005.
7 *China Daily*, 30 October 2007.
8 *Zhongguo xinwengang* (*China News* net), 28 October 2007.
9 Articles 199 and 200, *Criminal Procedure Law of the People's Republic of China* (adopted on 1 January 1997).
10 Harry Wu, *Laogai: The Chinese Gulag*, Boulder: Westview, 1992; Harry Wu (with Carolyn Wakeman), *Bitter Winds: A Memoir of My Years in the China's Gulag*, New York: John Wiley, 1994; Jean-Luc Domenach, *Chine: l'archipel oublié*, Paris: Fayard, 1992, contains the most detailed research on the history of China's prison camps and the way they have become integrated into the Chinese economy. *Laojiao* camps are also referred to as 're-education' camps in some Western accounts.
11 Rebiya Kadeer, an Uyghur businesswoman from Xinjiang who was nominated for the Nobel Prize for Peace in 2007, was sentenced to eight years imprisonment for sending such material to her husband in the United States. She has since been released and lives in exile in the United States.
12 *Criminal Law of the People's Republic of China* (extracts) in English and Chinese; *Country Report: China*, Home Office Immigration and Nationality Directorate (April 2005); Cohen, 'China's legal system in transition', 2005; Hu Juan, 'The development of the Chinese legal profession since 1978'; *China: Profile of Asylum Claims and Country Conditions*, Bureau of Democracy, Human Rights and Labor, US Department of State, Washington, DC, 20520, June 2004; *Country of Origin Research, China; Update to CHN32869.EX of 22 September 1999 regarding treatment of illegal emigrants repatriated to China; particularly information regarding treatment of those repatriated from Canada in May 2000*; Cohen, 'A slow march to legal reform', 2007, pp. 20–4.
13 *Xinhua*, 16 November 2006.
14 Amnesty International, *Report*, 2005.
15 Amnesty International, *Report*, 2005.
16 *Mainichi Daily News*, 2 September 2005.

17 *BBC News*, 5 and 14 September 2007.
18 *BBC News*, 3 January 2008.
19 *BBC News*, 20 November 2006.
20 Wu, *Laogai: The Chinese Gulag*, 1992; Domenach, *Chine: l'archipel oublié*, 1992.

11 Mass media

1 Liu Binyan, *A Higher Kind of Loyalty: A Memoir by China's Foremost Journalist*, London: Methuen, 1990, p. 155.
2 *Washington Post*, 24 January 2006.
3 *People's Daily*, 1 December 2006.
4 Yin Hong, Li Bin (editors-in-chief), *Quanqiuhua yu dazhong chuangmei: chongtu; ronghe; huxiang* (Globalisation and Mass Media: Clash, Convergence and Interaction), Beijing: Qinghua University Press, 2002.

12 Religion and ethnic minorities

1 The distinction between a religion and a cult is problematic and not solely in China: to a large extent it is a subjective determination. The Chinese authorities label Falungong a cult to deny it international legitimacy. Falungong leaders deny this and argue that they are a legitimate spiritual body.
2 Chan Wing-tsit, *Religious Trends in Modern China*, New York: Octagon Books, 1978.
3 Chan, *Religious Trends in Modern China*, 1978.
4 Chan, *Religious Trends in Modern China*, 1978, pp. 153, 156.
5 Gong Xuezheng *et al.*, *Minzu wenti yu zongjiao wenti jiangzuo* (Ethnic and Religious Issues), Beijing: Zhonggong zhongyang dangxiao (CCP Central Party School), 1994, pp. 163–4.
6 D. E. MacInnis, *Religion in China Today: Policy and Practice*, New York: Orbis, 1989, pp. 204–20.
7 K. Dean, *Taoist Ritual and Popular Cults of Southeast China*, Princeton: Princeton University Press, 1993.
8 Yang Zengwen (ed.), *Zhongguo fojiao jichu zhishi* (Fundamentals of Chinese Buddhism), Beijing: Zongjiao wenhua chubanshe (Religious Culture Publishers), 1999; K. K. S. Ch'en, *Buddhism in China: A Historical Survey*, Princeton: Princeton University Press, 1964.
9 Holmes Welch, *Buddhism under Mao*, Cambridge: Harvard University Press, 1972, p. 6.
10 Chan, *Religious Trends in Modern China*, 1978, p. 84; Welch, *Buddhism under Mao*, 1972, pp. 7–11, 389–407.
11 Yang Zengwen, *Zhongguo fojiao jichu zhishi*, 1999, p. 73.
12 Visits to Beijing and Alashan, Bayinhot, in Inner Mongolia, 2001; interview with monks, Yonghegong, 2001.
13 Interview with Tibetan Buddhist nun, London, May 2006.
14 John Gittings, *Real China: From Cannibalism to Karaoke*, London: Simon and Schuster, 1996, pp. 6–82.
15 Bob Whyte, *Unfinished Encounter: China and Christianity*, London: Collins, 1988.
16 *Christianity and the Reinvention of China*, Chatham House, 1 May 2007.
17 *BBC News*, 30 June 2007, 2 July 2007; 'Letter of the Holy Father Pope Benedict XVI to the Bishops, Priests, Consecrated Persons and Lay Faithful of the Catholic Church in the People's Republic of China', 27 May 2007 www.vatican.va.
18 *Financial Times*, 12 September 2007.
19 *Financial Times*, 20 September 2007; *BBC News*, 21 September 2007.

20 *BBC News*, 4 December 2007.
21 Regulation of religious and quasi-religious groups by national bodies is standard practice in the PRC. For further information on the regulation of religious organisations, see Michael Dillon, *Religious Minorities in China*, London Minority Rights Group International, 2001.
22 *Dangerous Meditation: China's Campaign Against Falungong*, New York: Human Rights Watch, January 2002. This is available at the Human Rights Watch website http://hrw.org/reports/2002/china. It is a particularly useful analysis of Falungong and the Chinese government's sustained attack on it because it is sceptical of source material that emanates from Falungong organisations in China and worldwide as well as information from the Chinese government in Beijing and subjects both to rigorous critical scrutiny.
23 *Dangerous Meditation*, 2002.
24 Sun Yat-sen, *Sanmin zhuyi* (Three People's Principles), 1924.
25 Mackerras, Colin, *China's Minority Cultures: Identities and Integration since 1912*, London: Longman, 1995; Mackerras, Colin, *China's Ethnic Minorities and Globalisation*, London: RoutledgeCurzon, 2003; Hansen, Mette Halskov, *Frontier People: Han Settlers in Minority Areas of China*, London: Hurst, 2005.

13 Gender and modernisation

1 *People's Daily*, 25 August 2003; *BBC News*, 24 August 2007.

14 Environment

1 *Xinhua*, 26 August 2006, via *Reuters*.
2 *Financial Times*, 10 July 2007.
3 *BBC News*, 26 September 2007; *Financial Times*, 26 September 2007; *China Daily*, 9 March 2007; *China View* (*Xinhua*), 26 September 2007.
4 Lu Yiyi, 'Environmental civil society and governance in China', Chatham House research paper, London: RIIA August, 2005.
5 *Xinhua*, 3 December 2005.
6 *China Dialogue*, interview 27 October 2006.
7 Elizabeth Economy, 'A blame game China needs to stop', *Washington Post*, 3 December 2006.

15 Government and politics

1 *Constitution of the People's Republic of China*, Beijing: Foreign Languages Press, 1954. Chinese text in *Jianguo yilai* Vol. 5, pp. 520–42.
2 The formal statement of its own work and status by the National People's Congress can be found on its website at http://english.gov.cn/links/npc.htm.
3 *Xinhua*, 12 October 2007.
4 *Financial Times*, 17 July 2007.
5 This should not be confused with the quasi-parliamentary National People's Congress.
6 This is remarkably similar to the form taken by factions in the Liberal Democratic Party (a conservative party in spite of its name) which has ruled Japan for most of the period since the Second World War.
7 "Three Represents" is inelegant and ungrammatical in English but unfortunately it has become the official translation for *san ge daibiao*.
8 *Financial Times*, 27 December 2007.
9 *South China Morning Post*, 6 March 2003.

10 *People's Daily* website.
11 *Xinhua*, 29 September 2006.
12 *BBC News*, *Financial Times*, 31 July 2007.
13 Tony Saich, *Governance and Politics of China*, Basingstoke: Palgrave Macmillan, 2004, pp. 195–201; Yawei Liu, 'Assessing China's villager self-government', Carter Centre China Elections Project, 3 November 2006; *South China Morning Post*, 'Victory for villagers in battle over "rigged poll" for chief', 2 May 2006; *South China Morning Post*, 'Police tackle "rural mafia"', 7 November 2006.
14 I was the subject of considerable derision from Chinese colleagues in a village outside Xi'an in 2005 when I bought what I thought was rather a fine ceramic ornament of the Cultural Revolution period depicting Mao and Lin Biao.
15 *Renmin Ribao*, 8 September 2006.
16 Lin Biao, *Long Live the Victory of People's War*, Beijing: Foreign Languages Press, 1965. This pamphlet was originally published as a leading article in *Renmin Ribao* on 3 September 1965 to commemorate the twentieth anniversary of the defeat of Japan at the end of the Second World War.
17 Sunil Janah, *The Tribals of India*, Calcutta: Oxford University Press, 1993; 'A spectre haunting India', *Economist*, 19 August 2006.
18 *BBC News*, 27 June 2007.
19 Jung Chang and Jon Halliday, *Mao: The Unknown Story*, London: Jonathan Cape, 2005.
20 More balanced and authoritative assessments of Mao's status and his place in the history of modern China can be found in Philip Short, *Mao: A Life*, London: Hodder and Stoughton, 1999, and Roderick MacFarquhar and Michael Schoenhals, *Mao's Last Revolution*, Cambridge: Belknap Press of Harvard University Press, 2006

16 Fourth- and fifth-generation leadership

1 *Financial Times*, 9 August 2006.
2 For example, *Renmin Ribao* (overseas edition), 27 September 2006.
3 *People's Daily*, 1 January 2006.
4 *People's Daily*, 18 November 2005.
5 *South China Morning Post*, 6 May 2006.
6 *South China Morning Post*, 13 November 2006.

17 Tibet

1 Patrick French, *Tibet, Tibet: A Personal History of a Lost Land*, London: HarperCollins, 2003, is a perceptive account of the relationship between Westerners and the Tibetan cause.
2 Melvyn C. Goldstein, *A History of Modern Tibet, 1913–1951: The Demise of the Lamaist State*, Berkeley: University of California Press, 1989, pp. 44–88.
3 Goldstein, *A History of Modern Tibet, 1913–1951*, 1989, pp. 44–88; see also Patrick French, *Younghusband: The Last Great Imperial Adventurer*, London: HarperCollins, 1994.
4 Dawa Norbu, *China's Tibet Policy*, Richmond: Curzon Press, 2001, p. 97.
5 Goldstein, *A History of Modern Tibet 1913–1951*, 1989; Melvyn C. Goldstein, *The Snow Lion and the Dragon: China, Tibet and the Dalai Lama*, Berkeley: University of California Press, 1997.
6 Tsering Shakya, *The Dragon in the Land of Snows: A History of Modern Tibet since 1947*, London: Pimlico, 1999, pp. 163–211.
7 Shakya, *The Dragon in the Land of Snows*, 1999, pp. 314–47.
8 Goldstein, *The Snow Lion and the Dragon*, 1997, pp. 61–75.
9 Shakya, *The Dragon in the Land of Snows*, 1999, pp. 381–2.

10 Goldstein, *The Snow Lion and the Dragon*, 1997, pp. 79–83.
11 Goldstein, *The Snow Lion and the Dragon*, 1997, pp. 100–11.
12 *South China Morning Post*, 29 June 2000.
13 *Press Trust of India*, New Delhi, 11 October 2000.
14 Personal communication from Tibetan nun.
15 *Financial Times*, 9 January 2000; *BBC News*, 8 January 2000.
16 *Agence France Presse*, 27 August 2000.
17 *South China Morning Post*, 30 September 2000.

18 Xinjiang

1 There is some evidence of links between Uyghur and Hui members of the Khufiyya Sufi order.
2 Wang Wenheng, *Xinjiang zongjiao wenti yanjiu* (Studies on Religion in Xinjiang), Urumqi: Xinjiang People's Press, 1993, pp. 93–5. These figures appear to reflect only the registered and officially sanctioned mosques and other bodies.
3 The Uyghurs use the Arabic and Turkic term *mazar* (tomb or shrine, *mezar* in Turkish) for the tombs of their founding *shaykhs* but there is also a tomb culture among the Hui (both within and outside Xinjiang), who use the term *gongbei*, a Chinese transliteration of the Arabic *qubba* (dome or cupola, after the dominant architectural feature of these tombs).
4 Reyila Dawuti (Rayila Dawud), *Weiwuerzu mazha wenhua yanjiu* (Studies of Uyghur Mazar Culture), Urumqi: Xinjiang University Press, 2001.
5 Thierry Zarcone, 'Le Culte des saints au Xinjiang (de 1949 à nos jours)', *Journal of the History of Sufism* 3 (2001), pp. 133–72.
6 Yining is the Chinese name and Ghulja the Uyghur name for the city which lies in the Yili (Ili) region.
7 The Chinese authorities initially suppressed information about these disturbances although details leaked out through émigré publications and the monitoring of local broadcast and print media by the BBC and FBIS. In-depth accounts, heavily slanted towards the Chinese government's perspective, were later published in Xu Yuqi and Chen Yishan (eds), *Xinjiang fandui minzu fenliezhuyi douzheng shihua* (Narrative History of the Struggle Against Separatism in Xinjiang), Urumqi: Xinjiang People's Press, 1999, and Ma Dazheng, *Guojia liyi gaoyu yiqie: Xinjiang wending wenti de guancha yu sikao* (The Interests of the Nation Are Above Everything: Observations and Reflections on the Stability of Xinjiang), Urumqi: Xinjiang People's Press, 2003. See also Michael Dillon, *Xinjiang: China's Muslim Far Northwest*, London: RoutledgeCurzon, 2004, and 'Uyghur separatism and nationalism in Xinjiang', in Benjamin Cole (ed.), *Conflict, Terrorism and the Media in Asia*, London: Routledge, 2006, pp. 98–116.
8 Chinese Communist Party Central Committee, *Central Committee Document No. 7 Record of the Meeting of the Standing Committee of the Politburo of the Chinese Communist Party concerning the Maintenance of Stability in Xinjiang* in Uyghur, 19 March 1996.
9 Wang Wenheng, *Xinjiang zongjiao wenti yanjiu*, 1993, pp. 91–2. A separate academy was also established in Yinchuan, the capital of the Ningxia Hui Autonomous Region, to train Chinese-speaking Hui imams.

19 Hong Kong

1 Steve Tsang, *Hong Kong: An Appointment with China*, London: I. B. Tauris, 1997, pp. 51–3; Philip Snow, *The Fall of Hong Kong: Britain, China and the Japanese Occupation*, Harvard: Yale University Press, 2003.
2 James L. Watson, *Emigration and the Chinese Lineage: The Mans in Hong Kong and London*, Berkeley: University of California Press, 1975.

3 Tsang, *Hong Kong*, 1997, pp. 83–94. Sir Murray became Lord Maclehose in 1982 on his retirement from the governorship.
4 Tsang, *Hong Kong*, 1997, p. 119.
5 The official history of the Legislative Council and an account of its current operation can be found on its website http://www.legco.gov.hk.
6 *BBC News*, 29 December 2007.

20 Taiwan

1 In Taiwan, the spellings Kuomintang and KMT are used as there is universal dislike of the *pinyin* spelling system used in the PRC.
2 This and subsequent sections rely on Chen Hongtu (ed.), *Taiwan shi* (History of Taiwan), Taibei: Sanmin, 2004; Huang Xiuzheng, Zhang Shengyuan and Wu Wenxing *Taiwan shi* (History of Taiwan), Taibei: Wunan tushu, 2004; John F. Copper, *Taiwan: Nation-State or Province?*, Boulder, Colorado: Westview, 1996, and Simon Long, *Taiwan: China's Last Frontier*, Basingstoke: Palgrave Macmillan, 1991.
3 Press release, Chinese Embassy in the United Kingdom, 25 January 2002.
4 *Economist*, 3 January 2002.
5 *Financial Times*, 27 June 2007.
6 *BBC News*, 20 July 2007; *Financial Times*, 21–22 July 2007. *BBC News*, 24 July 2007.
7 *Taipei Times*, 16 July 2007.
8 The Chinese character *yuan* refers to a court or courtyard, a hall, a college or other significant public buildings. For this reason it is not usually translated in the political context and administrative branches of government in Taiwan are normally known as the Five Yuan.

21 Western Development programme

1 *Xinhua* (BBC Monitoring), 20 June 2000.
2 *Xinhua* (BBC Monitoring), 18 November 2004.
3 *Xinhua* (BBC Monitoring), 4 February 2005.
4 Chinese Communist Party Central Committee, *Central Committee Document No. 7: Record of the meeting of the Standing Committee of the Political Bureau of the Chinese Communist Party concerning the maintenance of stability in Xinjiang*, 19 March 1996.
5 *Xinhua* (BBC Monitoring), 4 February 2005.
6 Delia Davin, *Internal Migration in Contemporary China*, New York: St Martin's Press, 1999.
7 Michael Dillon, *Xinjiang: China's Muslim Far Northwest*, London: RoutledgeCurzon, 2004.
8 Zhang Feng, 'Qu da Xibei: 1949 yilai Xinjiang yimin' (Head for the great northwest: Xinjiang migration since 1949), in Yu Zhen and Dawa Cairen (eds), *Zhongguo minzu guanxi he minzu fazhan* (Ethnic Relations and Ethnic Development in China), Beijing: Minzu chubanshe, 2003, pp. 76–405.
9 *Xinhua* (BBC Monitoring), 1 October 2004.
10 *Xinhua* (BBC Monitoring), 27 December 2004.
11 *South China Morning Post*, 4 August 2004.
12 Information Office of the State Council, *Regional Autonomy for Ethnic Minorities in China*, White Paper issued 28 February 2005, Section I.
13 Information Office of the State Council, *Regional Autonomy for Ethnic Minorities in China*, White Paper issued 28 February 2005, Section IV.

22 China and the world 1: strategic relationships

1 'Analysis', *BBC Radio 4*, 21 August 2006.
2 Toyota, 1984, witnessed by the author.
3 *Financial Times*, 14 December 2007.
4 *BBC News*, 28 and 30 December 2007.
5 *Peking Review*, Vol. 4, No. 28, p. 5.
6 *BBC News*, online, 10 April 2002.
7 Mure Dickie, 'China's food aid to North Korea soars', *Financial Times*, 21 July 2006.
8 Pudong, the area to the east of the Huangpu river in Shanghai, was mainly agricultural land until plans for its development were announced in 1990. It is now the financial and commercial district of the city with many impressive high-rise buildings, including the Shanghai Stock Exchange, which contrast dramatically with the nineteenth-century western-style buildings of the Bund across the river. Pudong International Airport, to the east of the financial district, is Shanghai's international transport hub.
9 Personal communication.
10 *BBC News*, online 24 April 2003.
11 *BBC News*, online 30 September 2003.
12 *BBC News*, online 15 and 19 September 2003.
13 *BBC News*, 23 September 2003.
14 *BBC News*, 13 August 2003.
15 *BBC News*, 30 August 2003.
16 *Financial Times*, 26 July 2006.
17 *BBC News*, 30 July 2006.
18 Richard McGregor, 'China's PM urges dialogue to defuse nuclear crisis', *Financial Times*, 21–22 October 2006; *South China Morning Post*, 20 October 2006.
19 *Financial Times*, 2 November 2006.
20 *New York Times*, 6 December 2006.
21 *The Invisible Exodus: North Koreans in the People's Republic of China*, New York: Human Rights Watch, November 2002, pp. 29–30.
22 *North Korean Refugees in China and Human Rights Issues: International Response and US Policy Options*, Congressional Research Service, Washington, DC, 26 September 2007, pp. 10–12.
23 'Human rights and the North Korea refugee crisis', Brookings Institution, 25 October 2007.
24 *Mainichi Shimbun*, Tokyo (BBC Monitoring), 19 September 2003.
25 *BBC News*, 8 August 2007, 4 October 2007.
26 *Bloomberg*, Seoul, 26 November 2007.
27 *Financial Times*, 24–25 November 2007.
28 *BBC News*, 11 December 2007.
29 *BBC News*, 14 December 2007.
30 *BBC News*, 26/27 June 2008.
31 V. B. Karnik (ed.), *China Invades India: The Story of Invasion Against the Background of Chinese History and Sino–Indian Relations*, Bombay: Allied Publishers, 1963.
32 *BBC News*, 21 April 2003.
33 *Hindustan Times*, 26 October 2007.
34 *Xinhua*, 16 December 2005; *BBC News*, 14 January 2008; *Xinhua*, 14 January 2008; *China Daily*, 22 November 2006.
35 In 1996, the National Assembly of Tanzania was transferred to the city of Dodoma, which was designated the new capital, but Dar es Salaam remains the administrative and economic heart of the country.
36 Alec Russell, 'The new colonialists', *Financial Times Magazine*, 17 and 18 November 2007.
37 Li Anshan, 'China and Africa: policy and challenges', *China Security* Vol. 3, No. 3, Summer 2007, pp. 69–93.

38 Philip Snow, *The Star Raft: China's Encounter with Africa*, London, 1988 is a comprehensive and reliable account of relations between the two.
39 *Agence France Presse*, 25 November 2007.
40 *Financial Times*, 23 and 24 February 2008.
41 *Financial Times,* 28 December 19th 2007; The website of the Export-Import Bank is at http://english.eximbank.gov.cn/profile/introduction.jsp.

23 China and the world 2: new neighbours to the west

1 Xu Yuqi *Xinjiang fandui minzu fenliezhuyi douzheng shihua* (History of the Struggle Against Separatism in Xinjiang), Urumqi: Xinjiang People's Publishing House, 1999.
2 *Vecherny Bishkek* (BBC Monitoring), 14 December 2001.
3 *Public Education Radio TV*, Bishkek (BBC Monitoring), 25 December 2001.
4 *Argumenty i fakty Kyrgyzstan* (BBC Monitoring), 9 January 2002.
5 *Vecherny Bishkek* (BBC Monitoring) 15 January 2002.
6 *Kabar News Agency*, Bishkek (BBC Monitoring), 10 January 2002.
7 *Komsomolskaya Pravda v Kyrgyzstane*, Bishkek (BBC Monitoring), 18 January 2002.
8 *Interfax Moscow*, 5 February 2002; *Kyrgyz Public TV* (BBC Monitoring), 15, 20, 25 February 2002.
9 *Economist*, 23 March 2002, p. 71.
10 *Los Angeles Times*, April 2002.
11 *Kazakh TV*, Almaty (BBC Monitoring), 18 January 2002.
12 *The Times*, London, 30 March 2002.
13 Chen Dasheng (ed.), *Quanzhou Yisilanjiao shike* (Islamic Inscriptions of Quanzhou), Fuzhou: Ningxia and Fujian People's Publishing House, 1984.
14 *Eastern Turkestan Information* Vol. 1, No. 4, November 1991.
15 *Eastern Turkestan Information* Vol. 2, No. 2, March 1992.
16 *Eastern Turkestan Information*, Munich, December 1992.
17 *Renmin Ribao* (*People's Daily*), 17 November 1992, cited in *Eastern Turkestan Information*. The edition of *Renmin Ribao* of that date circulated within China does not contain such an article, but it is possible that it appeared in the overseas edition which has not been available for consultation.
18 Nicole and Hugh Pope, *Turkey Unveiled: Ataturk and After*, London: John Murray, 1997, p. 284.
19 BBC Monitoring, 19 April 1993.
20 BBC Monitoring, 9 November 1996.
21 BBC Monitoring, 23 December 1996.
22 Pope, *Turkey Unveiled*, 1997.
23 Meetings with members of the Institute of Oriental Studies and Institute of Uyghur Studies of the Kazakhstan Academy of Sciences, Almaty, Kazakhstan, September 1994.
24 *Xinhua* (BBC Monitoring), 9 June 1998.
25 BBC Monitoring, 9 June 1998.
26 BBC Monitoring, 10 February 1999.
27 BBC Monitoring, 7 and 9 April 1999.
28 BBC Monitoring, 9 November 1991.
29 BBC Monitoring, 23 November 1993.
30 BBC Monitoring, 17 and 20 December 1991.
31 BBC Monitoring, 14 April 1992.
32 *Far Eastern Economic Review*, 3 December 1992.
33 *China Quarterly*, March 1993, p. 205.
34 BBC Monitoring, 5 April 1993.
35 *China Daily*, 11 September 1992; BBC Monitoring, 11, 12 and 15 September 1992.

36 *Eastern Turkestan Information* Vol. 2, No. 5, October 1992; *China Daily*, 10 September 1992.
37 Personal observation, Kashghar, 11 September 1992. There were no reports in the Chinese media of Rafsanjani's Kashghar visit although his discussions in Beijing and Urumqi were fully reported in the press and on television in the Chinese and Uyghur language programmes of Xinjiang Television (personal observation).
38 *Independent*, 25 August 1993.
39 BBC Monitoring, 21 February 1997.
40 *China Daily*, 31 October 2004; *Financial Times*, 9 December 2007.
41 BBC Monitoring, 26 April 1993.
42 *Reuters*, 27 August 1993.
43 *Guardian*, 25 August 1993; *BBC World Service News*, 25 and 27 August 1993; Jonathan Mirsky, 'China to defy US sanctions over missiles for Pakistan', *Times*, 27 August 1993.
44 BBC Monitoring, 5 July 1997.
45 BBC Monitoring, 25, 26 and 27 May 1999.
46 BBC Monitoring, 30 June 1999.
47 BBC Monitoring, 19 and 21 August 1999.
48 BBC Monitoring, 22 April 1998.
49 BBC Monitoring, 27 November 1998.
50 BBC Monitoring, 12 December 1998.
51 *Far Eastern Economic Review*, 30 November 2000, p. 8.

24 China rising and a 'harmonious society'?

1 *BBC News*, 10 July 2007.
2 'China's peaceful development road', *People's Daily*, 22 December 2005.
3 *Guardian*; *BBC News*, 26 June 2007.

Index

CPSIA information can be obtained
at www.ICGtesting.com
Printed in the USA
FSOW02n0109140916
24940FS